A FUNDAMENTAL
PRACTICAL THEOLOGY

Fortress Press Books
by
Don S. Browning

Religious Ethics and Pastoral Care
Theology and Pastoral Care series, 1983

*Religious Thought and the Modern
Psychologies*, 1987

A FUNDAMENTAL
PRACTICAL THEOLOGY

DESCRIPTIVE AND
STRATEGIC PROPOSALS

DON S.
BROWNING

FORTRESS PRESS   MINNEAPOLIS

To Robert W. Lynn
with appreciation for his contribution
to theological education

A FUNDAMENTAL PRACTICAL THEOLOGY
Descriptive and Strategic Proposals

First paperback edition 1996

All Scripture quotations, unless otherwise noted, are from the New Revised
Standard Version of the Bible, copyright © 1989 by the Division of Christian
Education of the National Council of Churches of Christ in the U.S.A., and are
used by permission.

Cover design: Pollock Design Group/David Meyer
Interior design: Pollock Design Group

The Library of Congress has cataloged the hardcover edition as follows:

Browning, Don S.
    A fundamental practical theology : descriptive and strategic
proposals / Don S. Browning
      p. cm.
    Includes bibliographic references.
    ISBN 0-8006-2518-8 (alk. paper)
    1. Theology, Practical. 2. Theology—Methodology. I. Title.
BV3.B76 1991   91-35269
                                              CIP

    ISBN 0-8006-2973-6 (paperback; alk. paper)

The paper used in this publication meets the minimum requirements of American
National Standard for Information Sciences—Permanence of Paper for Printed
Library Materials, ANSI Z329.48-1984.

Manufactured in the U.S.A.   AF 1-2973

          4   5   6   7   8   9   10

CONTENTS

PREFACE

S ome early readers of this work have said that I have established in these pages a new genre of theology. This goes beyond the claim I would make. In my view I have tried to give additional form to a growing conversation about the nature of practical theology. In the process, I have made claims about the nature of theology as a whole. Neither my efforts to clarify the nature of practical theology nor my efforts to redefine theology as a whole are distinctively new. Large portions of recent theology—from the dialogical and practical models of the two Niebuhrs, to the existentialism of Tillich, to the more recent political theologies of Jürgen Moltmann and Johann Baptist Metz and the liberation theologies of Segundo, Gutiérrez, and Míguez Bonino—have moved toward the category of the practical. In addition, Thomas Groome, Edward Farley, James Fowler, James Poling, Donald Miller, Lewis Mudge, and many others have tried, within the past decade, to broaden and redefine what used to be called *practical theology*—the church disciplines of preaching, worship, pastoral care, and religious education. Rather than create a new genre of theology, I simply have attempted to give additional form and elaboration to trends that have been gaining momentum in a variety of theological quarters.

Although the book has continuities with earlier directions in theology, my organization of a fundamental practical theology into descriptive theology, historical theology, systematic theology, and strategic practical theology is somewhat novel. It also may imply, in the minds of some readers, a strong criticism of earlier organizations of the disciplines of theology, especially on the North American scene. Although I do contrast my view with other perspectives, I do not claim that the others are wrong. Their purposes are different. My purposes are practical, and I believe that viewing theology as a practical discipline through and through leads to discoveries that will benefit theology, the churches, and theological education.

Although the book is complex, I hope that the three major case studies that I discuss throughout its pages will carry the reader along with minimum pain. Nonetheless, aids to reading may be helpful. I offer one if the reader promises not to take it with great seriousness. In the text that follows, the reader will be introduced to what I call the five dimensions (or levels) of practical reason. I call them the *visional*, the *obligational*, the *tendency-need*, the *environmental-social*, and the *rule-role*. A famous historian of Christianity, upon hearing about these five dimensions, noticed that the first letter of each word creates the anagram VOTER. A VOTER also might be seen as a person who exercises practical reason, but I will not push the point. I offer it as an aid to memory and a tribute to the clever person who suggested it.

The reader will note that at points throughout the book I use, although in a highly qualified way, the neo-Kantian moral psychology and philosophy of Lawrence Kohlberg. I do this without addressing the debate between Kohlberg and Carol Gilligan (Gilligan 1982). This is an important discussion, but to address the debate fully would have added many pages to a book that is already too long. Let me say this: Because Kohlberg's insights inform only one of my five dimensions of moral thinking (the obligational), the qualification my full system brings to Kohlberg anticipates some of Gilligan's objections to his formulations. Some of Gilligan's concerns with relationality are addressed by the way I relate the obligational dimension of moral thinking (level two) to the tendency-need dimension (level three), or, to say it differently, the way formal judgments about justice are informed by and help organize judgments about the premoral good. I hope that the moral framework I develop in the pages that follow helps synthesize Kohlberg's concern with justice and Gilligan's ethics of care and relationality.

Suggestions about how to use the book may prove helpful. This is not a textbook; it is more nearly a probe into a new way of thinking about theology and its relation to practical action. Yet it may be helpful in courses in seminaries and divinity schools. For those using the book in these settings, the steps of the following exercise may prove relevant. I describe this exercise in more detail in chapter 3. Early in writing this book, I began to convert in some of my classes the four movements of theology into a simple course assignment. The assignment entailed writing a paper and had the following steps: (1) Give a preliminary definition to an issue (personal, social, religious) that means a great deal to you and may have led you to come to divinity school. (2) Discuss briefly why this issue is important to you and what your *pre-understanding* (see p. 38 below) of it was before you began research on the paper.

(3) Interview someone who is also concerned with this issue. Describe how this person thinks religiously and ethically about this issue. (4) Choose two theological resources (I call them guides to the Christian classics) that address this issue. Summarize the way they define and normatively address the issue. (5) Compare and critically assess these two guides to the Christian classics. (6) Imagine communicating these two perspectives back to your interviewee, entering into her or his world view and preferred metaphysics and narrative. (7) Record ways in which your own pre-understanding of the issue has changed because of this exercise. (Address the entire paper, as nearly as possible, not to your instructor or even to the students in the class, but rather to your interviewee.) The four movements are implicit in these seven steps. But this is just one of the many pedagogical exercises that can be invented on the basis of the view developed in this book.

This book covers several concrete areas of practical Christian living—congregational care, religious education, theological education, clinical pastoral education (CPE)—and touches on the new discipline of church consultation. The book, however, is not exhaustive. I do not deal in detail with preaching or worship. The four movements of fundamental practical theology apply to these traditional practical disciplines as well. But to demonstrate this I will need to return to these disciplines at another time.

All books depend on the generosity, support, and good graces of many people besides the author. This book owes more debt than it can ever pay. I must first thank Robert Lynn, to whom I dedicate the book. He included me in a variety of projects sponsored by the Religion Division of the Lilly Endowment. These projects, especially the National Faculty Seminar on Congregational Education held at the Christian Theological Seminary, inspired me to broaden my thinking about practical theology to include the emerging field of congregational studies. I also express appreciation directly to the Lilly Endowment for a grant to the Divinity School of the University of Chicago that made possible the study leave for writing this book. I thank Dean George Newlands and Professor David Hamilton of the Faculty of Divinity of the University of Glasgow. During the autumn of 1989, while I served there as the Alexander Robertson Lecturer, they provided me with a comfortable office that enabled me to continue my work on this project. I wrote the bulk of the book at the Center of Theological Inquiry at Princeton, New Jersey, where I was a member for eight months in 1990. Parts of the manuscript were shared with the members of the center, and many intense conversations were held with, and much helpful criticism was gained from, specific members, most notably my friend Dean Lewis Mudge

of San Francisco Theological Seminary. I shared sections of this
book with the faculty of Candler School of Theology at an occasion
graciously hosted by my former colleague and friend Professor Rebecca Chopp, now of that faculty. A selection of the manuscript
was also shared at an international consultation on practical theology sponsored by the Department of Practical Theology at the
University of Tübingen. I gained immensely from these consulta-
tions and conversations and deeply appreciate all the responses
and evaluations that were shared with me.

I thank Franklin Gamwell, former Dean of the Divinity School
of the University of Chicago, who not only supported me in this
project with generous time for research and writing but also read
large sections of the manuscript and shared his usual sharp insights
and friendly challenges. Professors David Tracy, Robin Lovin, and
Philip Devenish constituted a pervasive community of dialogue that
helped shape the book—dialogue of the kind that makes the Divinity School one of the best environments in the world for inquiries of
this sort. I must give my special thanks to Robin Lovin. The phrase
naturalistic moment, which the reader will discover in the pages that
follow, I probably first heard from his lips.

I want to thank Professor Carl Dudley, of McCormick Theological Seminary, for not objecting too strongly to my characterization
of the research group that studied the Wiltshire Church. He reminds
me that theologians were not originally included on this team, not
because theology was overlooked, but because it was difficult to
think of a theologian interested in describing a congregation. This
is doubtless true. We agree that for one reason or another in the
early 1980s it was difficult to associate theology with the task of describing situations. The significance of these remarks will become
clear in chapter 6.

Ian Evison has helped me with a variety of projects over the last
five years. We have coedited three books, and he has helped me
in the preparation of the final manuscript of other books, including
this one. I have been most fortunate to have his intelligence, energy, and good judgment as a part of this and other projects. I also
appreciate Sister Kathleen Dolphin, who, with Ian, helped with the
editing. I also thank Michael Hayes and Bernard James for assisting
me with my research at the Apostolic Church of God.

And finally, I thank my family. My wife, Carol, who enters mentally and spiritually into all my projects, contributed her usual
intelligence and wondrous generosity. Beth and Chris, my daughter
and son, often provided me with an image of the young adults for
whom this book, in the last analysis, was written.

INTRODUCTION

FROM PRACTICE TO THEORY
AND BACK AGAIN

T his book is for anyone who has ever asked, In what way do
religious communities make sense? I use the word *sense* intentionally, as something of a substitute for the word *reason.*
Therefore, the question would be, In what way do religious communities exhibit reason or, more specifically, practical reason? To
push that question too quickly would be, I fear, a bit daunting. For
the moment, I will stay with the more general question.

Who would ask such a question? It probably would be people on the boundary—the boundary between religious and secular
life, between tradition and modernity, and between faith and reason
(Tillich 1966). This includes many people in modern Western societies—maybe most of us. Some individuals, of course, feel so secure
in their religious traditions that they do not consciously ask such
questions. Others are so alienated from religious traditions that they
cannot imagine how such traditions can make sense. Most of us
stand on the boundary: religious communities attract us; we may
even participate in them; but we also wonder if they make sense.

I sometimes imagine myself speaking to young people between
college and graduate school. They stand on this boundary, generally familiar with some form of religion, full of the secular world,
both trusting yet skeptical of tradition. To them and myself I offer
an answer to the question, Why should we trust the wisdom and
sense of these communities? Why, given these communities' falli-
bilities and ambiguities, their shortsightedness and weakness, their
increasing distance from centers of power, and their intellectual
unsteadiness, should late twentieth-century individuals with good
educations, concerns for the future of the human race, and a bit
of excess energy use this energy to support religious communities
such as churches and synagogues?

I ask those who have answered these questions both positively
and negatively not to close their minds permanently. They should

keep these questions open. Some true believers think that churches and synagogues are all-important. For them, I encourage a bit of philosophical skepticism—at least enough to get through the pages of this book. Others think that the church is a totally irrelevant vestige of Western culture that no longer has any function. To them I suggest that these communities may make more sense than they might first think. I certainly am addressing ministers in this book. In appealing to them, I will be addressing their more philosophical inclinations. I want secularists and philosophers to consider this book. I hope to show them how religious communities have rational dimensions although the rational never fully comprehends all that they are and do.

PRACTICAL WISDOM AND COMMUNITIES

I will be drawing into conversation several contemporary intellectual traditions. These include the group of recently reborn practical philosophies. This is the tradition of practical wisdom (*phronēsis*) or practical reason associated with Aristotle, Augustine, Aquinas, Hume, Kant, the American pragmatists William James and John Dewey, and the neopragmatists Richard Rorty and Richard Bernstein. These include also the hermeneutic theory of Hans-Georg Gadamer, the critical theory of Jürgen Habermas, the communitarianism of Alasdair MacIntyre, and many others. Most of these authors—especially Bernstein, Rorty, Gadamer, and MacIntyre—have pointed to the role that tradition plays in our practical rational thinking. It is not surprising that they help us understand how churches and religious communities are simultaneously "communities of memory" (Bellah et al. 1985, 152–57) and communities of practical reason. Robert Bellah builds on the thought of the philosopher Alasdair MacIntyre and the German political theologian Johann Baptist Metz to issue a call out of the depths of secular sociology for a rebirth of religious communities as communities of memory. Such communities are an antidote to the corrosive acids of Western individualism and liberalism. But Bellah does not go far in explaining how such communities make *sense*, that is, exhibit features of practical wisdom as well as tradition. A question central to this book is: How can communities of memory and tradition also be communities of practical reason and practical wisdom?

Simultaneous to the call for the rebirth of practical philosophy and return to communities of memory, there has developed a new inquiry known as *congregational studies.* Sponsored primarily by the Lilly Endowment, these studies have been dedicated to the careful historical, sociological, and theological analysis of those ignored religious communities called congregations. The suppositions of these studies have been that congregations and synagogues in some way touch the lives of most Americans, that the academic community has ignored them, and that when carefully and sympathetically interpreted they look much more interesting and complex than is often realized. The question that I bring to congregational studies is somewhat new. I will ask how these communities can be seen to make sense. How are they both communities of memory and communities of practical reason?

The phrasing of this question points to the last tradition of inquiry that I will use. This is the recent worldwide effort to reconceptualize what is commonly called *practical theology*. The field of practical theology has been throughout its history the most beleaguered and despised of the theological disciplines. The discipline of theology itself has had few friends, even in the church. To admit in academic theological circles that one is a theologian has been, in recent years, to court embarrassment. To admit that one is a practical theologian invites even deeper skepticism. To admit in a major university that one is a practical theologian has been to invite humiliation.

With the rebirth of the practical philosophies, practical theology itself has been reborn. Five years ago, few would admit being practical theologians. Today there is a rush among more dignified and well-established systematic and historical theologians to ask, After all, aren't we all practical? The epistemological climate has changed. The English word *practical* and the Greek word *praxis* are no longer words of disparagement. Ministers, social workers, and dentists take heart! The world may soon envy you! This is especially true if you can both act and think about or reflect on your action. If you can do both of these, you are a "reflective practitioner." Since the time, not so many years ago, that Donald Schön wrote a well-received book by that name, you have become far more appreciated and even admired (Schön 1983).

As an exercise in practical theology, this book may be too philosophical for some and too religious for others. From one perspective, it is a book in religiously oriented practical philosophy. From another perspective, it is a practical philosophy of religion. This is because the practical theology offered here is a critical practical theology. It is a practical theology that begins with the intuitions of faith but ends, when needed, with reasons and justifications for the practical actions it proposes.

With the reemergence of the practical philosophies, there has arisen a new fascination with terms such as *practical reason, practical wisdom, phronēsis, practice, praxis, justice, consensus, dialogue, conversation,* and *communication.* This fascination suggests that Western societies are desperate to find ways to make shared and workable decisions about the common good and the common life. The twin realities of modernity and liberalism have worked against the maintenance of shared traditions, social narratives, and communal identities. When it comes time to decide an issue about the common good, shared assumptive worlds are so fragmented that struggle, often unproductive, invariably ensues.

We are in a period of social reconstruction. On the one hand, we have relied in recent centuries too much on theoretical and technical reason to solve our problems. On the other hand, we have relied too much on blind custom and tradition. We swing from one extreme to the other because we lack a clear idea of how practical reason and tradition relate to one another. We now have returned to the category of the practical in search of a shared praxis that will enable us to either reconstruct tradition or to learn to exercise our practical wisdom without it. These seem the two basic choices. In each case—the exercise of practical wisdom *with* or *without* tradition—the debate is over competing images of what is variously called practical wisdom, practical reason, or *phronēsis.*

Practical reason is generally thought to be exercised by individuals. Most accounts of practical reason write as if it is always exercised in the form of a monologue. It is like individuals talking to themselves and going through the steps of practical thinking in the form of silent conversations. In this book, I am interested in how communities, and religious communities at that, exercise practical reason. In turn, I am interested in the way these communities make a difference in how practical reason works.

CAN THEOLOGY BE PRACTICAL?

To some of my colleagues at the university where I teach, theology is a mysterious and arcane discipline that one clever phrasemaker called "systematically articulated superstition." To the scholar who coined this phrase, theology is a totally mystifying subject hardly more respectable than phrenology, astrology, or alchemy. When such skeptics hear the phrase *practical theology,* doubtless the analogues that echo in their minds sound something like "practical phrenology," "practical astrology," or "practical alchemy."

More charitable critics still may have difficulty comprehending the distinctive ways in which theology can be thought to be practical. Older Scholastic definitions of theology that saw it as rational and deductive knowledge about God based upon indubitable first principles have been widely rejected. The great American philosopher William James, although no enemy of religion, made fun of theology. He did this largely, I think, because he associated it with the idealistic and Hegelian metaphysical religious systems so prevalent in Europe and America at the turn of the century (James [1897] 1956, 275-85).

More recent theologians—from Barth to Tillich, from a political theologian such as Johann Baptist Metz to a liberation theologian such as José Míguez Bonino, or from sectarian theologians such as Stanley Hauerwas to a public and philosophical theologian such as David Tracy—are much more likely to see theology as systematic reflection on the historical self-understanding of a particular religious tradition. Academic theology is less rationalistic, less deductive, and less apodictic than it once was. But when theology is seen as careful and systematic reflection on the self-understanding of a particular religious tradition such as Christianity, Judaism, or even Protestantism or Catholicism, interesting and puzzling concepts such as myth, story, legend, symbol, and metaphor begin to play important roles. This is true because religious traditions invariably express their self-understandings in the language of myth, story, symbol, and metaphor.

Although contemporary theology is less rationalistic, it may not seem less apodictic, impractical, and unrelated to the average person. A theologian as recent as Karl Barth saw theology as the systematic interpretation of God's self-disclosure to the Christian church (Barth 1936, 47-70). There was no role for human understanding, action, or practice in the construal of God's self-disclosure. In this view, theology is practical only by applying God's revelation as directly and purely as possible to the concrete situations of life. The theologian moves from revelation to the human, from theory to practice, and from revealed knowledge to application. A good deal of Barthianism is still present in modern theology. Barth's model of practical theology is partially right; many contemporary commentators, however, believe that it is partially, if not significantly, wrong.

BEGINNING WITH PRACTICAL CONCERNS

Theology can be practical but in more complicated ways than is comprehended by the Barthian model. Theology can be practical if we bring practical concerns to it from the beginning. The theologian does not stand before God, Scripture, and the historic witness of the church like an empty slate or Lockean tabula rasa ready to be determined, filled up, and then plugged into a concrete practical situation. A more accurate description goes like this. We come to the theological task with questions shaped by the secular and religious practices in which we are implicated—sometimes uncomfortably. These practices are meaningful or theory-laden. By using the phrase *theory-laden*, I mean to rule out in advance the widely held assumption that theory is distinct from practice. All our practices, even our religious practices, have theories behind and within them. We may not notice the theories in our practices. We are so embedded in our practices, take them so much for granted, and view them as so natural and self-evident that we never take time to abstract the theory from the practice and look at it as something in itself.

When a religious community hits a crisis in its practices, it then begins reflecting (asking questions) about its meaningful or theory-laden practices. It may take time to describe these practices so it can better understand the questions precipitated by the crisis. Eventually, if it is serious, the community must reexamine the sacred texts and events that constitute the source of the norms and ideals that guide its practices. It brings its questions to these normative texts and has a conversation between its questions and these texts. This community of interpreters will see its inherited normative sources in light of the questions engendered by its crisis. As its practices change its questions change, and the community will invariably see different meanings in its normative texts as its situation and questions change.

What happens next depends on how open and self-critical the religious community is. Confessionally oriented religious interpreters may stop the process here. More liberal or critically oriented religious interpreters (sometimes called *public churches*) may try to develop this new horizon of meaning by devising, when pushed to do so, various tests for the practical adequacy of these new meanings. In doing this, they may become somewhat more philosophical. They may even develop two languages, one religious and one more philosophical, to communicate these meanings to the outside world.

Finally, these new, reconstructed religious meanings and practices continue until this religious community meets a new crisis. This forces it to examine its new theory-laden practices that have only recently been put in place. Religious communities go from moments of consolidated practice to moments of deconstruction to new, tentative reconstructions and consolidations. Then a new crisis emerges and the community must launch into the entire process once more. It makes one a bit weary just to think about it. Yet that is much the way life works whether we admit it or not. That is why we often represent life in terms of metaphors of pilgrimage, trial, struggle, or, as did William James, "strenuousness" (James [1897] 1956, 221; Browning 1980, 211–36).

I have gotten more complex than I intended at this stage of the discussion. I have been forced to do so for one reason— the process of practical thinking, whether religious or secular, is indeed complex. To think and act practically in fresh and innovative ways may be the most complex thing that humans ever attempt. I wish it were otherwise. Life, especially modern life, would be so much simpler. Fortunately, we are not required to think and act practically in fresh ways all the time. If life were this hectic, this changing, and this unpredictable, we would surely fail. Modern life may be becoming so dynamic that we all will fail because we cannot keep up with the pace. Novel, fresh, and critical practical thinking helps us to establish more settled and predictable cultures governing our everyday behaviors. Our overheated and rapidly changing technological societies are requiring us to turn these corners of cultural deconstruction and reconstruction more often. They give us little time to catch our breath. This is why there is new concern, both inside and outside religious circles, about the nature of practical thinking in modern societies.

The difference between this view of theology as practical and the Barthian view is apparent. The view I propose goes from practice to theory and back to practice. Or more accurately, it goes from present theory-laden practice to a retrieval of normative theory-laden practice to the creation of more critically held theory-laden practices. Barth, in contrast, was an epistemological realist. He believed that the interpreting community should empty itself of its usual attempts to verify things morally, experientially, or cognitively. The believing community should conform itself totally to the Word of God revealed in Scripture (Barth 1936, 187–247). This, I believe, is a classic expression of the *theory-to-practice* model of theology. Such a model dominated most theological education in both Europe and North America in the middle decades of the twentieth century (Farley 1983a, 159–61). It also affected the thought and life of the churches.

FUNDAMENTAL PRACTICAL THEOLOGY

The view of theology I have outlined should not be seen as simply a subspecialty called *practical theology*. On the contrary, it is my proposed model for theology as such. I will be claiming that Christian theology should be seen as practical through and through and at its very heart. Historical, systematic, and practical theology (in the

more specific sense of the term) should be seen as subspecialties
of the larger and more encompassing discipline called *fundamental
practical theology*. Many will think this claim to be imperialistic.
I think that it is the natural outcome of the rebirth of practical
philosophy and its implication for theology. It is a consequence of
taking to their logical conclusion the theories of Hans-Georg Gadamer, Paul Ricoeur, and Jürgen Habermas; the pragmatism of William
James and John Dewey; and the neopragmatism of Richard Bernstein and Richard Rorty. I will say much more about these practical
philosophies in the pages to come.

These thinkers, in spite of their differences, share one fundamental idea, that is, that practical thinking is the center of human
thinking and that theoretical and technical thinking are abstrac-
tions from practical thinking. If one takes this seriously and relates
it to theology, it fundamentally changes the historic formulations
of the organization of the theological disciplines. It is a revolution long overdue. Rather than saying that theology is made up
of Bible, church history, systematic theology, and practical theology (as did the Protestant quadrivium) (Farley 1983a, 101–24), I
am presenting a different formulation. I argue that theology as a
whole is fundamental practical theology and that it has within it four
submovements of *descriptive theology, historical theology, systematic
theology*, and *strategic practical theology*. I use the phrase *strategic
practical theology* to refer to what is commonly understood as the
church disciplines of religious education, pastoral care, preaching,
liturgy, social ministries, and so forth. But here even these disciplines will be reconceived to have both an inner ecclesial and
public dimension.

STRATEGIC PRACTICAL THEOLOGY

Some of my colleagues have objected to the military or political
sound of the term *strategic*. It suggests to them images of ground, air,
or naval maneuvers in the midst of battle. Even worse, it suggests
complicated models of anticipation, calculation, and retaliation of
the kind associated with the elaborate nuclear strategies of the Cold
War era. One friend suggested that I use the phrase *fully practical
theology* in the place of *strategic practical theology*. The recommendation is a good one. It communicates the idea that although the
entire theological circle is practical, theology becomes fully or concretely practical only in the so-called strategic practical theological
disciplines. I have accepted his suggestion. In the pages that follow,
I will alternate between the two words *strategic* and *fully* practical
theology.

I realize that such organizations of knowledge, theological or nontheological, are of little interest to anyone who is not a specialist in theology. Yet changing how we see such issues makes earth-shaking differences in the way we think about a religious tradition. How we solve problems about the organization of theology makes a difference in how we think and act at the most concrete levels of our lives. In saying that we should move in theology from practice to theory and back to practice, I am saying more than meets the eye. First, in doing this in theology, I am simply following the nature of human thought. Human thought works that way. We never really move from theory to practice even when it seems we do. Theory is always embedded in practice. When theory seems to stand alone it is only because we have abstracted it from its practical context. We have become mentally blind to the practical activities that both precede and follow it.

Second, once we grasp the practice-theory-practice structure of all theology, the gulf disappears between our high-level theological texts and courses and the practical activity of religious education, care, preaching, and worship. The structure of theology and the structure of these concrete practices are the same. No matter what our practical religious activity, it has implicit within it the movements of descriptive, historical, systematic, and fully practical theology. In chapters 9 and 10, I will show this specifically in the areas of Christian education and pastoral or congregational care. I will make hints about how it works in homiletics and liturgy. This book is in many ways a systematic statement about the nature of practical theology. It does not, however, systematically cover all topics. I use Christian education and congregational care to *illustrate* that the rhythms of descriptive, historical, systematic, and strategic practical theology are not just divisions of the formal theological encyclopedia. They are movements of theological reflection in all practical religious activity, even the activities of education and care. One can even see them in the dynamics of theological education at the seminary or university level. In chapters 2 and 3, I will describe an educational experiment that shows this.

CENTRAL QUESTIONS

This short exposure to a new way of envisioning theology takes us ahead of the story. I am more concerned now to pose my central questions: Can religious communities be seen as carriers of practical reason? If so, What do their religious identities contribute to this practical reason? In asking these questions, I am posing both a normative and a descriptive question. I am asking, In what way *should* religious communities be understood as bearers of practical rationality? Is it justifiable to say that Christian communities are sanctioned by the ideals and norms of the Judeo-Christian tradition to be carriers and implementers of practical rationality? The descriptive question asks, In what ways *are* these communities carriers of practical reason although they may not always exercise it well and faithfully?

By focusing on practical reason, I mean to point to the use of reason to answer the questions, What should we do? and How should we live? The tradition of practical reason or practical wisdom has its origins in Aristotle's concept of *phronēsis.* Jesus used the word *phronēsis* in the Sermon on the Mount (Matt. 7:24) to refer to the "wise" persons who listen to the message of Jesus and build their lives upon it. Reason as *phronēsis* can be distinguished from *theoria* or theoretical reason, which is often thought to ask the more dispassionate, objective, or scientific question of What is the case? or What is the nature of things? It is also distinguishable from technical reason or *technē*, which asks the question, What are the most effective means to a given end?

To suggest that religious communities can be carriers of practical wisdom will seem to contradict various popular understandings. Some will say that religious communities are bearers of the revelation and will of God and this revelation sets aside all use of human reason. Others will say that these communities are anachronistic custodians of superstition and ignorance and certainly not carriers of practical rationality. It is my conviction, however, that these communities can and often do constitute powerful embodiments of practical rationality. Furthermore, their religious meanings can free practical rationality to function all the better. It is not that they exercise practical wisdom in spite of their religious symbols and convictions; they exercise practical wisdom *because* of their religious symbols and convictions. More specifically, I will be arguing that religious narratives and metaphors can function to enliven, energize, liberate, and make more effective the workings of practical reason.

A MAP OF THE ROAD

In what follows, I claim that practical reason has an overall dynamic, an outer envelope, and an inner core. Its overall dynamic is the reconstruction of experience. When inherited interpretations and practices seem to be breaking down, practical reason tries to reconstruct both its picture of the world and its more concrete practices. The overall dynamic of practical reason is a broad-scale interpretive and reinterpretive process; it is, as Gadamer would say, a "hermeneutic" process. I depend much on Gadamer's claim that there are important analogies between the interpretive process that he calls hermeneutics and Aristotle's understanding of *phronesis* or practical reason.

The outer envelope of practical reason is its fund of inherited narratives and practices that tradition has delivered to us and that always surrounds our practical thinking. In holding this, I have been influenced by Aristotle and contemporary neo-Aristotelians such as Hans-Georg Gadamer and Alasdair MacIntyre. I accept their general point that practical reason is always tradition-saturated. When practical reason tries to reconstruct experience in the most encompassing sense, it brings questions generated by the disruption of experience to its tradition-saturated ideals and practices.

I also hold there is an inner core to practical reason. The reversible reasoning to be found in the love command that reads, "You shall love your neighbor as yourself" (Matt. 19:19) exhibits this inner core as does the analogous golden rule, "In everything do to others as you would have them do to you" (Matt. 7:12; Luke 6:31).

I will give a mixed reading to these principles, blending certain strands of Kantianism with certain strands of Aristotelian teleology. I will do this, however, in such a way as to subsume the teleological to the more Kantian or deontological perspective. In Christianity, the religious tradition shapes this core of practical reason in various specific ways. But to say this does not mean that the inner core of practical reason cannot be distinguished from the outer narrative envelope of that tradition. Rather the inner core functions within a narrative about God's creation, governance, and redemption of the world. It also functions within a narrative that tells how the life and death of Jesus Christ further God's plans for the world. This narrative is the outer envelope of practical reason. It constitutes the vision that animates, informs, and provides the ontological context for practical reason.

Practical reason, I will argue, always has a narrative envelope. It is not necessarily specifically Christian. Because there is always some kind of narrative envelope around practical reason, the fact that Christianity has its specific envelope puts it in this respect on the same level as all other concrete forms of practical reason. The difference between so-called secular and religious forms of practical reason is not that the former is irreligious and the latter religious. The difference is between systems in which the religious framework (or at least the framework of faith) is explicit and where it is implicit. Practical reason is always surrounded by images of the world that are grounded on faith assumptions. Narratives and metaphors carry these faith assumptions. Some are vague and almost imperceptible. Others are explicit and clearly articulated. Christianity has an explicit narrative tradition that constitutes the envelope for a core model of practical reason.

To make this a genuinely practical book, and not just one about the theory of practical theology, I will illustrate my points around three rather extensive case studies of congregations. There was no grand scheme in choosing these congregations. They are simply three congregations that, for one reason or another, I was given the opportunity to study. One is an upper-middle-class church located in the northeastern part of the United States. It is called Wiltshire Methodist Church. The second is a middle-class, middle-American Presbyterian church called the Church of the Covenant. The third is an African American Pentecostal church on the South Side of Chicago near where I live and work. It is called the Apostolic Church of God. These churches, in various ways, are carriers of practical reason and exhibit many features of practical theological thinking. They do not always exhibit good practical theological thinking and action; that is not my claim. My claim is that they exhibit discernible features of practical theology and religiously informed practical reason—at least in some fashion and to some degree.

The thought of Reinhold Niebuhr and Louis Janssens will be principal resources for understanding the relation of the Christian narrative to practical reason. They will help fill out the theological and ethical submoment of practical theological thinking. Niebuhr will provide a version of the Christian narrative and some elements of a model of practical reason. Janssens, plus many other theological and philosophical sources, will help refine the model of practical reason implicit in Niebuhr, a model that I believe is consistent with the Christian message. After an extensive discussion and illustration of the nature of a fundamental practical theology with the submovements of descriptive, historical, systematic, and fully practical theology, I will try to illustrate how this view of theology can work in the regions of Christian education and congregational care. The argument will be long and complex, but I hope also to make it concrete. For this is the nature of practical theology—long, complex, yet concrete. There are no easy answers in a critical practical theology.

**PART
ONE**

FUNDAMENTAL PRACTICAL THEOLOGY

DESCRIBING THREE
RELIGIOUS COMMUNITIES

book on practical theology ought to be practical. If not fully practical, it should pertain to the practical. Doing theology in close connection with the description of situations gets to the heart of what makes theology practical. So I present the reader with three extensive case studies. I do this to juxtapose the view of practical theology developed here with descriptions of the situations faced by these three religious communities.

In the rather dense methodological chapters to follow, I argue that both practical theology and the description of situations proceed as dialogues or conversations. This is the hermeneutical model of practical theology that has grasped the attention of some of us in theological education. This view sees all understanding as proceeding in the form of a dialogue or conversation. Heidegger and Gadamer developed this model of understanding, but it has analogues in various aspects of American pragmatism. If I am to take this model seriously, my effort both to describe these congregations and to think theologically about them must take place as a kind of conversation. It is a conversation or dialogue in which I bring my questions and commitments to these congregations. In turn, I find myself confronted and questioned by their commitments and practices.

It is relevant, therefore, for me to state here that I am a professor in an interfaith divinity school at a research-oriented university. I belong to a liberal mainline Protestant church in the neighborhood of this university. This community, like most academic communities, is characterized by a political liberalism that is exceeded only by its tolerance for the myriad of life styles characteristic of students and urban professionals who live within its boundaries.

My church is quite different from the three churches that destiny has brought me to study. The agenda I brought to these

churches is very much different from the agenda these churches
have for themselves. The more I have confronted these differences,
the more I have gained fresh perspectives on my agenda and, at
times, questioned it. This is the nature of understanding as hermeneutical dialogue. And it is the nature of practical theology as
a slightly different kind of hermeneutical dialogue. One interprets
and even assesses the object of one's study, but one finds oneself
being interpreted and assessed in turn.

This happened to me in my study of and practical thinking
about these three churches. One was a liberal, upper-middle-class
Methodist church in an exclusive, suburban New England village.
One was a conservative, middle-class Presbyterian church in a
county seat in Ohio—a church close in style and social ethos to
the church of my youth. The third was a Pentecostal church located
only eight blocks from my home on the South Side of Chicago. As
close as it was physically, it was so far spiritually and culturally
from the world of my everyday life that it might as well have been
in a distant country. It was in the confrontation with this Pentecostal church that I experienced most directly the hermeneutical
and dialogical nature that characterizes all attempts to understand
and think practically about situations. .

I have chosen these three cases for several reasons. They will
provide illustrative material throughout the book to help make
some of my denser theological discussions clearer. Two of the
cases—Wiltshire Methodist Church and the Church of the Covenant—are already in the published literature from the fledgling
field of congregational studies (Dudley 1983; Slater 1989). I encourage the curious or skeptical reader to consult these works and join
in the practical interpretive process of understanding these religious communities. More important than that, since these two cases
already have been interpreted by a variety of disciplines, looking at
them again gives us an excellent opportunity to better understand
the complexities of what Paul Ricoeur has called the "conflict of interpretations" (Ricoeur 1974). In this context, we will be interested
in the conflict of interpretations between academic disciplines, not
as an abstract game in hermeneutics or interpretation theory, but
with regard to what these different interpretive perspectives have
to contribute to the clarification of practical action.

The reader must be warned now that these communities are
not always examples of good practical thinking. But each will show
us something crucially important about the way practical thinking
proceeds in a religious context even if that thinking is flawed. In
the pages to come, the reader will hear much about what I call the
thickness of practical wisdom. My position on the thickness or mul-

tidimensional nature of practical reason will distinguish what I have to say from most philosophical treatments of the subject. The cases I now briefly describe, if not always the best-imaginable examples of practical thinking in religious contexts, will reveal various aspects of this thickness of practical reason.

Finally, I was a member of both the team that studied the Wiltshire congregation and the team that studied the Covenant congregation, and thus I have chosen to use them as case studies. These two interdisciplinary teams, both sponsored through the beneficence and far-sightedness of the Lilly Endowment, each functioned—although for different reasons—like a group of value-laden cultural anthropologists. Both of the congregations were real, but to protect the innocent they have been given in the literature fictitious names and locations. I use them here because they were studies I was a part of and studies that have much to teach us about religious communities, the people who study them, and the nature of practical wisdom within the context of religious groups.

With the help of assistants I did the research on the Apostolic Church of God—the African American Pentecostal church. In the two Lilly-sponsored projects, the teams enjoyed the services of professional researchers who did the field and leg work for the group. The teams' members, individually and collectively, gave questions and guidelines to the researchers, who in turn did the interviews, collected the documents, gathered the social history, and so forth. In the case of the black Pentecostal church, my assistants and I did this work ourselves. The Lilly teams I worked with either visited their respective churches or interviewed their main actors, allowing us to gain a sense of immediacy and involvement with these churches. But this sense was more vivid in the work with the Apostolic Church. The richness of this church and the surprises that awaited me in my encounter with it give my practical theological conversation with this church a special place in this book. Throughout the book, as I already have indicated, I examine how religious experience and symbols interact with practical rationality in the shaping of the praxis of congregations. What I found in the Apostolic Church—near at hand but far from my previous experience—stretched to the limits what Gadamer would so inelegantly call my "pre-understanding." This is a concept I will discuss in the pages to follow.

The action and issues presented in these cases are, as is always the case with practical action, not completed. We leave the stories and the issues they contain in midstream. The reader will not know how they are finally resolved. This itself is an insight into the nature of practical action; it deals with issues that are fluid and that have

evolved out of old issues and fade into new ones. We never fully
know the final results of any of our actions.

I do not present these cases to instruct the reader on how to
run a church. I present them primarily to illustrate one view of
practical thought in a religious context. They will help us see the
complexity and richness of practical thought. They will help us see
the reason in practical religion and the religion in allegedly secular
practical thinking. Although I will often take sides and signal to the
reader the directions I think good practical thinking would take us, I
will not make definitive pronouncements. Although the information
about these cases is good, the complexity of practical thinking is
such that it is best for those standing outside the concrete situation
to be humble about their advice. In addition, just as several courses
of action can be shown to be wrong, often more than one course of
action can be shown to be good.

To involve the reader with these congregations as concretely as
possible, I invite you to imagine yourself as a friendly consultant to
each of them. By consultant, I mean nothing as weighty as a truly
professional consultant. I especially do not have in mind professionals who make their living consulting. Rather, imagine being a friend
to someone in one of these communities—someone who once, in
the midst of a conversation, asked you with a sense of both playful-
ness and seriousness the following question: "Where do you think
we should go from here?" Of course, even with a friend you can always beg off by saying, "Who, me? I haven't the faintest." I ask you
to resist this response, at least for a while. Instead, I invite you to
play with the question for a time and to do so even if, at first glance,
you have little sympathy with the situation, the religious beliefs of
those involved, or the issues that these congregations faced.

THE SHANGRI-LA BETWEEN TWO RIDGES

During the summer and autumn of 1980 and throughout 1981 a
team of four sociologists, two psychologists, one anthropologist,
one historian of religion, two theologians, one practical theologian,
and three professional church consultants was organized to study a
Protestant church in the northeastern part of the United States. The
Committee for Congregational Studies directed the project and the
Lilly Endowment sponsored it. The report of this study was published in a somewhat poorly titled book called *Building Effective
Ministry* (1983), edited by Carl Dudley. The study had two simple
purposes—to demonstrate the complexity and richness of congregational life and to show that to understand such religious groups,
several disciplines are necessary (xi). As a member of this re-

search group, I always felt uneasy with this rather bland statement of objectives. I believed that there was a deeper agenda, not so much hidden as unclearly perceived. For decades—possibly since the publication of Gibson Winter's *The Suburban Captivity of the Churches* (1962)—there had been the suspicion that in the United States the congregation was captive to the privatistic interests of families trying to raise their children and to develop emotional adjustment between the parents. The congregation was basically limited, it was argued, to helping the beleaguered American family accomplish these two tasks. The upshot of this view of the congregation (Parsons 1964) was that the more heroic leaders of the church, in both Protestant and Catholic circles, began to look with some disdain on the congregation's capacity to influence the wider public world. These leaders increasingly thought that it was the wider public world—government, education, the workplace, the economy—that truly shaped our society. Further, relegating the congregation to the realm of the family assured its powerlessness in modern societies. The early study edited by Dudley and the entire congregational study movement were efforts to refute this narrow, privatistic view of congregations. Before saying more about the purpose of that study, let me tell the story, in a preliminary way, of the congregation we named the Wiltshire Church.

The town of Wiltshire had about twenty-one thousand people. It rests between two ridges and is separated by only a few miles from a larger, more commercial, and more industrially oriented community that I will refer to as Springfield. Wiltshire's mayor reported that many of its residents see Wiltshire as a kind of Shangri-La providing a haven and protection from the competitive ethos of Springfield and other surrounding communities where most of its residents earn their living. I remember with some pangs of envy the lush green countryside, the sun-drenched yards and flower beds, and the attractive homes that both surround and make up the community of Wiltshire.

The community, founded in the 1600s, is old by North American standards. In the 1800s, a textile firm known as the Adams Company moved to Wiltshire and became the principal employer of the community. It had paid low salaries but took care of its people. Evidence of this could be found in the more than two hundred small homes still in town that the company had built for its workers. The owners of the Adams Company had built most of the present Methodist church, patterned oddly enough after a quaint Anglican church that the mill owner and his wife had fallen in love with during a visit to England in the early 1900s. For years the head of the Adams family invited the church board to his home annually. They established the budget for the coming year and calculated the projected pledges. Then the Adams patriarch wrote a check on the spot for several thousand dollars to make up the difference.

By the time Sid Carlson, the present minister, came to the church in the early 1970s, the congregation was stagnant. But the community of Wiltshire was not. It was booming. Its population had quadrupled over the last twenty years. Once primarily a company town in a rural setting, in recent years it had become the haven for executive-level young women and men who worked in nearby Springfield. The schools had mushroomed. During a secret visit to Wiltshire prior to accepting a "call" to the church, Sid Carlson discovered this potential.

After moving to Wiltshire with his wife and two daughters, Sid took a variety of decisive actions that both revealed his assertive leadership style and helped turn the church around. He removed 221 nonparticipating members from the rolls that totaled over seven hundred. He reduced the Sunday morning worship services, which averaged no more than 140 participants, from two to one. He reduced the size of the official board of the church. He renovated the church and the parsonage and put the church into debt for the first time in decades. He raised the average contribution to the church, which had been embarrassingly low (around twenty-five cents per member each week). He strongly emphasized the church school and the music programs. He began attracting young families. People liked Sid's plain-spoken and practical sermons. They liked the music. They called it the "best show in town." They joked that if a family couldn't afford a country club, the Wiltshire Methodist Church was a good substitute. The congregation grew rapidly.

Sid characterized his congregation as full of "wistful hearts." By this he meant people who were largely agnostic but came to church to give their children something more solid than they could provide by themselves. They were the kind of people who "are not biblically literate, people who wish that they could believe the message of the Christian Church but really find this difficult to do, people disillusioned with the American dream of the two-car garage and the house in the country—divorce—kids drinking and using pot—job conflicts—the plumbing leaking and your husband in San Francisco—the family needs as monumental" (Dudley 1983, 10). Sid Carlson admits that this situation leads to his emphasis upon the church school, and it informs both the subject matter and the manner of his preaching.

In the years before our study began in the early 1980s, both the community and the Wiltshire Methodist Church began to slow down. The population increase began to decline. Fewer children were attending the schools. Sid reached fifty and began working on a Doctor of Ministry degree. He later confessed that he failed his doctoral examinations. His ties with the Methodist church languished. He became concerned about retirement and whether he would have enough income to send his daughters to college. People in the church began to worry about their country club image, their perceived lack of a significant social ministry, and the lack of spirituality in the congregation. Two proposals that Sid was pushing with the official board of the church were meeting defeat. One was to renovate a poorly built and inadequately furnished Christian education building. The other would enable Sid to move out of the parsonage and buy his own home. He wanted equity in a home that would give him more financial security in retirement. But there was a major problem: It is the policy of the Methodist church not to allow ministers to own their parsonages. In fact, that denomination discourages long ministries. Sid already had been at Wiltshire for over ten years.

Sid was disappointed deeply by the resistance he met on these two projects. There were conflicts, accusations, and mutual recriminations between him and certain members of the congregation. Some people were resigning from the official board; some left the church.

This congregation was the subject of much description and analysis by the authors writing in Dudley's *Building Effective Ministry.* Sociological, psychological, ethnographic, church development, theological, and practical theological points of view were brought to the analysis of the Wiltshire Methodist Church. As I look back now, it seems that it was never clear why this team, representing a great string of modern academic disciplines, was lined up to study this beleaguered church. Dudley wrote in the preface, "The purpose of this book is to provide new routes into the social and spiritual dynamics of the local church. Renewed appreciation for the congregation should release new energy among the membership to challenge and enliven the whole Body of Christ" (xii). He seemed to be saying that if we lined up a half dozen or more disciplinary snapshots of the Wiltshire Church, both secular and religious types would all learn to love and appreciate congregations more. This expectation seems now a bit pious. Some of my students, after reading the case and examining the myriad of analytic perspectives brought to it, often loved and appreciated the church less. In spite of the great benefits that the book has afforded theological educators in recent years, I believe the efforts of our team lacked an integrating center. We failed to announce forcefully at the beginning of the book that all of these analytic and descriptive points of view were aimed at contributing vitally to the practical theological examination of this church and the practical theological task of making proposals about its future. Further, in that book we failed to implement that agenda thoroughly. Implementation of such an agenda is a task that I intend to illustrate in this book.

As we will see, this church had its own style of practical theological thinking. In addition, it exhibited some features of theologically informed practical wisdom. Its main problem was the highly restricted way in which it carried its practical reason forward. I will use this church primarily to illustrate the nature of descriptive theology. The various disciplines assembled in the Dudley book were principally interested in describing that church. The main limitation of the book was its inability to situate description within a larger theological task. Its authors did not have a sufficiently hermeneutical understanding of the task of description and therefore did not understand the intimate relation between description and the nature of practical thinking. I will say much more about these matters in later chapters, especially chapters 5 and 6.

My point, of course, is not that this is simply a shortcoming of this book. Such a thesis would be of limited interest. I reexamine the Dudley book because in many ways it exemplifies how churches use the social sciences.

THE CONVENTIONAL BUT RADICAL CHURCH

From the spring of 1983 to autumn 1987 a group of eleven scholars from different parts of the country met at Christian Theological Seminary in Indianapolis to discuss the renewal of Christian education. The Lilly Endowment sponsored this also and it was given the august title of the National Faculty Seminar on Christian Education. Although a few members were professional religious educators, most of us knew very little in a formal sense about religious education. The point was to bring religious educators together with theologians, philosophers, sociologists of religion, biblical scholars, and practical theologians to see if any new insights could be generated about what Christian education should be doing in our time. I tell you these things because they are part of the story, that is, the angle of vision that this group, as a special kind of study group, brought to the study of a congregation. Honestly and explicitly positioning the social location of the researcher is, as we will see later, an extremely important component of descriptive analysis in the larger practical theological task. The question to be put to any researcher is not only What did you learn? but also How did your interests and social location influence the questions that guided you?

The task of our seminar was to gain new insights into the way Christian education interacts with its congregational context. To further this goal, we decided to study the religious education of a congregation that had recently involved itself in significant social action. We decided to study a congregation that had become a *sanctuary congregation*. By sanctuary congregation, we meant a congregation that had decided to extend hospitality to Salvadoran or Guatemalan refugees—refugees who claimed they were fleeing persecution, torture, and possible death in their respective countries but whom the U.S. government had defined as illegal aliens. Sanctuary churches were part of a national movement of several hundred churches that broke the law and treated as political refugees deserving of hospitality and protection persons whom the United States had officially defined as economic refugees and, for that reason, said should return to their homelands.

The unusual aspect of this case is that the Church of the Covenant in Centerville was a rather conservative Presbyterian church in a conservative midwestern community. For example, after its pastor went to Washington in 1964 to march with Dr. Martin Luther King, Jr., he was asked to resign. And he did resign. What led this traditional church in a cautious and conservative community to break the law to fulfill its ministry? What were the educational processes that brought the church to vote for and support this action? How did the church think theologically and practically about this commitment?

Seeds that grew into this decision were planted at a retreat for elders, deacons, and clergy during January 1983. Paul Williams, an attractive and committed businessman, was asked to speak. He was a successful electrical contractor from another town. He identified himself as an "economic conservative," a Republican, and a person who tried to take his Christianity seriously. He challenged the leaders of the Church of the Covenant by insisting that the church could "not really be the church" unless it got "involved in loving its neighbor by reaching out to the world" (Slater 1989, 3). Williams had become involved with Central American refugees whose lives were in danger. He had been to El Salvador, and he challenged his audience to join with him to address this issue.

Shortly after the retreat, Paul Williams called the church and asked it to "provide hospitality" for a group of refugees from El Salvador who were traveling through the country speaking on the sanctuary movement. The session of the church debated the issue and referred it to the mission committee. In studying the issue, the members of the mission committee quickly arrived at the conclusion that there were refugees whose lives were in danger from death squads, guerrillas, and Central American governments. They also concluded that the Immigration and Naturalization Service may have contradicted its own legal framework and certain international traditions for addressing the needs of genuine political refugees. They also were reminded that the people in the Church of the Covenant were, in general, conservatives who would find it difficult to take an action that involved breaking the law or coming into conflict with the established foreign policy of their government.

Two women invigorated the early deliberations of the mission committee—its chair, Nan Carr, and one of her committee members, Hilda Mann. The committee's work and the interactions of Nan and Hilda testify to the fact that out of the tedious machinations of mundane committee work, existential struggle and creative breakthroughs do sometimes take place. The committee drafted position papers. Nan and Hilda spent long hours consulting by phone. Together they read Bonhoeffer on the cost of discipleship. Hilda was a professor at a nearby university and was finishing a dissertation on the relation of law and gospel in the writings of Martin Luther. She also was interested in Latin American liberation theology and issues on the relation of church and state. But the sanctuary question was real and not just academic. People were suffering. Breaking the law could lead to prison, fines, embarrassment, and disruption of life plans and goals. They wrestled with what the gospel seemed to demand. They agonized about the relation of the gospel to the law. One male member of the committee resigned. Hilda herself resigned for a period when gossip and innuendo about the committee started circulating through the church.

The committee consulted *The Nuts and Bolts of Sanctuary*—a publication put out by the Chicago Task Force on Central America. In June 1983, the mission committee asked the session to vote to inform the attorney general of the United States and their representatives in Congress that the Church of the Covenant supported the action of churches in the sanctuary movement. On June 19, the session confirmed this action, and the two pastors of the church wrote and signed a letter addressed to these officials.

The mission committee then turned to formulating a plan for educating the congregation on the sanctuary issue. Hilda Mann rejoined the committee. The plan was simple but comprehensive. It aspired to involve both the adults and the youth of the church. (This church had a huge youth program involving approximately 150 young people for a dinner and program every Thursday evening. The youth program was a central focus of the ministry of this church

and had been so since the coming of Hal Roberts, the present senior minister, some ten years earlier.) In addition to the adults and
youths in the church, interested outsiders from the community of
Centerville were also invited to participate in the sanctuary program. This set up a kind of dialogue between the church and the
community on the sanctuary issue.

The program was called "Latin America—Paradise Lost." It
consisted of a ten-week series of lecture-discussions presented at
10 A.M. Sunday morning with discussion continuing during coffee
hour after church. The committee attempted to balance different
points of view on the topic, but was never sure it adequately represented more conservative views. Members of the course were asked
to purchase and read Dietrich Bonhoeffer's *The Cost of Discipleship*
(1949). Pastor Roberts was invited to preach on scriptural texts and
topics relevant to the sanctuary issue, but he declined. He reported
that he was following the lectionary; in addition, he had decided
three years earlier to center his preaching on God's grace and the
tensions between gospel and law but declined to apply this message
to the sanctuary discussion.

At the conclusion of the ten-week course, the session appointed
a new study group to draft a resolution on sanctuary. Nan Carr was
the only member of the mission committee asked to be a part of
this drafting committee. When the session appointed the new study
group, Paul Williams announced that four Salvadoran refugees had
arrived in Centerville. Although the Church of the Covenant was
not officially asked then for help, certain members of the congregation started to help. The study group attended a reception for
the refugees.

The study group soon formulated a resolution. It built a case
that persecution of Central Americans was taking place, that the
Refugee Act of 1980 (Public Law 96-212) provided protection under
"Extended Voluntary Departure Status," that the U.S. government
through its membership in the United Nations was committed to
granting asylum to political refugees, and that the government ha-
bitually turned down approximately 95 percent of the applications
of persecuted refugees from El Salvador and Guatemala. It concluded with the statement, "Now therefore the Congregation of The
Church of the Covenant... meeting on January 29, 1984, publicly an-
nounces that this church will offer the protection of the sanctuary
to refugees from El Salvador and Guatemala, who have legitimate
fear of deportation to their homeland and persecution upon return"
(Slater 1989, 12). The resolution passed with a vote of 151 to 91.
The Sunday before the annual meeting when the vote was taken,
the associate pastor, Carl Gordon, preached a sermon that seemed

relevant to the vote. His text was Matthew 2:1-18 and his title was "The Trip Back Home." He drew a connection with the "civil disobedience" of the Wise Men who ignored the instruction of the authorities in order to protect the lives of Jesus, Mary, and Joseph—who themselves fled the land of Israel, where they were threatened with persecution, to become refugees in Egypt. Few people in the congregation missed the act of civil disobedience when they heard the Matthean words, "And having been warned in a dream not to return to Herod, they left for their own country by another road" (Matt. 2:12). Nor did they miss Jesus' status as a refugee when they heard the words, "Now after they had left, an angel of the Lord appeared to Joseph in a dream and said, 'Get up, take the child and his mother, and flee to Egypt, and remain there until I tell you; for Herod is about to search for the child, to destroy him'" (Matt. 2:13).

The practical theological thinking of the Church of the Covenant is the most discernible of any of these three churches. In addition, the structure of practical reason comes into play in this case most tellingly and more expansively than in the case of the Wiltshire Methodist Church. The multidimensional character of practical thinking is visible. Much of the inner core of practical reason was discerned by the lay members of the congregation with the professional ministers of the congregation contributing important aspects of the envelope of practical reason. Yet even this neat division of labor is not quite accurate. Some lay people, particularly Nan Carr and Hilda Mann, did much to contribute to an understanding of a crucial aspect of this envelope—the role of sacrifice and the cross in extending the reach of practical reason in a Christian context.

EMPOWERMENT IN A BLACK PENTECOSTAL CHURCH

In reporting on the Apostolic Church of God, I will depart from the method used in the cases above where pseudonyms were used for the names of the church, the minister, and members of the congregation. In discussing this church, I will use the real name of the church, the Apostolic Church of God, and the actual name of its senior minister, the Reverend Arthur Brazier. I will use pseudonyms only for the lay people and other members of the staff who have not achieved the prominence of Brazier. It would be impossible to disguise the identity of Brazier; I will not attempt it. Arthur Brazier already has achieved national prominence because of his early leadership in The Woodlawn Organization (TWO). This was a Saul Alinsky-style community organization that tried to gain for Woodlawn the political power necessary to overcome the ravages of its descent in the 1940s and 1950s to the status of one of Chicago's most notorious slums. The story of the early years of The Woodlawn Organization has been well chronicled in Brazier's *Black Self-determination* (1969), Charles Silberman's *Crisis in Black and White* (1964), and John Fish's exhaustive study, *Black Power/White Control* (1973).

Those of us who lived just to the north in Hyde Park had heard of Brazier and The Woodlawn Organization. We knew that in the early 1960s he had been the organization's most articulate representative and for a period its president. We also knew that TWO had been in conflict with the University of Chicago over the university's desire to purchase and develop for its own purposes some property in north Woodlawn—a project that threatened to displace poor people. In true Alinsky style, the battle between TWO and the University of Chicago had been a rallying point that had helped motivate and organize the constituencies of TWO. I was a member of the faculty of the university then. Students and friends of mine in the divinity school of the university had been involved in TWO.

Although I and other Hyde Park liberals knew something about Brazier as an activist, we knew nothing about him as a religious leader. Black religion was a mysterious and undifferentiated reality to white liberals in the 1960s. We saw and even participated to some extent in its political expression in the black civil rights movement. But we did not know the dynamics and power of its inner recesses—its Sunday worship, its congregational preaching, and above all its tremendous and developing music. I was not prepared for what I found the first Sunday I visited the Apostolic Church of God.

I was looking for an inner-city church that would allow me to study its practices of pastoral and congregational care. For some years I had thought that writers in pastoral care (or poimenics) needed to spend more time studying what pastors and congregations actually do in addition to making proposals about what they ought to do. I also had concluded that we should go beyond the clerical paradigm and study not only what ordained ministers do but what the congregation as a whole does—although often this is done under the guidance of the minister. I had tried my hand at this in an essay that reported on a study of the care practices of the church that I attend (Wheeler and Hough 1988). Now I wanted to study a church different from the liberal Protestant churches I knew. I wanted to study a church facing an entirely different set of problems. I decided to study an African American church on the South Side of Chicago.

I went to the Apostolic Church of God for the first time during the autumn of 1988. I was not aware that this was the church

pastored by the well-known Reverend Arthur Brazier. I went search-
ing for the church because I once had been invited to visit it by a
former black student at the divinity school who had served as its
director of music. As I approached the church in my car, I noticed
that the huge parking lot surrounding the church was full. I soon
discovered that automobiles were parked two abreast around the
entire block. Handsome, young, uniformed guards equipped with
walkie-talkies courteously suggested that the lot to the north of the
church might have an opening. It did not. I finally parked on the
street a block away.

The Apostolic Church of God is on the corner of Sixty-third
and Kenwood in the heart of Woodlawn. The neighborhood looks
something like the pictures of Berlin shortly after the Allied bomb-
ing during the last months of World War II. It is replete with empty,
burned-out, or otherwise disintegrating buildings, especially in the
east end of Woodlawn where the Apostolic Church of God is located. The church itself occupies a handsome red-brick building
that was little more than ten years old. It sat, however, in the
shadow of a huge, old abandoned warehouse marked by thousands
of crumbling bricks and hundreds of shattered windows. I learned
a few weeks after I started attending the church that the old warehouse was soon to be torn down and that the church was about
to build its second new sanctuary to contain its rapidly increasing
membership.

When I entered the church I was met by an usher whose uniform
was accented, as they say in the fashion business, by white gloves.
He took me to my seat. A sanctuary holding what I estimated to
be approximately twelve hundred black men, women, and children
spread out before me. Everyone seemed exceptionally well dressed.
The little girls wore beautiful dresses and the little boys white shirts
and ties. I soon learned that this was the second service of the
morning. The first service also had twelve hundred or more people
attending.

Facing me on a wide stage was a ninety-voice choir dressed in
robes matching the uniforms worn by the ushers. On the left of the
stage was a young black man playing a grand piano. On the right
of the stage was an ensemble of musicians playing what from my
experience was an unusual variety of instruments for a church—one
electric organ, one electric keyboard, a full set of orchestra drums, a
set of bongo drums, an electric guitar, and two trumpets. In front of
the choir was a row of fifteen or so handsome men (there was one
woman in the group) dressed in tasteful business suits. They were
obviously not members of the choir. Was this the church board?
Were they the staff? Whoever they were, they constituted a powerful

and reassuring background to the pastor when, in a few minutes, he stood to speak.

I noticed that there were no hymnals in the pews—only Bibles. The choir, which was precise, confident, and powerful, did not use music either. Everyone in the entire church seemed to know all the music by heart. What was this music I was hearing? Was it gospel? Was it rock? Was it something different from either of these? The soloist and choir were supported by a thunderous accompaniment from the organ, piano, and other instruments. As the music rose in intensity and force, one by one members of the congregation stood and extended an arm and hand in the direction of the soloist and, with closed eyes and bodies swaying with the beat of the music, seemed to receive some kind of direct nonsensory communication from a power that spoke through the music but came from beyond it.

The sermon opened themes that were paradigmatic of what I was to hear often during the months I worshiped at the Apostolic Church of God. The text came from 2 Corinthians 8:9: "For you know the generous act of our Lord Jesus Christ, that though he was rich, yet for your sakes he became poor, so that by his poverty you might become rich." The sermon emphasized the richness of the life of God and the richness of the gift of the Holy Spirit. This and other sermons I was to hear described the richness and power of the self of those believers who received the Holy Spirit. Such persons were sanctified. They were in fact veritable "saints" with an entirely transformed capacity to live a responsible moral life.

On this Sunday and over the following months, I heard a message that incorporated an extremely powerful and generous portrait of God as a source of affirmation and empowerment for the people of the Apostolic Church of God. This generous message of love, grace, recognition, and empowerment by the Holy Spirit was balanced with equally challenging demands to live a personal and social moral life at the highest level. Supported by electrifying music, forceful and eloquent preaching, and a rousing sense of joy and spontaneity, this demanding call for near moral perfection sounded amazingly light, bearable, unoppressive, and nonmoralistic to my white middle-class ears—and apparently to the ears of everyone around me. I did not feel that the black people in the pews beside me were being intimidated, frightened, repressed, or oppressed by the clear moral expectations bursting forth from the cascades of words of Arthur Brazier's sermons. Although his moral demands exceeded anything I had heard for years coming from the pulpits of mainstream Protestant churches, to these black people the gulf between the spiritual power that his sermons offered and the heightened moral expectations they stated seemed manageable indeed.

Brazier has been the minister of the Apostolic Church of God for over thirty years. His church is a member of the Pentecostal Assemblies of the World, a black spin-off of the spiritualistic wing of the Methodist church. But it is a long way from the Methodism of the Wiltshire Church and the kind of Methodism that gave rise to the Pentecostal Assemblies of the World. One thing, among others, that stands between them is the Azusa Street Mission in Los Angeles around the year 1906. Under the leadership of W. J. Seymour, an uneducated black minister, both blacks and whites became grasped by the Holy Spirit and began speaking in tongues. Out of this beginning a variety of black and white Pentecostal movements arose, such as the largely white Assemblies of God, the largely black Church of God in Christ, and the mainly black Pentecostal Assemblies of the World. Brazier is also a bishop of this denomination.

I came to this church primarily to study its pastoral and congregational care. More specifically, I came to enter into a practical theological dialogue with the church about the nature of the church's care. I did not know what I would find. I did not know whether a dialogue would be possible or even welcome. I simply knew that I wanted to do the research in order to illustrate some of my convictions about the relation of social science research to practical theological thinking. Also, I wanted to enrich my thinking about pastoral and congregational care by looking at some vastly different approaches from the ones I knew in the mainline Protestant churches. What I found in the Apostolic Church of God far exceeded in interest and power anything I expected in my most expansive dreams. I soon learned that I had much to learn from this church and that if anything, the practical theological dialogue that would occur between us might soon become one-sided—very much in favor of this church. Would I, as a reasonably respected scholar from the University of Chicago, have anything to contribute to the dialogue at all?

I found in this church a remarkable congregational care organization with several dimensions, all of which were guided by the mind, philosophy, and ethics of Arthur Brazier. In little over ten years, his church had grown from around five hundred to well over five thousand members. To address the needs of this small city of people, Brazier had constructed a variety of care initiatives. First there was the pastoral care leadership of Arthur Brazier himself. To understand this, one needed to grasp his compassion, intelligence, energy, and clarity of religious and moral vision. Although Brazier entered into virtually every aspect of the care life of the church, he also shared the responsibilities with others.

Among the great variety of structures, which I will review in detail in chapter 10, there was the Christian Action Lay Ministry. This was the idea of a lay woman who was also a professional psychologist. This was an extensive referral and counseling program that provided legal, marital, youth, job placement, college preparation, and substance abuse services to members and their extended families. Helen Barnes was the founder and volunteer director of the program. Through her I was soon introduced to a different model of relating Christianity to psychology, psychiatry, and the social service professions—different, at least, from what I was used to in much of my mainline Protestant experience. In this context the presuppositions of Pentecostal religious experience and ethics were clearly in control and guided the relation between Christianity and the psychological disciplines. For these people, the power that produced change in people was first of all the Holy Spirit and only secondarily human psychotherapy. As far as I could tell, the "triumph of the therapeutic" that Philip Rieff wrote about in the 1960s had not occurred in the Apostolic Church of God (Rieff 1966). Psychology and psychiatry were used, but they had not triumphed.

I decided I would concentrate on the congregation's care of families and couples. It soon became clear that a deep and abiding interest in the family was at the heart of Brazier's ministry. The problems of the black, inner-city family and their remedies received the great proportion of his energy—that is his preaching, counseling, programing, and public ministry. Family ministry, family care and counseling, and family ethics—these would be my angle of vision, my principle of selection, as I studied this church. I had always wondered how black families confronted the pressures of racism, bad neighborhoods, poor schools, inadequate income, teen-age gangs, and the ever-increasing intrusion of drugs to develop strong marriages and healthy, self-directing children. Although clearly there were many middle-class and upper-middle-class families in the Apostolic Church, it was likely that even they indirectly, if not directly, faced many of these same pressures.

The research took the form of a dialogue; I employed the value-active interview technique used by Robert Bellah et al. in *Habits of the Heart* (1985) and by Steven Tipton in *Getting Saved from the Sixties* (1982). I could soon see this would present new challenges that allegedly more objective social science research does not always directly encounter. Research as dialogue fully acknowledges the possibility that I might change this church or that it might change me. The focus of my practical theological dialogue with the Apos-

tolic Church would be a family ethic in the church that appeared
to exhibit what white liberals currently called male supremacy. I
soon discovered it was an ethic of male responsibility as well.
It was an ethic that proclaimed that men should be the spiritual
and intellectual leaders of their families. This was also associated
with a strong stance against divorce, cohabitation of the unmar-
ried, teen-age pregnancies, and adultery. My practical theological
dialogue with this church would center on the comparison of its
family ethic with the ethic of mutuality and equal-regard emerging
among feminists in the mainline Protestant churches.

The possibility that in this dialogue I might be converted was
brought home at the conclusion of my first interview with Helen
Barnes. She told me that she believed God was doing something
special in bringing me to her church. She said that it was her custom to invoke an experience of the Holy Spirit for everyone with
whom she comes into contact. With both confidence and warmth
growing in her voice, she promised to lead me into an experience
of the Holy Spirit. She predicted that I too would someday speak
in tongues. She took me to the prayer room in the church—the
room to which she had taken countless drug addicts, married couples, and other counselees. Praying for the gift and guidance of the
Holy Spirit was the first thing she did, I was told, before she started
counseling anyone. As we stood together there in the prayer room,
she looked deeply into my eyes as if to imply that whatever kind of
Christian I was when I came to her, sooner or later I would leave
as a "sanctified saint" speaking a new language and full of the Holy
Ghost. I felt the power of her certainty and deep conviction. I knew
that I stood before someone with a depth of religious experience
that far exceeded mine. I—with my liberal, intellectual Christianity,
my preoccupations with the relation of practical reason and religion, and my typically academic concerns for methodology—stood
before someone who believed that she had met God through the
Holy Spirit, and she believed that before our dialogue was over, she
would give that experience to me.

While we stood in the prayer room talking, another woman
poked her head in the door and uttered the ubiquitous words,
"Praise the Lord." These words are called out any time two members of the Apostolic Church meet one another. Following this,
Helen Barnes asked, "Is your daughter in Paris?" The answer was,
"Yes." Then as the door shut, Mrs. Barnes said to me, "Oh, you
never know where these kids are going to be these days. Paris?
The Riviera?" Such a remark could have fallen from the mouth of
a faculty spouse in the community around the University of Chicago. When I heard it in the prayer room at the Apostolic Church,

I knew that however far apart our worlds were, the distance was narrowing.

At first glance, the practical theology at the Apostolic Church seemed anything but an example of a critical hermeneutical or revised correlational approach—the approach I will champion in the rest of this book. Upon closer inspection, the contours of this method are discernible. In addition, the contours of practical reason, as I will define it, were also there. Brazier's theology of sanctification emphasizes the workings of the Holy Spirit more than does the theological ethics of Niebuhr. It will be with Niebuhr's thought that I will first illustrate the ways the Christian narrative can inform the logic of practical reason. Niebuhr will help us to discern the unique way in which Brazier's view of the Christian narrative informs the workings of practical reason within the context of the Apostolic Church. The range of practical reason is more limited at the Apostolic Church than it was at the Church of the Covenant. In this, Wiltshire Methodist Church and the Apostolic Church have more in common. The emergency surrounding the Apostolic Church may justify its more restricted focus. Although in some way less expansive, the power of practical reason at the Apostolic Church runs deep. Few churches I have ever known have done more for their people and their neighborhoods. Its theology was truly a "local theology," to use Robert Schreiter's important phrase (Schreiter 1985). Its religiously informed practical reason functioned in a limited circle, but within that circle it accomplished a great deal.

With these three cases in mind, I now turn to more theoretical discussion of the somewhat intimidating turns and twists of methodology in practical theology. Wiltshire Methodist Church, the Centerville Church of the Covenant, and the Apostolic Church of God will serve as illustrations of the process I will often discuss more formally. These illustrations will remind us that the leaders of these congregations, as well as each congregation as a whole, are practical theological thinkers.

EXPLORING PRACTICAL WISDOM
AND UNDERSTANDING

T he new vision of practical theology to be developed in these
pages will be greatly enriched by the contemporary turn to
practical philosophy. What is the importance of this turn? Why
should it interest all practical theologians be they ministers, lay
persons, or theological educators? Why should these philosophical
resources be as relevant to the Sid Carlsons and Arthur Braziers of
the world as they are to professional theological educators such as
James Fowler, Edward Farley, or Thomas Groome?

THE REBIRTH OF PRACTICAL PHILOSOPHY

The phrase *practical philosophy* refers to a loosely associated group
of philosophical positions that emphasize the importance of practical wisdom or *phronēsis* in contrast to theoretical reason (*theoria*)
or technical reason (*technē*). Since the Enlightenment, the modern experiment has been dedicated to the improvement of human
life through the increase of objective scientific knowledge (*theoria*)
that is then applied to the solution of human problems (*technē*).
The modern university has built itself on the idea of increasing
the cognitive and theoretical grasp of our social and natural environments. Issues pertaining to the goals of human action generally
are reduced to the technical solution of perceived problems. The
goals of action in modern societies increasingly are held to be self-
evident, or are viewed as a matter of individual choice, or are taken
over uncritically from the surrounding culture.

The rebirth of practical philosophy signals a wish to question
the dominance of theoretical and technical reason, to secure in our
culture and in the university a strong role for practical reason, and
to demonstrate that critical reflection about the goals of human action is both possible and necessary. Further, the rise of the practical
philosophies, especially as influenced by Gadamer, has brought into

closer relation historical thinking, hermeneutics or interpretation theory, and practical reason or ethics. This has brought a recognition that our present concerns shape the way we interpret the past. The reverse is also true. Solving our present ethical problems involves appropriating and reconstructing the past. These philosophical currents emphasize the importance of situations and how the situations of our inquiries inevitably color not only our practical thinking but all pursuit of knowledge and understanding.

We will see this in our three churches. Take for instance the Church of the Covenant. During the period of its sanctuary discussions, when that church interpreted the past, it often did so in light of the twofold question from the present about what it means to be both a good Christian *and* a good citizen. When the members of the Apostolic Church of God interpreted the Scriptures, they brought questions from their contemporary concerns over the state of the black family. We are not surprised to hear that these churches think in such a manner. The point of much of the recent turn to practical philosophy is that all thinking functions that way.

These intellectual currents are influencing theological education and the way we envision the structure and movement of theology. The organization of theological education shapes much of the self-understanding of ministers and other church leaders as well as the professors who teach in theological schools. The influence of these intellectual currents on theological education can be seen especially in Edward Farley's *Theologia* (1983a) and his more recent *The Fragility of Knowledge* (1988). The new centrality of the category of the practical also is visible in the proposals of John Cobb and Joseph Hough in their *Christian Identity and Theological Education* (1985) when they make "practical theological thinking" and "practical theology" the center of a reform of theological education.

There is additional evidence of the influence of practical philosophy on both theological education and practical theology. New definitions of practical theology can be found in Germany (Mette 1980; Klostermann and Zerfass 1974; Rössler 1986), Holland (van der Ven 1988; Firet 1987), England (Ballard 1986), Canada (Viau 1987), Latin America (Segundo 1976), and the United States. These formulations greatly enlarge the province of practical theology. Rather than envisioning practical theology as primarily theological reflection on the tasks of the ordained minister or the leadership of the church, as was the view of Schleiermacher (Schleiermacher [1830] 1966; Burkhart 1983), these newer trends define practical theology as critical reflection on the church's ministry to the world (Campbell 1972). In the United States, two volumes of essays have appeared that explicitly advance this newer picture of practical theology—a collection that I edited titled *Practical Theology* (Browning 1983a) and *Formation and Reflection* (Mudge and Poling 1987). In recent years we have witnessed the publication in the United States of several books dealing explicitly with the reconceptualization of practical theology. These books include some published by myself (Browning 1983a, 1983b), and by Fowler (1987), Gerkin (1986), Groome (1987), Schreiter (1985), Winquist (1981), Miller and Poling (1985), and McCann and Strain (1985). This publishing indicates the breadth and vigor of this renewed interest in practical theology and the growing influence of the practical philosophies.

RADICAL IMPLICATIONS

In spite of this interest in practical theology, the radical implications of the turn to practical philosophy have still not been comprehended fully in either ministry, theology, or theological education. It seems not to be understood that, if this philosophical turn is taken seriously, all humanistic studies, including theological studies, must be recognized as practical and historical through and through. In this view, all theology becomes practical theology. Historical theology, systematic theology, strategic practical theology, and what I will introduce as descriptive theology all become moments in a more inclusive fundamental practical theology. Furthermore, since much of the turn to practical philosophy presently emphasizes dialogue and conversation, these concepts will influence my basic definition of fundamental practical theology. I find it useful to think of fundamental practical theology as critical reflection on the church's dialogue with Christian sources and other communities of experience and interpretation with the aim of guiding its action toward social and individual transformation.

It may be difficult to see how the leaders and congregations in our three churches were doing practical theology as dialogue and conversation. They were doing it with different styles and with varying degrees of emphasis on the submoments of the total task. They were doing their practical theology out of vastly different situations and beginning points. This influenced how they interpreted their problems and looked for answers. Nonetheless, they all did practical theology more or less as dialogue, and I will soon illustrate how this was so. Clearly there was dialogue at the Church of the Covenant as its members inquired into the contemporary situation of Central American refugees, the practices of the Immigration and Naturalization Service, the past practices of the Church of the Covenant itself, and the witness of Scripture—all to the end of determining a consensus that would provide direction for their response to the refugee issue. In a very different way, Sid Carlson was in a contentious, troubled, unfree, and distorted dialogue with his congregation about the nature of his ministry and the purposes of the Wiltshire Church. The practical theological thinking done by Art Brazier may look the least dialogical. The immense authority that his congregation accorded to him gave him a wide range of initiative. But Brazier's practical hermeneutical dialogue between the situation of the Apostolic Church of God and the scriptural classics of the Pentecostal tradition was so sensitive to the situation of his members' lives that he too must be seen as doing practical theology as dialogue.

FEATURES OF GADAMER'S THOUGHT

Crucial features of the practical philosophies can best be understood by examining aspects of the thought of Hans-Georg Gadamer. Gadamer is a contemporary German philosopher in the tradition of Martin Heidegger, Edmund Husserl, Wilhelm Dilthey, and Friedrich Schleiermacher. These thinkers attempted to redefine and ground what academicians call the cultural or moral sciences (*Geisteswissenschaften*) in contrast to the natural sciences (*Naturwissenschaften*). Gadamer is the most recent thinker in this tradition who has attempted to find the philosophical ground for academic disciplines such as history, philosophy, psychology, sociology, and law. These are the disciplines that should study the meaning of the action of human beings considered as relatively free and intentional creatures. The central question occupying Gadamer and his predecessors is how to distinguish these disciplines from the prestigious natural sciences of physics, chemistry, and certain branches of biology—disciplines that study objects (in contrast to intentional human subjects) in the natural world.

Gadamer has developed the idea that all of these cultural disciplines are rooted in the fundamental structure of human understanding—a structure he describes under the model of "dialogue" and "conversation" (Gadamer 1982, 330). This is a very simple idea, the significance of which is difficult to grasp at first. When placed against the background of the thought of two of his predecessors, the significance of this concept of human understanding as dialogue becomes apparent. Dilthey thought that humans understand past historical epochs, for example, through an act of empathy; historians empty themselves and attempt an imaginative identification with the experience of the historical actors they are trying to understand (Dilthey [1900] 1972). Husserl thought, rather, that we understand meanings through an objective act of description that

involves pushing aside, neutralizing, or bracketing all our personal
prejudices and commitments (Husserl [1936] 1970).

Gadamer, following the lead of Heidegger, developed the view
that the kind of objectivity and self-emptying required by Dilthey
and Husserl was not only impossible to achieve but unfruitful in
promoting good understanding and adequate praxis. He said that
understanding was like a dialogue or conversation where we actually use our prejudices and commitments in the understanding
process. Gadamer calls these prejudices and commitments "fore-
understandings" or "fore-concepts" (Gadamer 1982, 235, 261). In
contrast to the Enlightenment project of expunging all biases or
prejudgments from understanding, Gadamer says that we must use
them positively. We understand things only in contrast or relation to
them. Our prejudices in the sense of fore-concepts should not dominate our understanding totally but should be used positively for
the contrasting light they can throw on what we study. As Gadamer
writes, "This kind of sensitivity involves neither 'neutrality' about
the object nor the extinction of oneself, but the conscious assim-
ilation of one's own fore-meanings and prejudices. The important
thing is to be aware of one's own bias, so that the text may present
itself in all its newness and thus be able to assert its own truth
against one's own fore-meanings" (238). I will carry these points
with me as I turn to a neglected aspect of Gadamer's hermeneutical philosophy—the relation of understanding and morality. This
topic is extremely important for the reconceptualization of practical
theology that I am attempting here.

UNDERSTANDING AND PRACTICAL WISDOM

Understanding and interpretation, whether in law, history, or theology, have for Gadamer a broadly moral concern with application.
Interpreters of Gadamer often overlook this point. It is this that
makes Gadamer's concept of understanding a bridge between historical reason and practical reason. Gadamer draws this relation
when he points out that Aristotle's concept of *phronēsis* or practical
wisdom may serve as a model of the process of understanding. The
key text is found in the middle of *Truth and Method* when he writes,
"If we relate Aristotle's description of the ethical phenomenon and
especially of the virtue of moral knowledge to our own investigation, we find that Aristotle's analysis is in fact a kind of model of
the problems of hermeneutics" (Gadamer 1982, 289).

Gadamer makes this point in discussing the role of application
in both his own view of understanding and Aristotle's concept of
phronēsis. The hermeneutic process aimed at understanding any

kind of human action—a classic text, work of art, letter, sermon, or political act—is like a moral conversation, when the word *moral* is understood in the broadest sense. The hermeneutical conversation is like Aristotle's practical wisdom because neither applies abstract universals to concrete situations. In both hermeneutical conversation and moral judgment, concern with application is there from the beginning. Gadamer says it more directly: "Application is neither a subsequent nor a merely occasional part of the phenomenon of understanding, but co-determines it as a whole from the beginning" (289). Understanding is a moral conversation shaped throughout by practical concerns about application that emerge from our current situation.

More than commentators have acknowledged, Gadamer sees hermeneutics as a broadly moral and practical enterprise that emerges out of the situations of our traditions of practice. When these practices become problematic, we try to orient ourselves by reexamining the classic sources that have shaped our present practices. The classic sources are generally religio-cultural texts and monuments. For Christians these texts and monuments are the Scriptures, the Hebrew and Greek sources that have informed them, and the major texts and monuments that have shaped the Christian tradition down through the ages. When seen from this perspective, understanding as interpretation and *phronēsis* as practical wisdom interpenetrate. Richard Bernstein astutely observes that it is a central thesis of Gadamer's *Truth and Method* that understanding, interpretation, and application are not distinct but intimately related. "They are internally related; every act of understanding involves interpretation, and all interpretation involves application. It is Aristotle's analysis of *phronêsis* that, according to Gadamer, enables us to understand the distinctive way in which application is an essential moment of the hermeneutical experience" (Bernstein 1983, 38).

This is the key to the relevance of Gadamer's practical philosophy for theology in general and practical theology in particular. Application to practice is not an act that follows understanding. It guides the interpretive process from the beginning, often in subtle, overlooked ways. Gadamer's hermeneutic theory clearly breaks down the theory-to-practice (text-to-application) model of humanistic learning. By analogy, it undercuts this model in theological studies as well. It implies more nearly a radical practice-theory-practice model of understanding that gives the entire theological enterprise a thoroughly practical cast.

Gadamer's theory of understanding not only breaks down the theory-to-practice model in the humanities and theology; it does this, as we will see in later chapters, in the social sciences as well. Richard Bernstein and Richard Rorty, with different degrees of debt to Gadamer, have carried hermeneutic theory into the philosophy of the natural sciences (Bernstein 1983, 173–74; Rorty 1979, 192–209). Earlier Thomas Kuhn's own variety of hermeneutic theory helped alert us to the tradition-laden nature of the natural sciences. These sciences, according to Kuhn, are not made up simply of raw empirical observations and replicable experiments that add up to sure and steady progress. They are made up of traditions and communities of observation and experimentation unconsciously guided by dominant paradigms that are not so much definitively disproved as relegated to the sidelines by boredom and lack of interest (Kuhn 1970, 41, 53). These hermeneutic thinkers have all undercut what philosophers call "foundationalist" preoccupations with anchoring knowledge on pure and undistorted sense impressions or something like a priori first principles or transcendental notions, that is, something certain, objective, and neutral. Both Gadamerian hermeneutic theory and North American pragmatism have blocked the bid by naive realism, positivism, and various forms of Kantian or phenomenological idealism to rid knowledge of history, tradition, finitude, and partiality. They have helped us understand how all cultural sciences (*Geisteswissenschaften*) and many if not all natural sciences (*Naturwissenschaften*) can best be understood as dialectical movements from traditions of theory-laden practice to theory and back to new theory-laden practices.

This rough equivalence of understanding and *phronēsis* is what I mean by the *envelope* of practical reason. I introduced this concept in the Introduction. It is distinguishable from what I call the *inner core* of practical reason. The envelope of practical reason is the focus of that larger task of reconstructing our experience by reconstructing, amending, or reconsolidating our more general picture of the world. The outer envelope of practical reason is made up of tradition-saturated images and visions of the way the world is at the ultimate edges of experience. The inner core of practical reason needs the envelope of this larger interpretive and hermeneutic process in order to have a sense of the wider reality in which it functions.

The practical nature of the hermeneutical process is even more interesting and complicated when viewed from the perspective of Gadamer's concept of "effective history." Gadamer develops the idea that the events of the past shape present historical consciousness. What does this mean? To answer this, Gadamer would point out that there is a "fusion of the whole of the past with the present" (Gadamer 1982, 273). This means something that common sense admits but may not fully understand. The past does not just die and exist as a frozen corpse totally inert, impotent, and unable to shape present events. The present is largely a product of the past. The past lives in the present whether we realize it or not.

This has implications for Christian theology. It suggests that when we interpret the classic religious texts of our past, we do not confront them as totally separate and alien entities. This is true for believers who interpret these texts and also for unbelieving interpreters. These texts are part of the sensibilities of believers and unbelievers before they begin their interpretive task, especially if they stand in any way within the Western religious heritage. Through our cultural heritage, these texts and monuments shape the fore-understandings that make up the practical questions we bring to our efforts to interpret them. Gadamer depicts the process of understanding as a fusion of the horizon of meaning surrounding the practical questions and fore-meanings that we bring to these texts and the horizon of meaning that the texts themselves project. The meanings of these classic texts already have shaped our questions (173–74, 331–41).

The idea that practical thinking moves from practice to theory to practice, not from theory to practice, can be illustrated by references to the Wiltshire Methodist Church. The members of Wiltshire are deeply embedded in practices that attempt to balance the demands of the corporate office with home and family as refuge—rhythms of life typical of upper-middle-class and upper-class suburbanites. These practices have meanings or theories. Some of my sociological colleagues on our research team characterized the theory of these practices as a typical Protestant ethic of work and upward mobility (Carroll, McKinney, and Roof 1983, 96). Our two psychologists called it an unconscious strategy of "expectancy" by which the congregation uses its pastor and religion to consolidate its drive toward success (Evans and Reed 1983, 48). James Hopewell used the myth of Zeus—who killed his oppressive father, Chronus—to get at the real unconscious theory behind Wiltshire's practices. Just as Zeus killed Chronus for the sake of liberation, Sid Carlson, the pastor at Wiltshire, is attempting to "kill" the Adams Company to liberate the church for a spiritual success commensurate with the financial and social success enjoyed by the church's members in their everyday lives (Hopewell 1983, 72–73). The rich questions that the members of Wiltshire Methodist ask of the texts and monuments of the Christian faith come out of the situation of their (largely unconscious) theory-laden practices. These practices and their theories constitute part of the fore-understanding that the congregation brings to its interpretation of the Christian message. The people of this church expect that their Christian resources will empower them to face the challenge of the world of success that they so energetically pursue. It is not clear, however, that the Wiltshire congregation can become sufficiently aware of its fore-concepts to keep from distorting the interpretive process. Our fore-concepts are necessary for interpretation, but we must be aware of them. If Gadamer is right about the structure of human understanding, what Wiltshire does (although not very well) in relating its practices and fore-concepts to its classics differs little from what any interpreter—even a scholar in the humanities—does in the process of understanding. There is a concern with application, however mute and unacknowledged, present from the beginning.

IMPLICATIONS FOR THEOLOGICAL STUDIES

If this is true—if there is a parallel between Gadamer's theory of understanding and what a religious community such as Wiltshire does—this gives us insight into the structure of theological reflection. Does Wiltshire have a stake in this question? Does it have a stake in how theologians and seminaries conceptualize the structure of theology? I think that it does. If Wiltshire's ministers understood the nature of theological thinking better, they might be able to lead the congregation to a more creative response to its problems.

So far I have not argued that Gadamer's hermeneutical theories are correct. I address my argument to those already attracted by the conversation or hermeneutical model of understanding. Guided by Gadamer's view of the practical nature of hermeneutics, I would like to propose a theory of the structure of theological studies. It is a theory that I hope will illuminate the theological thinking of Wiltshire Methodist Church, the Church of the Covenant, and the Apostolic Church of God.

My recommendation is simple. I propose that we conceive theology primarily as fundamental practical theology. Under this general rubric, I envision theology, as I already have suggested, as having the four submovements of descriptive theology, historical theology, systematic theology, and strategic or fully practical theology. These distinctions are not meaningful just within the confines of academic theology. They open the structure of theological reflection no matter where it occurs—in the pulpit, in the pastoral conversation, in the counseling room, in the setting of clinical pastoral education, in the educational situation, on the mission field, or in Christian social service.

This view differs from several well-known proposals for the organization of theology. For instance, it differs somewhat from Schleiermacher's organization of theology into philosophical theology, historical theology, and practical theology (Schleiermacher [1830] 1966, 25-27). Although Schleiermacher saw practical theology as the teleological goal and "crown" of theology, his view of theology still had a theory-to-practice structure. He understood theology as a movement from philosophical and historical theology to application in practical theology (91-126). It is true that this structure is altered by the fact that Schleiermacher understood the whole of theology as a positive science in contrast to a pure or theoretical science. By positive science, Schleiermacher meant "an assemblage of scientific elements which belong together, not because they form a constituent part of the organization of the sciences, as though by some necessity arising out of the notion of science itself, but only insofar as they are requisite for carrying out a practical task" (19). Such a view of theology clearly emphasizes its practical, conditioned, and historically located nature and makes all theology a basically practical task. It has, therefore, some affinities with the close association of historical reason and practical reason that we noticed in Gadamer's hermeneutic philosophy. Nonetheless, Schleiermacher saw theology in general as moving from historical knowledge to practical application; he had little idea how the practices of the church form the questions we bring to the historical sources.

My proposal also can be distinguished from other current understandings of the structure of theology. Paul Tillich divided theology into historical theology, systematic theology, and practical theology (Tillich 1951, 29). In the end, this too was a theory-to-practice model. Although Tillich granted that practical theology has a role in formulating the questions that systematic theology answers (33), his perspective clearly emphasized the theory-practice dichotomy. In his *Systematic Theology* he wrote, "It is the technical point of view that distinguishes practical from theoretical theology. As occurs in every cognitive approach to reality, a bifurcation between pure and applied knowledge takes place in theology" (1951, 33). Tillich softened this statement somewhat by affirming that all theology is an existential enterprise. Even so, meaning rather than the reconstruction of practice was his central thrust.

Both Schubert Ogden and David Tracy give heightened visibility to practical theology in their respective proposals for the organization of theology. Ogden indicates several ways in which he believes that practical theology is the application to practice of the truth of norms discovered by historical and systematic theology. He proposes a division of theology into historical, systematic, and practical theology. He gives a strongly cognitive definition of theology proper (systematic theology), characterizing it as "understanding the meaning of the Christian witness and assessing its truth" (Ogden 1986, 7-16). He distinguishes theology, as critical reflection on the "truth" of the Christian faith, from what he calls "witness." The faithful Christian witnesses to the gospel in the sense of confessing it. Theology as an academic enterprise assesses the truth of the Christian claims. Ogden would say that Arthur Brazier in his stirring sermons each Sunday gives witness to the faith; but, from Ogden's perspective, it would be erroneous to say he does theology, for he does not attempt to test the truth of his religious claims. Or at least he does not test them in the manner Ogden would call theology in the strict sense in which he uses the term.

A REVISED CORRELATIONAL APPROACH

In the following paragraphs I will advance, in spite of the clumsiness of the phrase, a critical correlational approach to fundamental practical theology. In doing this, I will be assisted greatly by the revisionist view of theology found in the work of David Tracy. I am attracted to this approach because I believe it most adequately connects two poles of theology that tend to split into separate camps. These two poles are the confessional approach (which sees theology as primarily witnessing to the narrative structure of the faith) and the apologetic approach (which defends the rationality of the faith and tries to increase its plausibility to the contemporary secular mind).

George Lindbeck has submitted these two approaches to theology to a stimulating discussion in *The Nature of Doctrine* (1984). He distinguishes between the *cultural-linguistic* and the *apologetic* approaches to theology. He then divides apologetic approaches into *propositional-cognitive* and *experiential-expressive* approaches (16). The cultural-linguistic approach sees Christian dogma as having a narrative structure that creates and shapes a particular form of life known as Christian. This view takes the linguistic expressions of a religion very seriously; it believes that our perceptions of experiences are formed by our language structures and not, as empiricists would have it, by the raw experiences themselves (39). The truth of Christian narrative, or for that matter the narratives of any religion, can never be demonstrated by any evidence outside it. Their only claim to truth is "categorical." This is not propositional truth that corresponds to reality or symbolic truth that gives expression to some deep and abiding experience (47). It is truth that has such inner coherence that it "makes meaningful statements possible" about what is considered "most important" (48).

Lindbeck's cultural-linguistic approach expresses with particular power a broad stream of contemporary theology. It has its roots in the confessionalism of Karl Barth. It is partly inspired by H. Richard Niebuhr, who emphasized in his work that all theology has a metaphorical base (H. Niebuhr 1963, 149–60). It has received particularly powerful articulation in the contemporary theologies of Stanley Hauerwas (1974, 1977, 1981), Johann Baptist Metz (1980), and Craig Dykstra (1981). These positions emphasize the way the linguistic structures of Christian stories and narratives shape the character and lives of Christian communities and individuals. They also emphasize how this happens without the help of either external philosophical categories or religious experiences independent of these narratives. This perspective attempts to advance theology without apologetics.

I will build on Tracy's critical correlational approach because it combines the best of the cultural-linguistic and the apologetic approaches. Of the apologetic approaches, it makes special use of the experiential-expressive view, although to some extent it employs the propositional-cognitive approach as well. It is cultural-linguistic because it is thoroughly hermeneutical; it recognizes that to a considerable extent the religious classics we interpret already shape us. Tracy grants that faith and confession precede reason; our thought is situated and historically shaped before it becomes conscious and critical. Gadamer influences Tracy profoundly, and on the question of the historically situated and conditioned nature of human knowing, Gadamer and Lindbeck are in profound agreement. Tracy grants that theology has a confessional beginning, but he does not end there. If one takes Gadamer's concept of effective history seriously and admits that all Western people live in pluralistic societies shaped by a variety of cultural and religious traditions, then one must admit a further, very important point that Lindbeck refuses to acknowledge: People living in modern pluralistic societies have a variety of confessional beginning points. If they are Christians or are in some way attempting to consult Christian classics, they tend to bring questions engendered by the conflict of their contemporary practices with these classics. The conflict between contending theory-laden practices means that their questions emerge out of the conflict between the Christian and non-Christian aspects of their lives. The question, for example, that the members of the Church of the Covenant put to their Christian classics grew from the conflict between images of citizenship and discipleship that the tradition of their church had mediated to them. This raised the

question: What do the Christian classics *really* say about the relation of citizenship and discipleship? We will see in chapter 9 that
in answering this question the Church of the Covenant used a variety of reflective procedures for which the cultural-linguistic school
cannot account.

Because the questions that we bring to our Christian classics are
ambiguous and shaped by a variety of sources, we should acknowledge the inevitable correlational nature of all theology. Lindbeck
does not. He, like Barth, seems to envision the possibility of listening to our religious narratives and hearing them and only them.
Tracy's view of theology is correlational; it correlates the confessional beginning point of theology with questions shaped both
by faith and by other aspects of our cultural experience. More
than that, Tracy's correlational theology is a "revised" or "critical" correlational program (Tracy 1975, 43–63). The meaning of
this becomes clear when Tracy distinguishes his correlational approach to theology from Tillich's. Tillich believed that theology is a
correlation of existential questions that emerge from cultural experience and answers from the Christian message (Tillich 1951, 36).
According to Tracy, his critical correlational method goes beyond
Tillich's. Tracy envisions theology as a mutually critical dialogue between interpretations of the Christian message and interpretations
of contemporary cultural experiences and practices. Stated more explicitly, Christian theology becomes a critical dialogue between the
implicit questions and the explicit answers of the Christian classics
and the explicit questions and implicit answers of contemporary
cultural experiences and practices. According to Tracy, the Christian theologian must in principle have this critical conversation with
"all other 'answers,'" from wherever they come (Tracy 1975, 46).

Before we determine what this means for practical theology, I
must say a word about Tracy's view of the organization of theology.
Tracy divides theology into fundamental theology, systematic theology, and practical theology. By beginning with fundamental theology
and defining it around questions of cognitive verification, Tracy
gives the impression that one must begin theological reflection by
establishing the cognitive and metaphysical grounds for judging the
relative adequacy of religious statements about God. The principal
criteria for the verification of the truth claims of theology are for
Tracy "transcendental" (52–56). Although his fundamental theology is built on the hermeneutical theory of Gadamer and Ricoeur,
he seems not to acknowledge that philosophical hermeneutics suggests a fundamental practical theology rather than a fundamental
theology concerned primarily with cognitive and transcendental
verification (49–52).

The strengths of Tracy's views, however, are easily applicable to a fundamental practical theology. Because of Tracy's critical correlational commitments, such a discipline would be a *critical correlational practical theology*. Fundamental theology, according to Tracy, determines the conditions for the possibility of the theological enterprise. If the conditions for theology are significantly influenced by the close association between hermeneutics and *phronēsis* as I outlined above, then fundamental theology would determine the conditions for the possibility of a theology that would be seen first as dealing with the normative and critical grounds of our religious praxis. This is what I mean by a fundamental practical theology. In refocusing Tracy toward a critical correlational practical theology, I am moving him closer to proposals first advanced by Matthew Lamb (1976, 1982) and Rebecca Chopp (1987).

When Tracy applies the critical correlational model to practical theology, the following definition emerges: "Practical theology is the mutually critical correlation of the interpreted theory and praxis of the Christian faith with the interpreted theory and praxis of the contemporary situation" (Tracy 1983, 76). I propose extending this excellent definition into a definition of the most inclusive and central theological enterprise, that is, fundamental practical theology. Fundamental practical theology would be the most inclusive understanding of theology, and the disciplines of descriptive, historical, systematic, and strategic practical theology would be submovements within this larger framework.

THE FIRST THREE MOVEMENTS

The description of theory-laden religious and cultural practices is the first movement of both theology and theological education. For want of a better term, I will call it descriptive theology. Its task is more important than its name. It is to describe the contemporary theory-laden practices that give rise to the practical questions that generate all theological reflection. To some extent, this first movement is horizon analysis; it attempts to analyze the horizon of cultural and religious meanings that surround our religious and secular practices. To describe these practices and their surrounding meanings is itself a multidimensional hermeneutic enterprise or dialogue. It would be a great mistake to believe that descriptive theology is simply a sociological task, especially if sociology is modeled after the narrowly empirical natural sciences.

Descriptive theology, however, would be close to sociology if sociology were conceived hermeneutically. A hermeneutic sociology sees the sociological task as a dialogue or conversation between the researcher and the subjects being researched (Hekman 1986). The researcher brings his or her pre-understanding into the dialogue with the actions, meanings, and pre-understandings of the subjects. Social-systemic, material, and psychological determinants are traced and explained as well as possible, but they are placed within the larger set of meanings that give them direction in the scheme of human action (Tracy 1981, 118; Ricoeur 1981, 131–44). These larger meanings that constitute the theory embedded in our practices invariably have a religious dimension. This is why hermeneutic sociology, when properly conceived, fades into descriptive theology. This is especially true when hermeneutic sociology is used within the wider task of practical theology. Practical theology describes practices in order to discern the conflicting cultural and religious meanings that guide our action and provoke the questions that animate our practical thinking. Because practical theologians already are embedded in their own preferred practices and theories, descriptive research is necessarily a historically situated dialogue.

Awareness by the researcher of the ideological nature of description marks the difference between the research done on the Wiltshire and Covenant churches and my research on the Apostolic Church of God. The psychologists, ethnologists, sociologists, theologians, educators, and historians making up these teams did not see their research, for the most part, as a hermeneutic conversation between their own presuppositions and the practices and meanings of their subjects. They did their research through surrogates, tried not to influence these congregations, and took little responsibility for their pre-understandings. Those proposing the hermeneutic view of descriptive research believe such detachment is impossible; both researcher and subjects are influenced and changed by the research itself. I call such research descriptive theology because when done by the practical theologian there will be special attention given to the influence of religion on the theory-laden practices being studied. Also, the practical theologian is interested in the full contextual meaning of the practical questions engendered by these practices. The hermeneutically informed practical theologian believes these questions help produce the fusion of meaning between situation and text. Thus, this descriptive task deserves to be called *descriptive theology.*

Questions of the following kind guide this moment of theological reflection: What, within a particular area of practice, are we actually doing? What reasons, ideals, and symbols do we use to interpret what we are doing? What do we consider to be the sources of authority and legitimation for what we do? The description of these practices engenders questions about what we *really* should be doing and about the accuracy and consistency of our use of our preferred sources of authority and legitimation. For those who claim to be Christian, this process inevitably leads to a fresh confrontation with the normative texts and monuments of the Christian faith—the sources of the norms of practice. Historical theology becomes the heart of the hermeneutical process, but it is now understood as putting the questions emerging from theory-laden practices to the central texts and monuments of the Christian faith.

This points to the second movement within theology and theological education. Historical theology asks, What do the normative texts that are already part of our effective history *really* imply for our praxis when they are confronted as honestly as possible? This is where the traditional disciplines of biblical studies, church history, and the history of Christian thought are located. In this scheme, these disciplines and all their technical literary-historical, textual, and social scientific explanatory interests are understood as parts of a larger practical hermeneutical enterprise. Their technical, explanatory, and distancing maneuvers are temporary procedures designed to gain clarity within a larger hermeneutic effort to understand our praxis and the theory behind it (Tracy 1975, 75–76; Ricoeur 1981, 149–64).

The technical literary-critical procedures within a larger hermeneutical dialogue are used more easily in the academic practical theology of the seminary and the university than in the confessing church. Different churches have different classics; they base their identity on different scriptural and creedal selections. They have different traditions of textuality. The Church of the Covenant's minister, Hal Roberts, preached primarily a message of grace. Although he followed the lectionary, he was somewhat like Karl Barth in interpreting every text to sound like Saint Paul's emphasis on justification by grace. Roberts never directly preached on the sanctuary issue. But his emphasis on grace was designed to address another issue stemming from Covenant's practice, that is, the potential conflict in the congregation that becoming a sanctuary church might create. Since Christians are justified by their faith rather than their deeds, all parties on any side of a debate would be justified, he seemed to say, despite the positions they might take. At a more popular level there were other texts with which members of the congregation entered into dialogue—principally the commandment to "Love your neighbor as yourself" and Paul Williams's use of the parable of the Good Samaritan. The point is that there were levels of textuality in the congregation. The final sanctuary action depended on a mosaic of interpretations, the parts of which addressed the different levels of practical reason.

The congregation even does its version of historical theology, but its practical hermeneutical character is clear. The Church of the Covenant returned to a few classic texts to deal with the refugee crisis sitting on its doorstep. In the theological academy, historical theology should be no less hermeneutical and practical. The academy, however, should provide the time and leisure to thematize more carefully the questions that are brought to the classic texts. It should also consider in a deeper and more inclusive way a wider range of relevant texts as well as attempt the distancing maneuvers more carefully than the worshiping religious community.

These comments on the textuality of the Church of the Covenant introduce an important point about hermeneutics. A hermeneutical dialogue with classic texts is not just a solitary conversation between one interpreter and his or her texts. In the situation of a congregation, it should be a community effort involving several people and their respective horizons in a dialogue with the classic texts. Frequently, as at Covenant, different members of the congregation concentrate on different sections of these texts. Hermeneutics, even in Gadamer's sense of dialogue and conversation, is a community process. The community as a whole, with members participating to varying degrees, enters a dialogue toward the end of achieving a working consensus—a consensus that may break up and be reformulated repeatedly.

This view of hermeneutics is implicit in Gadamer but not emphasized. Gadamer himself is close at times to the more individualistic model of interpretation found in Heidegger. Robert Corrington believes that although Gadamer is less individualistic than Heidegger, the American pragmatist Charles Peirce and the pragmatic idealist Josiah Royce formulated a more genuinely social view of the hermeneutic process. In *The Community of Interpreters* (1987) Corrington writes:

> The practical and social aspects of Gadamer's hermeneutics transcend the understanding of interpretation found in Heidegger. The isolated *Dasein* of Heidegger's *Sein und Zeit* remains unable to find a communal reality beyond the solitary reflections of a few thinkers and poets. Yet it does not follow that Gadamer has developed as rich a conceptual structure as that found in the later Royce.... The value of Gadamer's perspective is that it brings us to the threshold of the larger communal view and thereby transcends the Heideggerian model (44).

Peirce originated the semiotic and communal theory that Royce developed into the idea that interpretation always proceeds within a community. It can never be simply an individual matter.

In fact Peirce developed the idea that reality can never be known adequately by an individual. Our knowledge of reality is mediated by signs. To gain relatively reliable knowledge we need to rely on the interpretive skills of entire communities. Corrington tells us that for Peirce, the community of science and its mutually correcting investigators is the most adequate horizon for the quest for truth. Such a view makes the interpretive process future-oriented and open-ended. Royce transferred this image of interpretation to the church as the "beloved community" committed to the process of loving interpretation to achieve the good and true. In recent years, Peirce's ideas about interpretation as an indefinite, future-oriented, communal process have influenced greatly the critical theories of Jürgen Habermas and Karl-Otto Apel. The ideas of Habermas on this matter will be important to our argument at a later point (Habermas 1971, 91). For the moment, we should note that at the Church of the Covenant we see an example of a communal interpretive process. It illustrates the communal understanding of hermeneutics more typical of North American pragmatism than the European hermeneutical tradition. If this North American tradition were taken seriously, historical theology would be seen as a communally oriented interpretive process emerging from the questions of contemporary communities of praxis. This would be its character in the theological academy and, less systematically, in congregations. In chapter 9, I will investigate this issue in more detail around the question of religious and Christian education.

The third movement is systematic theology. Systematic theology, when seen from the perspective of Gadamer's hermeneutics, is the fusion of horizons between the vision implicit in contemporary practices and the vision implied in the practices of the normative Christian texts. This fusion between the present and the past is much different from a simple application of the past to the present. Systematic theology tries to gain as comprehensive a view of the present as possible. It tries to examine the large, encompassing themes of our present practices and the vision latent in them. The systematic character of this movement comes from its effort to investigate general themes of the gospel that respond to the general questions that characterize the situations of the present. This may entail questions that emerge out of such general trends as modernity, liberal democracy, or technical rationality. There is a role for systematic theology within a fundamental practical theology, but it is a submovement within a larger practical framework.

Two fundamental questions guide systematic theology. The first is, What new horizon of meaning is fused when questions from present practices are brought to the central Christian witness? The second is, What reasons can be advanced to support the validity claims of this new fusion of meaning? This last question points to the obligation of systematic theology to introduce a critical and philosophical moment into theology. There is, for instance, a role for transcendental judgments, as Tracy and others insist. They are one method for critically testing the metaphysical claims of the Christian faith. But practical claims of the Christian faith should be tested philosophically as well. In the order of things suggested here, metaphysical questions are the last validity claims to be defended, not the first. Christians and non-Christians collaborate in many areas without resolving their metaphysical disagreements. Furthermore, many reflective Christians justify their faith on practical grounds although they are unclear about the validity of its metaphysical claims. This does not mean that transcendental judgments in defense of metaphysical claims have no place in theology. Instead, we come to them gradually. Even then, we only develop good reasons for these claims, not definitive and universally convincing arguments.

My emphasis on the importance of defending validity claims places me in tension with Gadamer. Habermas and Bernstein have criticized Gadamer for being a traditionalist and for having no method to test the fusion of horizons that emerges out of the hermeneutic conversations (Bernstein 1983, 42–44; Habermas 1971, 301–17; 1979, 201–3). Developing criteria for testing the practical validity claims of the Christian faith is the task of theological ethics. Theological ethics generally is seen as a dimension of systematic theology. This, in fact, is the way it has been conceived in the history of the Protestant encyclopedia (Pannenberg 1976, 410). Without developing a foundationalist view of justifying validity claims that would be incompatible with the hermeneutical and pragmatic view of theology developed here, I will give below some suggestions for how systematic theology can advance what Bernstein calls "the best possible reasons and arguments that are appropriate to our hermeneutical situation in order to validate claims to truth" (Bernstein 1983, 153). Such reasons will not satisfy the foundational aspirations for absolute validity and total certainty typical of Cartesianism in science and philosophy or Kantianism in morals. They should constitute good reasons that can advance conversations between competing perspectives.

The link between the task of systematic theology and the life of our three congregations may at first seem weak. Doubtless many ministers and lay persons think it is. The relation becomes clearer when systematic theology is seen as a more orderly expression of a fundamental practical theology that addresses general issues and shared themes running through our practices. For instance, if you held a discussion between our three congregations, they would soon agree that in different ways they all are dealing with the forces of modernity. Yet they respond to these forces differently. They even have different interpretations of what these forces are and what they mean. It is the task of systematic theology to identify these and other common issues and then to search the Christian tradition for the common themes that will address these broadly practical and existential questions.

The religious thinking of these congregations and the task of the systematic theologian overlap. All three congregations are responding to common themes running through their practices. But the congregations always experience these themes from very specific and concrete angles. For instance, Sid Carlson with his educated and executive-level congregation faced the cognitive crisis of religious belief characteristic of modernity differently from Arthur Brazier's educationally diverse African American congregation. Sid Carlson acknowledged this crisis and characterized his congregation as "wistful hearts" who want to believe but cannot. Sid placed no demanding cognitive belief expectations on the members of Wiltshire Church. On the other hand, the congregation was aware that it was among the great beneficiaries of modernity. The religion of Wiltshire helped preserve an uneasy truce with modernity by asking the faithful to believe little. At the same time, it provided its members with an image of a warm and helpful God that would enable them to face the stresses that went with their accommodations to modernity.

Arthur Brazier helps his congregation cope with the pressures of modernity, but from a very different angle. The members of his congregation are anything but "wistful hearts" without genuine belief in God. Brazier is fully aware of the forces that make belief difficult—the pluralism of modern societies, the difficulty of maintaining plausible structures that support both religious belief and consistent morals, and naturalism that questions all belief in realities that cannot be seen or measured. But he does not answer these factors by lowering cognitive expectations. Instead, he supports his high cognitive expectations with artful use of intense and communally reinforced religious experience. Once one has received the Holy Spirit, the cognitive skepticism of modernity looks paltry indeed—even to the respectable number of professionals, scientists, psychiatrists, and social workers who belong to the Apostolic Church of God.

It has often been argued that systematic theology in the twentieth century has been sadly preoccupied with bolstering the cognitive claims of the Christian faith (Chopp 1987, 120–38). Although this statement would need to be nuanced before it could be sustained, there is little doubt that systematic theology has been concerned with the grounds for religious belief. Whether it was the turn toward religious experience in Schleiermacher and James; the turn to moral experience in Kant, Ritschl, and Bultmann; the neoorthodox reassertion of revelation in Barth and Brunner; the metaphysical turns in Tillich, Tracy, and Ogden; or the attempts of the followers of Wittgenstein to base religious belief on the linguistic system within a particular form of life—there indeed has been a widespread concern among systematic theologians with how religious belief can make sense for modern people. In the view advanced here, the themes of systematic theology would be first the common themes of praxis, in contrast to the concrete themes of praxis specific to a particular place and time. Further, it would be concerned with how modernity undermines these common themes of practice; its attention to how modernity threatens our beliefs would be subordinated to this. Tillich with his concern for the broad themes of human existence—finitude, anxiety, sin, and guilt—gets close to the tone of a systematic theology addressing the common themes of practice (Tillich 1951, 1963). If Tillich had been more consistently a critical correlational theologian and had clarified the links between meaning and practice, he then would exemplify the kind of systematic theologian advocated here.

These notes on the first three movements of a fundamental practical theology—descriptive theology, historical theology, and systematic theology—prepare us for the main concern of this book: a discussion of the structure and methods of what I am calling a strategic or fully practical theology.

3

PRACTICING STRATEGIC
PRACTICAL THEOLOGY

I use the phrase *strategic practical theology* to convey the complex, multidimensional character of this movement of theology. This is where ministers and lay persons who think about the practical life of the church really function. Here they make incredibly complex judgments of the most remarkable kind. If they are good practical thinkers, the richness and virtuosity of their work can contribute greatly to both the life of the church and the common good beyond it. Such persons are worth studying, understanding, and emulating.

Questions animate thinking. Questions are formed by the problems of life that impede our action. There are at least four basic questions that drive us to strategic practical theological thinking. First, How do we understand this concrete situation in which we must act? This goes beyond the question of the general features of the situation that systematic theology would address. It entails questions about this concrete situation in all its particularity. This consists of the special histories, commitments, and needs of the agents in the situation. It consists of the interplay of institutional systems and how they converge on the situation. And it includes an analysis of the various religio-cultural narratives and histories that compete to define and give meaning to the situation.

Second, strategic practical theology asks, What should be our praxis in this concrete situation? To answer this question, strategic practical theology builds on the accomplishments of the first three movements of fundamental practical theology. It brings the general fruits of descriptive theology and practically oriented historical and systematic theology back into contact with the concrete situation of action. It brings the fruits of historical and systematic theology into contact with the analysis of the concrete situation first begun in descriptive theology and now resumed in strategic practical theol-

ogy. The symbolic and actional norms that have come forth from
historical and systematic theology, shaped from the beginning by
practical concerns, are now brought into even more intimate relation with the particularities of the situation being addressed. But
a critical practical theology does not simply assert these norms. It
tries to defend them. This leads to the next question.

The third question is this: How do we critically defend the
norms of our praxis in this concrete situation? The critical defense
of the norms of action is what distinguishes the revised correlational approach to practical theology from all simple confessional,
narrative, or cultural-linguistic approaches. This step raises the
question of how practical theology sustains what Jürgen Habermas
calls "validity claims" (Habermas 1979, 2). To advance this aspect
of practical theology, I propose an alternative to Habermas's approach to validity claims. In contrast to his four validity claims, I
advance my five dimensions of practical theological thinking and
spell out the reasons one must advance to meet the obligations
that they entail.

The fourth question is: What means, strategies, and rhetorics
should we use in this concrete situation? This is the communication
question par excellence. This raises some classic questions of rhetoric. In the later chapters on religious education and congregational
care, this question will be quite visible. It poses the issue of *where
people are* and how ministry in its various forms takes the first step
and begins the process of transformation. For confessional, narrative, or cultural-linguistic approaches to strategic practical theology,
this last question—the question of strategies and rhetorics—often
is thought to be the totality of practical theology. They see practical theology exclusively as application, and application is thought
to entail communicative strategies of various kinds. In such a view,
practical theology is a technical discipline, the means to ends that
have been established outside the precincts of practical theology.
The vision of strategic practical theology advanced in these pages
differs considerably from this confessional view—a view that has
been dominant throughout the modern history of theology and
theological education.

Not only critical correlational practical theologians ask these
four questions. They are addressed by all practical theologians,
whether they are confessional, liberationist, liberal, neoorthodox,
or revisionist. It is not that some practical religious thinkers ask
these questions and others do not; it is rather that some practical theological methods take these questions self-consciously into
account and others do not. The virtue of the revised correlational
approach is that it takes these questions explicitly into account. In

different ways, Wiltshire Methodist Church, the Church of the Covenant, and the Apostolic Church of God all ask these questions, although not always clearly, consciously, and carefully.

This range of questions in strategic practical theology demonstrates the complexity of this movement of theology and this aspect of theological education. This is where the interpretation of present situations joins the hermeneutical process begun in descriptive theology and continued in historical and systematic theology. This is where these earlier steps join final critical efforts to advance relatively adequate justifications for new meanings and practices. Strategic practical theology is indeed the crown, as Schleiermacher said, of theology. But strategic practical theology is no longer the application to practice of the theoretical yield of biblical, historical, and systematic theology as it was in the old Protestant quadrivium. Concern with questions of practice and application, as Gadamer has argued, is present in theology from the beginning. Strategic practical theology is the culmination of an inquiry that has been practical throughout.

In strategic practical theology, the traditional fields associated with practical theology will still be present. These would at least include liturgics, homiletics, education, care, and social action ministries. My intention is not to be exhaustive or systematic but illustrative. In keeping with the move to go beyond yet include the clerical paradigm, strategic practical theology is concerned with the church's praxis in the world as well as within its own walls. For example, a practical theology of care is not just pastoral and congregational care; it must examine the church's strategy for creating and influencing the structures of care in the wider secular society. The same is true with education. A strategic practical theology is concerned not only with the Christian education of the faithful but also with the purposes of all education. Something similar holds true for liturgics and homiletics. These arts of ministry should not only be concerned with the church's internal worship and preaching; they also should be concerned with both the public liturgies and rhetorics of the church and the liturgies and rhetorics of the public.

In their various ways, each of our three churches exercised inner-churchly as well as public forms of these traditional realms of practical theology. At the Church of the Covenant, the sanctuary program was not a responsibility it assumed by itself. The church invited people from the wider community to participate, and many did. In participating with the community beyond its walls, Covenant developed a dual language—an inner-confessional language and a public language used to articulate convictions shared

with the wider community. Much of this wider community did not
affirm the theological grounds for these shared convictions. Surpris-
ingly, the Apostolic Church of God had the most evident dual focus
between inner-ecclesial and public ministries. Because of Arthur
Brazier's energetic participation in The Woodlawn Organization,
there were clear emphases on education, care, and social action
not only within the congregation but also in the public care systems, schools, housing programs, and job placement and creation
programs of Woodlawn. Brazier freely admitted that he had two languages, one he spoke within the church and one he spoke in his
social action in the community.

The conclusions of strategic practical theology play back on
the entire hermeneutic circle. The practices that emerge from the
judgments of fully strategic practical theology soon engender new
questions that start the hermeneutic circle again. Within the flux
and turns of history, our present practices seem secure only for a
period before they meet a new crisis that poses new questions that
take us through the hermeneutic circle again.

IMPLICATIONS FOR THEOLOGICAL EDUCATION

What would the movements of fundamental theology imply for theological education? What would they imply for its rhythms and
movements? The structure of theological education should follow
the structure of a fundamental practical theology. Understanding
this will solve many problems for theological students who wonder
about the relation of their theological education to the nature of
ministry. Once they understand the structure of theology and the
structure of theological education, they will have achieved a deep
insight into the structure of all acts of ministry—in education, care,
preaching, worship, or social action.

Theological education should be organized around courses and
educational experiences that focus upon: (1) descriptive theology
(which would help students learn the art of thick description of religious and cultural practices); (2) historical theology (guided by the
questions emerging from the first movement); (3) systematic theology (the search for generic features of the Christian message in
relation to generic features of present practices); and (4) strategic
practical theology (which establishes the norms and strategies of
concrete practices in light of analyses of concrete situations). This
would be done first to equip laity in their action in the world and
then for clergy as leaders and facilitators. These movements might
be organized serially over three or four years. They might be con-
current emphases throughout. Or key introductory courses might

plant the overall model in students so they could later organize
more specialized courses around that model. But how the movements are organized is less important than that they be recognized
and given attention. Both faculty and students would need to agree
that something like these four emphases constitute the practical
habitus of theological education (Farley 1983a, 35). In this view, the
distinction between university theological education and seminary
education would be modest; they would be the same except that
the seminary would give additional attention to the description of
the practices of ordained ministers and would work, at least in part,
on the strategic practical theology of ordained ministry.

THE ANALYSIS OF PERSONAL EXPERIENCE

The analysis of situations in practical theology is complex. Also,
ways must be found to include personal experience of the agents
participating in the action. The interpretation of situations seldom
is thought to include the personal histories that people bring to
praxis. This is a significant loss to practical theology and theological education in the church, the seminary, and the university. To
demonstrate how to include personal histories in the description
of situations I will take an excursion into the puzzling yet powerful
institution of clinical pastoral education (CPE). I do this to broaden
the understanding of what it means to describe situations anywhere
but especially in theological education.

Turning to CPE may seem parochial in the extreme. Although
I am discussing parochial things, I am trying to do it in a most
unparochial way. I argue that the issues that churches and theological education face are analogous to the issues that all practical
thinking and all education must face. The CPE model may give us insight into the personal dimensions of all education, both religious
and humanistic.

My proposal is simple. I recommend that some elements of
CPE be included in the four movements of theological education.
Although CPE is not beyond criticism, it provides important insights
into education for practical thinking and doing. It is especially relevant to education in fundamental and strategic practical theology.
CPE originated with Anton Boisen's suggestion that the minister
should study the "human document" as well as biblical and theological texts (Stokes 1985, 51–62). This proposal developed into a
widely popular supplement to ministerial education. Ministry students would spend ten to twelve weeks ministering to the patients
of a general or mental hospital under the guidance of an accredited
supervisor. Although the patient was the main focus in the early

days of CPE, the person of the ministerial student in her or his relation to the patient gradually became the center of attention. The methodology of the CPE movement varies from center to center and frequently degenerates into subjectivism and specialization. Frequently the student's interior perceptions and psychological history are the center of inquiry, and analysis of the total situation becomes peripheral. In addition, the guiding models of ministry that evolve in CPE are sometimes more appropriate to the specialized functions of the modern hospital than to other situations. This leaves the CPE student with narrow understandings of ministry to bring to the congregation and other nonmedical settings.

Most students, however, report receiving from CPE something absent from other aspects of theological education. The CPE concept, I believe, discovered an unsystematic practical hermeneutical model of learning. It gained its power from its rough approximation of the first of the four movements of theology—the movement of descriptive theology. Its strength was in describing present theory-laden practices, including the personal history of the student. In doing this, it helped students develop questions to bring to their historical and systematic theological studies. In facilitating this, CPE enlivened theological education. It brought Aristotle's and Gadamer's concern with application into the theological learning process from the beginning. It did this when the Protestant quadrivium and Catholic Scholasticism were functioning deductively from theory to practice. In Protestant quarters this meant moving from Bible, church history, and systematic theology to practical theology. In Catholic circles, it meant beginning with rationalistically conceived manuals of moral theology and applying their principles to concrete problems of conscience. The main weakness of the CPE model was its uncareful progression through the last three steps of the practical hermeneutical process: through historical and systematic theology to strategic practical theology.

In spite of this shortcoming, CPE has planted seeds that should be nurtured by a more adequate practical hermeneutical model. They are seeds to be nurtured not only in ministerial and theological education but in all praxis-oriented education. The insights of CPE should be moved out of the medical setting and into theological studies in the seminary and university and into the humanities as well.

This can be done if one broadens Tracy's revisionist correlational model of theology. A theology is revisionist if it critically correlates its investigations into the two principal sources of theology. These two sources are "Christian texts and common human experience and language" (Tracy 1975, 43). As we have seen, when this formulation is transferred to practical theology, the latter becomes "the mutually critical correlation of the interpreted theory and praxis of the Christian fact and the interpreted theory and praxis of the contemporary situation" (Tracy 1983, 76). When Tracy speaks about interpretations of common experience, he is electing common *cultural* experience and practice as one pole of the correlational process.

To connect Tracy's revised correlational model and CPE, one needs to refine Tracy's concept of "common human experience." James and Evelyn Whitehead do this in their *Method in Ministry* (1980). They recommend differentiating Tracy's "common human experience...into two separable poles of reflection," which they call *personal* and *corporate* experience (12). I propose we go one step further and differentiate common human experience into three poles or foci: (1) interpretations of the practices, inner motivations, and socio-cultural history of individual agents; (2) interpretations of relevant institutional patterns and practices; and (3) interpretations of the cultural and religious symbols that give meaning to individual and institutional action. This parallels Talcott Parsons's familiar threefold division of action into personality system, social system, and cultural system (Parsons 1964).

Elaborating a theory of action is not, however, my main purpose. In fact, I will later propose a fivefold division of action that further refines Parsons's threefold system. My intention now is to refine Tracy's theory of common human experience and use it to show the possible contributions of CPE to both theological education and humanistic studies. CPE is effective because it includes in its reflective processes interpretations of the personal dimension of practices. It may use psychology, particularly psychoanalytic theory, to help uncover the repressed archaeology of our personal narratives. Generally this is not necessary. CPE also includes interpretations of the hospital as institutional system. Occasionally it relates these two perspectives to interpretations of cultural and religious experiences that give meaning to the hospital experience; examples of these cultural and religious experiences are the fear of death and aging, the idolatry of youth and physical health, and the reverence for technical reason and medical heroism. The power of CPE does not derive from its concern with general or common experience. Its power comes from reflection on all levels of experience from the perspective of personal experience, that is, from the perspective of the student's personal experience and practice or the experience and practice of the student's community. This also entails description of personal religious experience, its institutional embodiment, and the special traditions from which it comes. The first movement of the theological task, the movement of descriptive theology, should not omit the intimate descriptions of our personal psychosocial and religio-cultural histories. I propose that fuller description of experiences and practices (from the personal to the institutional to the relevant religio-cultural) be more systematically included in both the first movement of theology and the first steps of theological education in any of its settings.

This first movement of theology and theological education, broadened to include the personal, is not an end in itself. To stop the theological educational process after this first step would be to leave it in subjectivism. But if this first movement, enriched by a deeper sense of the personal history behind our practices, is used to refine the questions (what Gadamer calls our "practical prejudices") that lead back to historical theology, systematic theology, and finally to the complexities of strategic practical theology, then the spirit of CPE can influence theological education in all its contexts in a healthy way.

Introducing the third, personal pole of descriptive theology raises a variety of additional questions. What methods would one use to uncover the relevant personal histories of agents in situations of praxis? What is relevant about my own history as I interact with the Wiltshire Methodist Church, the Church of the Covenant, and the Apostolic Church of God? If practical theology is a historically situated conversation designed to clarify the grounds for our praxis, my history, theological commitments, and personal and intellectual preoccupations are relevant to what I see and hear in my conversations with these churches. Who I am will influence these congregations in the very process of my dialogue with them. As I have already indicated, the team studies of Wiltshire and Covenant were modeled after more objective social science studies. These teams tried not to get involved in these churches. We collected information; we did not have a dialogue. In spite of this attitude, we sensed that we were influencing these congregations simply by collecting information. There were, Gadamer would insist, dialogic elements in these studies. My study of the Apostolic Church of God is intentionally hermeneutic in Gadamer's sense. A method such as that of CPE that would uncover the personal history behind individual practices is relevant to all hermeneutical dimensions of fundamental practical theology, especially descriptive theology.

For example, my religious background is liberal Protestant. For the past three decades I have been a member of one of the most liberal congregations in Protestantism. My congregation has dual affiliation with the Christian Church (Disciples of Christ) and the United Church of Christ. It is near the University of Chicago. An early minister, Edward S. Ames, was a professor of philosophy at the University of Chicago in the days that John Dewey and George Herbert Mead made pragmatism the dominant philosophical position in North American intellectual thought. During the 1920s and 1930s, Ames defined God as a social process undergirding the ideals of a society and helping to bring those ideals into reality (Ames 1929). This view of God, influenced directly by Dewey's *A Common Faith* (1934), helped undergird a form of agnostic Christianity that made this church almost indistinguishable from the Unitarian-Universalist church that occupied another corner on the same block. My teachers of religion in undergraduate school in Missouri also had been educated at the University of Chicago during the days when religious liberalism and pragmatism joined forces at that institution. But by the time I arrived at the university and my congregation in the mid-1950s, this older liberalism had waned.

Protestant liberalism came easy to me. I lived and breathed it at college and, before that, to some extent in my home church in northern Missouri. My pastor during my boyhood years had been educated at the feet of Chicago liberals at Culver-Stockton College. Unlike many young people who went to college and were shocked by their liberal professors of religion, I took their iconoclasms in stride. This religious liberalism of my youth and early adulthood was associated with what sociologists would call middle-class values. These included a healthy respect for reasonably hard work, higher education, monogamous and covenanted heterosexual marriage, and a social philosophy of democratic liberalism.

During divinity school, I gradually shifted from theological liberalism to neoorthodoxy. Even then, my neoorthodoxy had a liberal and critical flavor. The 1950s and 1960s were the heyday of Barth, Brunner, Bultmann, the two American Niebuhrs, and the process philosophy of Alfred North Whitehead and Charles Hartshorne. I gradually developed a theological stance that brought together the neoorthodox anthropologies of the Niebuhrs and Tillich with the process philosophy view of God found in Whitehead, Hartshorne, and William James (Browning 1966, 1980, 1987). My older liberalism, however, can be seen in my commitment to the revised correlational methodology. My indebtedness to the pragmatism that shaped theological liberalism can be seen in my fascination with Richard Bernstein's and Richard Rorty's attempts to relate North American pragmatism to the European hermeneutical tradition. The revised correlational approach permits me to bring together my more recent neoorthodoxy with my older liberalism. It begins confessionally, as does neoorthodoxy, pragmatism, and Gadamerian hermeneutics, but ends by pushing for critical appropriation and public reasons as far as needed.

The point of these biographical notes is to illustrate what descriptive theology must mean within a hermeneutic model. Description takes place within a dialogue or conversation. Cognitive distance and objectivity are important. But distance and objectivity are always relative and incomplete submoments within a larger historically situated dialogue between the person or group doing the description and the situations described. By giving some signals about my cultural and religious history I hope to show how personal and historical factors shape both my description and my practical theology. This also reveals the importance of the personal as an element to be described. This is the special focus of the CPE experience and should be introduced more systematically into theological education.

The reader will doubtless speculate about how my fore-understandings shaped my perceptions of the three congregations under consideration. In many ways, the Church of the Covenant was the congregation closest to my own history. It was in a county seat; so was the church of my youth. It was a Presbyterian church; the Disciples of Christ are an offshoot of the Reformed Protestant tradition. It was largely a middle-class, midwestern church; my home church was similar. The theology of the Church of the Covenant was largely neoorthodox, with its grand themes of the ambiguity and sinfulness of human existence, the sovereignty of God, and the necessity of God's grace for salvation. My theology is a synthesis of neoorthodoxy and liberalism. I should point out, however, that neoorthodoxy itself is a form of liberalism; it accepts biblical criticism and the role of symbolic language in interpreting theological dogma (Tracy 1975, 25–31). Against this background, I admired what the Church of the Covenant did in becoming a sanctuary church. I felt this way although Covenant was far less militant and thoroughgoing in its analysis and actions than my congregation in Chicago, which also had become a sanctuary church. My Chicago congregation placed far more responsibility on the government of the United States for contributing to the Central American refugee problem. The more militant liberalism of my present congregation conflicted a bit with the tamer liberalism of my younger years. So I was both sympathetic and impressed with how this settled and historically conservative congregation had taken such a radical step for its context.

On the other hand, I, like most of the team that studied it, felt little sympathy for the Wiltshire Methodist Church. Its theology was difficult to discern—not quite liberal, not quite neoorthodox, certainly not liberation or political theology. Yet when I visited that church, I felt strangely comfortable with the upper-middle-class couples mixing at the coffee hour. They looked very familiar to me. They looked much more average than I expected upper-middle-class and upper-class suburbanites to look. They looked like they had come from middle-class county seats. They seemed like people I had grown up with who had left their small towns, gotten educations and good jobs, and moved to their Shangri-La between two ridges. I could be critical of this congregation, but I felt at home.

I felt the most complex mixture of continuity and discontinuity in the Apostolic Church. It was black; I was white. It was Pentecostal; I was liberal, somewhat rationalistic, university-educated, and university-employed. It spoke about the Holy Spirit; no church I had ever belonged to spoke much about the Holy Spirit. It was bold, energetic, Spirit-filled, biblical, sanctified, extremely joyous, and gently rigorous about its expectations concerning personal morality. I came from a liberal religious community that reflected the attitudes toward personal morality typical of most sophisticated, urban, university communities. Personal morality for such communities is primarily a matter of personal taste. In the Apostolic Church, Christ and God are represented in direct, immediate, and highly personal terms. In my communities of faith, even those of my youth, God is discussed indirectly. Only rarely are God and Jesus spoken of directly and intimately as matters of firsthand religious experience.

In spite of these radical differences, I felt remarkably comfortable in this church. The intelligence of its sermons, the clarity and balance of its religious ethic, its emphasis on the importance of personal ethics and what I call family ethics—all these made contact with old interests and commitments that were not well satisfied by my current liberal ecclesial experiences. Although the Apostolic Church's emphasis upon religious experience was not continuous with anything I had known, my psychological interpretation of this experienced-based religion elicited both my sympathy and interest.

The main difference between my experiences of the three churches was the stance of my research. In the Apostolic Church, my active interview approach required a dialogue between the leaders of that church and me. I soon realized that before it was all over not only would I be asking questions of it, but the Apostolic Church would be asking questions of me. There is a place for psychology, psychoanalysis, and sociology in describing the personal and institutional histories of the agents of practical action. But these disciplines prove useful only when used as part of a larger hermeneutic and dialogical inquiry. Theological education and practical theology can profit from depth perspectives on the psychological and institutional infrastructures of religious practices. Some of this was done with reasonable success in CPE. A fuller and more systematic account of descriptive theology and the role of these social sciences must wait until chapters 4, 5, and 6. There I will sketch for the first time the five dimensions of practical reason and how they relate to the descriptive task.

PROXIMATE PROPOSALS FOR STRUCTURING

Several recent proposals concerning the structure of theology have either influenced my views or are similar to them. I will give brief attention to Juan Segundo, Joseph Hough and John Cobb, and Charles Wood. I will discuss more thoroughly the views of Johann Baptist Metz.

Segundo's conception of the hermeneutic circle, as stated in *The Liberation of Theology* (1976), is very close to mine. I am, however, uncomfortable with his rigid precommitments (9). I agree with Segundo's prejudgment that "partiality to the poor" is *in some way* part of the central witness of the Christian faith and can be used to measure the adequacy of the church's praxis in its various forms (33). But one suspects that Segundo is so attached to this prejudice, which is doubtless born of his experiences with the struggle of the Latin American poor, that he is insensitive to aspects of the Scriptures that this precommitment does not grasp.

The proposals in Joseph Hough and John Cobb's *Christian Identity and Theological Education* (1985) are also close to my own. These authors advocate making the capacity for "practical theological thinking" the goal of theology and the central task of theological education (104). In fact, I have in print strongly commended this book (Browning 1986; Browning, Polk, and Evison 1989). Yet in many ways their excellent proposals still are caught in a theory-to-practice model; their justifiable concern with Christian identity leads them to move from historical theology to practical theology in the theory-to-practice mode (Hough and Cobb 1985, 29–30).

I am deeply impressed with Charles Wood's definition of theology in *Vision and Discernment* (1985). Wood defines theology as "critical inquiry into the validity of the Christian witness" (20). Wood's view of theology as critical reflection on both Christian belief and activity clearly is congruent with my vision of a fundamental practical theology that is critical as well as confessional. But Wood comes dangerously close to a theory-to-practice model in his organization of the structure of theology into the five subdisciplines of historical theology, philosophical theology, practical theology, systematic theology, and moral theology (39–55). Because

Wood begins with historical theology and moves to practical theology, one detects the older applicational model. Wood tries to avoid this by using the concept of discernment—a category designed to bridge theory and practice. He further tries to avoid the applicational model by making systematic and moral theology follow and gain from practical theology. His model becomes a theory-practice-theory model. I believe it is theologically and philosophically preferable to use a thoroughly practical and hermeneutical model from the beginning—a model more consistent with the full implications of the turn to practical philosophy.

My idea of fundamental practical theology is close to Johann Baptist Metz's idea of a practical fundamental theology (Metz 1980, 5–8). Metz is a fundamental theologian trying to make fundamental theology practical. In contrast, as a practical theologian, I am expanding practical theology and making it a fundamental and critical discipline. The end result is very much the same. Metz and I agree that all theology is practical and that the Christian message is primarily practical in nature (Metz 1980, 50–70). He too emphasizes the primacy of praxis over theory and explicitly repudiates the traditional model of practice as the application of theory (50). He also believes in the importance of beginning theology with a description of contemporary practices, both religious and secular. This leads him to characterize contemporary secular practices as dominated by privatism and the "exchange principle" (a combination of market forces and technology). He also describes bourgeois religion as primarily in service to these trends (34–36).

My differences with Metz are small but substantial. I will mention two. First, Metz begins with a description of the contemporary situation, but he does this at a very general level. He describes the central, dominating, global trend—that is, the pervasive and ever-expanding supremacy of the exchange principle. In contrast to doing description at this most general level, I suggest beginning theology and theological education with differentiated description of the personal, institutional, and cultural dimensions of particular contemporary practices. Metz's very general analysis misses a great deal. For instance, even if the exchange principle and privatism dominate contemporary social practice, there are particular human responses to these trends that greatly complexify the range of contemporary practices. Metz's concern with the most generic features of the contemporary situation places his practical fundamental theology closer to systematic theology as I have defined it. He is describing very *general* features of contemporary practices and correlating them with general themes of the Christian witness. Although important, such an approach limits the range of practical issues that can stimulate practical theology. It limits practical fundamental theology to the *general* practical interests of systematic theology.

Second, Metz's model of practical fundamental theology is less dialogical and mutually critical than my vision of fundamental practical theology. For instance, Metz, in addition to having an extremely general interpretation of the contemporary situation, has little interest in describing the self-interpretations of contemporary practices. He does not have the interest of revised correlational theology in a critical conversation between diverse self-interpretations of contemporary practices and interpretations of the Christian message. A revised correlational practical theology is interested in the *identities, nonidentities,* and *analogies* between interpretations of contemporary practices and interpretations of the normative Christian events. Metz sees mostly nonidentity and discontinuity between contemporary practices and normative Christian practices. Insofar as nonidentity and discontinuity may dominate Metz's methodology, this precludes the possibility of hearing and seeing identities and analogies that also may exist. This is a problem for a religious practice that aspires to shape the public world. If Christians cannot discern identities and continuities between themselves and other actors, there is little chance that the church can form partnerships with secular and religious groups that share similar views on public issues. Discontinuities will always exist, but so will continuities and analogies. To tell the difference, the church must enter mutually critical conversations of the kind that Metz seems unwilling to advance. A stance like that of Metz would leave the public ministries of the Church of the Covenant and of the Apostolic Church of God without the critical methods necessary to undergird their programs that collaborate with groups outside their churches.

For instance, Metz seems to think that the praxis implications of his concept of *memoria passionis, mortis et resurrectionis Jesu Christi* need no test to discern their broader public validity (184–97). This is surprising since for Metz apologetics seems to consist of showing that secular programs of justice must make metaethical assumptions that require for their justification a Christian doctrine of a just God who suffers with and redeems the living and the dead. His apologetics stops with showing how other self-interpretations require Christian assumptions. Although this is important, practical theology should go further and enter a public and critical discourse about the validity claims supporting its praxis. Metz has little to say about this issue, and this distinguishes his proposals from mine.

CRITICAL PRACTICAL THEOLOGY

The phrase *validity claims* and the idea that fundamental practical theology should support its moral and cognitive claims invoke the critical theory of Jürgen Habermas. The world of Habermas seems far from the worlds of our three congregations. But these worlds are closer than we might initially believe. Habermas has gone beyond the preoccupation with ideology critique characteristic of Marxist analysis and the critical theory of Max Horkheimer, Theodor Adorno, and Herbert Marcuse. He has made a positive proposal for mediating between the conflicting interests of modern societies. He believes the self-justifying ideologies of interest groups must be uncovered and their distorted communication exposed and criticized. For this to occur, ideology critique must rest on a theory of undistorted communication.

For Habermas, a theory of undistorted communication depends on a theory of how various claims by individuals and groups are redeemed or validated (Habermas 1979, 2). Habermas believes that all communication implies the capacity to give reasons for or support the validity of claims being made. He believes all communication entails claims about the *comprehensibility, truth, truthfulness,* and *rightness* of what is said. To communicate well in supporting these four types of claims (what he calls "communicative competence") requires an ability to advance reasons for our actions that make sense even to those who do not share our presuppositions (Habermas 1979, 3, 57–58; 1981, 325–29). A revised correlational approach to practical theology must accept that obligation. This is especially true for any practical claims it might make on the public of which it is a part.

Habermas has been accused by commentators, especially Richard Bernstein and Richard Rorty, of developing a foundationalist drive for certainty in our social discourse (Bernstein 1983, 197–207; Rorty 1982, 173–74). Habermas's call for a discourse that provides for the systematic redemption of validity claims sounds foundationalist. It suggests that he believes certainty about factual perception and cognitive truth, about moral rightness, and about personal authenticity can be achieved. This search for certainty seems illusory from a pragmatic and hermeneutical point of view. Both pragmatism and hermeneutics know that all discourse is more historically situated, conditioned, and relative than foundationalist and Enlightenment views allowed. At times, Habermas's work seems like a continuation of the Enlightenment quest for certainty.

One need not lapse into the relativism of Richard Rorty in his *Philosophy and the Mirror of Nature* (1979) and *Consequences of Pragmatism* (1982) to avoid the foundationalism associated with the rationalist project of Descartes, the empiricist projects of Bacon, Hume, Locke, and the logical positivists, or Kant's quest for moral certainty. I hope to bring a concern with validity claims into a philosophical stance that relates pragmatism and hermeneutics. This is called for by a revised correlational practical theology that admits that the pursuit of knowledge begins with tradition. This is what the revised correlational approach has in common with Lindbeck's cultural linguistics, the confessionalism of Barth, and the narrative theologies of Stanley Hauerwas and Johann Baptist Metz. But the revised correlational approach proposes that within tradition-saturated and historically located beginning points, some claims to truth, rightness, and authenticity are more publicly sustainable than others. A revised correlational practical theology has a place for a nonfoundationalist yet meaningful concern with the redemption of validity claims. Richard Bernstein's pragmatism is less relativistic than Rorty's. His counsel is more appropriate to my position when he comments about Gadamer's avoidance of the question of validation:

> I have argued Gadamer really is committed to a communicative understanding of truth, believing that "claims to truth" always implicitly demand argumentation to warrant them, but he has failed to make this view fully explicit.... For although all claims to truth are fallible and open to criticism, they still require validation—validation that can be realized only through offering the best reasons and arguments that can be given in support of them—reasons and arguments that are themselves embedded in the practices that have been developed in the course of history. We never escape from the obligation of seeking to validate claims to truth through argumentation and opening ourselves to the criticism of others (Bernstein 1983, 163).

Bernstein's vision of the relation of pragmatism and hermeneutics will be a guiding strategy of this book. It functions to introduce a critical note into all communal discourse, even that within communities of religious faith. It says that all communal discourse begins in faith and is embedded in tradition. This is the wisdom of the cultural-linguistic, narrative, and confessional viewpoints. Bernstein asks that we take another step and have dialogues both within our communities and between diverse communities—dialogues that advance the best reasons possible for our positions although those reasons will never be definitive in the foundationalist sense of the term.

I divide the validity claims of a fundamental practical theology into five types of claims rather than Habermas's four. My five claims have analogies to his four but are derived differently and function differently. They are designed, like his, to enhance critical discourse in conflictive and pluralistic modern societies. His four and my five claims are useful as guides to critical dialogues between communities of diverse traditions and faiths.

The five validity claims that I propose reflect the five levels or dimensions of all forms of practical thinking, whether explicitly religious or avowedly secular. I call the dimensions: (1) the visional level (which inevitably raises metaphysical validity claims); (2) the obligational level (which raises normative ethical claims or claims of rightness in Habermas's sense of this word); (3) the tendency-need or anthropological dimension (which raises claims about human nature, its basic human needs, and the kinds of premoral goods required to meet these needs—a discussion that Habermas believes is impossible to conduct); (4) an environmental-social dimension (which raises claims that deal primarily with social-systemic and ecological constraints on our tendencies and needs); and (5) the rule-role dimension (which raises claims about the concrete patterns we should enact in our actual praxis in the everyday world). I will recommend the use of these five dimensions both for describing the theory-laden practices found in contemporary situations and for describing and critically assessing the Christian witness. The model can be used to guide description and interpretation at both poles of the revised correlational conversation—the pole of contemporary experience and the pole of the central Christian witness.

I cannot here amplify this division of validity claims that fundamental practical theology should address. I will do that in chapter 5. I now wish to assert only that a critical correlational practical theology must support its implicit validity claims if it takes part in the discourse of a free society aimed at shaping the common good. Here I agree with Bernstein. The arguments that a critical practical theology advances cannot be foundational arguments assuring absolute certainty. Its arguments can have the status of good reasons that, although not absolutely certain, can advance discourse about the action we should take.

A fundamental practical theology must be tested critically at a variety of points in the hermeneutic circle. Sketching out formally the types of validity claims that fundamental practical theology should address is the special province of systematic theology and theological ethics. The actual defense of the validity claims for the purposes of concrete praxis should occur in strategic practical theology.

AN EXPERIMENT IN THEOLOGICAL EDUCATION

I conclude with a brief illustration of what fundamental practical theology might mean for the teaching ethos of theological education. After completing an early draft of this chapter, I wondered what it might mean for teaching an introductory course in practical theology. Besides assigning a variety of theoretical readings, I made an assignment that required the students to use these four movements. I did this by asking them to choose a contemporary practical issue of vital importance to them. It was to be an issue so vital that it served as a basic motivation behind their interest in theological education. To aid them in their thick description of this issue (the first movement of a fundamental practical theology), I held a long evening meeting in which each of the nine students of this small class told the history of their interest in the issue. One student chose the tension between new age religion and Christianity. Another chose the way psychiatrists relate to the religion of their patients. Another was interested in the status and theological understanding of the newly emerging profession of lay ministers in the Catholic church. Another student chose homosexuality. Another chose the phenomenon of community organizations and the way various churches are using them as extensions of their public ministry. In all cases, the students had a significant history of existential concern with their chosen issues. Their initial task was to describe this history at several levels—their personal involvements and motivations, the institutional context of the issue, and the religio-cultural meanings that surrounded the issue.

This first step of descriptive theology was to be carried over into a major paper to be written for the course. The paper centered on an interview the student was to have with another person who was, in some way, dealing with the student's chosen issue. The students were to begin the paper with a thick description of their practices and attitudes as they related to their respective issues. More specifically, each student was to record her or his pre-understanding of the issue. For instance, the student who was concerned with homosexuality recorded his own prejudgments about it. The student concerned about the relation of new age religion to Christianity recorded his pre-understanding of that issue. Then they were to describe the personal, institutional, and religio-cultural situation of the interviewee as this related to the selected issue. The student interested in new age religion interviewed a manager of a new age bookstore. The student interested in psychiatry's handling of religion interviewed a psychiatrist. A student interested in cults interviewed an acquaintance who had converted to the Jehovah's

Witnesses. The student interested in homosexuality interviewed a gay graduate student. Their papers summarized these interviews and provided thick descriptions of the situation of both the student and the person interviewed.

Questions about practice (about what good practice would really be) emerged from these thick descriptions of both interviewer and interviewee. This led to the second movement—that is, historical theology. In the midst of this limited project, this movement was addressed by asking the students to present the argument of two serious books that served as guides to the witness of the Christian classics on their issue. The point was to investigate the historical sources from the angle of the student's description of contemporary practices, the theories implicit within them, and the questions that they pose. The student investigating homosexuality, for instance, chose Helmut Thielicke's *The Ethics of Sex* (1964) and James Nelson's *Embodiment* (1979).

The next task, which captured some features of systematic theology, was to lay out the general themes of these guides to the classic Christian sources as they related to the students' issues. The students were also to begin a critical dialogue between these guides in an attempt to determine their relative adequacy. In some projects, these two tasks were enriched by analytic insights from moral philosophy. The task, here, was to give the student an introductory exercise in making critical judgments about the relative adequacy of different interpretive theological perspectives anu advancing reasons why one view might be better than another. This is a large task that involves much more than I can discuss here or the students could adequately address in an introductory course. Nonetheless, they were introduced to the task of critically testing theological arguments. When this task was focused around a practical issue in which they were deeply interested, these students fulfilled this at a level typical of many third-year students.

The fourth movement gave the project its distinctively practical cast and distinguished it from the students' other theological studies. Here the task was to write the conclusions of their papers for their interviewees rather than for me, the professor. They were to attempt to communicate their critical comparison to this person. They were to communicate this position with sensitivity to the situation, views, and preferred symbols of this person. They were not to hide their own situations or pre-understandings on the issue. The students were to look for identities, nonidentities, and analogies between their pre-understandings and critical reflections and the situated views of their interviewees. The students also were to advance critical reasons for the more adequate position but were to do so in such a way as to make contact with the situation and pre-understandings of these persons. Most students went back to their interviewees and shared their papers with them. Hence, the entire project was a dialogue between the students and their subjects around issues that the classics of the Christian faith also address in some fashion. Virtually all the students reported a change—sometimes revolutionary—between their initial pre-understanding and their understanding of the issue at the conclusion of their dialogues. Because they were sensitive to the changes in themselves, they were also more sensitive to the changes this dialogue invoked in their subjects—changes that were sometimes modest and sometimes profound.

I explained to the students that not all classes in their theological education should be structured in this manner. I suggested, however, that they might better keep track of the twists and turns of their theological education if they saw it as entailing deeper investigations of each of these four movements, often considered more discretely and deeply than was possible in this large and synthetic assignment. Theological education should provide an opportunity both to see and to practice this process as a whole. It also should provide opportunities to delve deeply into the various movements and submovements considered both individually and in relation to the entire fundamental practical theological task.

This brief sketch of a fully practical theology process needs now to be followed by a detailed discussion of the nature of descriptive theology. The next three chapters are dedicated to this task.

PART
TWO

DESCRIPTIVE
THEOLOGY

4

THE HUMAN SCIENCES
AND HERMENEUTICS

In the following three chapters, the nature of descriptive theology will be illustrated at length. To do this, I will reconceptualize a description of the Wiltshire Methodist Church that was published in Carl Dudley's *Building Effective Ministry* (1983), an early book in the trend toward congregational studies. The story of the development of that volume is interesting in itself and relevant to the purposes of this book. From time to time in what follows I will go behind the scenes and discuss how the Dudley volume came about.

The description of the Wiltshire Church that follows is an exercise in descriptive theology. It begins in this chapter, climaxes in chapter 6, but lingers in chapters 7 and 8. I call it descriptive theology because I am formulating a place for theology as part of the *full* task of the description of situations. But I argue there is a place in the full descriptive task for other disciplines as well. One view says that one can use only the secular disciplines—possibly psychology, sociology, economics, or anthropology—to describe situations. Theology as such, this view holds, has no place in this endeavor. Theology, some people think, comes in only at the point of the answer to the problems situations pose.

This was the premise of the initial group convened to create the Dudley volume. When the group gathered in the spring of 1981 to get oriented to our task, there was no theologian or biblical scholar in the group. There were sociologists, psychologists, an anthropologist, a historian of religion, a professor of pastoral care, and some church consultants, but no one was invited to represent the theological disciplines themselves. We learned that our task was to study a local congregation. We were to help our society and the church regain their appreciation for the richness of congregational life. We were to demonstrate what the different academic disciplines could contribute to understanding and appreciating this richness.

We did this partially in reaction to the "church growth" movement, a conservative program and method designed to increase the membership of churches through evangelism. I sensed that our leaders wanted to show there were ways to understand congregations other than those preoccupied with the technologies of church growth.

I was surprised that the leaders had invited no one to represent a theological or biblical perspective. It suggested that theology had nothing to contribute to the understanding of congregations. It implied that understanding congregations was largely a matter for the social sciences. Some members of the team raised the question, "Don't we need a theological perspective?" The answer was, "Well, maybe we do." No one resisted the idea of a theological description of the congregation. But it was odd that the theological perspective was nearly left out. It was a sign that we had little idea at that time of what I am calling *descriptive theology*.

We did not understand the role of theology in description because we did not have a hermeneutical understanding of the descriptive task. Most of the scholars in that early study saw the social sciences as more or less objective and value-neutral disciplines. They did not understand how sociology, psychology, or anthropology could be seen as hermeneutic disciplines that fashion their studies on the model of a dialogue or conversation. They did not understand how their fore-understandings entered into their work as psychologists, sociologists, or anthropologists. All of the scholars were Christians. They were members of churches. They had their own theological predilections. Yet they did not ask how these precommitments entered into their social science descriptions of the Wiltshire Church. They did not initially plan to ask how their disciplines relate to a theological perspective on the congregation. In the language of Gadamer, they did not comprehend the relation of interpretation to tradition and *phronēsis*. They did not understand the role that application plays in the descriptive task from the beginning.

All of these descriptive perspectives had their implicit theological convictions that colored, however faintly, their description of the Wiltshire Church. In addition, the Wiltshire Church had its own theological self-interpretation. The descriptive task was really a hermeneutical dialogue between the team's theology and social philosophy and the theology and social philosophy of the Wiltshire Church. The theological commitments of the team were largely liberal. Some, although not all, had leanings toward political or liberation theology. In social philosophy, most of the team reflected many of the commitments of democratic liberalism sprinkled with socialist leanings. They believed in solidarity with the poor. They were, for the most part, to the left of the people of Wiltshire Methodist.

The theology of the Wiltshire Church centered around an individualistic message of empowerment. It was not unlike the message of the Apostolic Church of God. Both churches had messages of empowerment. Both mixed this message with varying degrees of individualism. The Wiltshire Church preached a message of empowerment to embattled middle- and upper-management executives who were under constant pressure from their demanding jobs and their hopes to enjoy a rich, protected, and wholesome family life. The Apostolic Church preached a message of empowerment to struggling, upwardly mobile African Americans who were about to enter, had entered, or were about to fall out of America's middle class. Both churches addressed the individual, but Wiltshire was far more individualistic. The Apostolic Church addressed the conscience of the individual person in the midst of his or her solidarity with family and community. To be fair, however, I must say that both churches presented their messages of empowerment by relativizing to varying degrees (the Apostolic Church more so and the Wiltshire Church less so) the very middle-class and upper-middle-class values they helped their people to achieve and maintain.

The description of the Wiltshire Church by our team was really a hermeneutical conversation between the political theology and socialist precommitments of many of the team's members and the church's gospel of empowerment. Only one side of the conversation, however, was reported in the book—the side of the team. This is not unusual; most social science studies report only one side of the conversation. This may be inevitable. It would be better if the social sciences were more honest and admitted this limitation of their investigations.

The structure of the Dudley book, and much of theology's present dialogue with the social sciences, follows a theory-to-practice model. The entire research project was conceived and executed before there was a wide awareness in either theology or the social sciences of the hermeneutic character of the human sciences. The introduction to part 2 of the book reads, "Separate disciplines are like primary colors of red, green, and blue. . . . [They] provide the basic building blocks of recognized theory that produce a consistent perspective in themselves and combine with others, without losing their integrity, to enrich the picture of the whole" (Dudley 1983, 36). In this quote, the disciplines of sociology, psychology, anthropology, and theology are treated like building stones that are put together to construct a representation of the Wiltshire Church. These theories are "applied" and a sharper, richer image of Wiltshire is the result. This is clearly a theory-to-practice model.

We see this quite decidedly in the title of part 2, "Basic Building Blocks: The Application of Theory" (33). But it can be seen even more decisively in the title of part 3. It almost paraphrases the theory-to-practice concept. It reads, "From Theory to Parish: Multidisciplinary Approaches to Effective Ministry" (153). This shows quite clearly that this volume was constructed around the idea of studying a church by using a series of discrete theoretical academic disciplines that would then be added together into a multidisciplinary whole and *applied* to both better understand the church and figure out what to do. The book exemplifies how the theory-to-practice view dominates our writing and educational models of church and ministry today.

THE INFLUENCE OF HERMENEUTICS

Hermeneutic perspectives are now having a significant impact on the human sciences. Sometimes these perspectives are directly influenced by Gadamer and Heidegger, but often they are inspired by other approaches that amount to the same thing. One can see this in Stephen Warner's engaging study of a northern California Presbyterian church in *New Wine in Old Wineskins: Evangelicals and Liberals in a Small-town Church* (1988). Although Warner did not invoke the European hermeneutic tradition, he got something similar from North American social psychology. In what follows, I will alternate between the phrases *human sciences* and *social sciences.* The phrase *social sciences* often suggests sociology and, perhaps, political science. The phrase *human sciences* is more inclusive and embraces a wide range of disciplines that study the "human" component of human action—disciplines such as psychology, psychiatry, sociology, anthropology, political science, law, and history. Some argue that the phrase can include theology insofar as it claims to be a science in this broader meaning of the term.

A theoretical discussion about the relation of theology to the human sciences is needed because much confusion about this question exists in the church and the wider culture. The great prestige of science extends for most people to the human and social sciences. Theologians and churches have increasingly both used and envied the human sciences. This is reflected in a number of phenomena: (1) The psychological disciplines have influenced the counseling and pastoral care disciplines of the church enormously. (2) Sociology influences liberation and political theologies, church planners, and the thinking of all educated church people.

(3) Anthropology, and especially the anthropological study of ritual and initiation processes, influence liturgics and religious education. (4) The psychology of moral development (Kohlberg, Gilligan) and developmental psychology (Freud, Erikson) have had tremendous impact on our understandings of both human and Christian maturity.

Much of theology's appropriation of the human sciences has been uninformed by sophisticated philosophies of science. It has been uncritical about the sense in which these disciplines are scientific, about their implicit values, and about how they may overlap or contradict the values of theology. Let me be clear: It is extremely important for theology—especially practical theology—to have a strong and positive relation with the modern human sciences. But the use of these sciences by theology must be as conceptually precise as possible—more accurate than it has been in the past.

Gadamer's hermeneutics has implications for the human sciences. He places the human sciences within his broader theory of understanding as dialogue and conversation. If all understanding is a dialogue, then any specific human science must also acknowledge that historically situated dialogue forms the wider context of its specific focus.

The title of Gadamer's great work is *Truth and Method*. By the word *method*, Gadamer had in mind the method of induction so widely used in the natural sciences and influential in the social sciences as well. The method of induction builds theory on the basis of uninterpreted observations of the phenomenon being studied. After repeated observations, it is believed that patterns in the data will begin to emerge. These patterns will suggest theories, models, and laws about the object of study. Gadamer begins *Truth and Method* by referring to David Hume, John Stuart Mill, and Herman Helmholtz as three important figures who established the importance of induction in the human sciences (Gadamer 1982, 5–7). Gadamer's book shows the inadequacies of this method in the human sciences and the need to ground them on a hermeneutical model of understanding. Gadamer's main complaint against "method" in the human sciences is this: It leads researchers to distance themselves both from their objects of study and from the cultural and religious traditions that form them. Paraphrasing Dilthey, Gadamer says that scientific method functions by "the establishing of a distance from its own history" (8). Scientific method as induction tries to eliminate the prejudgments (the prejudices) of its own history and tradition. In commenting on Gadamer, Paul Ricoeur has insightfully stated: "The methodology of the sciences ineluctably implies an assumption of distance; and this, in turn, presupposes the destruction of the primordial relation of belonging—*Zugehörigkeit*—without which there would be no relation to the historical as such" (Ricoeur 1981, 64–65).

The scientific method attempts to eliminate the effective history that shapes the consciousness of the researcher. In doing this, it attempts to eliminate, although never totally successfully, the fore-understandings so important to real understanding. Gadamer, as we have seen, built on Heidegger and went beyond the psychological approach of Schleiermacher and the objectivistic approach of Dilthey. Both Schleiermacher and Dilthey saw hermeneutics as a matter of understanding the deep intentions of the text or author being studied. Dilthey tried to do this with the same objectivity achieved by the natural scientists in their inductive explanations of the causes of phenomena in the outside world (Gadamer 1982, 153–214; Ricoeur 1981, 45–53). Both missed the importance for understanding of the historically situated nature of the interpreter (the historicity of the subject). Neither could adequately ground the human sciences and provide the appropriate context for specific sciences such as sociology, psychology, or anthropology.

To state adequately the relation of practical theology to the social sciences, we must examine the relation of hermeneutics to epistemology. By epistemology I mean, once again, what Gadamer meant by method, that is, the procedure for gaining knowledge in the so-called harder empirical sciences. The title of Gadamer's book is *Truth and Method*, but Paul Ricoeur reminds us that Gadamer never really answers the question of the relation of hermeneutics to method (Ricoeur 1981, 60). Although Heidegger clearly suppresses method (epistemology) in the name of truth (understanding), Ricoeur believes that Gadamer begins the process of getting them back together again. But Ricoeur believes that Gadamer does not get very far. He questions whether "the book deserves to be called *Truth AND Method*, and whether it ought not instead to be entitled *Truth OR Method*" (60).

This issue has analogous forms. They are the relation of truth and method, understanding and epistemology, interpretation and explanation, or narrative and theory. These parallel phrases all ask the question of the relation of hermeneutics to the specific human sciences. The answer to these questions sets the stage for an appropriate position on the relation of theology to the human sciences. On this question I follow Ricoeur, David Tracy, and in a more limited way the great German sociologist Max Weber. All of them have tried to develop a dialectical model for stating the relation of hermeneutics or understanding to explanation.

There is a modest move in the human sciences toward the hermeneutic model. Parts of this trend develop a dialectical relation between understanding and explanation. Other parts celebrate understanding with no place for explanation. I will illustrate these trends with reference to the social sciences I know best— psychology and sociology. The hermeneutical turn in psychology is exemplified by the psychoanalytic perspectives of Donald Spence (1982), Roy Schafer (1980), and Paul Ricoeur (1970). It can be found in social psychology in the work of Kenneth Gergen (1973). It is found in the sociological views of Robert Bellah, in Susan Hekman's *Hermeneutics and the Sociology of Knowledge* (1986), and in a modified way in the critical theory of Jürgen Habermas (1987).

PSYCHOANALYSIS AS PRACTICAL HERMENEUTICS

Psychoanalysis may have a modest role, as mentioned above, in uncovering the depth of our personal stories. But how is psychoanalysis to be conceived from the perspective of hermeneutics?

Roy Schafer states the position well for the disciplines of psychoanalysis:

> It makes sense, and it may be a useful project, to present psychoanalysis in narrational terms. In order to carry through this project, one must, first of all, accept the proposition that there are no objective, autonomous, or pure psychoanalytic data which, as Freud was fond of saying, compel one to draw certain conclusions. ... What have been presented as the plain empirical data and techniques of psychoanalysis are inseparable from the investigator's precritical and interrelated assumptions concerning the origins, coherence, totality, and intelligibility of personal action (Schafer 1980, 30).

Schafer believes Freud had two primary narratives. One concerned the taming of the bestiality of the young infant through the frustrations of growing up and the prohibitions of the Oedipal drama. The other narrative is the story of tension increase and tension reduction; it is the Newtonian narrative of the structure and functioning of our libidinal instincts (32). Schafer believes that the two narratives borrow from one another, interact, and function, at times, to make Freud's clinical interpretations narratively incoherent. In view of this position, it is clear where Schafer would stand on the issue of the relation between understanding and epistemology, interpretation and explanation, narrative and theory. For Schafer, the human sciences collapse into hermeneutics, explanation into interpretation, theory into narrative. All becomes understanding, interpretation, narrative.

Paul Ricoeur advances a position quite different from Schafer's and closer to my own. Ricoeur believes that psychoanalysis has a double language. In *Freud and Philosophy* (1970) he argues that Freud's psychoanalytic perspective is made up of a mixed language that he calls the language of energetics and the language of meaning or narrative (5–7, 160). The language of energetics is from the theory that Freud borrowed from physics and hydraulics about how energy systems function in the material world. The language of energetics explains how libidinal energy works according to the rhythms of tension increase and discharge. Without fully addressing the scientific adequacy of that theory as applied to human sexuality, Ricoeur pitches his lot with a hermeneutic model that finds a place for theory within a larger framework of narrative and a place for explanation within a context of understanding.

Ricoeur believes that Freudian energetics adds "realism" to hermeneutics (431–39). It helps us to make observations about the subpersonal forces that our meaning-making capacities respond to and guide. Our bodily regularities do not determine our egos (our *cogitos*), but they constitute a context of givenness that our freedom must take into account. Ricoeur would distinguish between theories about our biological givenness and the narratives humans invent to respond to and guide these natural needs, wants, and tendencies. Although our natural desires are revealed through our linguisticality, and are never experienced simply as brute external forces, they still follow certain regularities that can be more or less captured by theory. According to Ricoeur, it is the situation of psychoanalysis as a "practice" and a "work," that is, a praxis, that requires the twofold language of narrative and meaning *along with* the language (and theory) of force, need, and desire. Hence Ricoeur, in contrast to Schafer, Heidegger, and even Gadamer, holds in tension the poles of understanding and explanation, narrative and theory. In what follows, I will do the same. This is one of the many reasons I maintain a distinction between the narrative-obligational dimensions of practical reason and what I call the tendency-need dimension. Our meaning-making and our practical wisdom (and they are intimately related) respond to but are never dictated by the regularities of our tendencies and needs. A theory of what these needs are and how they regularly work is, as Ricoeur claims, useful for both hermeneutics and practical reason.

To claim that psychoanalysis is a practice or work is to see it as an exercise in practical reason. If we accept Gadamer's claims about the close relation of hermeneutics and *phronēsis*, psychoanalysis and most psychotherapy should be seen as practical hermeneutical attempts to reconstruct through dialogue the experience of the client. Since this reconstruction comes through dialogue, it necessarily entails a reconstruction of the experience of the therapist or counselor as well. Research and inquiry, in the context of therapy, are dimensions of the wider task of the practical reconstruction of experience, both the client's and the therapist's.

HERMENEUTICS IN THE SOCIAL SCIENCES

Kenneth Gergen develops a view of social psychology similar to Ricoeur's understanding of psychoanalysis. Gergen is aware of the practical context of all research in social psychology. He believes that the social sciences "can fruitfully be viewed as a protracted communications system" (Gergen 1973, 310). He shows how the values of social psychologists shape both their research questions and their answers (311). He demonstrates how social psychology influences the values of society. Learning what social psychologists are saying about society frequently induces people to resist these interpretations, thereby invalidating the conclusions that these scientists once had good reason to hold. "Herein lies a fundamental difference between the natural and the social sciences. In the former, the scientist cannot typically communicate his knowledge to the subjects of his study such that their behavioral dispositions are modified. In the social sciences such communication can have a vital impact on behavior" (312). Without invoking the names of Gadamer or Ricoeur, Gergen is developing a hermeneutical view of social psychology. Psychology is basically a conversation designed not to predict and control but to open the minds of researchers to wider possibilities for creative living.

Gergen's position is paralleled in sociology by Robert Bellah and his associates, especially the writings of his former student Stephen Tipton (Bellah 1983a, 1983b; Bellah et al. 1985; Tipton 1982). On the North American scene, the work of Robert Bellah is the most daring present attempt to advance a hermeneutic understanding of sociology. Bellah is influenced by both Gadamer and his American interpreter Richard Bernstein (Bellah et al. 1985, 330). Bellah repudiates the model of sociology as a natural science. He rejects the idea of sociology set forth by Hobbes in his *Leviathan*—the idea that sociology is an exercise in technical reason designed to find means to fulfill arbitrary human desires. Instead he follows Plato, and more specifically Aristotle, and he therefore envisions sociology as both a moral and technical discipline designed to establish the ends, and the means to accomplish the ends, of the good society (Bellah 1983b, 45–46). All of the social sciences, he claims, should be seen as exercises in *phronēsis* or practical reason and not, as Hobbes thought, as sciences of society based on technical reason.

How would Bellah ground the moral horizon of sociology? What place would there be in this discipline for what Ricoeur calls distance, explanation, or theory? Bellah would establish the normative ground of sociology hermeneutically, that is, with reference to tradition. In the appendix of *Habits of the Heart* (1985), entitled "Social Science as Public Policy," Bellah argues for a new relation between sociology and moral philosophy (298). He wants the boundaries between sociology and the humanities to fall. The following passage is crucial to understanding what I am calling descriptive theology and its relation to the social sciences:

> It is precisely the boundary between the social sciences and the humanities that social science as public philosophy most wants to open up. Social science is not a disembodied cognitive enterprise. It is a tradition, or set of traditions, deeply rooted in the philosophical and humanistic (and, to more than a small extent, the religious) history of the West. Social science makes assumptions about the nature of persons, the nature of society, and the relation between persons and society. It also, whether it admits it or not, makes assumptions about the good person and a good society and considers how far these conceptions are embodied in our actual society. Becoming conscious of the cultural roots of these assumptions would remind the social scientist that these assumptions are contestable and the choice of assumptions involves controversies that lie deep in the history of Western thought. Social science as public philosophy would make the philosophical conversation concerning these matters its own (301).

In view of their necessary embeddedness in tradition and culture, the social and human sciences become disciplines that further "social self-understanding or self-interpretation." These disciplines bring the "traditions, ideals, and aspirations of society into juxtaposition with its present reality. By probing the past as well as the present, by looking at 'values' as much as at 'facts,' such a social science is able to make connections that are not obvious and to ask difficult questions" (301).

For social scientists as public philosophers to do their task, they must take responsibility for understanding the stories and narratives that shape the present. They must come to know the ideals within the narratives from the past (our effective history) that provide the values by which the present is judged. "The social scientist as public philosopher," Bellah tells us, "also seeks to relate the stories scholars tell to the stories current in the society at large and thus to expose them both to mutual discussion and criticism"

(302). Bellah is saying we need narratives of what Gadamer calls our effective history, of how we got from the past to the present.

In developing a hermeneutic theory of the human sciences, Bellah does not throw out all concerns with the empirical, the explanatory, or the theoretical. He simply locates them as moments within the larger hermeneutical task. There is still a place for technical social science—for counting, for predicting, for analyzing the forces of class, race, occupation, and income. Bellah writes, "The practical social scientist can certainly use the quantitative data that the technological scientist prefers and the latter can use qualitative data and even hermeneutic interpretation" (Bellah 1983b, 59). When the hermeneutic social scientist is running the show, hard quantitative data and explanatory theory are seen as accounting for conditions or constraints to which humans respond with their freedom and their interpretive frameworks from the past. These constraints are not hard determinations before which humans are passive and unfree. In wanting to relate hermeneutics and understanding to explanation and epistemology, Bellah is closer to Ricoeur than he is to Gadamer and Heidegger.

There is a fundamental difference, according to Bellah, between technical and hermeneutic social science. Technical and hermeneutic social science treat the subjects of their research differently. This difference is more moral than methodological. Bellah puts it this way: "This is to say once again that social science is a moral science as well as a cognitive enterprise and that the relations between the social scientist and those who are studied must be moral rather than manipulative" (59). It is for this reason that Bellah and his associates in *Habits of the Heart* use what they call the "active interview" as their primary tool for gathering information on their subjects. It is a method designed to engage their subjects in dialogue. Bellah admits that he and his team did not come to their conversations empty-handed. "Rather," he tells us, "we sought to bring our preconceptions and questions into the conversation and to understand the answers we were receiving not only in terms of the language but also, so far as we could discover, the lives of those we were talking with" (Bellah et al. 1985, 301).

Bellah insists his team did not impose their ideas on their subjects. But they did try to probe their subjects' thinking, uncover assumptions, and evoke their subjects' feelings and thoughts. Bellah believes that the active interview has advantages over the survey questionnaire and poll data based on fixed questions that do not begin a conversation. In the latter, data of sociology take on the aura of "natural facts" rather than meanings taking shape within an ongoing historical conversation. The conversation and dialogue

that are the core of social science research are not just a matter
of Bellah and his team talking to their subjects; they talked to the
voices of tradition as well. Through the voices of their subjects,
they heard the voices of the biblical and philosophical traditions
that have shaped North American life. They even heard the voices
of the modern social sciences as these disciplines have shaped the
thinking of their subjects.

Bellah is setting forth what some would call a critical social science. The word *critical* invokes the tradition of the Frankfurt school
of social science and social theory. Critical social science or critical
social theory tries to break down the walls between social science
and social ethics. It is an approach to social science that puts explanation and methodology into the service of the norms and values
that would guide social transformation.

The writings of Jürgen Habermas are the most visible and articulate representative of the tradition of critical social science in
the Frankfurt tradition. Although Bellah is now drawing close to
that school, there is a difference. Bellah would anchor the norms
and values informing his sociological work within tradition itself
as hermeneutics helps us understand it. Habermas consults tradition, but goes beyond hermeneutics to ground the norms of
his critical social science in his theory of communicative action
(Habermas 1979, 202–5). The difference between grounding the
norms of a critical social science hermeneutically or on the basis of a theory of communicative action gets to the heart of the
debate between Habermas and Gadamer, a debate I will touch on
later. In grounding his norms historically and hermeneutically—
primarily on what he calls the scriptural and republican tradition
of North American history—Bellah raises the crucial question of
which aspects of these histories he trusts and how he makes his
decisions. Furthermore, how did he choose these particular traditions since other traditions inform North American life as well?
Some would argue that in grounding his norms on tradition alone,
Bellah does not in fact ground them at all; he advances no rationally articulate principle that would give reasons why some
aspects of tradition are affirmed and other aspects rejected. In
following this course, Bellah is closer to Gadamer than he is to
Habermas.

I will further discuss this later. For the moment, I must address
one final issue in Bellah's hermeneutical sociology—the role of religion in a hermeneutical human science. Remember Bellah's words:
"Social science is not a disembodied cognitive enterprise. It is a
tradition, or set of traditions, deeply rooted in the philosophical
and humanistic (and, to more than a small extent, the *religious*)

history of the West" (Bellah et al. 1985, 301; emphasis added). If the social and human sciences are rooted in a tradition, if that tradition inevitably influences their interpretive perspectives (their pre-understanding and prejudices), and if that tradition has religious dimensions, does it follow that the interpretive horizon of the social sciences is colored by the religio-cultural backgrounds of the researchers?

Bellah says it does. This is how he and his colleagues wrote *Habits of the Heart*. The two traditions that claimed their commitments were the biblical tradition (both Old and New Testaments) and the republican tradition. Although the republican tradition reflects the Greek and Roman contributions to the formation of Western democratic institutions, these two traditions came together and became a single tradition at the formation of the American republic. Their coming together is especially visible in the thought and life of Thomas Jefferson. Jefferson drew actively on both of these traditions. He drew on the republican tradition in the Declaration of Independence when he wrote that "all men are created equal," in his commitment to citizen participation in government, and in his concern that government be responsible to the will of the people (Bellah et al. 1985, 30). At the same time, he brought the biblical tradition to bear on his republican principles. He was willing to measure human justice with God's justice. Bellah tells us, "In considering the continued existence of slavery, Jefferson wrote, 'Indeed I tremble for my country when I reflect that God is just; that his justice cannot sleep forever.' The profound contradiction of a people fighting for its freedom while subjecting another to slavery was not lost on Jefferson and gave rise to anxiety for our future if this contradiction were not solved" (31).

The authors of *Habits of the Heart* use the ideals of these two traditions to guide their interpretive perspective. Their interpretive framework has a religious dimension. And they claim that *all social science perspectives*, not just theirs, have hidden in the background not only pre-understandings and prejudices shaped by effective history but an effective history with religious dimensions. In this respect, all fully honest social science—even naturalistic, technical, and positivistic social science—has a religious dimension, although it may be unconscious. This can be demonstrated for all the human sciences. I have tried to show how this is true in the psychotherapeutically oriented psychologies (Browning 1980, 1987). All the human sciences are, at least at their horizons, a kind of descriptive theology. The difference between explicitly hermeneutic human science and more positivistic human science is that the former is more aware of how this is the case.

A distinction needs to be made between social science theories and the full historical reality of the social science researchers. The latter clearly and always have a religious dimension. This is the case for even those researchers who ostensibly reject their religious traditions. In ways they do not understand, they are still saturated with those traditions; they form an implicit context of hope, trust, faith, and moral sensibility that shapes consciousness even if the positive religious doctrines are no longer affirmed. I can document this best in psychotherapeutic psychology. In recent years a host of books have attempted to uncover the religious backgrounds of some of the great twentieth-century psychologists and the way these backgrounds influenced their psychologies. The lingering influence of Freud's Jewishness has been thoroughly investigated by Rieff (1959), Klein (1985), Bakan (1958), Gresser (1989), and many others. Even the influence of Christianity, mediated through Freud's Christian nanny, has been brilliantly investigated by Paul Vitz (1988). The American Protestant influences on the consciousness of Carl Rogers have been investigated by Lewis Brandt (1982). The Presbyterian influences on the psychology of B. F. Skinner have been discussed by Shea (1974), Fuller (1986), and Browning (1987). Investigations have uncovered how religious commitments shaped the psychological thought of early American psychologists such as William James and other great nineteenth- and twentieth-century psychologists (Karier 1986). Religious tradition shaped the descriptive work of each of these psychologists.

But it was not just that their historical consciousness had a religious dimension; this consciousness actually influenced their core psychological concepts. Unthematized aspects of their religious consciousness not only spilled over into their professional and intellectual life and unwittingly colored how they used their allegedly value-neutral psychological concepts; this religious consciousness also shaped their basic scientific concepts. For example, Jung envisioned the workings of the archetypes to have the same irresistible and sovereign qualities as the Calvinistic God of his childhood. The Jewish emphasis on the Law is transmuted but still visible in Freud's view of health as the ego's control over the id. Rogers's early Protestantism may have shaped his psychotherapeutic concepts of acceptance and unconditioned positive regard. Skinner's strong emphasis on the ubiquitous power of environmental reinforcement may have been shaped by his own early exposure to the Presbyterian doctrine of providence. All of this means that in these figures, social science description had a religious dimension that touched its theoretical core. There is a quasi-theological component to social science description. It is not at the *center* of social science, but it is at the horizon, and the horizon influences the center.

If this is true for the researcher, it is even more true for the subjects of social science research. The people and groups studied by the social or human sciences are also concrete historical actors shaped by histories that have a religious dimension. All Western people are shaped to some extent, even if they consider themselves atheists or agnostics, by an effective history with a religious dimension. The great religious monuments and classics of a culture are a part of effective history, shaping our sensibilities, even when we do not believe we are actually believers. This is true for not only the West, but also for the great Eastern cultures, which have their religious classics as well.

Social science research is, in part, a dialogue between the religious horizons of researchers and the religious horizons of the subjects of research. This is true even if religion as such is not the central focus of the research. If the religious horizons of the investigator and subject are in the background, they will inevitably influence both what is seen and how it is evaluated. We soon will see how this works in the social science study of a human group such as the Wiltshire Methodist Church.

FOCUS AND HORIZON IN SOCIAL RESEARCH

All research in the human and social sciences has a focus and a horizon, a foreground and background, a center and periphery, or, as William James called it, a topic and object. I am using these pairs of terms as more or less parallel. Such terms invoke a variety of closely related intellectual traditions such as gestalt psychology (Lewin 1951), American pragmatism (James [1912] 1971, 90–91), and process philosophy (Whitehead [1929] 1960). All of these traditions hold that there is a center and periphery to human perception. That which is excluded from the center, focus, or topic continues to influence our perceptions as horizon, background, periphery, or object.

This model of perception suggests how the full description of situations can employ the various human sciences. These different disciplines are distinguished by what constitutes the focus or center of their inquiries. In addition to their focus, these disciplines have necessary horizons (peripheries, backgrounds, objects) made up of the effective histories of the researchers. These effective histories have religious dimensions. These effective histories and their religious dimensions influence both the theoretical concepts of the science and the nonthematized consciousness of its researchers.

This says the same thing as Gadamer and Bellah have already said, that is, that the social and human sciences function out of the traditions that shape the cultures in which they operate. I add the point, readily admitted by Bellah, that if the social sciences are hermeneutic, they also have a religious dimension. That point is not clear in Gadamer.

Although each science has its horizon in tradition, it also has its special focus or topic. In biology, this may be the biological infrastructures that influence behavior. In psychology, it might be the regularities of human development. In sociology, it might be the factors of class, race, gender, or education that influence behavior. The concern may be explanatory. The methodology may emphasize empirical observation in the narrow, factual sense of that word. It may aim for the development of theoretical models that attempt to account for the biological, psychological, or sociological factors that influence human behavior. But at the horizon of these disciplines, the larger frameworks of effective history have a pervasive influence. If Gadamer and Bellah are right, there is no alternative to this. If it were not so, there would be no effective understanding achieved in the human sciences. The human sciences fade at their edges into religious perspectives. Insofar as they function within the Western tradition, they may fade at their edges into some sort of Jewish and Christian perspective.

The idea of descriptive theology is not completely foreign to the human sciences. When they are used explicitly within fundamental practical theology, what is implicit in the so-called secular human sciences becomes explicit. The religious and theological horizon is made clear and direct. Interpretations of situations are made from a directly theological perspective. The human sciences can be used within descriptive theology and their explanatory interests employed to account for biological, psychological, and sociological factors that influence but do not determine human behavior. Here they would function within an explicit theological context, not unlike how they function within their implicit religious contexts in the human sciences as such. When seen from this perspective, descriptive theology is not a freak among the human sciences; it makes explicit what is often implicit within the human sciences themselves.

For descriptive theology to gain justification, it must do what any hermeneutical social science must do; it must make its normative religious and ethical assumptions explicit and test them critically. I will argue below that hermeneutic social science requires a critical social science. Analogously, descriptive theology requires critical defense of the religious and ethical frameworks it uses to describe the individual and social realities it attempts to understand.

The interests of descriptive theology are practical. These interests dominate all efforts to understand. The concern of descriptive theology is to capture in all their richness the basic questions practical theology takes back to its classics. Its interests are practical because, in the end, it wants to appreciate and criticize current social, cultural, and ecclesial practices. The integrating core of descriptive theology is the structure of practical reason, both its core and its envelope. The structure of practical reason provides the framework for descriptive theology; it also guides the normative reconstructive task of the entire fundamental practical theological project. *Phronēsis*, as I will account for it, guides both the descriptive and the normative-critical task. In fact, it is useful to see the focus of the special human sciences as illuminating different aspects of *phronēsis*. In the following chapter, I give a preliminary account of the five dimensions of practical reason to illustrate further what I mean by descriptive theology.

5

PRACTICAL MORAL
THINKING

D escriptive theology aims for a thick description of situations. It greatly helps practical theology if that thick description can be rendered in the same categories used to guide its normative reconstructions. In this chapter, I will present an outline of the five dimensions of practical reason. These five dimensions help guide description. They also help guide the critical business of establishing the norms of praxis.

Before turning to this, I want to identify, in a preliminary way, the central religious question emerging from the practices of each of the three churches we are examining. The reader must be warned: Even to identify these central questions is a hermeneutical act. There is no way to say objectively that these are the central questions. The questions that seem central to me are shaped by my own history of practices. To identify the three churches' central questions is a fusion of horizons between their questions and mine. Were I to become the minister, leader, or consultant to one of these churches, the question we would decide to address would be a synthesis of our different histories of practice. Nonetheless, to identify how I see their respective central questions will advance the goal of using their stories to illustrate the nature of practical theology that I am proposing.

Identifying these questions at this stage is to do so in a *thin*, in contrast to a *thick*, way. It is not the task of descriptive theology to discern a question in some simple, logical way. The task is to describe it in its thickness. The task of descriptive theology is to describe a question in all of its situated richness. This is basic for the later task of strategic practical theology. To address, to communicate with, to support, or to transform situations is to make contact with them in their fullness. The best churches, ministers, lay leaders, and religious actors are not only those with the best answers; they are those with the best grasp of the questions in their richness. Reverend Brazier is my candidate for the religious actor in these three churches with the best grasp of the situation of his congregation. It is not just that he is an exciting and moving preacher, although he is that. Rather he is the most effective of these religious actors because he can describe powerfully the questions his people are asking. When he presents practical theological answers, they generate explosive excitement. His people believe he has good answers; they believe even more deeply that he knows the right questions.

I will now make an initial interpretation of the three churches' basic questions. Later I will bring out the fuller richness of these questions. Even the thin description is important because it keeps us in contact with these cases. The central question of the Wiltshire Methodist Church is: How does a church balance the needs of its own leaders and members with the needs of others? This is the question raised by the proposal to build a new religious education building. This is also the question raised by Sid Carlson's desire to go against the long-standing traditions of the Methodist church and own a home rather than live in the parsonage. At first glance one might say, "Oh, what trivial issues." And indeed, from one perspective they are. From the perspective of the starving people of Ethiopia, the refugees of Cambodia, Central America, and Asia, the AIDS crisis, and many other tragic issues that afflict our globe, these issues may at first glance appear unimportant. Nonetheless, their resolution requires a method of practical thinking and one that is attuned to the particularities of the situation at Wiltshire. The question is not abstract; it does not ask in some ahistorical and universal way how we balance our own needs with the needs of others. It asks, How do these people whose children have been shunted to the periphery of abundant facilities in an affluent community provide for their religious education? It further asks, How should this aging minister who leads this affluent flock be provided for in his old age? These questions will be addressed in chapter 6 and then again in chapter 11.

The central question facing the Church of the Covenant deals with balancing the requirements of citizenship with the demands of Christian discipleship. To respond to Paul Williams's appeal to address the plight of Salvadoran refugees, this church had to decide whether or not to break the law. A church whose practices had centered primarily around its ministry to youth was suddenly confronted with a challenge to these settled actions. This was not just the abstract question of whether civil disobedience is ever justified; it was the concrete question of whether to provide hospitality to three living, breathing refugees (Rosa, Juan, and Oscar) and break a law, an act that might end in imprisonment. This question will be addressed specifically in chapter 9.

Finally, the central question facing the Apostolic Church of God is the ethics of the black family. In addition to discrimination and the threats to the black family of inner-city urban life, new challenges from feminism and affluence were confronting Brazier's congregation. His congregation faced other problems such as whether to build a larger sanctuary and a school to attract more families with young children back to the Woodlawn neighborhood. But the linchpin of Brazier's ministry is a theology and program to reconstruct the black family. This will be the special concern of chapter 10.

THE CENTRALITY OF THEOLOGICAL ETHICS

All of these issues are genuine practical issues. All of them can be addressed by the classic practical theological disciplines—religious education, pastoral care, liturgics, homiletics, social outreach and service. I believe that theological ethics and moral theology must enjoy a central position for these traditional strategic practical disciplines to gain their proper orientation. The praxis of these strategic practical disciplines must be informed by theological ethics if they are to avoid sentimentality and achieve powerful implications for our lives.

By theological ethics I mean two things. First, I mean the theoretical and critical form it takes in systematic theology. And second, I mean the concrete and contextually nuanced form it takes in strategic practical theology. Theological ethics in the first sense is more abstract. It is an abstraction in the same way that systematic theology is an abstraction. The intent of both is practical; both systematic theology and theological ethics are concerned with living the Christian life. As part of the larger task of a fundamental practical theology, theological ethics in its abstract form attempts to gain the distance required to make general statements about the norms of practice—statements that find their meaning as they arise out of and return to the concrete challenges of living. The moment of theological ethics within systematic theology is not, when rightly understood, a return to the theory-to-practice model. Theological ethics in this sense is a transitional moment of gaining distance within a task that is practical from beginning to end.

Theological ethics is important for all the strategic practical theological disciplines. For instance, the central task of worship may be the dramatic reenactment of the goodness, moral seriousness, and love that comes from God through Jesus. Without a theological ethics that works on the meaning of God's goodness and its implications for the good human life, our liturgical gratitude for this goodness is vacuous. Without a theory of the moral seriousness of God and its implications for our moral obligations, our dramatic reenactments of God's forgiveness and empowering grace are, as Bonhoeffer said, cheap and sentimental (Bonhoeffer 1949). The same is true for the verbal announcement of these religious truths in preaching the Word. Our proclamations of grace and forgiveness must be closely related to discernments of the practical obligations of the Christian life. I will make these points in far more detail with regard to religious education and congregational care in chapters 9 and 10.

Although theological ethics in both its forms has a special importance for strategic practical theology, the main point of this chapter is to illustrate its importance for descriptive theology. To describe situations thickly, it is useful to understand the formal pattern of practical thinking. To describe situations is to describe how people think and act practically in specific contexts. To describe situations is to describe the forms of *phronēsis* that actors use in concrete situations. This chapter will seem abstract. It is abstract. I do not apologize. The task is to develop an abstract model that can accomplish several things—help describe human practices in concrete situations, account for the formal features of practical thinking, and highlight the special features of Christian practical thinking. The interest in developing such a model is driven from the beginning by practical interests—a concern with application. When this model is placed once again within the context of fully practical theology, the applicational interests that are always there come fully into view.

Although the task of descriptive theology logically precedes the task of historical and systematic theology (and its dimension of theological ethics), it is necessary to establish the formal categories that guide descriptions in descriptive theology. Hence, my question for the pages that follow becomes, How can the five dimensions of practical theological thinking be derived and how can they be used for both descriptive theology and the purposes of a strategic practical theology within a revised correlational methodology?

The interests of this chapter are primarily formal. The specific content of a Christian theological ethics will be developed with the help of Reinhold Niebuhr and others in chapters 7 and 8. At the same time, my decisions in this area have not come out of thin air. They have come from the interaction of practical experience and reflection. It is for this reason that the following sections have the form of an autobiography.

My interest in theological ethics has gradually developed over the years. The motivating forces are primarily practical. I have found it necessary to do work in ethics to make headway in the field in which I was really trained. What is that field? It is an area called Religion and Psychological Studies. It covers a variety of interests—the psychology and sociology of religion, the dialogue between theology and the social sciences, and the traditions of pastoral care, especially as they have interacted with the modern psychologies. My interests have centered on the dialogue between theology and the modern psychologies (Browning 1966, 1973, 1980, 1987) and pastoral care (Browning 1976, 1983b). In pursuing these matters, I became aware of the ethical dimensions of the modern psychologies. Most of the modern psychologies, I slowly concluded, were not simply opposing scientific schools distinguished by their varying scientific methodologies and different explanations of the facts. Freudianism, humanistic psychology, behaviorism, Jungianism, and Freudian revisionist perspectives such as ego-psychology (Hartmann and Erikson) and self-psychology (Kohut) differed from one another partially because they implicitly held alternative moral views of the good person and the good society. I investigated this theme rather systematically in *Generative Man* (1973), *Pluralism and Personality* (1980), and *Religious Thought and the Modern Psychologies* (1987). Furthermore, I gradually began to discover quasi-religious dimensions to some of the modern psychotherapeutic psychologies, especially in the deep metaphors that animate and give coherence to their basic scientific models. I slowly concluded that some of the conflicts and correspondences between theology and psychology had something to do with the ethical and religious commitments that informed both disciplines. This led me to a hermeneutical understanding of the psychological and social sciences. This view says that in spite of their intentions to achieve value neutrality, these disciplines are historically relative and are embedded in a variety of moral and religious assumptions about the nature of persons, societies, and even the ultimate features of the world.

My interest in the dialogue between theology and the modern psychologies was ultimately practical. I was interested in how theology and the modern psychologies could relate to inform the care exercised by the church and the care disciplines of secular society such as psychotherapy, social work, and psychiatry. In fact, this is what finally led to my interest in practical theology. It was from the beginning a concern to relate theology and the social sciences to inform caring practices in concrete situations.

I soon realized that to make headway with these practical concerns, I needed to know more about ethics, both theological ethics and moral philosophy. Everywhere in my thinking about care, counseling, and human development, I was running into moral and ethical issues. There were the implicit moral images of the good person in the modern psychologies. There were questions about the general moral norms of the care disciplines themselves, secular or religious. And there were the concrete moral problems that suffering people bring to their counselors and therapists, whether religious or secular.

KANTIANISM VERSUS UTILITARIANISM

Hence, in the mid 1970s, I began a wide-ranging reading program in theological ethics, modern moral philosophy, and the history of ethics, especially the history of the concept of practical reason. I became acquainted with the two great schools of modern ethics—the Kantians and the utilitarians—that have battled, and are still battling, to guide liberal democratic societies through the thickets of their moral challenges. I learned that both of these systems were highly rationalistic and, in differing degrees, antagonistic to the moral claims advanced by the religious traditions of Western society. The Kantians believed that the ethical had to do with those maxims that could be universalized or generalized. The right thing to do, Kant (1724–1804) told us in his *Foundations of the Metaphysics of Morals* ([1785] 1959), was to "act only according to that maxim by which you can at the same time will that it should become a universal law" (39). This was his understanding of the nature of practical reason. He called it the "categorical imperative." It put duty before happiness and dictated that the morally right could be conceived—in fact by logic had to be conceived—as independent of our passions and the natural human drive toward happiness (29, 35). One can find evidence of Kantian modes of thought in the neo-Kantian perspectives of American moral philosophers John Rawls (1971), Alan Donagan (1977), and Alan Gewirth (1978). Kantian perspectives have influenced modern theological ethics tremendously, especially in the tradition of Ritschl, the neoorthodox theologies of Barth and Bultmann, the contemporary theological ethics of Paul Ramsey, and the Jewish religious ethics of Ronald Green.

Utilitarians are the other great school of moral philosophy competing for leadership in modern democratic societies. Utilitarianism got its start with the British moral philosophers Jeremy Bentham (1748–1832) and John Stuart Mill (1806–73), was developed by later

British philosophers such as Henry Sidgwick (1962) and G. E. Moore (1965), and has been vigorously represented in recent decades by R. B. Brandt (1959), J. W. Ewing (1965), and Russell Hardin (1988). Although there are important differences between utilitarians, they hold in common the belief that "obligation is the principle of utility, which says quite strictly that the moral end to be sought in all we do is *the greatest possible balance of good over evil* (or the least possible balance of evil over good) in the world as a whole" (Frankena 1973, 34). Utilitarians decide moral issues by trying to determine the aggregate good, that is, what will produce the greatest nonmoral or premoral good for the largest number of people. Their views always require some theory of value or nonmoral good in ways that Kantian theories do not, unless they become modified as happens in the work of neo-Kantians such as Rawls, Green, or William Frankena.

Utilitarian theories are a species of teleological perspective in moral philosophy and determine the morally right with reference to consequences, that is, what will increase the amount of premoral or nonmoral good in the world. By premoral or nonmoral good, utilitarians have in mind all the ways we use the words *good* or *value* to refer to the things we like, find pleasant, or in some way find enhancing for our health, wealth, joy, or general welfare. Hence nonmoral or premoral values and goods can include things as diverse as food, transportation, education, sexual pleasure, peace of mind, or even compact discs. It would be improper to call these goods strictly moral goods; we do not ascribe moral qualities as such to our automobiles, our evening dinner, the corner school house, or, for that matter, the ability to read a book. Automobiles, food, or even education are possible goods that can either be used morally or immorally; they are themselves nonmoral or premoral goods rather than moral goods as such. Whether or not they are moral, from the utilitarian point of view, depends upon whether they can be organized, coordinated, and arranged to produce the greatest good for the largest number of people.

Utilitarianism has influenced the positions of some contemporary theological ethicists and moral theologians, notably the situation ethics of Joseph Fletcher (1966). Fletcher distinctly defines the Christian concept of love as *agapē* as a matter of utilitarian calculation designed to enhance the good of the neighbor. A less situationally stated and more rule-oriented form of utilitarianism can be found in the theologically oriented medical ethics of Richard McCormick (1984).

Kantianism and utilitarianism are competitors in liberal societies for a rather simple reason. Liberal democracies need formal and procedurally oriented mechanisms for resolving conflicts. Such societies gravitate toward procedures that de-emphasize the various moral traditions that people bring to their moral disputes. The Kantian principle of universalization and the utilitarian principle of the aggregate good seem to be useful neutral courts of appeal for people who begin their moral disputes with vastly different presuppositions.

THE NARRATIVIST CHALLENGE

I also learned about the narrativist challenges to these two great rationalist contenders for the guidance of liberal democratic societies. Narrative theory has had an increasingly powerful impact on recent moral philosophy, moral theology, and even moral psychology (Dykstra 1981; Vitz 1990). Narrative approaches to ethics have been defended in recent years by Hans Frei (1974), Stanley Hauerwas (1981), William McClendon (1974), Johann Baptist Metz (1980), and Michael Goldberg (1982). The narrative approach's most vigorous proponent in moral philosophy is Alasdair MacIntyre (1981, 1988). In fact, it is remarkable to see the convergence between the narrative emphasis in moral theology and the narrative emphasis in the precincts of allegedly secular philosophy. In both of these forms of narrative theory, moral philosophy that depends on general rational principles, be they Kantian or utilitarian, is rejected in favor of the narratives or stories that shape a particular community's tradition and the character and virtues of the individuals in that tradition.

Stanley Hauerwas has been the most articulate theological proponent of this view. In his most comprehensive book, *A Community of Character* (1982), he argues that it is impossible to abstract a general ethical principle or even a substantive ethic from the narratives and stories that make up the Christian tradition or from the narrative of any tradition (4). The narratives carry the moral sensibilities of the tradition. Rational moral principles and theories of nonmoral good become meaningless when abstracted from these stories. Hauerwas and MacIntyre agree that liberal Western democracies have tried to suppress their moral and religious traditions. These societies try to solve their moral conflicts on minimal commonly affirmed rational moral principles. But they are failing. The common traditions and narratives that give a society a shared moral vision are collapsing in these liberal societies. MacIntyre asserts that the Enlightenment project of justifying morality by providing a philosophical defense of basic moral principles has failed:

> The project of providing a rational vindication of morality had
> decisively failed; and from henceforward the morality of our
> predecessor culture—and subsequently of our own—lacked any
> public, shared rationale or justification. In a world of secular ratio-
> nality religion could no longer provide such a shared background
> and foundation for moral discourse and action; and the failure of
> philosophy to provide what religion could no longer furnish was
> an important cause of philosophy losing its central cultural role
> and becoming a marginal, narrowly academic subject (MacIntyre
> 1981, 48).

MacIntyre differs from Hauerwas in his more forthright desire
to build a place for reason in ethical deliberation. In *Whose Justice?
Which Rationality?* (1988) he argues that reason is always dependent
on tradition (7–10)—a position I will discuss more fully. He writes,
"So rationality itself, whether theoretical or practical, is a concept
with a history: indeed, since there are a diversity of traditions of en-
quiry, with histories, there are, so it will turn out, rationalities rather
than rationality, just as it will also turn out that there are justices
rather than justice" (9). But even here, Hauerwas and MacIntyre
would agree; even if there are moral rationalities embedded in the
narratives of a particular tradition, it is impossible to abstract them
from these traditions and give them intelligibility independent of
the traditions that gave them birth. It is clear that Hauerwas and
MacIntyre, in their different ways, give support to a confessional
approach to theology and to a cultural-linguistic perspective like
George Lindbeck's. Their concerns give rise to a theological method
that a revised correlational approach can affirm—but only in part.
A correlational approach can affirm that all practical theology, as
all knowing, begins in a confessional and narrative-bound context
or situation. It differs from the narrative approach in its more ro-
bust optimism that some relative distance can be acquired in some
cases so that common values and rational principles can arise out
of diverse traditions to guide our practical dialogues in pluralistic
societies.

TENDENCIES, NEEDS, AND THE PREMORAL GOOD

At the same time that I was reading in these two traditions—the
rational principle views and the narrativist perspectives—I was
also reading in the scientifically informed literature that claims
modern moral discourse needs insights from biology, sociobiology, ethnology, and modern evolutionary theory. I was an associate
editor of *Zygon: A Journal of Science and Religion* and had friend-
ships with leaders in the science and religion discussion such as

Ralph Burhoe, Philip Hefner, Karl Peters, and Arthur Peacocke. This led me to take seriously, at least as an interesting hypothesis, the claim that insights from these naturalistic disciplines into common features of animal and human behavior could inform moral deliberations. This argument is an old one. It was put forth in its most ambitious form by the sociobiologists E. O. Wilson (1975, 1978) and George Pugh (1977). Wilson and Pugh believe that evolution has given human beings a discernible genetic code that is adapted to a range of average expectable environments. This genetic code constitutes the ground of our basic wants, tendencies, and biopsychological needs. These needs and tendencies determine what we value and disvalue, what we need for survival and enjoyment, and what is harmful to survival and enjoyment. Wilson, Pugh, and the other sociobiologically oriented moralists never quite say it this way, but in substance claim that this genetic code structuring our basic psychobiological tendencies and needs constitutes a species-relevant core determining the premoral values and goods that are essential for human life and flourishing. For this reason, disciplines such as biology, sociobiology, and comparative ethology can contribute to ethics by developing a core theory about our basic human premoral wants, tendencies, and needs and the values and goods that satisfy them.

Wilson in his early work was a determinist and unable to distinguish between moral and premoral goods. He thought that if he knew our basic biological wants, he was a long way toward knowing what our morality should be. Pugh was a more sophisticated moral theorist and used his sociobiological analysis to develop a theory of the premoral good that informed a basically utilitarian theory of moral obligation (Pugh 1977, 119, 392-94). He distinguished clearly between moral and premoral values. At the level of moral values he was teleological and utilitarian, and at the level of nonmoral or premoral values (fundamental human tendencies and needs) he was a naturalist and highly informed by the biological and psychobiological disciplines.

Even more sophisticated statements of this perspective were advanced by Mary Midgley in *Beast and Man* (1978) and Peter Singer in *The Expanding Circle* (1981). Singer combines a neo-Kantian or Rawlsian theory of moral obligation with sociobiological theories of kin altruism and reciprocal altruism. Evolution has made us social creatures who live to protect and enhance our own genes through our offspring and kin (kin altruism). We also enter into various reciprocal arrangements of mutual help with our neighbors (reciprocal altruism) (Singer 1981, 12-17). Reason and our enduring capacity to think impartially and reversibly (from the other person's point of view) extend and complete our kin and reciprocal altruism to include progressively wider areas of social experience, that is, persons and groups beyond our families, neighbors, and natural groups. These might include distant strangers and sometimes even enemies (91–123).

Midgley, on the other hand, never states an explicit moral principle but builds a general picture of what sociobiologists and other naturalists can contribute to ethics. They can help us better understand our multiple and conflicting human wants and tendencies and help us learn to live within our "central needs" (Midgley 1978, 193). For Midgley, our instincts and our capacity for reason complement each other. We have multiple and conflicting instinctual tendencies. As Midgley writes, "Human needs are multiple. *Bonum est multiplex*" (190). Midgley would agree with Wilson and Pugh that our instinctual heritage carries within it the structure of our evaluative responses to the world that constitute the bedrock of our specieswide structure of premoral values and disvalues. Because of the richness and variety of human instincts and because different environments call out different facets of these instincts, reason and tradition are called to guide and mediate between our basically positive but conflicting instinctual potentialities (42, 189, 209–17). Midgley goes beyond the reductionist sociobiology of the early E. O. Wilson, who thought our instinctual wants constitute the total source of our morality. There is evidence that Wilson has himself gone beyond this position (Wilson 1978). But Midgley's position was clear from the beginning. For her, this structure of wants and central tendencies provides a core of premoral goods within which reason, tradition, and culture must stay; yet she also refines the moral in the fuller sense of the word.

In my reading, I also became aware of other levels of moral thinking, what I now call the environmental-social dimension of practical moral thinking. My reading in evolutionary theory and its implications for moral thinking helped uncover this facet, which has to do with how our natural and social environments place constraints on our needs and tendencies. These constraints tell us which of our many conflicting wants and needs can be actualized and satisfied within the limits of the social and natural environment. This dimension of practical moral thinking further concerns how these environmental factors limit the amount of our human satisfaction.

And finally, I became interested in the most ordinary level of moral rules and roles. By this I mean not only those general rules such as "do not tell lies" or "always keep your promises" that Kant studied. I had in mind such rules as "you should return your library books punctually," "you should pay your taxes," "a man should be the head of the house," "you should not have sex before marriage," or "it is all right to have sex before marriage." Some people equate the entirety of moral thought with these concrete rules. Other people think that these rules are peripheral to moral thought. What is important, they believe, is the higher order of general principles that control these concrete rules. I increasingly became convinced that these concrete rules and their related social roles are important. But they also are *thick*. By this I mean that they have behind them a range of implicit or explicit assumptions or judgments at many different levels or dimensions. When I began thinking this way, I began constructing what I called the five dimensions of practical moral thinking.

THE FIVE DIMENSIONS OF MORAL THINKING

One can see in this brief intellectual biography the emerging outlines of the five dimensions of practical moral thinking that I first mentioned in chapter 2. As I reviewed the contemporary literature, I began to believe that there was a portion of the truth in all of these perspectives. It seemed to me that the narrativists were quite right that our moral thinking begins in the context of specific traditions and that these traditions are carried by particular narratives, stories, and metaphors that shape the self-understanding of the communities that belong to the tradition. I came to call this the *visional* dimension of practical moral thinking.

I also became convinced that within these traditions and between the conflict of particular traditions, the workings of human reason gradually elaborate general principles of obligation that have a rational structure. These general principles of obligation that Kantianism or utilitarianism discussed might indeed be embedded within the narrative structures of these traditions. But these principles can be identified and can gain some relative independence from the narratives in which they are originally embedded. It is not that narratives are unimportant and incidental, as the liberal tradition has held. They very definitely contribute something original and profound to these general moral principles. Nonetheless, moral principles with common structures can be identified within differing narrative traditions, and this reality is important for dialogue between these traditions. I began calling this the *obligational* dimension of practical moral thinking. Within the context of Judaism and Christianity, the principle of neighbor love ("You shall love your neighbor as yourself" [Lev. 19:18, 34; Matt. 22:39]) and the golden rule ("Do to others as you would have them do to you"

[Luke 6:31]) are the chief examples of general principles of obligation. It is important to note that these principles have received at
different times both Kantian and utilitarian interpretations.

I also grew to believe that moral thinking in both religious and
secular contexts always had some theory of the central tendencies
and needs of our human nature. These theories were often quite
implicit and unsystematic. Moral perspectives make use of different aspects of their implicit theories of human nature depending
on the kind of problem being confronted. These tendencies and
needs may include very basic items such as the need for food,
water, sex, and warmth, or the need for security, belongingness,
self-respect, and self-cohesion, or even the need for actualization of
our higher-cognitive and creative powers (Maslow 1954, 147). They
might be organized by a system such as that devised by George
Pugh, who divides fundamental human values into selfish values
(values associated with individual welfare and survival), social values (values that motivate individuals to contribute to the welfare
of the group), and intellectual values (values that motivate efficient
rational thought) (Pugh 1977, 115). In addition, there are culturally
induced needs that may have a distant relation to more fundamental
psychobiological needs. On the surface, however, they seem to be
the products of tradition, history, and fashion. Although the mere
existence of these needs, whether basic or culturally induced, never
in itself justifies their actualization, I increasingly was convinced
that our higher-order moral principles always function to organize,
mediate, and coordinate these needs and tendencies both within
individuals and among individuals. I called this the *tendency-need*
dimension of practical moral thinking.

And finally, I eventually came to call the dimension of social-
structural and ecological constraint the *environmental-social* dimension and the most concrete level of actual practices and behaviors
the *rule-role* dimension. These are the five dimensions or levels of
practical moral thinking—the *visional*, the *obligational*, the *tendency-
need*, the *environmental-social*, and the *rule-role*. The logic of their
relation, how they interact, their presence in the Christian classics,
the distinctive way that Christian theological ethics might fill them
out, their relation to the older tradition of *phronēsis*, the different
forms these levels take in different moral systems, and the way they
are used in practical theological reflection are issues I will address
in later chapters.

At this point I can make a number of statements about these five
dimensions, and here I am going beyond what we need in the way
of formal categories to guide description. The visional level constitutes the envelope of practical reason. A particular relation, which

I will elaborate later, between the obligational and tendency-need levels constitutes the inner core of practical reason. The visional level defines the world view within which the inner core of practical reason works. This vision or envelope does several important things for practical reason. I show in some detail in chapters 7 and 8 how the Christian vision (at least Niebuhr's view of it) shapes the inner core of practical reason. The obligational level mediates between our implicit theories of premoral good (at the tendency-need level). On the other hand, the tendency-need level gives content to the obligational level; it provides implicit or explicit theories and hierarchies about the premoral goods of life that must be morally organized. Finally, social-systemic and ecological restraints show us the limits within which the moral ordering of goods must take place. Some of these limits can be changed and some cannot, but both these types of restraints must be confronted and respected. The rules and roles of life are the settled results of reflection at the higher levels.

All concrete rules and roles are pregnant with assumptions and judgments at these higher levels. All of this will be further elaborated. I propose that we use these five dimensions both to describe the thickness of situations and to guide our critical thinking about their reconstruction. Human situations are created by the struggles of practical action and practical reason. If I become involved in the situation of the Wiltshire Methodist Church, that church becomes part of the situation of my action. That church's action is an exercise in practical reason; it is trying to reconstruct its praxis in light of challenges facing it. I bring my own history of praxis, which is my history of practical reason designed to maintain and reconstruct my action. At every point, the five dimensions of practical moral thinking can be used to describe action—the action of the church, the action of those who might intervene (a consultant, perhaps myself), or the action of the individuals in the church (Sid Carlson, the chairperson of his board, etc.). As Clifford Geertz has taught us, action is thick; it has many levels, symbolic components, structures, and drives (Geertz 1973). The description of situations must be thick as well.

It would be nice to claim I had some elegant method for deriving these five dimensions. As the reader can tell, I did not so much derive them as construct them. This is why I told the story of my early reading in theological ethics and moral philosophy. I did not derive them through rigorous transcendental analysis of the kind associated with Kantianism, Husserlian phenomenology, or various brands of transcendental metaphysics. That type of analysis assumes that the mind is endowed with certain structures or built-in assumptions that ordinary thought necessarily presupposes. That kind of analysis might argue that the five dimensions are necessary presuppositions of the very possibility of thinking morally. I am not prepared to make such strong claims.

At most, these five dimensions have been developed through something like the "reconstructive science" that Jürgen Habermas has used to develop the four validity claims presupposed by competent communicative action (Habermas 1979, 8–15). Habermas distinguishes a reconstructive science from transcendental philosophy on the one hand and the empirical sciences on the other. A reconstructive science is not built on the logical and a priori structures of the mind without which thought and communication cannot be conceived to take place. Nor is a reconstructive science built on the ordering of collections of empirical observations of events. Rather, reconstructive sciences, especially as they are used in determining the competencies that go into good communication, are "sciences that systematically reconstruct the intuitive knowledge of competent subjects." These reconstructions, according to Habermas, "like all other types of knowledge have only a hypothetical status" (9). They are tested by how well they organize our experience.

I make this kind of claim for my five dimensions of practical moral thinking. They are reconstructions of intuitive experience of what goes into practical moral thinking, whether conventional or critical. In the case of conventional practical thinking, the five dimensions are uncritically assumed and unthematized. In the case of critical practical thinking, they are conscious, thematized, and open to tests of various kinds. I call them dimensions of practical thinking because they generally interpenetrate so smoothly that we are unaware of them as differentiated aspects of experience. I occasionally use the metaphor of *levels* in contrast to *dimensions* to communicate that the visional and obligational dimensions are more comprehensive and influence our interpretations of the lower three levels. Nonetheless the so-called lower levels also influence the form and sometimes reshape the substance of the more comprehensive visional and obligational levels. Each of the five dimensions must submit to tests about its validity in ways similar to Habermas's consent of validity claims.

I invite the reader to try the five dimensions on for size and comfort. My claims for their usefulness are open-ended and modest. Do they help us describe the situations of our practical action? Do they help us think critically about the norms and strategies of our practical action? I believe that they will carry us a long way. It is my present conviction that every instance of practical moral thinking that I have ever confronted sooner or later revealed these five dimensions. We will see all of these dimensions functioning in our three congregations. The dimensions will help us understand the situations of these congregations. They will help us analyze the practical thinking that the congregations do. They will guide our practical theological dialogue with these congregations.

6

DESCRIBING
THE WILTSHIRE CHURCH

A model that integrates a selected number of human sciences needs to be set forth. I will claim that although each of the human sciences has a distinctive focus, they relate at the level of their respective horizons. The social sciences must have what Ricoeur calls an epistemological or explanatory submoment. The various psychologies should have their explanatory submoments, and the various sociologies should have theirs. But they also have their horizons, which are shaped in complex ways by their effective histories and the religious dimensions of those histories.

This model will be illustrated with the four disciplines that were central to Dudley's *Building Effective Ministry:* psychology, sociology, cultural anthropology, and theology. By using the term *anthropology* for one of the disciplines, I am bringing together two closely related perspectives. One was put forth by Melvin Williams and was called *ethnography.* The other was developed by James Hopewell and was called *literary symbolism.* Williams by profession was an anthropologist and Hopewell a historian of religion. Their methods for understanding the Wiltshire Methodist Church overlapped. They both concentrated on the symbolic expressions of the church. I bring the two together under the general rubric of *cultural anthropology.*

Talcott Parsons's division of social action into personality, social system, and culture is similar to my division of practical reason into five dimensions. The main difference is that I differentiate the cultural system into visional and obligational levels of practical reasoning. Concrete social practices are complex expressions of various forms of practical reasoning and can be described in the terms of their five dimensions.

For the purpose of describing concrete social practices, it is best to list these five dimensions from the concrete to the more abstract. Action is (1) made up of concrete practices (rules, roles, communication patterns); (2) motivated by needs and tendencies; (3) limited and channeled by social-systemic and ecological constraints; (4) further ordered by principles of obligation; and (5) given meaning by visions, narratives, and metaphors. Below is a diagram (Figure 1) representing the thickness of human action and practices. It also parcels out the disciplines of psychology, sociology, ecology, and cultural and social anthropology as special foci within the wider rubric of descriptive theology. The diagram should be read from the bottom upward. What is above the line representing concrete practices is really not *above* these practices; rather what is represented as above is really embodied *in* the practices. What is above simply represents the thick and theory-laden nature of these practices.

The parceling out of the disciplines we are considering should be seen as suggestive and illustrative, not definitive. The diagram represents the special focus of each discipline and not the effective history that surrounds the discipline.

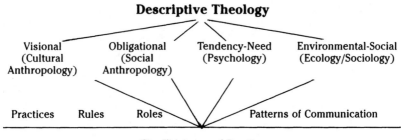

Descriptive Theology

| Visional (Cultural Anthropology) | Obligational (Social Anthropology) | Tendency-Need (Psychology) | Environmental-Social (Ecology/Sociology) |

Practices   Rules   Roles   Patterns of Communication

The Thickness of Practice

Figure 1
The structure of practical reasoning and descriptive theology's use of the special focus of the various social sciences to describe its various dimensions.

To say that psychology focuses on human psychobiological tendencies or sociology on institutional tendencies should not obscure the influence that traditions have on their theories and researchers. The focus of anthropology is the symbolic system of human groups. In the case of the Wiltshire Church, Williams and Hopewell are interested in the web of meanings that constitute its identity. At times, they uncover the obligational patterns that govern Wiltshire Church and the principles that give it coherence and weight. At other times, they focus on the narrative pattern, sometimes unconscious, that provides a sense of continuity over time.

Theological descriptions of human action also focus on the symbolic dimensions of it. They do it from a self-declared and explicit angle of vision. That angle of vision is some interpretation of what is ultimate, sacred, and divine. If theologians are Christian, they will use some interpretation of the Christian faith as the key to what is ultimate, sacred, and divine. In the case of the Dudley book, there were two theological interpretations of the Wiltshire Church. One was done by David Pacini and the other by Joseph Hough. Although they had different orientations to theology, their interpretations were primarily a process of measuring or assessing the degree to which the lived reality of the Wiltshire Church conformed to the ideals of the Christian faith as they understood them. Theological interpretation of actual communities is a process of measuring the *isness* of that community by some normative vision of what the community should be. Hough and Pacini were practicing a form of descriptive theology. What they saw, however, did not differ radically from what the other disciplines saw; this is because the other disciplines studying Wiltshire Church had their own implicit theological dimensions.

Descriptive theology can use all of the human and social sciences; their special explanatory foci can add power to the insights of descriptive theology. But descriptive theology uses these special foci within an explicit and critically grounded theological horizon. Having a religious horizon does not distinguish descriptive theology from the other human sciences. What distinguishes it is that its religious horizon is explicitly Christian and critically defended.

I begin the description of the Wiltshire Methodist Church at the most concrete of the five levels of description—the level of concrete practices and the rules, roles, and patterns of communication that they exhibit.

THE CHURCH'S PRACTICES AND COMMUNITY

The practices of the Wiltshire Church are part of the practices of its wider community. The community of Wiltshire in recent years had combined escapism and activism. Comfortable upper-middle-class families escaped the pressures and dangers of the city to enjoy the protection and relaxation of a Shangri-La located between two ridges. It was a community of activity with a boom mentality; this new influx of people had brought about growth in its schools, churches, and real estate industry. Sid Carlson, the new minister of the Wiltshire Church, had advanced this mentality of growth. He had taken decisive action to streamline the church, increase its attractiveness, and preach a gospel that appealed to busy, harried, and basically secular people who were looking for meaning within a life that was good but not without problems. In recent years, there were signs that the boom was drawing to a close. Sid was growing older. He wanted to invest in his own home. He wanted to expand facilities for Christian education. Both proposals met resistance.

On the surface, these practices look simple. But they are thick. They interweave many strands of motivation; social, environmental, and ecological context; moral principle; and narrative. One could begin to analyze them by looking at any one of these strands. I choose arbitrarily to examine first tendencies and needs.

TENDENCIES AND NEEDS

Psychology is the discipline most able to comprehend the tendency-need dimension. A dimension within descriptive theology is a special focus. It does not exclude the other dimensions; they are always in the margins of the discipline in question. To convey the idea of the circular and interacting relation of the various dimensions and the disciplines that uncover them, I begin with the relatively concrete tendency-need dimension of human life.

Barry Evans and Bruce Reed wrote a chapter for the Dudley book entitled "The Success and Failure of a Religious Club: A Psychological Approach." Evans was a consultant with the College of Preachers at the Washington Cathedral and Reed was the director of the Grubb Institute of Behavioral Studies. Their professional work was situated at the junction between research and consulting. They saw their descriptive psychological work as basically value-free and objective. In their essay they wrote, "In analyzing an organization, our approach is to collaborate with its members and attempt to *describe* the realities of the situations rather than to *evaluate* them" (Evans and Reed 1983, 41). But this team was anything but strictly objective. Rather, they were practicing a hermeneutical psychology that had within it what Ricoeur calls an explanatory or epistemological moment. Rather than invalidating their work, the hermeneutical horizons of their psychological description gave it value and intelligibility.

Evans and Reed drew on the "basic assumptions" theory of groups put forth by W. R. Bion in his famous *Experiences in Groups* (1961). Bion studied how groups form basic assumptions or shared attitudes that function to defend the group against threats. Bion describes three recurring basic assumptions, each of which gives rise to characteristic patterns of relatedness between members of the group and between members and leader. These basic assumptions are *dependence, expectancy (or pairing)*, and *flight-fight* (40).

Dependence is the unconscious assumption that the group's survival depends on being sustained by a powerful leader, institution, or ideal. Expectancy is the unconscious assumption that the group's survival depends on producing a new leader who will deliver the group from its present plight. Flight-fight is the assumption that the group's survival depends on vanquishing or avoiding an enemy, institution, or idea that threatens it.

Evans and Reed brought together these categories and the history of the Wiltshire Church. They believed that before the coming of Sid Carlson in 1970, the church was in a basic assumption of *dependence.* Wiltshire was a company town both serving and cared for by the Adams Company. The Wiltshire Church had been planned and financed with money from the Adams family; a patriarch of the family paid off the annual budget deficit. Evans and Reed say Wiltshire Church during this period was the "private chapel" of the Adams family.

Sid Carlson's arrival and the new community growth put the church in an attitude of *expectancy.* The new executive families joined with the assertive style of Sid Carlson to develop an unconscious sense of expectancy that he would lead them to growth and spiritual prestige. The church prospered by centering on the needs of its new members who had come to Wiltshire for safe haven and rest from their demanding professional commitments. Denominational ties suffered. Public ministries, social service ministries, and missions received little attention. According to Sid, the church was "the place that provides nurture and caring for those who must go out of the sanctuary and do battle in a fundamentally positive and exciting world" (Dudley 1983, 30). Few demands were made on the members of the Wiltshire Church; there was little they were asked to believe and little that they were asked to do to change their lives.

At the time of the study, Evans and Reed believed that the period of expectancy was waning and that disillusionment was setting in. It was a despair over the collapse of the "myth of success." During this period, the pastor and the congregation were in "collusion"—protecting one another from facing this collapse.

The analysis of Evans and Reed is more social-psychological than strictly psychological. I have said that psychology focuses on how psychobiological tendencies motivate human action. I still hold to that. Evans and Reed do not concentrate on the needs themselves, which they assume. They study the styles and attitudes that groups adopt to meet these needs. This is what they mean by "basic assumption."

Evans and Reed's use of this model, however, is not purely neutral, explanatory, and predictive. It is also evaluative. Their explana-

tory "if-then" or independent-dependent variable type thinking is
only a submoment of a largely interpretive framework that goes beyond being strictly descriptive and non-evaluative. It is clear that
they are not happy with the Wiltshire Church. Where does their
evaluative attitude come from? It comes from two sources, and they
are far more closely related than Evans and Reed realize. The first
source is the functionalist model of religion that they employ. Good
and healthy religions are, from their perspective, functional; they
meet human emotional needs. This is the main reason for the success of the Wiltshire Church. It was successful because it met the
needs of its current congregation "*insofar as these reflect the dominant needs of the town of Wiltshire*" (51). But these needs, from the
standpoint of Reed and Evans, were largely socially induced and
not basic. They were creations of a town attempting to handle the
emotional turmoil connected with the pursuit of upper-middle-class
success. Evans and Reed distinguish between "pseudofunctional
religion" and "functional religion" (52). Pseudofunctional religion
meets inauthentic, nonbasic, and socially induced needs. Functional
religion, on the other hand, does two things: It meets more abiding
and fundamental human needs, and it invokes a reflective process
in the minds of its adherents. In functional religion, this reflective
process is primary, and the pursuit of the fulfillment of human needs
is secondary (53). Trying to be scientific by following the function-
alism of Freud, Durkheim, and Parsons, Evans and Reed call the
religion of Wiltshire Church pseudofunctional. It met inauthentic
emotional needs and failed to create a reflective process that would
expose this inauthenticity.

But their analysis leaves questions unanswered. Nowhere in
their discussion do they develop a theory of authentic or basic
human needs. They assume that there are such things and that the
needs aimed toward the maintenance of upper-middle-class success
are not part of them. But one detects more than the functionalist
theory of religion behind their negative evaluation of Wiltshire. One
detects the horizon of their own pre-understanding of churches—
their own ecclesiology—formed by their own interpretation of the
Christian classics. As psychologists, they stand within a broader
religio-cultural tradition. If I am correct, they are not unique; all
psychologists and all social scientists stand within a tradition that
they cannot fully suppress. This tradition colors what they see and
is an integral part of their description of what they study. We see
it in this case. Evans and Reed are doing more than explaining
the basic psychological assumptions of the Wiltshire Church. They
do more than assess the religion of this church functionally. This
functionalist evaluation is also guided by their vision of normative

Christianity. Even though earlier they said they simply describe and do not evaluate, by the end we see that practical interests have guided them from the beginning. In the last paragraph of their study, Evans and Reed finally allow the full hermeneutical and practical interests of their work to shine forth when they write, "The promised outcome of the gospel is that those who get this right will become God's servants to those who are helpless." The Wiltshire Church, from their perspective, did not get the Christian message right. Although Evans and Reed do not refer to themselves as hermeneutic psychologists, their work is nonetheless an excellent example of a hermeneutic psychology that has within it an explanatory and naturalistic moment. It is also a hermeneutic psychology that borders on descriptive theology.

ENVIRONMENT AND SOCIAL CONTEXT

A team of distinguished sociologists—Jackson Carroll, William McKinney, and Wade Clark Roof—wrote a chapter offering a sociological account of the Wiltshire Church (Carroll, McKinney, and Roof 1983). This chapter illustrates many of the features I associate with my environmental-social dimension of practical thinking. Roof and McKinney are well known for their insightful *American Mainline Religion* (1987). Because they are distinguished sociologists of religion, their chapter is a window on the methods and assumptions of sociological description of religion.

By the environmental-social dimension of practical reason, I mean reason's effort to grasp the social-structural and ecological factors that place material constraints on our human needs. Contexts or situations in their fullest sense are constituted by much more than these two factors; they in fact exhibit all of the five dimensions of practical moral thinking. In the narrow sense meant here, I refer more specifically to the constraints of social structure and natural ecology. This dimension contains some material features associated with Marxist concerns with patterns of work and economic productivity. It also goes beyond Marxist preoccupations by looking at ecological constraints as well. These sociologists show how these factors relate to the context of the Wiltshire Church.

Their chapter had a revealing title: "From the Outside In and the Inside Out." The title conveys the main point of their contribution: All human organizations, even the church, are significantly shaped by their social and ecological context. This social and ecological context influences the mind-set that churches bring to the Christian message. Although these external factors were potent in shaping this congregation, these sociologists do not hold that they *determined* the mind-set of Wiltshire Church in all respects. Carroll, McKinney, and Roof are not sociological determinists. The internal life of the congregation and the influence of the Christian message can shape environmental forces. This is the meaning of the title that emphasizes both the "outside in" and the "inside out"; the inside can influence the outside. In the case of Wiltshire, these sociologists believe that its inner message is so bland, its boundaries so diffuse, its expectations for its members so undemanding, that in reality the trends and values of the wider community do have the upper hand.

This chapter exemplifies the difficulty of avoiding a hermeneutical stance. Regardless of its strong *focus* on the external social-systemic and ecological factors shaping the Wiltshire Church, the perspective that pervades this chapter clearly comes from the theological pre-understandings of these authors. Although they are interested primarily in the external social and ecological factors, they are also interested in the meanings that the people of the town and church gave to these factors. These authors follow Max Weber more than Karl Marx or Émile Durkheim. Like Weber, they emphasize the *interaction* of cultural ideals—in fact religio-cultural ideals—with social-systemic and material factors. In spite of the priority they give to external factors, much of their chapter sounds very close to the cultural and symbolic analyses found in the chapters by Williams and Hopewell and by theologians Hough and Pacini. But they do not account for the practical interests that both motivate and color their sociological work. They do not explicitly acknowledge the ways in which their chapter is not so much an objective sociological study as it is a dialogue and a conversation where the voices of the researchers are not directly heard but are yet very much in control. They do not, as Gadamer and those involved in the turn toward practical philosophy ask, make explicit the close relation between *phronēsis* and sociological reason.

The major external sociological trend they assume is the increase in modern societies of technical or purposive rationality and the related drift toward bureaucratization and privatism. The analysis of these broad modern trends, first powerfully explicated by Max Weber in his various writings ([1904–5] 1958, 181–83), has been expanded and detailed by a host of sociologists, particularly Talcott Parsons (1960, 60) and Jürgen Habermas (1984, 143–271). Technical or purposive rationality attempts to achieve increasingly efficient means-end relations for the realization of human needs and desires. Some theorists claim that technical rationality has become the dominant fact of life in modern societies, conditioning and shaping all other aspects. Over the last hundred years, Wiltshire has changed from an agricultural community into an industrial town (indeed a company town) and more recently into a residential community for executives and bureaucrats involved in the technical rationality of the modern insurance and other information-intensive industries.

Technical rationality brings bureaucratization and privatism in its wake. It inevitably accentuates the separation between the world of work and the world of home, residence, family, and intimate interpersonal relations. As Robert Bellah has so aptly put it, people in modern societies become utilitarian individualists in their corporate offices and expressive individualists at home in their private lives (Bellah et al. 1985, 32–35, 46). The new population of Wiltshire of the 1950s and 1960s was shaped by this split between public purposive rationality and domestic privatism and expressiveness.

According to our sociological team, this broad social-structural dynamic shapes the external world of Wiltshire, the community itself, and its Methodist church. Here are the demographic statistics that Carroll, McKinney, and Roof give to document these "outside" factors. Wiltshire had undergone rapid growth, is youthful, and is affluent. Its population of twenty-one thousand marks a fourfold increase from the 1940s. While the central city of Springfield lost 9 percent of its population between 1950 and 1960, Wiltshire's population increased 210 percent. It was, in fact, during that period the fastest growing suburb in the Springfield area (Carroll, McKinney, and Roof 1983, 86). In 1970, 42 percent of the community's residents were under eighteen, and 28 percent were in the prime childbearing ages, twenty-four to forty-four. Its median age was only 26.1, significantly lower than the rest of the region of Springfield (87). Its public school enrollments increased 61 percent from 1963 to 1970, but finally began to decline in the 1980s.

It became one of the wealthiest communities in the region. In 1981 (we must remind ourselves that salaries have increased significantly in the last decade) 10 percent of the families had incomes of over fifty thousand dollars a year. There were four times as many families with incomes over fifty thousand dollars as there were families with incomes under ten thousand dollars. This affluence is explained by the fact that 45 percent of Wiltshire's employed residents were in professional or managerial positions.

But these forces intermingle with other social realities. These authors have a section on the "social perceptions" or the "social worlds" of the Wiltshire community. This is the view from the inside out. Much of what they say overlaps with the more distinctively cultural, literary-symbolic, and theological analyses to which we will soon turn. They show the relation of privatism and individualism to the Wiltshire community's ethic of hard work, its emphasis on the family, and its appreciation for the virtues of honesty, punctuality, and persistence. These values and virtues, our trio tells us, are something the old-timers of Wiltshire (the farmers and the workers and managers of the Adams Company) and the newcomers (the management and executive types) share (97). Old-timers and newcomers share what culturally oriented sociologists have called the Protestant ethic. Since Max Weber's *The Protestant Ethic and the Spirit of Capitalism* ([1904–5] 1958), the Protestant ethic hypothesis has been one of the most celebrated and established concepts in the sociological literature. It holds that everywhere Protestantism (especially variations of the Reformed tradition) thrived, it unleashed a vision holding that the proximate goal of life was systematic, strenuous, honest, and persistent work. In the Reformed Protestant groups, this work was a sign that one was saved (the ultimate goal of life), a sign indeed of one's election by God.

Later, in more secularized times, hard work became a sign of one's general worthiness. Although both the older and the newer families of Wiltshire hold this ethic, the new families give it a new twist. They are far more consumer-oriented than the old-timers. They are far more inclined to limit their work morality to the Monday to Friday world of the office. Their time away from work is for private interests, warmth, expressiveness, and the enjoyment of their consumer worlds of large homes, expensive automobiles, stereos, country clubs, recreational centers, good eating, and the fellowship of a friendly, thought-provoking, but not too demanding form of the religion of their childhoods.

Even here, our sociologists believe the Wiltshire Church is formed primarily by forces outside of itself—by the values of the wider community. Wiltshire Church is Methodist, but the Methodist tradition influences its present identity little. Wiltshire Church is Christian, but the pastor characterizes most members as "wistful hearts" who are basically "secular and agnostic" (Dudley 1983, 10). Carroll, McKinney, and Roof characterize the theology of the Wiltshire Church as featuring a God who is warm, secure, basically in charge of the world, and supportive of the ambitions and values of the Wiltshire people. The God of Wiltshire "loves individuals, calls them to fulfill their potential as individuals, forgives and supports them when they fall short and are hurt, and blesses them with the good life. There is an especially strong belief that individuals are called to fulfill their potential and must refuse to give up or to sell themselves short" (102). God has become basically a support to the self-actualization of the children and adults of Wiltshire Church and a comfort and support for those undergoing the trials and tribulations that afflict them in their struggles to succeed.

This sociological chapter exhibits some but not all of what I have called the environmental-social dimension of moral experience. It illustrates primarily the social-systemic forces bearing down on Wiltshire. It says little about the ecological forces that play on Wiltshire. They are doubtless there. It has had the richness of soil and the climate to be an agricultural community. It had the sources of power and the materials to support a textile factory. The only ecological factors that these sociologists mention are the two ridges that provide a natural haven, refuge, and protection from the wider urban conglomerate of which it is a part. Here ecology is seen primarily as a resource for private life. Carroll, McKinney, and Roof help us see that, but they do not go further. In the end, a fuller description would have much more to say. At the least it would begin to hint at the limits of the life style of Wiltshire. Such an analysis might begin to ask: What would happen if the entire world reproduced Wiltshire's life style with its single-family dwellings, its automobiles, its green and manicured grass, its playgrounds, schools, and golf courses? How much water, energy, fertilizer, lumber, brick, asphalt, glass, cement, and food would the world need to provide these things to all? Can the world's ecological system sustain a generalization of Wiltshire?

The sociological team was more subdued than Evans and Reed in revealing the hermeneutical nature of their work. But clues as to their precommitments are strewn throughout their chapter. Rather than being a limitation, these precommitments give their work perspective. I wish they had taken explicit responsibility for their prejudices and the tradition that forms them. Had they done this, they would move from their illusory hope of doing value-free sociology to the hermeneutical and critical sociology that Bellah advocates. The chapter reveals the following: Their religion would heal the public-private gap, would make the situation of the poor a central issue for the church, and is not very interested in what they call the "private" issues of "drugs in the schools, tension and divorce in families, alcoholism for particular persons" (99). In spite of their concluding words that "sociological analysis will not prescribe to the church what it should be or do," it is clear that in addition to their descriptive and explanatory *focus*, their analysis assumed a wider religious vision that implied the Wiltshire Church was not living up to its mission. In ways they did not fully understand, their sociological account bordered on descriptive theology.

VISIONAL AND OBLIGATIONAL DIMENSIONS

I will review the visional and obligational dimensions together. I distinguish them for reasons that I hope will be clear as my argument unfolds. The distinction is important for constructive practical theological thinking and action. The distinction is also important for descriptive theology. The distinction I draw between vision and obligation parallels the distinction in moral philosophy between religion and morality. Drawing this distinction for both descriptive and constructive purposes will make us more sensitive to the many different ways humans relate religion and morality. Using the broader terms *vision* and *obligation* will make us aware of not only how official religions relate to morality but also how quasi-religious visions relate to moral beliefs.

By visional dimension of practical moral thinking, I mean the narratives and metaphors that a community tells to state and justify its identity. By identity I mean communities' or persons' symbolic self-representation of their origins, present self-understanding, and destiny. By obligational dimension, I mean the implicit or explicit principles that state what a person or group is morally obligated to do. Sometimes the narratives of a community or person directly state these principles. Sometimes these narratives relate to these principles in other ways. What I refer to as the visional and obligational levels of practical reason others often refer to as culture, that is, the system of narratives, signs, symbols, and rules that gives meaning and significance to the actions and practices of a group.

I will examine how two ethnographers and two theologians interpreted the cultural (visional and obligational) dimensions of Wiltshire Methodist Church's practical thinking. As we have seen, a visional level of interpretation has infused the psychological and sociological explanations through and through. Explanation and interpretation have proceeded hand-in-hand even in these allegedly objective explanations.

If this is so, were the psychological and sociological explanations helpful? Were they complementary? I think that the answer is yes to both questions. It is important to gain some insight into the broad social-systemic trends that purposive rationality unleashes in modern societies and the way these affect the practices of concrete religious communities. But it is also important to have the psychological investigation into tendencies and needs as a supplement to the sociological. Social patterns are inert unless they interact with certain tendencies and needs of human nature. These broad trends are meaningless unless they pattern certain describable regularities of human *desire*. Purposive rationality interacting with human de-

sire tends to produce a distance between public and private, work
and intimate expressivity. With the appearance of Sid Carlson, desire took the form of an expectancy that the emerging way of life of
Wiltshire would receive fulfillment and religious justification.

But there was nothing mechanically inevitable about the ways
in which purposive rationality interacted with human desire to produce the patterns of the Wiltshire community and the Wiltshire
Methodist Church. These sociological and psychological trends
were patterned and given significance by Wiltshire's system of cultural symbols (or religio-cultural visions). We already have seen
how the Protestant ethic shaped the separation between work and
private life that purposive rationality tends to create. There is
more to say about the cultural or visional dimensions infusing the
practices of the Wiltshire Church. To this we now turn.

Although the psychological and sociological explanations are
useful and anticipate cultural interpretations, the cultural as such
was not their focus. The cultural *is* the focus of the studies by Melvin
Williams and James Hopewell. Both refer to their perspectives
as ethnographic. Hopewell supplements his ethnography with resources from the literary-symbolic approach. Both draw on cultural
anthropology. The characterization of themselves as ethnographers
refers to the participant observation method that cultural anthropologists use to interpret the system of signs and symbols of the
groups they study. Cultural anthropology and ethnography are extremely useful for uncovering the interplay of the narratives, signs,
and symbols that make up the visional and cultural dimensions of
practical thinking and action.

Both Williams and Hopewell have a slight weakness from the
standpoint of my position. Neither fully acknowledges the hermeneutic nature of his cultural analysis. Both get close to this, but
neither makes it entirely explicit. Since the hermeneutic grounding
of their cultural interpretation is not explicit, the contribution of
their cultural descriptions to practical thinking and practical theology is not immediately clear. A practical motivation guides their
work from the very beginning—one, however, that is not clearly
acknowledged.

The hermeneutic and practical stance of Williams is clearer
than Hopewell's. Williams is a cultural anthropologist who has
contributed to his discipline through ethnographic or participant observation studies of black congregations. These studies
are recorded in *Community in a Black Pentecostal Church* (1974).
Williams believes that it is through participant observation that
the anthropologist is able to understand the network of symbolic
meanings that gives a group its identity. In studying the Wiltshire

Church, Williams applies the polarities of the ritual process first clarified by Victor Turner in his important *The Ritual Process* (1969). Turner develops the idea that all rituals move back and forth between what he calls "structure" and "*communitas.*" The moment of structure in the ritual process functions to consolidate the assumed and sedimented habits, patterns, hierarchical roles, and social structures of the everyday world. The moment of *communitas* deconstructs this assumed structure and emphasizes a nonhierarchical, unstructured, and intimate set of relations without regard to status, wealth, or property. Williams omits telling us that in primitive societies, where Turner derived his concepts, moments of *communitas* are associated with changes of the state of the ritual participants and is a transitory moment on the way to the reinstatement of structure and order. Nonetheless, he applies these categories to the Wiltshire Church. He claims that the central issue is the conflict between those who would have the church conform to the *structures* of the bureaucratic world (the world of purposive rationality) and those who want an intimate face-to-face community—a *communitas.*

Williams's treatment is brief and not entirely successful. More relevant is his claim that ethnographic research is basically practical and designed primarily to help the group being observed. His description of participant observation research exhibits many of the features of the hermeneutic conception of the human sciences. Following the work of J. P. Spradley on the ethnographic interview, Williams acknowledges that the ethnographic interview assumes the particular perspective (Does he mean pre-understandings?) of the interviewer. Furthermore, he claims that such research when applied to congregations "should be useful to members in resolving their own congregational predicaments" (Melvin Williams 1983, 58). Just as Gadamer has suggested, application guides description from the beginning.

From the perspective of hermeneutic social science Williams lacks any concept of effective history—specifically the effective history from which Williams writes his ethnographic report of the Wiltshire Church. He makes no admission or any defense of the angle of vision from which he describes the symbolic patterns in that congregation. Yet his precommitments are easily discerned. Williams came prizing intimate relations, fluid structure, and non-hierarchical role patterns. These precommitments give his analysis of the symbolic culture of Wiltshire a hue, a flavor, and an evaluative feel that it would not otherwise have. In summary, cultural anthropology, like the other disciplines examined above, should be seen as a hermeneutic social science.

James Hopewell's ethnographic description is more detailed and more novel. It is also supplemented and amplified by his significant posthumously published book, *Congregation: Stories and Structures* (1987). Hopewell was important in stimulating the current wave of congregational studies. As director of Emory University's Rollins Center for Church Ministries, he played a significant role in arguing for congregational studies in theological education. I will attend to both his article in the Dudley volume and his above-mentioned book.

Hopewell supplements his ethnographic approach to symbolic culture with the literary theories of Northrop Frye (Frye 1957). Hopewell is a practitioner of the currently fashionable semiotic approach to the study of culture. This approach sees cultural meaning as primarily a configuration of signs and metaphors organized by systems of rules or codes. The leading practitioners of semiotics are such figures as Clifford Geertz in the United States, Roland Barthes in France, and Roman Jacobson and Vladimir Propp, who are associated with the Moscow-Tartu school. Hopewell draws mainly from Geertz supplemented by the literary theories of Frye.

Narrative is the key, for Hopewell, to understanding the web of signs, metaphors, and rules that make up the culture of any group or congregation. A narrative to some extent is a group's history. But it is more than just the sequence of events that make up that history. A narrative is the story that a group tells to give significance to a particular sequence of events. Hopewell holds a complex and sometimes taxing theory of narrative. He claims a narrative is made up of *plot, setting,* and *characterization.* A plot is the storyline assigned to the history of the group. A setting is the world view implied by this plot. Characterization is what Hopewell, following Geertz, calls the "ethos or pattern of values" or "genius" of a group (1983, 71; 1987, 103–7). Ethos refers more to the ethical tone or feel of a group than to its world view as such. Or to put it in my terminology, it has more to do with obligation than it does with vision, although it deals more with moral character than moral principle. (My obligational level has more to do with moral principle than with moral character, although it is concerned with the latter as well.) Hopewell believes that the ethos or ethical tone of a group is significantly shaped by the group's implicit myth (1987, 107–11). (I will make the analogous point that the obligational level of practical thinking is shaped significantly by a group's or individual's religio-cultural vision.) This is true even of congregations. In fact, according to Hopewell, it is especially true of congregations. How is this so?

Hopewell explains that in addition to some version of the Christian story that constitutes their official narrative identity, all congregations have a latent mythic narrative as well. Hopewell implies this makes up the actual identity of the congregation. To get at this latent mythic narrative one has to go back to plot and setting. One has to gain an imaginative grasp of the plot and ask what people are *really* saying when they tell their church's story. Hopewell exercises his imagination by reviewing the great myths of the Western cultural tradition. He believes that the subconscious narrative of a church will correspond to one of those myths. He also looks for the setting or world view of this narrative. He does this by giving members of a congregation a rather elaborate questionnaire designed to uncover that world view.

In doing these things, Hopewell reveals that his semiotics is deeply influenced by the literary theories of Northrop Frye. To this extent, his semiotics is more theory-bound than some. He follows Frye in believing that there are typical archetypal patterns by which human imagination has negotiated the challenges of life in the Western tradition. These are not archetypes in the Jungian sense but rather archetypes in the more historical sense; they are a fund of imaginative patterns that have arisen out of the experiences of groups in the West. All particular examples of narrative imagination in the West draw on this fund of archetypal patterns and their attendant world views (1987, 47, 49, 61). This is true of the mythic narrative behind the story that Wiltshire Church tells about itself.

Hopewell believes that the latent myth of the Wiltshire Church parallels the Greek myth of Zeus, the father of gods and humans. The myth goes like this. Chronus, the original father of the gods, was saturnine, heavy, and dull. He also had the revolting habit of eating his children. Zeus was the last-born of Chronus. By deceiving Chronus, Zeus managed to escape being swallowed by his father. In addition, he further tricked Chronus into vomiting up his brothers and sisters, who then joined Zeus to inaugurate the Olympian age. A titanic battle was required before Zeus's dominance was secured. After a colossal struggle and using a combination of power and subterfuge, Zeus was victorious.

Hopewell believes this myth exposes the latent meaning of the Wiltshire Church. Under the domination of the Adams family, the church was ruled by aging and dull powers who remind us of Chronus. After a secret visit to Wiltshire prior to his call (Sid actually disguised himself during the visit), Sid came to the church and quickly deposed the old leadership (the old official board was asked to resign, and the old church secretary and choir director left). Like Zeus, Sid defeated the dull and aged through deception, cleverness, and power.

After his victory, Zeus was seen as the protector of law and morals and the punisher of evil. He was a moral authority willing to push for what is right. Zeus controlled the gods and humans with thunderbolts and severe penalties. Sid, as the years go by, controls people through embarrassment and ridicule.

In the beginning, life under Zeus was good. Zeus was jovial. On Olympus the gods lived serenely in merriment and laughter. Life under Sid at the Wiltshire Church is also jovial. The Wiltshire Church is the "best show in town." "If you can't join the Wiltshire Country Club, join Wiltshire Church."

And finally, the Greek gods under Zeus, although very much like humans, were in reality immortal. Although they were subject to certain kinds of accidents, they could not be destroyed. In an analogous way, the people of Wiltshire Church under Sid seem to enjoy a similar invulnerability or, more accurately, exude an aura of invulnerability (1983, 71–76; 1987, 178–91).

During later years of Sid's ministry, however, the myth of Zeus has seemed to crumble. Sid has passed fifty and is becoming saturnine himself. He is concerned about his security, failed his Doctor of Ministry examinations, and has admitted he is in psychotherapy. His moral rule is collapsing. The church is reacting negatively to his proposal to purchase the parsonage. The congregation is confused about and resisting construction of a new educational building for children and youth. There are mutual accusations and a breakdown of trust. The former joviality and humor are gone. The sense of immortality and invulnerability has begun to crack.

Hopewell follows Frye in grasping the synchronic world view of a group. Frye believes that the storehouse of world views in the West is finite. There are basically four—comic, romantic, tragic, and ironic (Hopewell 1983, 70; 1987, 57–62). On the basis of Hopewell's world view questionnaire, Wiltshire Church had the highest ironic and the lowest romantic scores he had found in any of the thirty churches he had studied. An ironic world view, according to Frye, holds that life is to be lived without illusions and without recourse to the sacred. Its religious sensibilities are empirical; it seeks knowledge and wisdom through the integrity of human experience. On the other hand, a romantic world view sees life as a heroic adventure and finds religion in the charismatic search for communion with God. Wiltshire's world view is the opposite of the romantic and a near-perfect exemplification of ironic spirituality.

What are we to make of Hopewell's engaging ethnographic and literary-symbolic approach to the culture of Wiltshire Church? Does it add something to the psychological and sociological descriptions? Does it help capture the visional level of practical experience and does it help us to see the relation of the visional to the obligational?

Hopewell's semiotics (it is a particular approach among many semiotic options) does add something to the psychological and sociological perspectives without contradicting them. In fact, the three perspectives very much cohere; they all see Wiltshire Church as living at the end of a period of expectancy, increase, advance, and enhancement. Yet each has a slightly different focus. Seen from the perspective of Hopewell's semiotics, the emotional needs studied by psychology and social-structural conditioning studied by sociology become elaborated into an unconscious narrative about the defeat of the chronic forces of death and dullness and the victory of joviality and immortality. These religio-cultural meanings are not totally independent of the emotional and social-systemic forces. Yet the cultural meanings that semiotics uncovers are responses to these forces and give them a particular elaboration. The culture of joviality gives the emotionality of expectancy a particular significance. Expectancy can take other symbolic forms. The culture of joviality gives the sociological forces of purposive rationality a particular significance. Purposive rationality may have vastly different meaning in an inner city where industry abandons no longer profitable operations depriving people of jobs—purposive rationality affects the life of the Apostolic Church of God this way. The culture of joviality gives purposive rationality a particular meaning for the upper-middle class of Wiltshire. All of these perspectives tell us something, and the semiotic analysis of Wiltshire's culture has added something distinctive. It all helps uncover the various dimensions of practical experience at Wiltshire Church.

Yet the full meaning of these levels of analysis is seen only when placed in the broader hermeneutical context. Hopewell's semiotics is like the other perspectives; it is the focus of a wider hermeneutical interpretation in which Hopewell's pre-understandings are part of the interpretive process. Hopewell has explicit Christian theological pre-understandings that he does not account for in his theory of interpretation. In his article in the Dudley volume, we see them only faintly. In his book *Congregation*, they become much clearer, and the extent to which his cultural and semiotic analysis is also a hermeneutic interpretation becomes more obvious. We learn in his book that Hopewell himself was on the border between ironic and tragic world views (1987, 63–64). Hopewell wrote his book while he was dying of cancer. He confesses that the spiritual resources that move him are a synthesis of ironic and tragic views of Christianity. He shares the ironic view that sees God's action as infused throughout ordinary events. But he also interprets Christianity with a tragic

world view. This view sees people as morally flawed agents breaking
the moral law of God but also finding their redemption through submission to this very same law (1983, 70; 1987, 60). Hopewell tells us
he takes an ironic-tragic view of his approaching death. He comes
to his impending death with little hope of either comic release or
romantic miraculous intervention. Instead, he looks for signals of
God's love in the empirical acts of kindness from his friends and
family. And he finds God's transcendence through submission to
God's rule and the destiny God has assigned. This is the heart of
tragedy.

Then Hopewell adds something of extreme importance for this
discussion. He writes, "The tragic irony that I tell about my mortal
body reflects something of the approach I make to understanding
congregations" (1987, 64). He confesses, in effect, that an ironic-
tragic interpretation of the Christian faith is the hermeneutical
pre-understanding he brings to his semiotic description of the cultures of congregations. Hopewell tells us he did not just neutrally
describe the symbolic meanings of the Wiltshire Church. He did not
accidentally discover the analogies between Wiltshire's latent narrative and the myth of Zeus. From the beginning he described the
culture of Wiltshire from the perspective of his own ironic-tragic
view of Christianity. When he uses the myth of Zeus to characterize the unconscious meanings of this church, we detect Hopewell's
view that this myth is seriously incongruent with the Christian story.
Hopewell's semiotic interpretation is really a dialogue between his
ironic-tragic view of Christianity and the radically ironic view of
life found in the Wiltshire people.

Hopewell's semiotic analysis is flawed in this respect: It does
not fully describe what he actually does. It is not adequate to the
full scope of the narrative of the Wiltshire Church, and it does not
fully account for the role that his Christian precommitments play in
his descriptions. Hopewell is not just describing how the myth of
Zeus figures in the unconscious of the congregation of the Wiltshire
Methodist Church. He is interpreting both the myth of Zeus and
that church's version of the Christian story, and interpreting both
of these stories from the perspective of *his* version of the Christian
story. Hopewell's analysis of his semiotics does not adequately account for the complex hermeneutical nature of his efforts to grasp
the culture of the Wiltshire Church.

As a result, the richness of the narrativity of the Wiltshire
Church is underestimated. There is, after all, a particular version
of the Christian story being told there. And it does interact with
the latent patterns that the myth of Zeus suggestively illuminates.
But Hopewell does not acknowledge the possibility that the myth

of Zeus may be collapsing partially because the Christian story has been told there. Although inadequate, the Christian story told there may have been sufficiently powerful to sow the seeds of collapse for the myth of Zeus. The turmoil at the Wiltshire Church may be more than the beginning of the end; it may be the beginning of a new beginning. The wider meanings of the gospel—meanings that neither Sid nor his congregation fully understands—may be hastening the end of the dominance of the Zeus myth.

The gospel preached at Wiltshire Church reinforced the self-actualization of the individuals in the congregation. In Hopewell's semiotics, his version of structuralism gives us a more static understanding of the narrative of the Wiltshire Church than we need. I do not use structuralism in the sense associated with Claude Lévi-Strauss, with the formalism of Jean Piaget and Lawrence Kohlberg, or with the archetypal structuralism of Carl Jung. I mean the more historically formed quasi-structuralism that Hopewell inherited from Northrop Frye. This quasi-structuralism leads Hopewell to think that the fund of Greek myths more or less exhausts the mythic possibilities of the human imagination and that the comedic, ironic, romantic, and tragic perspectives more or less exhaust the fund of possible world views. This quasi-structuralism functions more like a genuine structuralism than Hopewell admits. In Hopewell's description, the synchronic aspects of the narrative dominate the diachronic. Hence, the Wiltshire Church appears stationary. It seems to be trapped in a myth that is breaking down. But this may seem true more because of Hopewell's quasi-structuralist semiotics than because the actual narratives of the church are not moving forward.

Paul Ricoeur's critique of structuralism applies to Hopewell's quasi-structuralism. Ricoeur makes a crucial distinction between what he calls the *sense* of a narrative and the *referent* of the narrative. The sense is the immanent meaning of the narrative; it is both the internal system of codes and rules that govern the lexical meaning of terms and the fund of associated commonplaces that make up the ordinary usage of a language. A narrative also has what Ricoeur calls a referent. This is the world of meanings that the narrative projects in front of itself as it points toward the future (Ricoeur 1981, 171–76, 280–87). Metaphor is the linguistic unit that gives birth to a creativity in narrative that goes beyond the immanent sense. Since part of the narrativity of the Wiltshire Church entails the preaching and hearing of a version of the Christian story, important questions arise. What is the interaction between these two fields of meaning—the field of the myth of Zeus and the field of the Christian story? Is it possible that as the myth of Zeus was a drag on the Christian story so Wiltshire's version of the Christian story also subtly transformed the myth of Zeus? Ricoeur's critique of structuralism opens the possibility that meanings may not be rigidly settled and that narratives can transform each other. This is the possibility we will carry with us as we turn to the explicit attempts to render a theological interpretation of the Wiltshire Church.

DESCRIPTIVE THEOLOGY'S VISIONAL DIMENSION

Each of these disciplines had an explanatory focus that earned it the right to be called psychology, sociology, anthropology, or ethnography. But each had a horizon that has faded into theology. This horizon was evident in spite of the fact that most authors attempted to inhibit their theological commitments. Each perspective had a theological fringe partially because its practitioner was Christian and contributing to a book that addressed the church. My argument, however, is that the human sciences are necessarily hermeneutical; for this reason, quasi-religious commitments inevitably will appear in the horizon of all of these disciplines. The examples studied here are not unique. Some theological horizon, although it may not be Christian, informs all instances of the human sciences. Because of this, we cannot ask a discipline to shed its religious depths. But we can ask that it take responsibility for it, acknowledge it, and when appropriate attempt to justify it.

Descriptive theology attempts to describe the visional and obligational dimensions of situations from an explicitly theological perspective. But the descriptive theology that I envision goes further. It attempts to describe the religious dimensions of a situation and then offers a critical theological evaluation of that situation. Then it goes further still. It tries to keep the theological description and evaluation in contact with the other dimensions of practical experience—the tendency-need, the environmental-social, and the unconscious semiotic dimensions that form the subtext of a group's life. It does this by describing the meaning-laden or theory-laden character of actual practices. Obviously, the cultural anthropological perspectives and the theological perspectives overlap. Many of the techniques associated with semiotics can be used by explicitly descriptive theology. The difference is that explicitly descriptive theology confesses openly its hermeneutical character and takes critical responsibility for its theological pre-understandings.

Two authors in Dudley's book were charged to bring a theological perspective to the Wiltshire Church. As I indicated earlier, this congregational study was first conceived without an explicitly theological perspective. This was a telling omission. It was as though the description of situations—even the situation of a Christian congregation—could proceed completely on the basis of human sciences outside of theology. But finally, Joseph Hough and David Pacini were invited to throw their respective theological lights on Wiltshire Church.

Hough and Pacini both believe that Wiltshire Church is in the grips of a conflict between two linguistic fields. One is provided by the culture of the Wiltshire community, and one is provided by an interpretation of the Christian story. Pacini believes that the linguistic field of the Wiltshire community dominates the Christian linguistic field. For Pacini, the secular culture of Wiltshire dominates its theology; together they project an ideology that depicts God as the great supporter of the modern tendency to solve conflicts through democratic consensus. Pacini believes that, on the whole, the Christian narrative told at Wiltshire is contentless. It has sold out to a consensual democracy that is itself an attempt to handle the breakdown of authority in societies dominated by purposive rationality (Pacini 1983, 133–54).

For our purposes, Hough's description is more useful. It sees a genuine conflict between the secular-cultural and Christian fields of meaning. But he believes that the meanings of the secular-cultural field, although strong, are somewhat transformed by the Christian meanings. Hough's theological interpretation is the only perspective in the Dudley book that holds out the possibility that new meaning may be breaking forth in the Wiltshire Church and that this meaning may be Christian. All the others—the psychological, socio-ecological, anthropological-ethnographic, even Pacini's theological view—see the Wiltshire Church as trapped in a system of closed meanings determined primarily by its emotionality, its social-systemic and ecological context, or its cultural-linguistic subtext. Even Hopewell, as we saw earlier, uncovers the myth of Zeus in the culture of the Wiltshire Church but does not show us how it interacts with the congregation's interpretation of the Christian story. In *Congregation* Hopewell does sometimes show how a congregation's Christian story interacts with and transforms its mythic subtext (1987, 171–72). He does not do this in his essay for Dudley. Hough's explicitly theological description is the most charitable description of the Wiltshire Church in the Dudley volume. As critical as he is, Hough is sensitive to signs of grace, hope, and transformation at Wiltshire.

It surprises me to see this, but it should not. It should not be surprising that an interpretive perspective informed by a gospel of justice, grace, and forgiveness can discern better than others the signals of justice, grace, and forgiveness at the Wiltshire Church.

In many ways, Hough's article approaches a model of descriptive theology in a practical theology context. From my perspective, however, it falls short of fully incorporating important human science submoments in its descriptive theological work. It has an implicit practice-theory-practice logic and it adapts its descriptive work to it. Hough makes a decided effort to describe the central *practices* of the Wiltshire Church. He notes its music program and the judgment that it is the best in the area. He notes the strong emphasis on preaching; Sid is considered a good and clear homilist. Wiltshire is considered to have the best religious education program in the area, involves a large number of adult leaders in this program, and is still growing even though the school population is declining. There is a strong emphasis on ministry to the ill, although Sid does most of the calling. Worship and communion are highly valued. The ministry of the church, however, is primarily a ministry to the members of the church in their moments of need.

Then Hough moves from a description of the practices of the congregation to a description of the theory behind these practices. Here he is relying on a questionnaire investigating the theological beliefs of the congregation. Only a small percentage of the congregation ever turn to God for guidance. God is primarily a source of comfort and inspiration who gives courage and strength in times of crisis and stress. Jesus is primarily a moral example. Jesus also reveals the spark of the divine in all human beings. But Jesus does not challenge the present order; instead he loves his children and "exhibits courage and honor and good sportsmanship" (Hough 1983, 114).

Then Hough moves into a dialogue between the theory of these practices and Hough's interpretation of the Christian story. It is not a fully critical dialogue. Nonetheless, it exhibits some of the features of a hermeneutic conversation that begins with the description of theory-laden practices, moves back to a confrontation with the Christian classics, and then returns to a critique of these theory-laden practices. Hough examines the theory of the Wiltshire practices, that is, its ecclesiology. He makes this interpretation from the perspective of his interpretation of the ecclesiology of the early Christian church. Hough's interpretation of this early ecclesiology is just that—an interpretation; other interpretations are possible. I will not attempt to judge its correctness. I am more interested in using the overall logic of his analysis to illustrate features of descriptive theology.

Hough interprets early Christian ecclesiology under the rubric of the body of Christ. He makes three points. First, using Barth, he says the church as the body of Christ is a *human community*

that shows forth an attitude of joy and gratitude and is marked
by face-to-face relations, mutual speaking and hearing, and mutual
assistance (120). Second, the church as the body of Christ is a community "for the poor." This is seen in Jesus' renunciation of riches
and power in the wilderness. It also is seen in the synagogue reading of the passage from Isaiah that Jesus applied to himself: "The
spirit of the Lord is upon me, because he has anointed me to bring
good news to the poor. He has sent me to proclaim release to the
captives and recovery of sight to the blind, to let the oppressed
go free" (Luke 4:18-19; Isa. 61:1-2). Hough follows Luise Schottroff
and Wolfgang Stegemann in believing that in these words "Jesus is
turning established Jewish theology on its head; not only are the
poor to be included in the covenant people, they were the object of
God's special concern" (125). Being the church means being *with*
the poor, not just ministering *to* the poor. And finally, the body of
Christ is a "community for the world" (126). Jesus became human
not just for human beings but for the whole world. God's covenant is
not just with humans, it is with the whole of creation. The fulfillment
of the covenant with Abraham is the covenant with Noah, which is
in fact a covenant with the whole of creation. Human dominion over
the world is like God's; it is for the fulfillment of creation, not its
exploitation. The Christian story and its view of the mission of the
church have ecological implications for all of creation as well as
soteriological implications for humans.

It is not surprising that from the perspective of this ecclesiology, Hough finds the Wiltshire Church wanting. It does not have
a deep identification with the poor. It supports instead an upper-
middle-class ideology of success. It is not a community concerned
with the ecological integrity and fulfillment of the whole of creation.
Some of the themes of the gospel are heard at Wiltshire Church. But
the struggle between the linguistic field of secular private refuge
and public success *and* the linguistic field of the Christian story is
resolved primarily in favor of the secular message.

But not completely. Hough sees hints of a struggle for a deeper
identification with the body of Christ. He sees this in Wiltshire
Church's high valuation of communion. He sees it in the effort
that goes into the church school and the church's struggle to leave
something of value to the congregation's children. He concludes, "In
short, Wiltshire Church partakes very much in the paradox of the
people of God. It is at once a self-centered, fractured, and culture-
bound community of like-minded persons, and at the same time,
by the miracle of grace, it is the body of Christ symbolized in the
bread and wine, called to be for each other and for the poor and for
the world" (130). Hough sees the body of Christ in the dissatisfac-

tion that many members have with the present state of the church. He sees it in their hunger for more. The Christian story may be transforming the Wiltshire Church ever so slightly.

The purpose of explicitly descriptive theology is to capture the questions that guide the move to historical and systematic theology and the return to the concreteness of strategic practical theology. In chapter 5, I risked a preliminary statement of the central question of the Wiltshire Church. It went like this: How does a church balance the needs of its own leaders and members with the needs of others? When I first phrased that question, it sounded thin and insignificant. I hope now that it sounds thicker and weightier. From one perspective, the question simply addresses the particular form that sin takes at the Wiltshire Church. This sin is, as Reinhold Niebuhr would say, the inordinate self-interest of all people, including the congregation of the Wiltshire Church (R. Niebuhr 1941, 190–91). Sid wants his own home. Some people want a new educational building for their children. There is little concern for the poor and for the world outside Wiltshire. This sin, as Hough would say, leads Wiltshire Church to fall short of the demands of the body of Christ.

Our understanding of this inordinate self-concern is enriched when amplified by the multidimensional analyses provided above. Evans and Reed help us see how it takes the form of an emotionality of expectation—an almost magical investment in Sid Carlson's powers. The sociologists help us see how this inordinate self-concern is embedded in the social-systemic patterns of purposive rationality; in the separations between private and public, home and work; and in the individualism, privatism, and sentimentality that such self-concern unleashes. The cultural anthropologists help us recognize the mythic structure undergirding this inordinate self-concern at the Wiltshire Church—the unconscious fantasy that the old and dull had been vanquished and a new life of joviality and immortality had been inaugurated. All of these levels greatly amplify the richness of the practical theological question emerging out of the struggles of Wiltshire Methodist Church. It is one thing to simply ask the abstract question, What is the relation of self-concern to concern for others? It is quite another thing to ask: How are people who are pervasively afflicted by the sin of inordinate self-concern, who by their luck of being on the right side of purposive rationality have been thrust into the seductions of a protected community, who therefore have difficulty bridging the distance between public and private life, who feel full of expectation and relief over being in this situation, who even fantasize it lasting forever—how do these people address the relation of self-concern to the concern for others? The formulation of thick questions is an essential part of descriptive theology and the first step of a fundamental practical theology. The formulation of thick questions is necessary for a rich retrieval of the classic meanings of the faith at all points in the hermeneutic circle. But it is particularly important for the full and rich communicative task at the stage of strategic practical theology.

I have labored long and hard to formulate this question. Doubtless it is still inadequate. Further, it is probably formulated far too much from my angle of vision. I am an outsider. Descriptive theology functioning in the concreteness of the Wiltshire situation would make the elaboration of that question a community endeavor. It would never come all at once. It would not have the neatness of my formulation. It might never become fully explicit. Yet if good practical theology were occurring, it would be the product of an ongoing process that would guide and perpetually renew the reflection of this congregation. This question can take its present form only if a hermeneutical horizon with a religious dimension is brought to the interpretation of the Wiltshire situation. We saw such horizons implicit in the human science perspectives and explicit in Hough's interpretations. Hough, however, could have profited from the explicit focus of the other disciplines and what they have to offer to a description of the other dimensions of practical thinking and action.

If descriptive theology is to be rich, thick, and dense, that is, if it is to comprehend the multidimensional fabric of practical reason, it must touch the five dimensions I have illustrated. Of course, in the sermon, the theological tract, the actual moment of care, and the immediate task of education, these five dimensions in their analytic austerity vanish into the art and grace of poetry and the immediacy of fresh and spontaneous religious language. The exercises of dissection in this book are like stopping a moving picture to examine the frames one at a time. Such exercises are important to clarify what goes into a good movie, but they are no substitute for assembling with artistic flourish the entire reel, coordinating it with sound and light, and letting it play. Learning to do live and moving practical theology is something like this. But even then, it does not start with bits and pieces. It starts with the whole—a description of some practices and their meanings. It then gains interpretive and critical distance and gradually returns to reconstruct the whole. It does this time and time again.

PART THREE

SYSTEMATIC THEOLOGY AND THEOLOGICAL ETHICS

7

THEOLOGY, ETHICS, AND THE FIVE DIMENSIONS

Were the purpose of this book to present a fully systematic fundamental practical theology, then my earlier statements about historical and systematic theology would need to be elaborated. Practical theology moves from descriptive theology and its formation of questions back to historical theology, systematic theology (and theological ethics), and finally to strategic or fully practical theology. To be fully systematic I would now need to present expansive treatments of historical and systematic theology.

Although not repeating what I have said already about historical and systematic theology, with regard to historical theology I need to add this: Christian practical theology, by virtue of being Christian, will give special weight to classic Christian texts. But it needs to listen to the classic texts of other traditions as well, especially those non-Christian texts to which Christianity has itself listened. This means listening to the texts of Hebrew Scriptures and the Greek and Roman texts that the biblical authors read and partially incorporated. This especially means attending to the Greek classics that influenced the Israel of Jesus' day and that further influenced the Gospels and Epistles that make up the New Testament. We now know, thanks to the important work of New Testament scholars such as Hans Dieter Betz, Abraham Malherbe, Gerd Theissen, and many others, that the early Christian writings are a mélange of Jewish and Greek histories. We know also that those Christian writings' distinctively Christian elements derive from the unique way early Christianity put together Greek and Hebrew worlds. With this in mind, I will state again that historical theology is not the cool, objective, and distanciated study of the theological ideas of the past. It is a practical process of putting the theory-laden questions that emerge from contemporary praxis to the great religious monuments of the religious tradition.

The thick descriptions of descriptive theology should guide the reappropriation of the classic texts and monuments. The five dimensions can guide biblical interpretation. Too much scriptural interpretation stays at the visional and obligational levels of meaning. We tend not to examine how texts interpret human needs or the pressures of the social-systemic and ecological environments. We now have an excellent fund of new literature that investigates the social environment of early Christianity. Wayne Meeks, Gerd Theissen, John Gager, and others have contributed to this literature. Their work illuminates how the different New Testament theologies interact with their rich social contexts. Theological appropriation of this research has been slow. Unfortunately, I will not advance it here. My effort will be once removed. But the direct reading of the biblical texts from the perspective of the five dimensions is essential, and possible.

I also need to add these words about systematic theology: Systematic theology shares the practical character of all theology. It is concerned with general rather than concrete aspects of situations. In his *Systematic Theology*, Paul Tillich, a systematic theologian par excellence, correlated Christian answers with the broad polar elements that constitute the ambiguities of existence (Tillich 1951, 174–85). They are present to varying degrees in all situations. Although at times Tillich attended to how these ambiguities worked in certain historical epochs (fate and death at the end of the Roman Empire, guilt and condemnation in the Middle Ages, and emptiness and meaninglessness in the modern era), it was not his habit to study the questions emerging from highly concrete situations (Tillich 1952, 57–63). As I pointed out earlier, Johann Baptist Metz primarily relates his practical theology to the general features of modernity created by the "exchange principle" (Metz 1980, 32–47). There is a place for these general analyses of human situations, but life begins and ends in more concrete contexts. A fundamental practical theology starts with full descriptions of concrete situations and relates more general features of situations to the richness of the concrete. It is for this reason that as we turn to Niebuhr we must keep the thick description of the Wiltshire Church's situation in mind. That question will lead us to the issue of Christian love— how self-love, love for the other, and self-sacrifice are related in the Christian life.

THE RETURN TO REINHOLD NIEBUHR

In this and the following chapter, I advance a definition of theological ethics as part of systematic theology. As I have said already, there are two forms of theological ethics. One is part of systematic theology and the other a part of strategic practical theology. The latter form addresses the full immediacy of concrete questions about practices. In contrast, theological ethics in systematic theology is part of that transient moment of relatively distanciated reflection when we try to grasp the general features of Christian ethical thinking as they relate to some features of life. It is at most only a passing moment between concrete practical interests and consequent concrete practical acts.

Reinhold Niebuhr commonly is considered the most powerful theological ethicist of the mid–twentieth century. He was also a highly engaging practical theologian. But in his monumental, two-volume *The Nature and Destiny of Man* (1941, 1943), he was a theological ethicist. His concerns were systematic. He addressed the great general features of the Christian faith and the general basic trends of the modern world. But both before and after writing this systematic piece, he was concerned with a variety of concrete problems—the anguish of industrial civilization, its inequalities, the labor movement, race relations, war and peace issues around World War II, the Korean conflict, and the Vietnam struggle. His concerns were practical and hermeneutical in Gadamer's sense, although his work appeared long before Gadamer's writings.

It is, however, with Niebuhr as a theological ethicist that I am concerned at the moment. From one angle, his *The Nature and Destiny of Man* is a work in systematic theology. From another, it is a work in theological ethics. It is an excellent illustration of how systematic concern with the major theological themes of Christianity sheds light on its central ethical implications. The concrete questions that preoccupied Niebuhr are in the background of this text, and it will not be his questions that I bring to his theological ethics. It will be the questions of our three churches. Niebuhr's systematic position will be treated as primarily a transient moment of distanciation located between the concrete practical questions coming from these congregations and the concrete strategies that the practical theologian must entertain.

I will use Niebuhr as a guide to the Christian classics. I do not say he is totally reliable and that no other theologian is worth using. Other theologians, both ancient and modern, will be brought into dialogue with him. Nor does using Niebuhr substitute for fresh confrontation with these classics. But practical theology depends heavily on other theological disciplines. My use of Niebuhr is a confession of my dependencies and something more.

I want to develop the Christian content of the first four of the five dimensions of practical thinking by uncovering their presence in his thought. The most concrete rule-role level is not discernible in *The Nature and Destiny of Man* precisely because it is a work in theological ethics rather than a fully practical theology. Niebuhr is often said to be the theologian to return to if late twentieth-century theology is to renew itself. By uncovering these dimensions of practical thinking in his thought, I will illustrate how they function within Christian ethics and, at the same time, strengthen Niebuhr's own ethical program.

Yet my goal goes even beyond this. I plan to uncover the implicit discourse ethic that can be found in Niebuhr and bring this into conversation with the discourse ethic of Jürgen Habermas. By discourse ethic, I mean an ethic for conversation and decision-making between conflicting parties in complex democratic societies. In relating Niebuhr and Habermas, I will raise a question important for any discourse ethic that might contribute to practical theology. It is the question of the relation of religion to morality and the more specific question of the relation of the Christian story to an ethics of discourse.

NIEBUHR'S NARRATIVE OF THE CHRISTIAN FAITH

Before uncovering the first four dimensions in Niebuhr's ethics, we should grasp the narrative structure of his theology. My concern for this follows directly from my view of the visional level of practical moral thinking. I claim that all practical thinking, even allegedly secular practical thinking, contains a vision of the purposes of life. Often this is only implicit, as Basil Mitchell (1980), Peter Strawson (1966), and Iris Murdoch (1970) have argued. This vision, as Hauerwas, Metz, and others have claimed, often takes a narrative form. Sometimes a narrative is very difficult to discern. Even when it is practical, thinking will reveal what I call deep metaphors that suggest something about how the world *really* is. I have shown how this works in the practical thinking of modern psychotherapeutic psychology (Browning 1987). Tensions can develop between these metaphors that create, if not a full narrative, then a storylike dynamic. To show how this is so in Niebuhr's work I (1) start with a rendition of the basic narrative in his theology, (2) identify how deep metaphors interact in this narrative, and then (3) uncover the other dimensions of practical reason implicit within the narrative. The dimensions of practical reason are implicit in the narrative. The questions posed by the above three steps will be in the background as we use Niebuhr as a guide to the Christian classics. In this chapter I will give attention to the thick questions of the Wiltshire Church—how to balance the needs of its own leaders and members with the needs of others. This will cause me to examine the nature of Christian love and the relation of self-fulfillment to self-sacrificial love on behalf of others.

Niebuhr's theology consists of two narratives, not one. There is first a story of God's activity in creating the world and second a story about God's salvation of this world when it falls. The two stories are related but also to a degree independent. The first is a Jewish story, and the second is a Christian story. It is wrong to tell the first story, as some theologians do, completely from the perspective of the second more strictly Christian story.

GENERAL REVELATION

The first story begins with creation. God is the Creator of the world. God is in all respects good and the ultimate Source and Judge of moral right and wrong. Reinhold Niebuhr can say, along with his brother H. Richard Niebuhr, that the Christian story is built around the nature and action of God. God's nature and action are projected into the very structures of creation. God is revealed in these created structures as "Creator, Judge, and Redeemer" (R. Niebuhr 1941, 132). These three metaphors capture the human experience of God in what Niebuhr calls God's "general revelation" (131). God's self-revelation occurs in God's created works. Humans experience at the edge of consciousness a sense of the holy that "contains three elements, two of which are not too sharply defined, while the third is not defined at all" (131). These three elements are the manifestations of God as Creator, Judge, and Redeemer. When Niebuhr says that two are only slightly defined and one not at all, he is saying that the third element, the experience of God as Redeemer, is present in general experience but not articulated sufficiently to be adequately named. It is adequately named only in God's self-revelation in the acts of the prophets and the ministry of Jesus.

Niebuhr's belief that Scriptures witness to the self-manifestation of God in general experience makes him a correlational theologian somewhat like Tillich and Tracy. This truth about the narrative structure of his theology is not widely acknowledged. God as Creator is revealed in a pervasive sense of "reverence" and "dependence upon an ultimate source of being" beyond our finite powers. God as Judge is experienced in a sense of "moral obligation laid upon us" by something beyond ourselves. God as Redeemer is experienced in a dimly felt "longing for forgiveness." Although these are felt aspects of human experience, Niebuhr tells us that "all three of these elements become more sharply defined as they gain the support of other forms of revelation" (131). There are biblical foundations for the belief that God is known in fragmentary ways in general revelation. Paul tells us that those who do not acknowledge God have no excuse, "for the invisible things of him from the creation of the world are clearly seen, being understood by the things that are made, even his eternal power and Godhead" (132; Rom. 1:19-20). The reality of God as Judge and Redeemer, however, can be seen more dramatically against the background of the reality of human sin. But God as Creator does have a purpose for the human race. It is that humans should freely live with one another in "mutuality" and "brotherhood" and grow toward fellowship and enjoyment with God.

NATURE AND SPIRIT

The story becomes complicated. Humans were created finite and free. The interplay between these two realities leads humans to become anxious and to sin. Niebuhr's doctrine of original sin is the most creative and profound aspect of his version of the Christian narrative vision. It is a combination of Pauline, Augustinian, and Kierkegaardian theological anthropologies, one that is also attentive to the insights of Freud, Darwin, and Marx. Humans in their finite freedom are created by God as a synthesis or dialectical relation between nature and spirit. Both nature and spirit must be included in the biblical affirmation that humans are made in the image of God. As a part of nature, humans are subject to its "vicissitudes," "necessities," "impulses," and "brevity" (R. Niebuhr 1941, 3). But humans are also spirit. Spirit is the human capacity to transcend imaginatively one's finitude—one's conditionedness by nature—and to relate reflexively not only to one's self but to the eternal as well. Although humans have the capacity for reason—that is, the capacity to grasp intellectual forms and make generalizations—Niebuhr believes that spirit's capacity to take one's self as an object of reflection is something different from reason. The emphasis on spirit rather than reason as central to human uniqueness distinguishes all biblical anthropology from either Greek or modern anthropologies (155). To say that humans are a dialectic of nature and spirit is not to say that they are a dualism of material body and immaterial soul. Spirit is nature or body with the capacity to transcend itself, look at itself, and relate to itself.

FINITUDE, ANXIETY, AND SIN

Because humans are spirit and transcend themselves to survey their situations, they also become anxious about the insecurities, indefiniteness, and limitless possibilities of finitude. It is not the finitude and creatureliness of humans but their "anxiety about it" that tempts them to sin (R. Niebuhr 1941, 168). Humans are insecure and anxious about their natural contingency, and they seek to overcome this "by a will-to-power which overreaches the limits of human creatureliness" (178). Reflecting on the biblical story of the temptation, Niebuhr brings together Kierkegaard's concept of anxiety with Karen Horney's concept of the will-to-power. He boldly asserts, "Anxiety is the internal description of the state of temptation" (43–44, 182). Human beings do not sin and fall because they are finite or bodily or part of nature or insecure; they fall because they are so anxious about these realities that they try to secure themselves by inordinate self-regard and will-to-power at the expense of their neighbors. But it must be stated emphatically that Niebuhr does not see the Christian story as denying the human right to have *ordinate* self-concern; it is *inordinate* self-concern that is the essence of sin.

The fall is a mythic and existential representation of the universal way humans use and misuse their freedom. Sin is unbelief, the loss of faith in the supportive providence of God. Although sin primarily manifests itself as pride and the will-to-power, it can also take the form of sensuality—the drive to escape from the unlimited possibilities of freedom by immersion into the "mutable good" and "natural vitalities" of life (186). This is the form of sin, as some feminists have suggested, so open to women in Western societies (Goldstein 1960). Sin does not just affect us individually; the lives of groups and nations are also subject to anxiety and the inordinate self-concern of sin. Although all humans are equally sinful as a general condition of their lives in the world, some sins are greater than others and can be amplified more than others by the corruptions of power. All people are equally sinful, but they are not equally guilty. Some are clearly more guilty than others (R. Niebuhr 1941, 223).

SIN, PASSION, AND PRACTICAL REASON

Sin affects the totality of human potentialities—spirit, passion, emotion, reason, and intellect. All of these are subject to inordinate self-concern. Sin affects all human efforts to erect rational and disinterested systems of morality and government. Because of this, Niebuhr is suspicious of all Enlightenment attempts to erect totally rational moral arguments. But here a caution is in order: Although Niebuhr does not believe in the *purity* of practical reason, he still believes there is a place for it in Christian ethics. The same is true with regard to our natural vitalities, passions, and emotions. Although they too are inflamed by inordinate self-regard and affected by spirit and the contingencies of history, Niebuhr believes there is a place in Christian ethics for intellectual efforts to grasp their structure. Both of these points are relevant for our delineation of the dimensions of practical reason to be found in Niebuhr.

Although practical reason and our animal vitalities (our tendencies and needs) are distorted by sin, neither of these anthropological capacities is completely lost. Niebuhr sees abundant evidence in the Bible, church history, and general human experience that the essence of humans—the *imago dei*, the memory of a former blessedness—is not totally lost in the fall of humans. Humans in their freedom have the capacity to contradict their essential nature and its affections and rationality. But they cannot lose these capacities completely (R. Niebuhr 1941, 269). Nonetheless, once sin has set in, humans are trapped in a never-ending circle of inordinate self-interest, pride, and distrust that corrupts, although it does not destroy, practical reason. This circle of self-interest frustrates God's goals for humans—mutuality in intimate affairs, brotherhood and sisterhood in public affairs, and fellowship with the divine.

GOD AS JUDGE

God as Sovereign, however, will not tolerate the divine purposes for humans being frustrated forever. It is against the background of the situation of sin and fallenness that humans experience even more intensely, both in general and special revelation, God as Judge and Governor. God as Judge is not an arbitrary tyrant or unfeeling magistrate. Rather God as Judge is the ongoing manifestation of God's seriousness and constancy in holding forth the conditions for the fulfillment of humans. These conditions are primarily love and justice. But against the background of sin, both God's own nature as love and justice and the continuing presence of the essential nature of humans in spite of sin are experienced as judgment (R. Niebuhr 1941, 276–80). These two factors bring us to know vaguely that we are both guilty and unable to do anything about it. This is the basis of Paul's statement, "But in fact it is no longer I that do it, but sin that dwells within me" (Rom. 7:17).

In the history of Israel, this judgment is most intensely experienced in the messages and condemnations of such prophets as Isaiah, Amos, and Jeremiah. What is vaguely present in general experience becomes clearer in the emerging history of special revelation. Special revelation is the explicit self-revelation of God in the events of history; it provides a perspective from which to interpret the more inchoate signs and signals of general experience. The prophets are particularly powerful in condemning the national sin and pride of Israel—its belief that its nationalistic ambitions and self-interests were coterminous with God's intentions in history.

JESUS AND GOD THE REDEEMER

Jesus stands in the history of special revelation as its fulfillment. He fulfills yet transforms both the messianic and the prophetic tradition of ancient Israel. The prophetic tradition, although powerful in showing that the political defeats of Israel were due to Israel's own unfaithfulness, was left with an unanswerable dilemma. Why do innocent and righteous individuals and nations suffer (R. Niebuhr 1943, 42–47)? In his mission and message, Jesus addressed this issue by transforming the question. Jesus transformed popular messianic expectations that the Christ would deliver the nation of Israel either through force or through perfect fulfillment of the Jewish Law (15–46). Jesus fulfilled messianic expectations by amplifying the messianic themes of Isaiah. He answered the prophetic dilemma about the suffering of the righteous by denying the very possibility of a perfectly righteous individual or nation. The two transformations came together around the themes of Jesus as the Suffering Servant and the meaning of the crucifixion. These two themes reveal both Jesus as the Messiah and the nature of God.

Jesus is the Christ not because of his power or legal purity, but because in his life and death on the cross he takes on the sins, sufferings, and punishments of the world. This is the essence of Jesus' action in the world and a symbol of the nature of the divine. The implied answer of these deeds and symbols to the prophetic question of why the just suffer is this: Although there is a difference between good and evil people in this world, the good are also sinners and fall short. The implied answer to messianism was that it is neither through power nor legal purity that the kingdom of God becomes manifest; it is rather through God's self-revelation as the Suffering Servant who overcomes evil by taking on the sins of the world through forgiveness and grace. Niebuhr writes that Jesus' reign and interpretive work contain "the two offensive ideas that the righteous are unrighteous in the final judgment and that God's sovereignty over history is established and his triumph over evil is effected not by the destruction of the evil-doers but by his own bearing of the evil" (46).

AGAPĒ AS SACRIFICIAL LOVE

This is the meaning of love as *agapē* that shows forth the inner character of the love of God and the love of Jesus. Love as *agapē*, according to Niebuhr, is self-sacrificial love, the love that takes on itself the suffering and sin of others (R. Niebuhr 1943, 68-97). Sacrificial love is the essence of God and the perfect norm of the Christian life—a point that addresses the Wiltshire question. It is a love that can neither fulfill itself nor justify itself in human history. Mutual love and brotherhood and sisterhood are the highest possibilities for life amid this broken, finite, and sinful world (81-90). This is an important but debatable formula in Niebuhr to which I will soon return as I cope with the Wiltshire situation.

THE GRACE AND FORGIVENESS OF GOD

This love of God does not just mediate forgiveness; it communicates grace as well. In the letters of Paul grace is the love of God that gives both forgiveness and a power outside ourselves that renews our faith, frees us from insecurity, mitigates the corruptions of self-interest over both practical reason and our vitalities, and strengthens our capacity to live the morally righteous life. As Paul says, "I have been crucified with Christ; and it is no longer I who live, but it is Christ who lives in me. And the life I now live in the flesh I live by faith in the Son of God, who loved me and gave himself for me" (Gal. 2:19-20; R. Niebuhr 1943, 106-27). Although the gift of grace breaks the hold of sin over the self in principle, it does not completely do so in fact. Even the faithful are still sinful and always in need of the justifying grace of God. The meaning of the resurrection is not that God assures the triumph of good over evil. It means rather that in spite of grace's power to mitigate sin and in spite of the signs of the coming kingdom of God, the final defeat of sin and fulfillment of the kingdom can never occur on the plane of human history (47-52). "Sin is overcome in principle but not in fact. Love must continue to be suffering love rather than triumphant love" (49). The final fulfillment must wait upon the action of God. This is the meaning of the symbols of the "second coming" and the "Second Adam" (48).

NIEBUHR AND THE WILTSHIRE CHURCH

This summary of the narrative line of Niebuhr's theology illustrates how theological ethics differs from fully practical theology. The contextuality of Niebuhr's thought is largely absent from his principal systematic statement in *The Nature and Destiny of Man*. The environmental-social concerns that he does discuss pertain to the philosophical ideas that shaped the modern mind, particularly the Christian view of human nature in relation to rationalistic, naturalistic, and romantic alternatives (R. Niebuhr 1941, 26-92). I will soon analyze further these environmental-social dimensions in Niebuhr. But practical theology, although it needs a theological ethic as an indispensable yet transient moment, brings its thick questions immediately into conversation with the Christian ethical classics. We need systematic theological ethics but must distinguish it from strategic practical theology. We must understand how much more needs to be done if systematic theological ethics is to advance genuinely practical enterprises.

Niebuhr's theological ethics can be used to describe the Wiltshire Church. He can contribute to descriptive theology. He does not have a multidimensional theory of action with which to weave a theological perspective together with anthropological-ethnographic, psychological, and socio-ecological perspectives. That is, it is not explicit in his work. But his distinctively theological perspective, especially his emphasis on the concept of original sin, adds something important to what we learned from the authors of the Dudley volume. It is interesting to observe that none of these authors, even the theological authors, ever used the category of sin. They never spoke of the shape of sin, original or otherwise, at the Wiltshire Church. It may have been implied, but it was never made explicit. But the category should not be avoided. In Niebuhr's mind it is a fundamental category of philosophical anthropology as well as a confession of the Christian faith. Original sin was for him a fundamental empirical truth. When he uses *empirical* in this way, he is developing a view of the empirical inspired by European phenomenology and the radical empiricism of William James (R. Niebuhr 1941, 74; 1955, 129–30). Sin is not an empirical reality in the form of discrete sense data; this has been from the days of Descartes the model of the empirical in the natural sciences. Rather, sin is empirical in the sense of a broad pattern of experience that must be given symbolic form if we are to grasp adequately its pervasive presence.

The question is not whether there is sin, but the shape that it takes. In the case of the Wiltshire Church, it takes the shape of a genteel privatism and careerism, a bifurcation between public and private, a neglect of larger public issues, an unreflective appropriation of the inner logic of technical or purposive rationality, messianic expectations about the powers of its minister to give religious sanction to the congregation's strivings, and an unconscious and prideful hope that time, death, and the past will be vanquished and replaced by immortality and joviality. This is the shape that original sin takes in the Wiltshire Church. But if one takes Niebuhr seriously, the startling truth is this: The people of the Wiltshire Church are no more sinful than anyone else. Their sin simply takes a peculiarly modern and civilized form. But here is the other side of

Niebuhr's formula: They indeed may be more guilty. Because they are near seats of power and wealth, because of their possibilities, they are no more sinful, but they may be more guilty. Niebuhr would offer powerful additional perspectives to a descriptive theology of the situation of the Wiltshire Church, but it would be all the more powerful if brought into contact with a fuller theory of human action that differentiates the five dimensions I have presented. This would help us understand the shape and complexity of sin as it manifests itself in this situation.

There are other ways in which Niebuhr's theological ethics might contribute to the descriptive theology of this church. Of the three metaphors of God at the heart of the Christian narrative, Wiltshire emphasizes God the Redeemer. Wiltshire's theology makes little reference to God as Creator or Governor. Just as there is little reference to God as Governor, there is little reference to the category of sin. The people of Wiltshire face hardships and challenges. They are harried and overworked. They face marital strains, divorce, and alcoholism, but sin is not part of their self-interpretations. Nor do they have a sense of being measured by the expectations of God as Judge. Niebuhr offers more to descriptive theology, but that will come out in the pages to come.

THE OBLIGATIONAL DIMENSION

The dimensions of practical reason can be found in Niebuhr's normative theological ethics. They are implicit but beg to be brought into the open. I will not only uncover these dimensions, but I will illustrate their meaning with regard to the Wiltshire Church. In later chapters, I will do the same for the Church of the Covenant and the Apostolic Church of God. I will show the ways these dimensions make *sense* from the perspectives of both the envelope and core of practical reason. Let us recall that the specific question of the Wiltshire Methodist Church dealt with how a church balances the needs of its leaders and members with the needs of others. The question raises the theological issue of the relation of self-sacrifice to self-fulfillment and mutuality. Since we have seen what this question in all its thickness means for Wiltshire, I now bring it to the Christian classics with Niebuhr as our guide. In bringing this question to his theological ethics, I will be creating a new horizon of meaning and a critical practical theology.

Since I already have provided an overview of the visional and narrative structure of Niebuhr's theology, I turn now to the obligational level of practical thinking. The narrative structure of Niebuhr's theology represents God as moral Judge and Governor.

But the metaphor of God as Judge has its full meaning only in relation to the metaphors of God as Creator and Redeemer. God's judgment is not an end in itself. It is designed to facilitate God's original plan. It helps fulfill creation and opens us to redemption. The metaphors of Creator, Judge, and Redeemer find their meaning as they interact in a narrative that tells a story about God's action in the world of fallen humans.

But this still leaves the question, What is the moral structure of God and what does it mean for the obligations of humans? How does the obligational structure of the Christian narrative, as Niebuhr depicts it, relate to what I call the tendency-need dimension of practical thinking? In other words, how are my dimensions two and three (the core of practical reason) defined in Niebuhr's view of the Christian narrative?

Although Niebuhr constantly speaks of God as Judge, he says very little about the actual content of this concept. Nonetheless, at least three things can be said. God as Judge is *universal.* Hebrew prophets preach clearly that God's interests in justice and liberation go beyond Israel. Amos tells us that Yahweh delivered not only Israel from Egypt but "the Philistines from Caphtor" and the "Arameans from Kir" (Amos 9:7; R. Niebuhr 1943, 23). God's justice is universal and *impartial.* God makes the "sun rise on the evil and on the good, and sends rain on the righteous and the unrighteous" (Matt. 5:45). There is no favoritism; the wealthy, the powerful, even the righteous are no more the objects of God's special favor than the poor and the sinner. In this sinful and broken world, God is specially concerned to bring the poor and downtrodden to equality and new levels of dignity. Finally, God's justice is *teleological,* a word that Niebuhr does not use but that is, nonetheless, relevant. Although the formal character of God's moral seriousness is universal and impartial, it is nevertheless interested in the fulfillment of human need. The hungry must be fed, the naked clothed, the imprisoned freed, the unemployed given work.

The trickier issue for both theological ethics and practical theology is what these characteristics of God mean for human obligations. On the one hand, Niebuhr seems to say that mutuality in the sphere of intimate relations and brotherhood and sisterhood in the area of political life are God's will for our moral lives. On the other hand, he seems to say it is the self-sacrificial way of the cross that God wills for all spheres of life.

In some places Niebuhr says that sacrificial love is the "perfection of man" but a perfection that is "not attainable in history" (68). Niebuhr tells us that among the possibilities of finite and sinful history, "mutual love is the highest good" (68). This suggests that mutuality is second best, a compromise with sinfulness, and not the true end of life. Niebuhr defines mutual love as the "concern of one person for the interests of another" that "prompts and elicits a reciprocal affection" (69). Although Niebuhr states that self-sacrificial love is the unattainable perfection of the Christian life, he also states that it is the presupposition for the fulfillment of mutuality: "The self cannot achieve relations of mutual and reciprocal affection with others if its actions are dominated by the fear that they may not be reciprocated. Mutuality is not a possible achievement if it is made the intention and goal of any action. Sacrificial love is thus paradoxically related to mutual love" (69).

Niebuhr makes his point even more emphatically when he writes, "The Cross symbolizes the perfection of *agapē* which transcends all particular norms of justice and mutuality in history" (74). By this, Niebuhr means that the *agapē* of Christians should rise above the attempt to harmonize human interests and vitalities. He acknowledges that the harmonization in mutuality of human interests is desirable, but "it can never be a final norm" (74). "For sinful egoism," he tells us, "makes all historical harmonies of interest partial and incomplete; and a life which accepts the harmonies as final is bound to introduce sinful self-assertion into the ethical norm" (74).

Hence, Niebuhr speaks of two kinds of love. One is love as *agapē* and is self-sacrificial. The other is love as mutuality and seeks a kind of reciprocity. In Niebuhr's mind love as mutuality overlaps with justice; they both seem marked by fairness and equality. Brotherhood and sisterhood in political life also have the abstract form of justice. *Agapē* is the presupposition of the possibility of the justice implicit in sisterhood and brotherhood in political life just as it is the presupposition of mutuality in intimate relations (246–48). Niebuhr believes that the justice in mutuality and in brotherhood and sisterhood always becomes calculative and self-interested under the conditions of sin; for this reason, it cannot be the norm of the Christian life although it is the best that history can expect.

There are confusions and misplaced emphases in Niebuhr's thought on this issue. He is not so much wrong as misleading in his presentation of Christian ethics. Yet he is very close to being right and very creatively so; his thought is worth the small amount of reworking that is required. And this reworking is relevant to a proper understanding of the situation of the Wiltshire Church.

I have several complaints. First, Niebuhr confuses mutuality and brotherhood/sisterhood as they might be essentially conceived with their distortions under the conditions of finitude and sin. In response to this, I will argue that imperfect mutuality and justice cannot be the norm of the Christian life, but the ideal of perfect mutuality and justice, although never attainable, most certainly can be. And indeed that ideal seems to be the norm of the Christian life for Niebuhr throughout the chapter entitled "The Kingdom of God and the Struggle for Justice" in *The Nature and Destiny of Man* (244–86).

Second, because Niebuhr elevates self-sacrifice as the norm and treats mutuality and justice as concessions, his ethic downplays the role of self-concern and self-regard in the Christian life. Niebuhr admits, as we saw above, that ordinate self-concern has a place in the Christian life. With the coming of sin, ordinate self-concern becomes inordinate. In Niebuhr's handling of love as mutuality, the love that seeks a response always seems inferior. This obscures the fact that Niebuhr does provide a place in the Christian life for natural and ordinate self-concern.

Finally, as Niebuhr sometimes confuses the ideal of mutuality with fallen and self-interested mutuality, he also confuses reason in its wholeness with reason infected with sin. This is why Niebuhr appears at times to reject a role for practical reason in Christian ethics. Along with that, he seems to reject the Catholic tradition of natural law in which reason plays a significant role. Catholic natural law ethics saw a role for reason both in discerning the law of justice and in discerning the needs and tendencies of human beings that ethics helps fulfill. Both forms of reason were seen as natural capacities. The first form of natural law some writers called the *ius gentium* and the second form the *ius naturale*. The first was reason comprehending just relations between humans ruled, sometimes, by different civil laws (*ius civile*). The second was reason comprehending our essential animal nature that ethics should stay within and fulfill (Weinreb 1987, 44–49). In attacking the Greek emphasis upon rationality as the essence of humans (R. Niebuhr 1941, 4–11, 30–33) and in demonstrating how sin corrupts all manifestations of reason (194–98), Niebuhr appears at times to be eliminating any of these forms of natural law. But this is not quite true.

Niebuhr clearly maintains a place for both practical reason and natural law in Christian ethics. He preserves a place both for reason discerning the requirements of justice for humans (*ius gentium*) and reason discerning the fundamental structure of our human nature (*ius naturale*). Niebuhr says in one place that in spite of the fact that spirit and sin distort our animal vitalities and our reason, natural law thinking "has nevertheless a tentative validity" (271). Although sin distorts reason, it does not destroy it totally. Reason has, for Niebuhr, the capacity to think the right, but it cannot resist sin and self-interest when it passes over into action. Reason serves both the self-as-subject and the self-as-actor. In a remarkably lucid and profound passage, Niebuhr writes,

> Reason is in fact in an equivocal position between the self-as-subject and the self-as-agent, between the self as transcending itself and the anxious self in action. It is the servant of both. Its universal judgments, its effort to relate all things to each other in a system of coherence, can be alternately the instrument by which the self-as-subject condemns the partial and prejudiced actions of the sinful self, and the vehicle of the sinful self by which it seeks to give the sanctity of a false universality to its particular needs and partial insights (284–85).

In this passage Niebuhr both affirms and shows the limits of what we would call today the Kant-Rawls-Kohlberg penchant for universalization in ethics (Kohlberg 1981, 191–210). The problem with reason is not that it is totally incapable of good judgments. Its problem is that in the split second between thought and action, practical reason succumbs to degrees of sin. Still, its capacity to universalize and discern human need can enable it to validly judge our actions and those of others. Reason is not totally trustworthy, but it is not irrelevant. The renewing and cleansing power of God's *agapē*, forgiveness, and grace strengthens practical reason although it does not purify it completely.

Because of sin, practical reason never functions with purity in the heat of action. But practical reason never functions purely for another reason as well. The final activity that hammers out actual rules of justice in history is a compromise between sinful reason and the limitations of finitude. The two together mean all decisions between conflicting groups are compromises. Practical reason can make its contribution, but the final product is always a compromise of conflicting perspectives. Niebuhr writes, "Such rules of justice as we have known in history have been arrived at by a social process in which various partial perspectives have been synthesized into a more inclusive one. But even the inclusive perspective is contingent to time and place" (R. Niebuhr 1943, 252). Not only does sin make our compromises partial, but the contingencies of time and space further make them limited and provincial as well.

These issues are important for an adequate descriptive theology of the Wiltshire Church. They are also important for an adequate critical practical theology. If *agapē* is defined as self-sacrifice and seen as the norm of the Christian life, then judgment about the Wiltshire Church becomes even deeper. But if mutuality and brotherhood/sisterhood are seen as norms (though in reality they will never be fully achievable), then one's view of Wiltshire changes. If mutuality and sisterhood/brotherhood have a place for self-regard and self-actualization, then Wiltshire looks different again. It suddenly looks far more human, even Christian, for the people of Wiltshire to work on the various needs that they bring to that church. Their needs for fellowship and recognition, their concern for their children, and their needs for relaxation and refuge from the tribulations of the work pressures of purposive rationality—all these look like they might have some place in the Christian life if mutuality is the center of the Christian life. Then the questions would be: Do the people of the Wiltshire Church take other people's needs for these things as seriously as they take their own? Or rather: Do they give more weight to their own needs than they do to others?

These questions point to the critical task that is a part of all good theological ethics and practical theology. Starting with Niebuhr as my guide, I am advancing a critique of parts of his theological ethics. It is both an internal criticism and a test against the demands of practice, not only the practices of the Wiltshire Church but, as we will see more fully later, the practices of feminists and minorities.

TENDENCIES AND NEEDS

Niebuhr rejects a rigid application of either practical reason or natural law in apprehending the natural structures of human beings. Humans are, after all, historical creatures of freedom and spirit. Our natural vitalities are through and through qualified by spirit and self-transcendence. Nonetheless, our natural vitalities do lay some claim on our historical existence and must inform our ethical thinking. Niebuhr sets forth his position on these matters in the following important passage:

> Since man is deeply involved in the forms of nature on the one hand and is free of them on the other; since he must regard determinations of sex, race and (to a lesser degree) geography as forces of ineluctable fate, but can nevertheless arrange and rearrange the vitalities and unities of nature within certain limits, the problem of human creativity is obviously filled with complexities. Four terms must be considered in his situation: (1) The vitality of nature (its impulses and drives); (2) the forms and unities of nature, that is, the determinations of instinct, and the forms of natural cohesion and natural differentiation; (3) the freedom of spirit to transcend natural forms within limits and to direct and redirect the vitalities; (4) and finally the forming capacity of spirit, its ability to create a new realm of coherence and order. All these four factors are involved in human creativity and by implication

in human destructiveness. Creativity always involves both vitality
and form (R. Niebuhr 1941, 26–27).

This is an extremely important passage in Niebuhr that most commentators do not take seriously. It says several things about the
tendency-need dimension in Niebuhr's thought. It first tells us that
our human instinctuality and our natural vitalities have forms and
regularities. In contrast to Freud, who saw our instinctuality as
basically fluid, or B. F. Skinner, who saw humans as fashioned by
external reinforcements, Niebuhr believed that the nature in our
humanness has enough structure both to limit and guide our moral
thinking. There is a naturalistic moment in Niebuhr's theological
ethic. It is not a thoroughgoing naturalism like that found in E. O.
Wilson's early work where all ethical norms are derived directly
from our biological substrata. Thus I call it a naturalistic moment,
not a naturalistic ethic.

In Niebuhr's view, the forms of our natural vitalities are flexible limits within which moral arrangements must stay. These
natural vitalities possess certain implicit unities—certain natural
harmonies—that always must be respected. When Niebuhr said
these things, he was setting forth a natural law thinking that would
be very relevant to the ecological problems that were to intensify
in the decades that followed.

Although nature has form and structure, it is flexible, subject to
a variety of arrangements, and needs the further ordering power
of our moral principles—what I have called the obligational dimension of practical thinking. Niebuhr's ethic would order human
vitalities by mutuality, justice, and brotherhood/sisterhood even
though they are themselves never pure. Sin distorts both the natural harmonies of our instinctuality and the ordering power of
mutuality and justice. In spite of these limitations of both our instinctuality and practical reason, our instinctuality must inform our
faulty mutuality just as mutuality and justice are needed to further order instinctuality. Finally, because both our vital impulses
and our moral principles provide simultaneously order and distortion, each requires the liberating and empowering infusions
of *agapē* and grace. A Christian morality requires all three—the
unities of eros or instinctuality (the tendency-need dimension),
the refinements of mutuality and justice (the obligational dimension), and the forgiveness and empowerment of *agapē* (the visional
dimension).

Niebuhr is cautious about listing the aspects of our instinctual
natures that lay claims on our moral life. Nonetheless, he does
indeed list some. Human sexuality and its differentiation into male-

ness and femaleness are central natural factors for Niebuhr (260). Natural instincts to survive, primal needs for attachments, needs for material acquisition, needs for group relatedness (26–54)—these are also vital needs that motivate life and provide it with basic unities.

Although Niebuhr said novel things about this naturalistic moment in Christian ethics that have interesting implications for a reconstructed theory of natural law, Niebuhr never fully developed them. I will return to the task of reconstructing Niebuhr on these issues in the paragraphs ahead.

THE ENVIRONMENTAL-SOCIAL DIMENSION

The environmental-social dimension as I define it is difficult to discern in *The Nature and Destiny of Man*. Niebuhr gives little direct attention there to social-structural trends and dynamics such as purposive rationality, structural differentiation, bureaucratization, and so forth. He gives no attention whatsoever to ecology. That issue had not emerged in Niebuhr's time as it has in ours. In addition, he simply assumes analyses he had made in his earlier writings of such trends as industrialization and the class struggles that Marxists describe so well.

The theory of class struggle does inform subtly the very limited environmental-social discussion in *The Nature and Destiny of Man*. But it gets transmuted into a broader discussion of how Christian anthropology compares to other philosophical anthropologies in Western thought. It is not, however, just a discussion in the history of ideas. Niebuhr shows how these philosophical traditions have been carried by certain social classes to rationalize their positions.

He shows how the older idealistic rationalism associated with Plato and Aristotle provided the hierarchical and idealistic justification for the authoritarian structures of feudalism. Romanticism, he claims, was a reaction to both feudalism and the emerging naturalistic rationalism unleashed by the Enlightenment. Some forms of romanticism provided empowerment for various lower-class self-assertions, some of which ended in fascism. Other forms of romanticism fueled the utopian ideas of Marxism. And finally, modern naturalistic rationalism provided some of the justification of the middle classes (R. Niebuhr 1941, 49–53). Niebuhr's analysis here opens up the relation between technical rationality and the bourgeois classes that is so visible at the Wiltshire Church. It has similarities to Hopewell's discussion of the empirical irony and "wistful agnosticism" of that church. Throughout *The Nature and Destiny of Man*, Niebuhr is generally aware of the interaction of thought and social context. Strategic practical theology can learn from Niebuhr but must go further.

A RECONSTRUCTION OF NIEBUHR

Niebuhr's theological ethics should be reconstructed mainly at levels two and three—the obligational and tendency-need levels that are the inner core of practical reason. This reconstruction also has implications for the narrative structure of his theology.

THE OBLIGATIONAL DIMENSION

I have hinted at the reconstruction needed. This is the need to make mutuality and sisterhood/brotherhood the goals of the Christian life and to derive sacrificial love from these more basic structures. This reconstruction is needed not only to make Niebuhr's ethic more consistent with the historical witness. The reconstruction is needed for practical reasons as well. It is important to help answer Wiltshire Church's question of how the needs of the self are balanced with the needs of the other. But the reconstruction I offer also comes out of the practical experience of relating Christian love to minority communities and to women (Andolsen 1981; Gudorf 1985).

It must be pointed out that Niebuhr mitigates the extreme emphasis on *agapē* as self-sacrificial love that Anders Nygren introduced in his monumental *Agape and Eros* (1953). Unlike Nygren, Niebuhr does not make a radical distinction between eros and *agapē*. He believed that Nygren properly emphasized *agapē*'s character as disinterested and unconditioned by the value or merit of the other. But he believed Nygren made the contrast between *agapē* and eros too absolute and even contradicted the teachings of Jesus in Matthew 7:11.

In spite of the elevated position Niebuhr gave to eros, he still understated its proper role in Christian love. In recent years the work of the Catholic moral theologian Louis Janssens has informed my thought on this issue. He believes that *agapē* should be defined as mutuality and equal regard. In holding this, he intends to revive the Catholic tradition of Christian love as *caritas* associated with Augustine, Aquinas, and more recently Martin D'Arcy (1959), Robert Johann (1955), and Daniel Day Williams (1968). In his 1977 essay "Norms and Priorities in a Love Ethics," Janssens offers an extended meditation on the second half of Jesus' love commandment ("you shall love your neighbor as yourself") and the golden rule. Neighbor love was offered by Jesus and reaffirmed by Paul as the summary of the Jewish Law and the heart of their respective messages (Matt. 22:37-39; Mark 12:30-31; Luke 10:25-28; Gal. 5:14; Rom. 13:9). It is notable that Niebuhr says little about neighbor love in *The Nature and Destiny of Man*.

Following the work of Gene Outka, Janssens believes that the underlying meaning of all the New Testament formulations of neighbor love is that "love of neighbor is impartial. It is fundamentally an equal regard for every person, because it applies to each neighbor qua human extent" (Janssens 1977, 219). Insofar as Janssens emphasizes impartiality, he sounds similar to both Niebuhr and Nygren. Indeed, at this point, Janssens's formulation sounds Kantian; it invokes, with some justification, a concept of moral obligation centered in impartial, universalizable, and reversible thinking associated with Kant's categorical imperative or John Rawls's theory of justice as fairness.

Then, suddenly, this Kantian and abstemious sounding principle of impartiality takes on in Janssens's thought a tone quite foreign to Nygren and Niebuhr. Janssens applies the impartiality that *agapē* requires both to one's own self and to the other. He writes, "In accord with the impartiality of *agapē*, we maintain that one is to have equal regard for self and for others, since the reasons for valuing the self are identical with those for valuing others, namely that everyone is a human being" (220). Janssens, along with Outka, argues that valuing one's self as well as the other is a manifest obligation implicit in the principle of neighbor love (Outka 1972, 219).

This ethic goes beyond reciprocity. I should not just regard the other equally *if* the other regards me equally. Niebuhr sometimes speaks of mutuality in such conditional terms, and then proceeds to see it as an inferior ethic that is only tolerable as a compromise with sin. But this is not the meaning of equal regard or mutuality for Janssens. My self-regard ideally should count for no less and no more than my regard for the other. Janssens admits that under the pressure of sin mutuality as equal regard is always sliding into calculating reciprocity, but he does not make Niebuhr's mistake of advancing the corrupted form of mutuality as its only definition.

Equal regard, then, is the inner rational structure of the Christian ethic. It forms the rational structure of both mutuality in intimate affairs and brotherhood/sisterhood in public affairs. Equal regard is the normative structure of practical reason—its inner core. It is a rationality, however, that depends on certain beliefs—most specifically the belief that all persons are ends rather than means. In contrast to the way neo-Kantians like Rawls, Gewirth, and Donagan build the case on the rational agency of humans, Janssens builds on the biblical affirmation that all humans are children of

God and made in God's image (Janssens 1977, 219). The rational
capacity for reversible thinking plays a part in love as mutuality
and equal regard. It helps me make judgments recognizing that any
claim I make on another, that person has the right to make on me.
Taking the other's view in one's imagination and reversing roles in
this respect—this is the rational core of practical reason.

But this rationality functions in the context of beliefs about
treating humans as ends that formal reversibility does not itself
provide. Janssens makes a significant gesture toward the Kantian
concept of practical reason without yielding to its overwhelming
rationalism. Janssens, and the contemporary British philosopher
of religion Basil Mitchell, are Kantians but with a difference. They
believe that the idea of respect for persons can be built more satisfactorily—more in keeping with the fullness of our intuitions about
the status of persons—if it is anchored on the Jewish and Christian
concept of humans as *imago dei*. This concept is truer to our intuitions about the status of humans than any philosophical analysis
of human agency (Mitchell 1980, 131–32).

Janssens, like Niebuhr, maintains the importance of self-
sacrifice and the cross in Christian life. But Janssens does not make
self-sacrifice the goal and norm of the Christian life the way Niebuhr and other Christian writers have done. For Janssens, mutuality
or equal regard (and he would happily add the analogous concept of sisterhood/brotherhood in political life) is the norm and
self-sacrifice is its extension. Self-sacrifice is derived from mutuality and equal regard; it is the extra mile we must travel to help
bring a situation of conflict and disharmony into mutuality again.
Janssens states unequivocally, "In short, self-sacrifice is not the
quintessence of love.... Self-sacrifice is justified derivatively from
other regard" (Janssens 1977, 228). As long as humans are a part
of fallen and sinful historical existence, as long as mutuality perpetually falls into unbalance and premature reciprocity, sacrifice is
needed. This is true not because self-sacrifice is the goal of life; the
fellowship of mutuality and equal regard is the goal of life. Sacrifice
is the necessary step required to bring equal regard back into focus.
It is precisely the forgiveness and grace of God's own outpouring
agapē that make our sacrificial *agapē* possible. For neither God nor
humans is sacrifice as such the goal of life either in or beyond
history. The goal is fellowship and enjoyment between God and humans, and mutuality, sisterhood, and brotherhood between humans
themselves. Because sin will never disappear—and for that reason
mutuality can never be perfect—self-sacrifice will always and everywhere be a part of the Christian life even though it is neither its
proximate nor its ultimate goal.

TENDENCIES AND NEEDS

Niebuhr believed that our natural vitalities have form and must inform our concrete moral judgments. The view that our natural vitalities have form follows directly, as Niebuhr sees it, from the Christian understanding of the nature of God and the goodness of God's created order. To say that God is good is to say that God is a perfect unity of vitality and form. To say that creation is good is to say that in its essence it too is a unity of vitality and form (R. Niebuhr 1941, 12–18, 26–53). Because of this, Niebuhr finds a place in Christian ethics for natural law to inquire into the natural structures of human existence. Because of our sinfulness and our historicity, this natural law must be flexible and humble.

Niebuhr's position on the role of this naturalistic moment in theological ethics could have been stronger if he had developed a clear concept of the premoral good. The concept of the premoral good has a firm place in Catholic natural law and is widely used in modern moral philosophy as well. Modern moral philosophers, like William Frankena, often refer to it as the "nonmoral good" (Frankena 1973, 9–10). Janssens develops an excellent discussion of premoral good. Judgments pertaining to the premoral good deal with the various ways we speak about the good in a distinctively nonmoral, in contrast to a moral, sense. Premoral goods are not directly moral goods because we do not attribute to them moral qualities as such. But we do indeed see them as objects or experiences that are good to pursue. Janssens writes that they are "realities in us and outside of us which, because of their properties, provoke in our experience a positive reaction in the sense that we enjoy them and welcome them as 'valuable' and hence 'worthy' of promotion (*prosequendo*)" (Janssens 1977, 212). These might be life, health, pleasure, joy, friendship, education, a good meal, or a good automobile. All of these things are good under certain circumstances, but we do not call them moral goods. Premoral goods are in themselves neither moral nor immoral, although they can become organized so as to become either.

The classic term in moral philosophy for premoral goods is the *ordo bonorum* (Janssens 1977, 229). According to Janssens, all moral judgments should bring together into a unity the *ordo caritatis* (the order of love defined as mutuality and equal regard) and the *ordo bonorum* (material judgments about relative premoral goods). The *ordo caritatis* is absolute and formal; it applies primarily to our inner disposition as this guides our actions toward the other. The *ordo bonorum* is relative and relates to all the particular premoral goods that the formal norm of mutuality should both actualize and mediate between. All concrete and genuinely moral actions are a synthesis of the formal *ordo caritatis* and the relative *ordo bonorum.* For action to be truly moral, the formal character of the *ordo caritatis* (equal regard) must be given the dominant and guiding position. The two together, with the *ordo caritatis* guiding the *ordo bonorum*, are the full meaning of the inner core of practical reason as I am defining it in this book.

In his gesture toward a naturalistic moment, Niebuhr accounts in his ethics for some features of the premoral good or *ordo bonorum.* But he does not develop his insights extensively. He does respect, however, two important ideas that Janssens develops further. First, Niebuhr holds that our natural vitalities have certain intrinsic forms, unities, and harmonies. Second, Niebuhr believes that because of human self-transcendence, our historical experience complexifies all natural vitalities. Janssens affirms and develops both these ideas.

For instance, Janssens says there are certain unities, harmonies, and hierarchies in our premoral values that ethics must respect. In saying this, he is not equating premoral values with instinctuality or natural vitalities. Yet he clearly sees them as shaped to a degree by natural wants, needs, and tendencies. With this in mind, it is important to notice that different premoral values do not "hold the same rank and position in the hierarchy of values" (Janssens 1977, 229). Further, he believes that the social and psychological sciences can help identify these natural hierarchies. He explicitly mentions that Abraham Maslow's humanistic psychology is "helpful for moralists" in clarifying the "distinction between lower and higher values" (229). He could have suggested many others. Some premoral values are more urgent than others; for instance, health must be restored before learning can proceed. Some premoral values are more foundational than others; life is necessary for actualizing any other value. Probability is relevant; when chances are small that a higher value can be realized, it is better to settle for the lower one. The premoral values protected by institutions, because of their range and usefulness to many, may take precedent over the premoral values of particular individuals (229–30). In short, there are all kinds of calculations, judgments, and assessments about consequences that one must do at the level of the *ordo bonorum.* But, if one follows Janssens, one does this under the rubrics of the formal and universal demands of the *ordo caritatis*, that is, mutuality and equal regard.

This is not the calculation of a utilitarian that seeks the greatest good for the largest number. It is the calculation of one dedicated to the justice of all under the rubric of equal regard. It attempts to actualize as much premoral good as can be distributed equally under the prior commitment to mutuality in intimate affairs and brotherhood/ sisterhood in political affairs. It is basically what Frankena has in mind with his "mixed deontological" principle that combines justice and beneficence but in such a way as to give priority to the formal principle of justice (Frankena 1973, 43).

Although there is a naturalistic moment in both Niebuhr and Janssens, its claim is made more flexible by the way they understand how human historicity and self-transcendence interpenetrate our desires, wants, needs, and tendencies. Niebuhr asks us to keep in mind "the freedom of spirit to transcend natural forms within limits and to direct and redirect the vitalities" (R. Niebuhr 1941, 27). Janssens says something similar when he suggests that culture adumbrates our premoral goods and that moral theology should do critical reflection on "the realization of premoral values made possible by increasing cultural acquisitions" (230). To point up the historicity of our premoral values does not imply that in time all of our traditional concrete moral norms will disappear. Nor does it mean that all newly evolved premoral values are advanced. It means only that there will be change. Some changes will disturb natural hierarchies and limits. Others will be enriching.

In any case, ethical reflection begins with conflicts among the premoral values that have evolved in a society at a particular time. For instance, modern means of transportation—cars, trains, and airplanes, for example—are premoral goods typical of advanced societies. They meet some basic human needs—the desire to move our bodies, to acquire a livelihood, and to be with loved ones. Humans always have needed to move across space and have used either their own two feet, the horse, the wheel, the buggy, or cars, trains, and airplanes. It is not unjust that medieval humans were denied cars and trains; these premoral goods were unavailable. It may be unjust that premoral goods are not equally available to everyone living in modern societies. Premoral goods and the concrete moral norms that are related to them are historical. Also, the pursuit of the premoral goods of travel may conflict with other premoral goods such as clean air, safety, or the goods associated with other institutions that require fuel and energy. At that point, one might need to inquire into which needs and tendencies (natural unities, harmonies, or hierarchies) are *more basic* to determine what sacrifices in contemporary travel arrangements need to be made. Although our premoral values evolve with historical development, both Janssens and Niebuhr find a place for that naturalistic moment in ethical reflection that may provide critical leverage on contemporary social arrangements of these values.

Niebuhr and Janssens could both agree with yet criticize the contemporary moral philosopher Michael Walzer in his emphasis on the historicity of all human values, either moral or premoral (Walzer 1983). They would both agree that moral reflection must take seriously contemporary organizations of premoral goods and values and the strains and conflicts they produce. If 95 percent of the people in a community enjoy air conditioning in their homes, one cannot say to the 5 percent that do not, "Oh, humans really don't need it anyway; we never had it before." It may be true that we once got along without air conditioning, but to conclude we do not need it now overlooks the historicity of the premoral value, that is, that very wide sectors of a community now enjoy it. All things being equal, if a premoral enjoyment has emerged in history and is widely available, it is legitimate for those who do not have it to demand it. If, however, supplying residential air conditioning for an entire society, and then possibly the whole world, exceeds our natural resources, pollutes the air, destroys the ozone, and increases cancer-producing radiation, then we have relevant naturalistic considerations that provide a critical leverage on these historically developed premoral goods. This point is relevant to the evaluation of the possible generalizability of the life style of the Wiltshire community.

To speak of a naturalistic moment does not slight the role of tradition in shaping a society's patterns of premoral goods. A community does not start anew on the basis of scientifically verifiable natural laws. In the case of Wiltshire, it does not wipe clean its history—the history of the Western world, the emergence of post–World War II suburban communities, the rise of purposive rationality, and all the other historical traditions that formed this community. Instead, a community starts with the particular pattern of premoral and moral values that has evolved historically and then uses the naturalistic moment to test and rearrange some of these values. Starting the other way, forgetting history and tradition, was the agenda of the Enlightenment. It is still the agenda of the naturalistically conceived sciences. But this project is now coming to a halt. Human sciences will never provide us with the information to construct a social superstructure founded on verified scientific knowledge.

NATURAL LAW

In discussing the tendency-need level of practical moral thinking in chapter 5, I referred to Mary Midgley. Midgley and Niebuhr both discuss the relation of our natural vitalities to our formal moral reason, and these discussions are amazingly similar. They agree that human instincts have both vitality and form and that human instinctuality has patterns; these contentions are not unlike those made by romanticists and naturalists. Midgley and Niebuhr both believe that this unity of vitality and form at the level of impulse is unstable and needs ordering at higher levels—the levels of tradition, culture, and reason. They differ in accounting for this instability. Midgley holds that humans have a large number of instincts and are responsive to a myriad of stimuli that arouse conflicting responses. For instance, we need both independence and dependence, trust and autonomy. We need food, water, warmth, but also need safety, self-cohesion, and the recognition of others. The list could be extended. Midgley joins the older voice of William James and a variety of contemporary theorists in seeing humans as the most richly instinctual of all creatures even though these instincts are highly plastic. Niebuhr would agree with this but would also emphasize how our instincts are amplified by our capacity for self-transcendence, historicity, anxiety, and sin. Both would affirm that nature in humans is a combination of vitality, order, flexibility, and distortion.

Midgley and Niebuhr bear resources for a reconstructed natural law theory in the sense of *ius naturale* (in contrast to *ius gentium*, which pertains more to natural judgments about justice). It would differ from older rigidly teleological natural law perspectives. These older theories, put forth by Stoicism, Ulpian, Aquinas, and the Scholastic tradition of Catholic moral theology, developed the idea that nature had a rigid, single teleological goal for each entity. The eye was for seeing, the sexual organs were for procreation, and so forth. The task of life was to live consistently within the specific ends of nature. The perspective put forth by Niebuhr and even more graphically by Midgley offers an entirely new model for natural law thinking. The task is not to fulfill the static goals of nature. The task, instead, is to stay within the range of human central tendencies. Midgley writes, "Central factors in us *must* be accepted, and the right line of human conduct must lie somewhere within the range they allow.... These general motives are innate, but they are wide. Guidance within their limits comes from balancing their various possible expressions with one's other motives, in the light of a proper system of priorities" (Midgley 1978, 81–82). This presents an entirely different model for that form of natural law thinking that attempts to grasp the nature in human nature. It is not a model of rigid and fixed natural ends, but one that envisions a flexible range of tendencies that must be kept in balance with reference to the selective pressures of our social and ecological environments. Such a view of natural law (in the sense of *ius naturale*) can constitute a crucial but limited naturalistic moment within a larger hermeneutical approach to theological ethics.

WILTSHIRE CHURCH'S HIERARCHY OF VALUES

Most of the interpretations in Dudley's book were negative about the Wiltshire Church. This was as true of the social science perspectives as of the theological perspectives. I conclude this chapter with these questions: Does my discussion of the place of the premoral good in ethics make a difference for my descriptive theology of the Wiltshire Church? Does my effort to establish a naturalistic moment within a hermeneutic ethic make a difference in how Wiltshire is perceived? What would this naturalistic moment mean for a strategic practical theology for Wiltshire's situation?

Only one of the essays in Dudley's volume discussed systematically the premoral goods that the people of the Wiltshire Church pursued. Evans and Reed in their psychological interpretation discussed the various "basic assumptions" (dependency, expectancy) that the Wiltshire congregation used to meet their *needs.* But this team neither identified nor evaluated those themselves. To do this the authors would have had to ask: Are the needs that the Wiltshire people pursue through their religion historically created? Can they be justified at this stage of history? Are they needs that everyone is entitled to pursue? Or are they pseudoneeds and unjustifiable? Are they unjustifiable because they are not basic? Or are they unjustifiable because they cannot be pursued without denying the basic needs of others?

The question of the status of the needs and tendencies pursued by the people of the Wiltshire Church is a relevant theological question. It is relevant but also neglected. It is pertinent because the doctrine of creation that says that creation is good gives humans a right to pursue their ordinate human needs. It is not sinful to have an ordinate amount of human self-concern about one's own needs and self-actualization. Not only does this follow from the doctrine of creation; it follows also from the nature of love as equal regard. Love as equal regard simply assumes that we have a right to be concerned about our own needs and the needs of our families and loved ones. But it places on us the additional stricture that we cannot claim more for our needs than we will allow others to claim for theirs.

This means that the people of the Wiltshire Church should be permitted to take their own needs seriously. What do their needs appear to be? Elsewhere, I suggested that the language of needs is quite complex and should be differentiated. It is useful to distinguish between (1) *basic* human needs, (2) *existential* needs, (3) *technical* needs, (4) and *culturally induced* needs. According to the view developed here, people are theologically justified in pursuing their *basic* human needs as long as they do not infringe on others and as long as they help others pursue theirs. Furthermore, they have a right, within the context of their religion, to pursue the satisfaction of their *existential* needs. Existential needs are basic human needs but not in the psychobiological sense of the term. They concern the insecurities and anxieties created by human self-transcendence, finitude, and contingency. Religion has everywhere specialized in addressing and meeting these needs. This is true, and with justification, of the religion at the Wiltshire Church; that religion, as we saw earlier, persistently emphasizes the love, faithfulness, strength, and renewing grace of God as answers to these existential needs. The religion of all three of our churches profoundly addresses these needs. Wiltshire Church is no different on this score from the Church of the Covenant or the Apostolic Church of God. Whether or not the meeting of existential needs is ideologically distorted depends on the whole context of values being promoted or denied by a church's total ministry.

In an age when technical or purposive rationality dominates, the people of a church such as Wiltshire do not turn to religion to find the means to meet their material or *technical* needs. The people of the Apostolic Church of God do, but not the affluent people of Wiltshire. Because of this, religion gets mixed with the realities of earning a living for the people of the Apostolic Church in ways it does not at Wiltshire.

The problem here is with the *culturally* induced (or at least culturally amplified) and moral needs of the Wiltshire Church. According to my discussion of the historical and cultural elaboration of premoral values, humans are justified in pursuing such needs and values as long as they do not conflict with other important needs, both within themselves and in others, and thereby create more premoral disvalue than premoral value. But that is precisely the issue at Wiltshire. There is every reason to believe that both the Wiltshire community and the Wiltshire Church have exceeded the range and amount of premoral goods that they can justifiably pursue.

Most of the needs of the Wiltshire congregation are both basic and culturally relative. They are culturally relative ways of working out basic and authentic human needs. Their needs for belonging, their concern for their children, their thirst for metaphysical assurance, and their drive to develop a religious world image that makes sense out of the tensions of their lives—all of these are basic human needs that are either psychobiological or existential.

At Wiltshire Church they take a unique historical form. They are worked out within the context of the modern split between public and private worlds that technical rationality has created. Further, they are aggravated by anxiety and sin and are therefore inordinate. Meeting the congregation's needs requires more wealth, more of the world's resources, more of the world's energy, and more of the world's space than can be justly spared within the ecological limits of our finite world.

But it is extremely important to certify the humanity of the needs and desires of the people of the Wiltshire Church. This is necessary for an accurate theological assessment of their situation and for an adequate strategic practical ministry with these people. None of the interpretive perspectives of the Dudley volume adequately acknowledged this. The premoral goods that the people of the Wiltshire Church want are human and part of the goodness of creation. In their ordinate form, they reveal what it means to be creaturely, finite, and a part of rhythms of the natural order. Some people may question this. If they do, I claim that the naturalistic moment within hermeneutic Christian ethics makes it possible to give reasons supporting a view of what is natural and basic. However, in spite of the light that reason and science can throw on these issues, our discussion will never be totally objective. A hermeneutic understanding of the human sciences shows that to be impossible. Nonetheless, our human sciences, especially the more naturalistic and observational sciences such as biology, psychobiology, ethology, and sociobiology, may through their multiple observations, their experimental variations, their comparative procedures, and their repeated reexamination of the data over time gain some relative objectivity and grant some stabilization to our historically and culturally conditioned observations about our humanity. Such discussions are relevant for a proper evaluation of the Wiltshire Church. They are even more important for interpretations and normative proposals in areas of medical ethics, reproductive technology, and family ethics. Such considerations are essential if historically situated hermeneutical ethics are to have some defense against total relativism.

ARE WILTSHIRE CHURCH'S NEEDS HUMAN?

What can be said in defense of the fundamental humanness of the needs of the Wiltshire people, even though they find culturally relative and inordinate expression? Psychobiology and sociobiology present a variety of lists and schedules of fundamental human needs that are suggestive. None of these lists is definitive, but some do have the support of observations, evidence, and reasons that can help stabilize disputes over the nature of our premoral goods and the *ordo bonorum*. Certainly, as Janssens claims, Abraham Maslow's famous hierarchy of human needs (physiological needs, security, love, self-esteem, and self-actualization) is suggestive (Maslow 1954). But George Pugh proposes a more updated and empirically supported list. Pugh divides human values and needs into primary and secondary categories. Primary values and needs are innate psychobiological products of our evolutionary heritage (Pugh 1977, 7–8). Secondary values are products of human intelligence and culture; they constitute, as Pugh defines them, a kind of utilitarian form of practical reason (7, 61–62). We have a need for this second class of values in a derived sense; they serve and coordinate the primary values. Because our primary values are part of our very psychobiological existence, we more or less unconsciously take them for granted. Pugh claims that there are three kinds of primary values—*selfish* values, *social* values, and *intellectual* values (115). In developing this rather simple categorization, Pugh has synthesized a huge amount of empirical information from biology, ethology, psychobiology, psychology, and sociobiology. What is important is his claim that social and intellectual values (generally thought of as spiritual values) are basic psychobiological needs and a product of evolutionary inheritance just as the so-called selfish values. Selfish values are essentially survival values associated with the welfare of the individual.

The social values are the most interesting for our purposes because they are so present at Wiltshire Church. Social values motivate the individual to contribute to the survival of the group; they are often called altruistic values. Humans have social needs to belong to, cooperate with, and sustain the groups to which they belong. Pugh points to both the kin-selection theory of altruism (animals feel altruistic toward those who share their genes) and reciprocal altruism (animals reciprocate and become attached to those who help them). These altruistic values motivate humans as well as primates and lead us to form groups (almost primatelike troops) for mutual protection and care (227–96).

Each of these primary needs and values can be elaborated culturally and has been so at Wiltshire Church. But these needs and values are basic and fundamentally human as well. They are among the ordinate needs and interests that humans have as part of their creatureliness and finitude. The human needs of the Wiltshire people to meet their children's basic survival needs and to educate them, to find group cohesion and solidarity, to attend to their own needs for rest and recuperation, to find some religio-intellectual coherence, and to build models of their world—all of these needs are human and must be respected. From an evolutionary point of view, they are part of what humans do to both live and live well. From a theological perspective, they are part of the goodness of creation. From the perspective of the ethics of equal regard, the sin of the Wiltshire people is not their possession of these needs but the inordinate claims that they make on their behalf.

A practical theology of the Wiltshire situation would need both to affirm the humanness of fundamental aspirations of the Wiltshire congregation and to critique their inordinate manifestation. Growth toward a responsible Christian solution could move in either of two directions. The Wiltshire people could use their remarkable resources to work toward helping all the world achieve what they have. The formal pattern of practical reason could lead them to work impartially to universalize their privileges to all. But it is becoming clear that this solution is not realistic if we consider the fourth dimension of practical reason—the environmental-social dimension. The ecological limits of nature and of our productive systems constitute intractable constraints on exercising this option. Although some increase in the world's wealth seems absolutely essential to meet the basic human needs of its populations, it now seems necessary to pursue a second course. Wiltshire as a church must find ways to limit the privatism and consumerism of its community's style of life. Wiltshire now exhibits features of the core of practical reason. Demands are being made to extend the privileges of the adult community to include the minister and children. But the circle of inclusion is too small. Even in this limited circle, Wiltshire Church cannot fulfill the dictates of the core of practical reason—an ethic of equal regard. Conflict at Wiltshire Church is not occurring because the demands of the minister or those made for the children are unjust as such. Rather the conflict is occurring because these exercises in practical reason expose the overextended claims of the adults.

In view of the constraints of this world, an ethic of equal regard for the Wiltshire people must entail an ethic of sacrifice. This sacrifice would not be an end in itself; it is a necessary act to restore the mutuality and equal regard between Wiltshire and its surrounding communities. It will require sacrificial efforts to restrain its own privatism and consumption, increase its giving to others, and provide the resources for others to meet their legitimate needs. The specific resolution of controversies about a new church school building and about Sid Carlson's retirement rests within a larger spiritual reorientation of the congregation's priorities and spiritual mode of being-in-the-world.

8

WISDOM AND THE
HISTORICAL TURN

Most interpretations of the Wiltshire Church in Dudley's volume assumed a strong, almost Nygren-like definition of Christian love as self-sacrificial love. They leave the impression that the Wiltshire congregation was wrong in having its wants and needs. Churches should not meet the needs of their people, the message seems, but rather the needs of others.

I put the accent elsewhere. The understanding of *agapē* as equal regard suggests that the Wiltshire congregation has every right within a Christian understanding to pursue its needs. Its members do not have a right to do so *inordinately*. Their needs are no more important than those of others. The ethic of equal regard requires them to take the needs of others as seriously as their own. Even more, if there are clear and obvious imbalances, they are obligated to work on behalf of others. If they go to God in trust and openness, God will empower them to do this. This shift in theological perspective is ethically, pastorally, and strategically important. It provides an entirely new theological and pastoral stance from which to transform the Wiltshire Church. It makes it possible to both affirm and critique the congregation's interests. Judgment either changes people through fear or hardens their hearts. Love and affirmation that support people in the critical examination of their lives are the essence of revitalizing change.

This issue does not pertain solely to the Wiltshire Church. It drives to the heart of the estrangement between the reigning theologies in the mainline denominations and the hearts of their people. Most of these churches are declining. There is evidence that their theologies bring this about. The sociologist Benton Johnson has presented a diagnosis of this situation (Johnson 1982). Since Jeffrey Hadden's ominous warning in *The Gathering Storm in the Churches* (1969), it is accepted wisdom that there is a growing theological split between clergy and laity. Johnson believes that the influence of neoorthodox theology, including the theology of Reinhold Niebuhr, helped create this situation. It was not that the clergy were social activists and the laity were not. It was rather that the clergy were pessimists and forecasters of doom while the laity persisted in their American, future-oriented optimism. The Niebuhrian doctrine of original sin plus Niebuhr's elevation of self-sacrificial love over mutuality affected the preaching of ministers educated in the 1940s, 1950s, and 1960s. When liberation theology became popular, it brought additional appeals to a self-sacrificial service that denied one's own needs and the needs of one's family, neighborhood, and friends. Johnson argues that a more optimistic Christian vision nearer the liberalism that preceded neoorthodoxy is now needed. This is needed if church leaders are to communicate again with the laity.

Johnson's message is important but not entirely accurate. We do not need more optimism. We need more faithfulness to the humanity of the Christian message. We should admit that humans have Christian justification to pursue their ordinate human needs. All fundamental human needs are part of the goodness of creation and can be brought to a love ethic of equal regard. This is a message for all Christians. It is especially a message for women, minorities, and all who have been manipulated and controlled by exhortations to love others and not assert themselves (Gudorf 1985). In a different way, it may be a message that the people of the Wiltshire Methodist Church need as well. They, like all people, can confront their idolatries more freely if they understand them as distortions of fundamental and legitimate human needs. The Apostolic Church of God has heard this message better than either Wiltshire or Covenant.

PRACTICAL REASON IN A THEOLOGICAL CONTEXT

The Wiltshire Church raises important issues about the nature of practical reason within a theological context. I have tried to include a naturalistic moment in practical reason and theological ethics. I used it to analyze and criticize the needs and wants of Wiltshire people. I have acknowledged the historicist claim that our language of needs is historically situated and relative. Niebuhr said this himself. But when historically elaborated needs and tendencies conflict or overstep the constraints of the environment, he permitted a limited critical role for natural law—what I called the naturalistic moment. But this gives rise to a possible challenge: Do both Niebuhr and I combine a naturalistic and hermeneutic approach to practical reason in ways that simply will not work?

FOUNDATIONALISM AND NONFOUNDATIONALISM

My earlier formulations of the five dimensions of practical reason, in chapter 5 and elsewhere, had something of a foundationalist tone. I referred favorably to Kant at level two. This may suggest that I believe the obligational dimension can be derived through transcendental analysis of the metaphysical presuppositions of common moral experience, like Kant in *Foundations of the Metaphysics of Morals* ([1785] 1959, 3-9). At level three, I invoked a role for common human needs as the human sciences might understand them. Foundationalism tries to anchor moral thought on some objective beginning point whether it be transcendental judgments, empirical facts, or intuited and indubitable first principles (Bernstein 1983, 8-16). Because I find *some* role for reason and the human sciences, it may appear that I side with the foundationalists.

This is not so. My earlier published formulations saw the five dimensions as aspects of a larger hermeneutic conversation (Browning 1983b, 49). But I did not make this case with sufficient strength. If one accepts the historically situated nature of all knowledge, including religious knowledge, what does it mean for the five dimensions? If one agrees up to a point with MacIntyre, Gadamer, Bernstein, Rorty, Lindbeck, and Jeffrey Stout about the historicity of all thought, what would this mean for testing the multiple judgments of practical reason? Do each of the five dimensions disappear into relativism? If two communities have historically specific judgments at each of the five levels, can they get beyond these historically situated beginning points? Is dialogue possible?

Would, for instance, the naturalistic moment in ethics be possible? If empirical judgments are colored by the tradition of interpretation we bring to them (as Kuhn, Davidson, Gadamer, and Rorty assert), is it possible to make reliable judgments that clarify the fundamental needs and tendencies of human beings—the *ius naturale?* If moral judgments at level two are also historically situated, is equal regard as the rational core of both love and justice a fiction? Is there no way to mediate between equal regard and other principles of obligation? Is turning to uncritically appropriated tradition our only alternative? If I start out with precommitments to a particular vision and narrative about the world, is there nothing I can do to advance reasons for or against one vision or world view in contrast to another?

My answer is this: Although it is impossible to advance absolutely foundational, crystal-clear, and totally objective judgments at any of the five levels, the historically situated nature of practical thinking does not prevent us from advancing good reasons for what is better or worse. Richard Bernstein is right. Although reasons are never totally objective, some arguments are better than others. Bernstein writes, "If we take our historicity seriously, then the challenge that confronts us is to give the best possible reasons and arguments that are appropriate to our hermeneutical situation in order to validate claims to truth" (Bernstein 1983, 153). Although Bernstein leaves us with this insight, he says nothing to help us in understanding how a community might find these best possible reasons.

PRAGMATISM AND PRACTICAL REASON

The position elaborated with the help of Niebuhr places practical reason within communities of tradition. Niebuhr believed that both our measure of mutuality and our perception of human needs are historically conditioned. This is why he held that unnuanced appeals to natural law are unworkable though, as we have seen, he never completely threw them out. Niebuhr is consistent with the hermeneutical emphasis in Gadamer. In *The Self and the Dramas of History* (1955), Niebuhr used Martin Buber's thought to develop a dialogical understanding of human existence not unlike Gadamer's. He even anticipated the strong emphasis on responsiveness, dialogue, and conversation that appeared in his brother H. Richard Niebuhr's later *The Responsible Self* (1963). In terms of contemporary discussions, Niebuhr was Aristotelian in his understanding of the dialogical and tradition-based content of practical reason.

Aristotle emphasized the role of tradition and community in the formation of *phronēsis*. He did this when he emphasized in *Nicomachean Ethics* the role of habit, virtue, and character in the discernment of the goods of life (1941a, bks. 2–5). Recognizing these goods is largely a matter of perception. The education of our habits, virtues, and character shapes our capacity to perceive the good (bk. 1, ch. 9). This education occurs in community and these communities have traditions. This suggests that tradition shapes our initial capacities to discern both the lesser goods of life and the highest good for humans. When Stanley Hauerwas in *Character and the Christian Life* (1975a) demonstrated how Aristotle articulated the role of tradition in the shaping of practical reason, he provided a great service for the theological community. He was right. He advanced a philosophical defense for what theological ethics tends to do, that is, affirm tradition as the context for its moral reflection. This insight, as important as it is, is partial. More needs to be said.

Both Niebuhrian neoorthodoxy and Gadamerian hermeneutics can affirm this Aristotelian role for tradition. So can North American pragmatism. William James once said that tradition has developed a casuistical scale "for the philosopher far better than he can ever make it for himself.... The presumption in cases of conflict must always be in favor of the conventional recognized good" (James [1897] 1956, 206). This does not mean that James believed tradition always holds the final word in moral deliberations. But he did believe that we always begin with tradition and that our pragmatic moral thinking experiments with reworking resources from the past. These past resources are veritable storehouses of wisdom. Niebuhr fed on the ethos of pragmatism and anticipated the neo-Aristotelianism of Gadamerian hermeneutics.

Niebuhr's views resonate up to a point with the holism and hermeneutical philosophy of neopragmatist Richard Rorty. Rorty too criticizes the Enlightenment drive toward objectivity and sees our moral statements as finding their meaning within a larger holistic web of beliefs and traditions (Rorty 1979, 318). Rorty interprets pragmatism as developing an understanding of knowledge that does not start with objective foundations; pragmatism sees knowledge as claims that gain consensus within an ongoing conversation among people who share social meanings (9, 171). Niebuhr would never have equated the verification of moral deliberation with Rorty's view of consensus as what "keeps the conversation going." But he would have agreed that tradition and community dialogue shape moral discourse.

Jeffrey Stout is another neopragmatist with views similar to Rorty's. He has used his version of philosophical holism and pragmatism to give philosophical justification, even if ambivalent, to the role of religion in moral deliberation (Stout 1981, 1988). Richard Bernstein has contributed by concisely summarizing this recent convergence of Aristotelianism, hermeneutics, and pragmatism (Allen 1989). Niebuhr can rightly take his place in this conversation. At points he is in tension with these converging views, but this tension is productive.

ARISTOTLE, HUME, AND NIEBUHR

Niebuhr emphasizes sin and historicity, but he envisions a larger role for both rationality and experience in moral deliberation than this Aristotelian-pragmaticist-hermeneutic discussion allows. There was a role for rationality and experience in Aristotle as well. Aristotle said that we must be persons of virtue before we can discern the good. This suggested that a community must form us in order for us to have these virtues. But he also recognized that new situations in life could test our fund of tradition-formed virtues and that a principle of rationality was needed to refine the wisdom of our virtues. Aristotle identified this rational principle as a mean and defined it as a point between two extremes or vices, "one of excess and one of deficiency" (1941a, bk. 2, ch. 6). The specific task of *phronēsis* is to discern and apply the rational principle that would supply the mean between the excesses. It performs this task for virtues such as courage, temperance, liberality, and justice.

At times Aristotle seems to claim little more for reason than the eighteenth-century philosopher David Hume. Hume held that practical reason is passive and can provide only technical means for ends that are themselves supplied by the passions (Hume [1751] 1957, 4–5). But as Norman Dahl has pointed out in his able *Practical Reason, Aristotle, and Weakness of the Will* (1984), Aristotle does more than this. Practical reason, according to Dahl, is far more active in Aristotle than in Hume. In Aristotle, practical reason has the capacity to review rationally the history of ends supplied by our virtue-shaped passions and determine their relative and lasting value. When reflective review finds these tradition-shaped ends lacking, practical reason can supply a more adequate rational principle that mediates between the extremes, thereby guiding us in a more satisfactory total direction (49–66).

Hume, on the other hand, saw practical reason as primarily serving the passions. He overlooked the ways our community-shaped virtues shape our passions. Reason for Hume at best gives weight to one set of passions in contrast to another by assessing their respective consequences and overall social utility (Hume [1751] 1957, 105; Dahl 1984, 23–25; MacIntyre 1988, 301). In contrast to Hume, practical reason in Aristotle actually helps shape the ends of our action as well as the means-ends technologies for achieving these ends. In Aristotle's model practical reason refines, tests, and criticizes ends that our tradition-shaped virtues first provide. But some neo-Aristotelians, such as Gadamer and Rorty, overlook this role for reason and reflective review and subsume practical reason totally to tradition-based communities of consensus.

I think Niebuhr goes beyond this. Certainly my reconstruction of Niebuhr with the help of Janssens goes beyond this. Both give more weight to the reason in practical reason than Gadamer and Rorty, and probably MacIntyre. We can grant that practical reason lives off community-shaped virtues and passions. Because of this, the virtues and passions must be seen as a part of practical reason. Practical reason would be empty without them. Nonetheless, there are ways in which the reason in practical reason can play back on the traditions that form it. It can criticize these traditions and help stabilize conversations designed to achieve consensus. To show this I will return to Aristotle.

The neo-Aristotelians in philosophy and theology correctly show the role of tradition and virtue in Aristotle. But they have underplayed the role of principle and rationality. In the current debate over the relative strengths of ethics of virtue and ethics of principle, the role Aristotle gives to principles is generally underestimated. Aristotle held that justice is the master virtue (1941a, bk. 5, ch. 1). Guided by the principle of proportionality it avoids the extremes, selfishness, and self-emptying (bk. 5, ch. 3). Proportionality is a rational principle. It establishes ratios of worth "according to merit" (bk. 5, ch. 3). Distributive justice is determined not according to need or strict equality but according to relative worth and merit. Hence, according to Aristotle, a free man has more merit than a woman, child, or slave. Justice between a free man and these other humans is proportionate to their relative worth and merit. Proportionality is clearly a principle and a principle that can be rationally articulated.

Although it is a principle and can be rationally stated, it does not stand independently of background beliefs—beliefs that have been formed by a community's tradition. What is proportionate in this geometrical sense depends on the political customs of the Athenian city-state, a state that gave the political privileges of citizenship only to certain free and propertied men. It denied these privileges to women and slaves. This social fact determined the criterion of worth and merit. This kind of observation leads MacIntyre, Stout, Hauerwas, and others in the narrative school to hold that morality is entirely tradition-dependent. I argue that morality depends on tradition in many respects, even most respects, but *not* all respects. I invoke Niebuhr, and my revision of Niebuhr, in defense of my case.

THE LIMITS OF NEO-ARISTOTELIANISM

Niebuhr had a rationally articulate principle for addressing issues of justice. It was the principle of mutuality in intimate affairs and brotherhood/sisterhood in social affairs. In my reconstruction, I gave both the abstract character of equal regard. Although Niebuhr saw this principle as the rule of justice in the context of fallen humanity, my reconstruction made it the moral norm of human life and not just a concession to fallenness. It is not difficult to see the remarkable difference between Aristotle's principle of justice as proportionality of merit and justice as mutuality and equal regard. They are different formal or rational principles. On the one hand, the principle of proportionality says that as A's worth is to

B's so A's resources should be in relation to B's resources. The principle of mutuality and equal regard has, on the other hand, the logic of reversibility and universality. It says that in order to avoid self-contradiction, any claim that A makes on B, A in turn must allow B to make on A. Furthermore, the principle of equal regard is willing to generalize or universalize this principle of reversibility and say that the principle applies not only in A's relation to B but in A's relation to all others like B.

These principles, which can be stated rationally, are still influenced by background beliefs provided by tradition and the narratives that carry it. Aristotle knew a story about the status and worth of diverse sorts of people that differed from Niebuhr's and, indeed, from the early Christians'. These narrative traditions collided when the early Christian house churches expanded into the Greek polis. The laws and ethics of the Greek city-state dominated city life during the first century of the Christian era. Christians then (and Niebuhr and other Christians today) believed that all humans were made in the image of God and were ultimately equal in God's sight. This was true in spite of the transient inequalities of life that being born a woman or slave might foist upon a person. Wayne Meeks has shown this in *The Moral World of the First Christians* (1986). The Christian house church treated men, women, and slaves with an ethic of mutuality and equal regard. The ethic of the house church directly contradicted Aristotle's theory of proportional justice that dominated the surrounding Greek polis (11–17, 110–14). Christian initiates were likely to hear "that with their clothing they had 'stripped off the old human,'... 'putting on' in his place the 'new human, Christ,' in whom 'there is no slave nor free, no Jew nor Greek, no male and female' " (Meeks 1986, 113; Col. 3:9-11; Eph. 4:22-24; Gal. 3:27ff.). There were, in the later Pastoral Letters, calls to return to the old Aristotelian hierarchies. But according to Meeks, the Pauline churches in Corinth, Rome, and elsewhere were quietly yet dangerously in tension with them. Later Christian theologians, such as Niebuhr and Janssens, stated these early breakthroughs as systematic ethical positions formulated around the idea of love as equal regard.

It is useful to distinguish between the beliefs or narrative background of a moral principle and the moral principle itself. Similar moral principles can often be found in different background traditions and narratives. We see this when we find moral principles in Kantian, neo-Kantian, and certain religious contexts that are formally similar to the principles of neighbor love and the golden rule in the Judeo-Christian tradition. The narrative contexts of these philosophical and religious principles differ from the narrative contexts of similar principles within the Jewish and Christian traditions. This might be explained by saying that the Kantian perspectives are secularized forms of the Christian ethic; they make assumptions about the status of human beings that have evolved out of the Christian belief that humans are made in the image of God. There is truth in this, but it does not exhaust the discussion. It does not explain why principles like neighbor love and the golden rule, with their features of reversibility and universalization, are found in religious and cultural contexts around the world in both ancient and modern times, contexts that probably did not influence each other, at least not originally (Erikson 1963, 233). In addition, overstating how tradition forms our moral thinking—as the hermeneutic, historicist, and cultural-linguistic schools do—leads us to overestimate the difficulties of having productive conversations and entering shared projects with people from other traditions. It blinds us to the similarities of moral thinking in different contexts. It obscures the ways that shared experiences shape the thought of those who begin in vastly different narrative contexts.

PRACTICAL REASON BEYOND ITS TRADITION

Historicists overlook the role of brute experience in the formation of our moral thinking. Yes, our narrative traditions form our moral thinking, but the thickness, resistance, and intractability of experience poke irresistibly into our linguistic forms and make their testimony. This is why our natural moral thinking at the level of the *ius gentium* gravitates toward the principle of equal regard rather than toward Aristotelian proportional, ethical-egoist, or utilitarian theories of obligation. We meet something in the other—any human other, be it woman, slave, or person from another race— that tells us that the person thinks, feels, and listens like we do, and has talents like ours and therefore must be a *person* in many respects like us. Analogously, our brute experience helps us to gain deeper and deeper insights, beneath our narrative traditions, into the tendencies and needs of our basic human nature.

In making these statements, I moderate the extreme claims of historicist perspectives by appealing to the radical empiricism of certain strands of North American pragmatism, especially William James. I argue that the revised correlational method of practical theology requires both the hermeneutical *and* the radical empirical perspectives. Although we always interpret experience from the perspective of our fore-knowledge, experience *can and does talk back*. MacIntyre is correct—images of justice are greatly shaped by their narrative traditions. But our ongoing social experience—our

brute experience of other people's claims, counterclaims, personhood, and needs—leads us to new knowledge that reshapes our
concepts of justice.

Similarly, we interpret our human tendencies and needs first
by inherited narrative traditions. Yet brute reality and the ongoing
experience of our human nature do at times intrude and teach us
nuances about ourselves that our cultural-linguistic traditions lead
us to overlook or obscure. Radical empiricism's view of experience
does not contradict the narrative view. It makes it less rigid. It shows
how experience, as well as narrative, informs both our principles
of obligation and our perception of human needs and tendencies. It
helps us see how, on some occasions, the wisdom of narrative and
experience can inform and sometimes confirm one another.

What is radical empiricism? Why do I invoke it to show that
practical reason always starts within tradition but is not confined to
it? Practical reason can kick at the edges of tradition and take small
but important steps outside it. This is because our reflective and
generalizing powers work not only on the linguistic and symbolic
materials that traditions provide but also on the thick and brute
aspects of experience that do not completely yield to the linguistic
constructions we place upon them. We saw a radical empirical strain
in Niebuhr in his theory of general and special revelation. Niebuhr
held, we should recall, that evidence of God as Creator, Governor,
and Redeemer can be found in human experience in general. He
saw this as both a biblical idea and a tenable philosophical position. Niebuhr did not believe that the cultural-linguistic categories
of tradition and the narratives of special revelation were the only
sources of knowledge about God. Experience does things that break
through the edges of our linguistic structures. Although Niebuhr
never directly invokes the radical empiricism of William James and
other pragmatists, there runs throughout his thought a general critique of the positivistic empiricism associated with Cartesian and
Lockean epistemologies. He launches this critique in the name of a
larger empiricism clearly consistent with the major features of radical empiricism. Such arguments are especially evident in *The Self
and the Dramas of History* (1955, 129).

It is precisely the radical empirical element of classic North
American pragmatism that the current confluence of hermeneutics
and pragmatism omits. Rorty, Bernstein, and Stout are among the
most prominent persons who are weaving hermeneutics and pragmatism together. They all ignore the radical empirical element of
pragmatism. The radical empirical element in different ways runs
through the thought of Peirce, James, and Dewey. It concerns a
level of bodily interaction with the environment that is below our

higher-level linguistic construals. William Dean in *American Religious Empiricism* (1986) and Nancy Frankenberry in *Religion and Radical Empiricism* (1987) reintroduce radical empiricism into the neopragmatist revival. Frankenberry argues that Rorty's and Stout's hermeneutic and linguistic construal of pragmatism, although accurate to a point, goes too far. Frankenberry succinctly summarizes radical empiricism and distinguishes it from classic empiricism and neopragmatism: "On this view, before ever undertaking the comparatively high-level discriminations of the world by means of the senses or linguistic forms, the subject is aware of itself and others as causally efficacious powers interacting with a world of qualitative values where memories of the past and anticipations of the future are felt as given" (84). Radical empiricism describes this diffuse yet persistent testimony of experience beneath our tradition-laden linguistic forms. The revised correlational method assumes something like this view of experience in its drive to correlate tradition with contemporary experience.

Niebuhr's doctrine of special and general revelation also assumes something like it; nuances of God's creative, governing, and redeeming power are felt in our common experience; they permeate our linguistic forms as well as being shaped in turn by them. The possibility of a revised theory of natural law that can provide stabilizing moments in a historically situated moral conversation also can be clarified by radical empiricism. When our tradition-laden linguistic forms either conflict or seem inconclusive about what our basic human tendencies and needs really are, then the testimony of our ongoing psychobiological experience and the insights of the human sciences may provide stabilizing insights that are relevant to public discussion. At the obligational level, our ongoing direct experience of the agency, initiative, and resistance of other persons may convince us that they are indeed persons and need to be treated according to the principle of equal regard.

This blend of historicism and radical empiricism makes sense if one makes the traditional pragmatic distinction between the beginning of an inquiry and its direction or end. All inquiry begins in historically situated contexts. We interpret the world, our ongoing experience, and the challenges of life out of tradition-shaped contexts. This is the truth of the antifoundationalist and historicist perspective. But when we start thinking and inquiring about the challenges that confront us, our reflection goes in two directions simultaneously—toward the past and toward the future. It goes *backward* to the founding or classic monuments that have formed us. Then our practical reflection goes forward to test the adequacy of this witness to experience, our present situation, and the future.

Although our grasp of experience is always shaped at first by the cultural-linguistic perspective that we bring to it, there are ways to vary perceptions, feel more deeply, compare, control variables, and gain a partial, limited, yet meaningful distance from this beginning point. We cannot test our classic traditions against experience in any simple or univocal way. Nor can we test experience solely against the classic traditions. But we can have a dialogue between them. Such a dialogue requires avenues to experience through reason and a broader empiricism of a kind that the hermeneutical and historicist schools do not fully understand. Frankenberry says it well when she writes,

> Assuming a dialectical relation between experience and interpretation, the problem becomes one of critically incorporating both as a paired phenomenon in a theory that does not displace either by the other.... From the perspective of radical empiricism, the near collapse of experience into its interpretations is as unempirical as was an earlier disabling antithesis between experience and interpretation. Once experience and interpretation come to be regarded as indistinguishable within the hermeneutic circle, any testing of the one in terms of the other is rendered either very unlikely or extremely precarious (68).

Practical reason within the context of the hermeneutic circle begins in historically situated contexts, moves backward to understand more deeply the classical ideals that have formed it, but further tests the adequacy to experience of these retrieved formulations as we move forward into the future. This is close to the classic pragmatist theory of verification. We know the truth not by its roots (or foundations) but by its fruits (where it takes us). This is the way practical reason works in situated communities of moral inquiry, reflection, and action.

THE LOGIC OF PRACTICAL REASON

In contrast to the Enlightenment and empiricist cultural projects that dominated the nineteenth and twentieth centuries, I propose a modest use of reason and experience as stabilizing factors within a larger historically situated hermeneutical dialogue. Reason and experience, as used here, do not wipe the slate clean of tradition. But they can build small islands of clarification and stability within larger fractured and conflicted traditions. The historicist and hermeneutical perspectives have been important in calling our positivistic and scientific age back to an appreciation of tradition. Yet if representatives of historicist and hermeneutical perspectives like MacIntyre, Stout, and Bernstein have not plunged us into complete relativism, they leave us on the brink. I want to outline briefly how rational principles and empirically described experience can play a modest role within a hermeneutically conceived understanding of practical reason.

A hermeneutically conceived practical reason contains several kinds of rationality as submoments within it. These various rationalities help create a social objectivity that facilitates deliberation and consensus both within and between traditions. As we saw, when the five dimensions of practical reason are used descriptively, there is room for various distancing maneuvers that aid in seeing the infrastructures of experience more fully. When a hermeneutically conceived practical reason is used normatively, something similar is true. Various logics function as submoments within the whole. These submoments help extend the realm of social objectivity.

By social objectivity I do not mean the crystal-clear, cold objectivity that positivistically oriented science believed it was creating throughout most of modernity. Instead I mean an objectivity that widens the scope of social agreement by clarifying the structures of our experience and helping us come to terms more adequately with the givens of nature, human nature, and our social and ecological environments. This objectivity is a socially achieved objectivity (certainly not an absolute objectivity). But it is an objectivity that wins consensus because it indeed grasps more adequately some of the intractable givens in experience. It is the kind of objectivity that one associates with a critical-realist position in the philosophy of science. It acknowledges that we bring our fore-concepts to experience and always construe experience partially in terms of them. It holds, however, that careful attention to experience over time shows that some tradition-laden theories address our moral and epistemological problems better than others. As William James said, some hypotheses help us do things with experience better than others (James [1909] 1970, 28; James [1907] 1955, 41–64). For this reason, we assume that some of our cultural-linguistic forms are more in contact with the givens of experience than others.

CONVENTIONALITY

Doing things, however, with the givens of human nature, society, and the natural is not the first modus operandi of practical reason. Practical reason operates first by the logic of conventionality. It tries to reason about the world in the way custom and tradition has taught. It tries to interpret and implement both its moral and premoral values according to the consolidated patterns society offers. This is true for the way we interpret our needs and tendencies,

our general moral principles, our concrete rules, and our view of
the world in which these are placed. Insofar as we do this naively,
we follow the logic of *conventionality*. We reason thusly: Because
everyone has done it this way, I should do it this way.

RECONSTRUCTIVE MEMORY

When our conventional patterns are seriously challenged, appear to
break down, or become confused by competitors, the next step is
the *reconstruction of memory*. In order to determine how to proceed
freely in the future, we must use practical reason to discern how
it has been formed by the past. Starting with its current practices
and the meaning attached to them, we turn *phronēsis* toward the
monuments (texts and events) that have provided it with its norms
and ideals—however fragmentarily, confusedly, and incompletely.
We ask, What do our traditions *really* say about what we should
do? When we ask this question—the hermeneutical question par
excellence—we will get a thick, rich answer containing elements
from all the five levels. The fruit of this labor should, in fact, be
the return to our practices with an enriched view of the five dimensions of practical reason. But we do not depend alone on either
conventionality or the reconstruction of memory. We supplement
these logics with others.

DISCERNING HUMAN NEEDS

Introspective Induction

Convention and reconstructive memory (the hermeneutical turn)
give us our first orientation to the fullness of practical reason.
Yet it is still an inherited practical reason; it has not been tested.
In this testing, how do we examine more deeply what we really
want and need? We learn about our genuine human needs not
only from convention and reconstructive memory. We learn from
the brute aspects of our experience. Many who have gone through
psychotherapy believe that it exemplifies how people can work
through, to a degree, their learned cultural-linguistic constructs and
gradually gain a deeper sense of their true feelings, needs, and tendencies (Gendlin 1962; Rogers 1957). Norman Dahl may be right
that this process has the logic of induction, albeit an introspective
induction. It not only follows the logic of the practical syllogism
that says, "I am thirsty, this is water, I will drink" (Dahl 1984, 26–
29). The logic of introspective induction in psychotherapy not only
tests means-end relations, that is, how best to achieve the goal of
finding something to drink. Introspective induction also may induc-

tively test the validity of the major premise—the premise about ends. It may say, "I thought I wanted water but I was really simply anxious and tense—I wanted love and affirmation." After drinking countless glasses of water and still feeling dry, introspective induction concludes, "Water was not really my sole end and goal; I also need companionship." In spite of the importance of the cultural-linguistic perspective in the interpretation of our tendencies and wants, practical reason uses, in part, the logic of induction. It says, "*If* I assume I want love in addition to water and then act on this over time, *then* possibly I will feel better."

It is possible that a group will think similarly. Take an Alcoholics Anonymous group. The logic might go like this: "We thought we wanted alcohol, but after much suffering we discovered that we really want love. *If* we let our friends love us, *then* possibly we will feel more whole." Practical reason may use introspective induction as one of its sublogics. Does something like that happen in the group processes of the Wiltshire Methodist Church and, perhaps, the Apostolic Church of God—the two churches that most directly wrestle to order human wants and needs? I think it does.

Comparison

The logics of reconstructive memory and introspective induction may combine in another kind of logic—the logic of comparison. The alcoholic may say, "I thought I wanted alcohol because my fun-loving Irish Catholic tradition taught me to interpret my loneliness and anxiety as a need for alcohol. But my reconstructive memory," he may add, "has taught me that excessive drinking plays no basic role in the classics of the Christian tradition. Instead, they tell me much about my need for love." Hence the logic of reconstructive memory may provide a new hypothesis to be tested by the logic of introspective induction. Whether the old hypothesis about the need for alcohol or the new hypothesis about the need for love is the stronger can be tested, in part, by introspective induction over a long time. It depends on how acting on the latter hypothesis helps actualize a wide range of other goods as the person moves toward the future. This entails a comparison between the two hypotheses "I want alcohol" and "I want love." The hypothesis "I want alcohol" was provided by the logic of convention (what my friends have always done must be good), and the hypothesis "I want love" may have been provided by reconstructive memory (possibly mediated through a therapeutic group). But the comparison is significantly aided by a faltering, tentative testing of these two hypotheses against the fundamental needs of the alcoholic's human nature and the other realities of experience. It is the faith of the Christian that the hypothesis provided by the classic Christian sources will be sustained when tested this way.

Other groups, even churches, use such tests. This was particularly visible in the Apostolic Church of God, as we will see in later chapters. Its people had such a fresh openness to experience that they were always publicly comparing their experience before becoming Christian with present experiences of acting on their Christian hypotheses. I became convinced that although their Christian categories provided powerful perspectives for the interpretation of experience, the brute aspects of their human nature and external experience "spoke back" with an affirmative vote for the hypotheses of tradition. In many ways, the people of the Apostolic Church were radical empiricists.

Objective Empiricism

Not only the logics of conventionality, reconstructive memory, introspective induction, and comparison, but other *more objective empirical logic* may be used to test our knowledge of our deepest needs and tendencies. The alcoholic may learn something from the experimental sciences about how destructive alcohol is to the human brain, the heart, reproductive capacities, and social relations. The alcoholic may learn something about the effects of alcohol on animals such as monkeys, dogs, or cats that are in some ways physiologically similar to himself. This more objective and naturalistic knowledge can teach the alcoholic something about his deeper needs and tendencies. In addition, this more objective and experimentally derived knowledge might provide a hypothesis that could supplement the hypotheses of reconstructive memory and introspective induction. This experimental information might suggest the hypothesis, "If I continue to drink, I will harm myself." This knowledge would function as a small and limited index within a much larger historically situated practical reflective process. Alcoholics Anonymous may succeed precisely because its blend of religion and practical therapeutic reflection artfully crafts a complex synthesis of practical reflective logics reinforced by powerful, loving, consistent, and ongoing group supports.

DISCERNING SYSTEMIC CONSTRAINTS

These rationalities used to describe our human needs have much in common with the rationalities we use to describe the constraints of our social and ecological environments. Clearly, our narrative traditions say much about social-systemic and ecological realities.

For instance, the Judeo-Christian tradition tells us that we live in a finite world with clear natural limits. It tells us that although nature is good, it cannot satisfy all wants for all people. Further, these natural constraints imply, according to this tradition, that no social system can satisfy all human wants all the time. All social systems are frustrating. Total and complete human fulfillment is impossible in this world. But the human consequences of various social systems and the results of various accommodations with nature can be assessed. Both conventional rationality and reconstructive memory provide the first frameworks for the assessment of these contexts.

Other refinements are also useful. Intuitive, comparative, and empirical rationalities have their subordinate roles in analyzing social and ecological contexts just as they do in describing our fundamental human needs and tendencies—as I tried to show at length in chapter 6.

THE LOGIC OF EQUAL REGARD

Most philosophical perspectives acknowledge that humans pursue the premoral good through some kind of teleological logic. They pursue the goods that meet their basic human needs through goal-oriented practical activity. Kant pointed this out in his discussion of the hypothetical imperative. From Aristotle, Aquinas, and Hume to the modern utilitarians Bentham and Mill, the goal-oriented logic of some brand of teleological thinking has had a central place in certain types of ethical thinking. In discussing the logic of the tendency-need level of practical reason, I acknowledge the importance of a teleological moment.

But I side with Kant, and more recently Alan Donagan (1977), who claim that a deontological ethic is closer to the genius of the Christian ethic. It need not be the one-sided deontological ethic championed by Kant. It can be a deontology that includes teleology but places it in a secondary yet prominent position. This is basically what I have done in subordinating a concern with the *ordo bonorum* to the logic of mutuality and equal regard as formulated by Niebuhr and Janssens. This retains the teleology of the hypothetical imperative but subordinates it to the categorical imperative. More concretely, it affirms that all humans have the right to satisfy their premoral goods but only as this is consistent with a universalizable equal regard for others.

What is the logic of equal regard? I have already hinted it has the structure of reversibility and universalizability. It has the logic of being able to reverse our claims; any claim we make on others they should be able to make on us. And it has the logic of universalizability; this reversibility should be in principle generalizable to all social actors who impinge on my action. In short, the principle of equal regard has the logic of the golden rule and neighbor love. Paul Ricoeur has made a powerful statement of this subordination of teleology to deontology in his meditation on the golden rule. He interprets the command to "do unto others as you would have them do unto you" to mean that we are to do *good* unto others as we would have them do *good* unto us (Ricoeur 1989). We have seen already that Ricoeur's formulation of the relation of teleology to deontology fits Frankena's mixed deontological theory.

The principle of neighbor love as equal regard is a product not only of revelation. It is also a product of the interaction of reason and experience. As Kohlberg and his school have argued, our moral experience of other people's agency pushes us bit by bit through successive transformations in our moral thinking toward a more fully reversible and universalizable logic of moral obligation. The more we interact with people, the more their subjectivity impinges upon our experience and the more we must recognize their otherness and treat them with genuine equal regard. Few people arrive at this level of moral thinking. Fewer live by it consistently. It by no means explains moral development totally. Yet our cognitive moral thinking does seem to push toward more comprehensive reversibility.

The principle of obligation toward which the mind naturally gravitates and the principle of obligation that the Christian tradition reveals tend to converge. What the Christian's reconstructive memory suggests and what moral experience pushes us toward seem to cohere and reinforce one another. But they may not always reach their goal simultaneously. Christians may hear the Christian story throughout their lives and hear time and again the call of neighbor love. But their own moral development may only gradually approximate this ideal as they move, as Kohlberg has described, through egocentrism, to conventionality, to utilitarianism, to a more genuinely adequate reversible and universalizable principle of obligation (Kohlberg 1981, 147–68). Their Christian convictions may facilitate this growth, but the experience of dealing with the datum of others' subjectivity also pushes them in this direction. This is a phenomenon that a radical empirical perspective on experience helps us to understand. For just as we feel the weight and thickness of our own human nature breaking into our cultural-linguistic traditions, so we feel the weight and reality of other persons' subjectivity breaking through. Aristotle's principle of justice as proportionality is not only relative to his cultural situation; in the end it is inadequate for the moral tasks that face human beings. Sufficient experience over time with women and slaves helped, in the end, to lead to the recognition that they have the same deliberative powers, the same self-reflective capacities, and approximately the same tendencies and needs as free and propertied men. Our experience teaches us that they are persons deserving equal regard.

Our Christian heritage reinforces what our experience tells us and even adds more weight. It tells us that in addition to being rational agents with feelings and wants, humans are children of God and made in God's image. Grounding respect for persons on an analysis of human agency and rationality as done by Kant and the neo-Kantians is valid enough logically and ethically. They correctly show that our experience of other people's reason pushes us in the direction of respect and equal regard. It is not that the Christian tradition and reason are opposed. Rather, the Christian narrative about humans reflecting the image of God adds metaphysical weight that leads us to take the personhood of others all the more seriously.

Finally, although the principle that should guide practical reason at level two has the deontological structure of reversibility, universalizability, and impartiality, we must not understand this as a foundationalist principle. The reversibility and universalizability of equal regard have, in my view, a historically situated character. No person or group ever exercises this principle in a completely pure way. Although reversibility and universalizability make equal regard sound as though it allows no variability in time or space and would arrive at precisely the same conclusions no matter where it is exercised, this is not the claim being made here. This principle is always limited by its contextual locations. It is limited by the premoral goods that are brought to it to be adjudicated. Equal regard is limited by the specific socioeconomic and ecological constraints that it confronts in specific situations. Equal regard may entail dividing five loaves or fifty depending on the extent of the drought and the limits it places on the supply of grain. These constraints do not alter the *formal structure* of equal regard. Equal regard can be limited by those who are identified as appropriate members of the conversation, by those who are in situations similar to the parties in conversation, or by those who will or will not be affected by the action. Hence, these principles never function with crystal-clear, ice cold objectivity. They do inject a drift, however, in all conscientious conversations that requires participants to be alert to the boundaries of their conversations. They require all participants in principle to be willing to extend the deliberations to include individuals, groups, and members beyond those originally thought relevant.

When the religious concept of the *imago dei* reinforces the principle of universalization, moral conversations can in principle extend to the universal community. In a time of mass media and growing global awareness, we are coming to the awareness that our various moral conversations do have repercussions to the end of the world.

DESCRIPTIVE GENERALIZATION

Full practical reason has additional logics and additional tests. Logics are even available to test the metaphysical claims implicit in the visional level of our practical reason. Practical reasoning takes place within assumptions about the ultimate context of the world. Aristotle's understanding of practical reason is placed within a metaphysic that associates the truly good with an Unmoved Mover. This Unmoved Mover is the final cause of all that exists as well as a model for all finite quests for the good. The highest good for humans, according to Aristotle, was to fulfill the function that made them unique. This was their rational capacity that, when exercised in free contemplation, exhibits the self-sufficiency and intrinsic enjoyment of the Unmoved Mover. Kant too, in the end, placed his view of practical reason within a larger view of the ultimate context of life. This was a concept of God that functioned as a postulate of practical reason; it functioned as an idea about the way things really are. Moral reason, Kant believed, requires this postulate to sustain the hope that virtue and happiness will come together, if not in this life then in the next (Kant [1788] 1956, 128–36). In modern systems of thought, models of practical reason also are always surrounded by larger visions of the way the world is. I have given special attention to how this works in the modern psychologies where models of optimal ego functions (which invariably follow some model of practical reason) are surrounded by metaphysical models, be they mechanistic (Skinner), hydraulic (Freud), or organic and harmonistic (humanistic psychology) (Browning 1987).

Even here, there are logics that can test the relative adequacy of these visions. This gets us into the complex question of metaphysical verification. I will not carry the conversation far; to do so would move my argument beyond its proper scope. At least this much needs to be said. The role for metaphysics that I envision is as a humble enterprise that functions primarily to stabilize conversations that are historically situated. No definitive and fully rational metaphysical system will ever be generated. Even if such a system were developed, it would be only modestly useful in practical thinking. Metaphysical systems are extensions and generalizations of historically generated metaphors and narratives. Our metaphysical reflection has the same motivation as our other cognitive endeavors, that is, our practical interests.

Nonetheless, some visions and their metaphysical implications are more adequate than others. Some are more adequate to the assumptions about the world implicit in our practical activity and more adequate to our experience of the thick and obdurate facts of our human nature and the outside world. Reasons can be advanced why one vision may be more adequate to the fullness of experience than others. These reasons are always historically situated and never definitive in any narrow rationalistic sense. From my perspective, the Whiteheadian method of descriptive generalization of the basic features of experience is more useful than the transcendental deductions of the kind associated with Kant or, in modern theology, Karl Rahner and, at times, David Tracy (Tracy 1975, 52–63). Descriptive generalization recognizes that all descriptions are interpretations but that some interpretations of basic features of experience can be generalized further than others. In contemporary discussions, the relational view of the world put forth by the process philosophy of William James, Alfred North Whitehead, and Charles Hartshorne is more generalizable and adequate to experience and contemporary knowledge than the older substantialist view. This does not mean that the truth of process philosophy has been proven definitively in a way that should stop further discussion. It means that good reasons can be advanced to support it and that a moral system informed by this vision of the world may be on more solid ground than one based on a substantialist or mechanistic perspective.

But my point is not to settle metaphysical disputes. It is, rather, to show that each dimension of practical reason specializes in a form of rationality. Although most moral conversations make progress primarily through dialogue and tests at levels two, three, and four, there are times when tests of the most all-encompassing visional level become relevant and necessary. This is because the visional level forms the background beliefs that influence all other levels of practical reason. Groups and individuals with differing visions of life often have much in common in the way they think about moral obligation and human need. But frequently they do not. Clarity about the different types of rationality in *phronēsis* and the influence of our visions on them does not give us mathematical formulas for solving moral disputes. It may, however, greatly open our conversations, make them more flexible, and give us new tools for widening the space of social objectivity.

NIEBUHR'S IMPLICIT DISCOURSE ETHIC

In this chapter I have amplified what I find implicit in Reinhold Niebuhr's understanding of the relation of practical reason to narrative
traditions. Although he believed reason is historically situated and
distorted by sin, he thought it had a place in both discerning our
moral obligations and divining our human nature. He did not spell
out the subrationalities of a tradition-informed practical reason. I
have tried to do this.

Extending Niebuhr in this way clarifies a crucial move in his
thought—toward what is now called discourse ethics. Niebuhr encouraged all the critical ethical reflection that humans can muster.
He also knew that, in the end, decisions in the church, outside
the church, and between the church and the world are products
of compromise and the balance of power. They are products of
consensus between the best thought, the vested interests, and the
relative power of the persons and groups involved. Discourse and
good moral thinking play a role, but they are never pure and are
always accompanied by self-interest, power maneuvers, and compromise. Practical reason can only improve decisions; it does not
make them perfect.

Niebuhr does not deny the role of rational discourse in form-
ing concrete rules for a group or society. The highest ideals of a
tradition and the exercise of natural human rationality play their respective roles. Out of the heat of conversation between historically
conditioned and self-interested parties, the final concrete rules of
justice emerge by "a social process in which various partial perspectives have been synthesized into a more inclusive one" (R. Niebuhr
1943, 252). Rational discourse and higher ideals play their role,
but concrete norms of law are "compromises between the rational
moral ideals of what ought to be, and the possibilities of the situation as determined by given equilibria of vital forces" (257). All
societies have some central power or government, but they also
are held together by diffuse balances of power between diverse interest groups and localities (257). All societies are constantly in
danger of falling under the control of this central organizing force
or splintering under the forces of the competing groups. In democracies, the constitutional establishment of free speech, criticism,
and constant review helps avoid the extremes of totalitarianism
and anarchy (263, 268).

According to Niebuhr, this blend of rational group deliberation
and compromise is not instituted in democracies because human
nature is benign and totally trustworthy. It is instituted because
humans are sinful, self-interested, and in constant need of the judg-

WISDOM AND THE HISTORICAL TURN

ment of critical discourse. Niebuhr writes in *The Self and the Dramas of History:*

> The health and justice of the community is preserved, not so much by the discriminate judgement of the whole community as by the effect of free criticism in moderating the pretensions of every group and by the weight of competing power in balancing power that might become inordinate and oppressive. Democracy in short is not a method that is effective only among virtuous men. It is a method that prevents interested men from following their interests to the detriment of the community (R. Niebuhr 1955, 198).

Niebuhr could easily join the contemporary struggle to state moral philosophy as a theory of discourse rather than a theory of the thought processes of individual, isolated moral thinkers. Individuals may think morally, but they never do it alone. Moral thinking by definition deals with other people, and eventually they insist on being part of the process that affects their lives. Niebuhr had an embryonic discourse ethic of the kind that today we associate with Jürgen Habermas, Karl-Otto Apel, and others. In contrast to these theories—especially that of Habermas, which we will review—Niebuhr stated much more positively the relation of religion to ethics. The view that follows, although inspired by Niebuhr, extends his position in light of my earlier reconstruction of his views on love and justice. After completing this task, I will turn to a conversation with Habermas and his friendly critic, Helmut Peukert.

THE CHRISTIAN NARRATIVE AND PRACTICAL REASON

Moral philosophers often argue that ethical thinking has no necessary relation to religion. Yet it is fashionable among theological ethicists such as Hauerwas and Metz and historicists such as MacIntyre, Rorty, and Stout to claim that practical reason has little or no autonomy from the tradition and narratives of a community. Even these thinkers, who are in principle open to considering how the Judeo-Christian tradition informs practical reason, do not show how this might be possible.

By using and extending the narrative line of Niebuhr's theology, I want to sketch several ways the Christian story informs practical reason. I already have argued that the inner core of practical reason has a *mixed deontological structure.* This phrase, borrowed from William Frankena, shows practical reason to have a dominant deontological logic of equal regard with a subordinate teleological moment that promotes the increase of the premoral good. I find this structure of practical reason embedded in the Christian narrative in the love command and the golden rule.

What does Niebuhr's version of the Christian narrative contribute to the inner core of practical reason? Hauerwas and Metz correctly suggest that the Christian narrative contributes something essential to practical reason. They are wrong in arguing that practical reason has no independence from this narrative. To say that it has a modicum of independence does not mean, of course, that it is completely independent. It means, instead, that practical reason and our narrative traditions relate interactively. I argue that we can discern the form of practical reason within the Christian narrative but that we discern it within other narrative contexts as well. The Christian narrative adds very important ingredients to the functioning of practical reason—ingredients that are important to all the levels of practical reason I have been discussing.

With my amendments to the Niebuhrian view of Christian narrative in mind, let us review how the three great metaphors of God as Creator, Governor, and Redeemer help form the outer envelope of practical reason and influence its inner core.

GOODNESS OF THE CREATED WORLD

First and foremost, the metaphor of God the Creator bestows the ontological status of goodness on all the created world. This metaphor endows all genuine human needs and tendencies and all basic patterns of the created natural world with the status of premoral goodness. The category of premoral goodness is especially useful for understanding the relevance of the doctrine of creation for practical reason. The goodness that God the Creator bestows on creation is not directly a moral goodness in the stricter sense of that term. Moral goodness, as I use the term, refers to principles of obligation that mediate between conflicting premoral or nonmoral goods. It is best to interpret the words "God saw everything he had made, and indeed, it was very good" (Gen. 1:25) as assigning premoral goodness, in contrast to a distinctively moral goodness, to the divine handiwork. It means that our fundamental humanness—our thirst, hunger, sexuality, longing for others, desire to create and to build, and need for self-regard and the regard of others—is good in this basic premoral sense. So too are other beings and their needs—the birds, reptiles, fish, animals, and insects of the world. In their own lives and in their needs, they are good. Yet in the abundance of life and the copious needs and wants that exist in all beings there are both the potential and reality of conflict. This conflict requires moral ordering, and giving moral order is a responsibility of humans as moral creatures. This gets to the heart of the dominion or special moral responsibility that humans, under God's guidance, have over creation (Gen. 1:26).

From the standpoint of practical reason, the metaphor of God the good Creator means that all premoral values are assigned a *prima facie* goodness and thereby permitted into deliberation. They receive a voice before the court of practical reason. The doctrine of creation asks practical reason to take seriously into its deliberations the nature that is both inside and outside us as well as the nature intertwined with culture. Practical reason builds on, refines, and tests the myriad of premoral goods whether confronted in their more pristine state or mediated through custom, habit, and tradition.

SPECIAL STATUS OF HUMANS

The metaphor of God as Creator assigns a special status to humans, who are made in God's image. This is generally considered the most fundamental contribution of the Hebrew and Christian narratives to the workings of practical reason. We already have seen how Niebuhr relies on this. We have seen how Basil Mitchell believes that this assumption about the sacredness of humans is more consistent with our moral intuitions about the value of persons than are Kantian assumptions about individuals as rational agents. This suggests that the Judeo-Christian narrative tells practical reason that not only are other people like me, not only are they rational and self-reflective like me, but they are also sacred beings made in the image of God. Therefore, their claims must be taken with equal seriousness to my own. Although the creation narratives add special weight—special sacredness—to the personhood of others, the thickness of my experience of the agency and rationality of others also, as the Kantians insisted (but without invoking radical empiricism), teaches me that they are ends and not means. Hence I learn that others are ends from two sources, but my Christian story gives a deeper meaning and weight to this insight and requires practical reason to take others with even more radical seriousness.

LIMITS OF LIFE

The metaphor of God the Creator informs practical reason about the limits of life. God the Creator creates humans as creatures and not gods. The creation narrative depicts humans as subject to both the rhythms of nature and the limits of finitude and death. All human wants, needs, and tendencies are in some way good in the premoral sense, but not all can be reconciled harmoniously with one another. Natural hierarchies must be respected; some premoral goods coordinate better with a wide range of other goods. Also, the finitude of life prevents us from realizing all our wants and needs. The realities of death require practical reason to deliberate, choose, develop priorities, and resolve conflicts between opposing goods struggling for existence. The doctrine of creation reinforces what practical reason through its radical empirical experience also gradually learns—that the limits of nature and human institutions place constraints on practical reason that it must recognize and accept.

The doctrine of creation informs our image of the constraints of life that the fourth dimension of practical reason must inevitably acknowledge. But the doctrine of creation tells practical reason something that its own radical empirical experience may not discern, that is, that not only does life have limits but these limitations are, in God's inscrutable wisdom, deemed to be good.

PRINCIPLE OF OBLIGATION

The metaphor of God the Governor both reveals and reinforces practical reason's guiding principle of obligation. The Hebraic and Christian doctrine of God reveals and reinforces the element of active impartiality implicit in *agapē* as mutuality in intimate affairs and brotherhood/sisterhood in public life. Both mutuality and sisterhood/brotherhood contain the rational structure of equal regard. To say that they have an inward rational structure—a core, so to speak—is not to say that they are only rational principles; they are living active patterns of human interaction. But these patterns of interaction conform to the rational elements of impartiality, reversibility, and generalizability.

God reveals this principle because throughout both the ancient Hebrew and primitive Christian depictions of God, God's justice and love are everywhere shown to be actively impartial. The wealthy, powerful, beautiful, and talented are no more objects of God's favor than are the poor, despised, and humble. Ronald Green in *Religious Reason* (1978) has shown better than anyone the analogies between the impartiality of practical reason when conceived in Kantian and neo-Kantian terms and God's impartiality as revealed in Scriptures. Both the Hebrew and Christian Scriptures abound with references to God's impartiality. Deuteronomy tells us that "The Lord your God is God of gods and Lord of lords, the great God, mighty and awesome, who is not partial and takes no bribe, who executes justice for the orphan and the widow, and who loves the strangers, providing them food and clothing" (Deut. 10:17-18). In the Sermon on the Mount we are asked to imitate God and love all neighbors impartially, even our enemies. In this we are asked to be like our

"Father in heaven; for he makes his sun rise on the evil and on the good, and sends rain on the righteous and on the unrighteous" (Matt. 5:45).

Although God's love and justice are impartial, they are also active and function to balance and enhance the poor and down-trodden against the injustices of others. This is the proper meaning of God's preferential action for the poor. God does not prefer the poor in any fundamental or ontological sense; if that were so God would work to maintain the poor in their situation of poverty so that God would always have the poor around in order to prefer them. God's preferential action means instead that because God is impartial, God works actively to bring the poor and disadvantaged back to a situation of equal regard and mutuality.

If Green is correct, then God is the perfect exemplification of the impartiality that makes up the inner rational core of practical reason. We saw something like this in Niebuhr's image of God as universal and impartial. This means that God reveals the structure of what I have called the obligational level of practical reason in God's own character and activity.

According to my argument, the direction of our natural ca-pacities for practical reason is also toward the impartiality and universalization of equal regard. As Kohlberg has pointed out, to handle the pressures and conflicts of social experience, practical reason tends to move toward universal impartiality and finds it pro-gressively more adequate. Although the revelation of God's justice in the sacred history of Israel and the Christian narrative reveals the rational core of practical reason, it also reinforces our fragmen-tary, unsteady, yet discernible capacity to discover that rational core in the process of living. It is one thing for practical reason to per-ceive or conceive the structure of equal regard and mutuality; it is another thing to act on it. In the gap between thought and ac-tion, anxiety and the inordinate self-interest of sin raise their ugly heads. But there are other aspects of the Christian narrative that assist practical reason to confront and overcome sin.

CONGRUENCE OF VIRTUE AND HAPPINESS

In the justice embedded in God's character as Governor, God as-sures the eventual congruence of virtue and happiness. In this principle, as is well known, is Kant's answer to the question of the relation of religion to practical reason. Practical reason does not re-quire religion in order to function; Kant thought that this capacity was indigenous to pure practical reason. But as Kant argues in his *Critique of Practical Reason*, God is a postulate of practical reason required to complete the rationality of the categorical imperative ([1788] 1956, 128–30). For Kant, the idea of God aids practical reason in giving grounds for the belief that in the life to come, virtue will indeed be rewarded by happiness.

It should not be surprising to see a similar idea in Niebuhr. Kant himself acknowledges that his concept was consistent with Christianity. Niebuhr repeatedly points out that because of sin, justice and love will never be fully victorious on the plane of history. This is partially the meaning of the Suffering Servant. Although love and justice are never perfectly fulfilled in history, Christians can be sustained by the faith that they are ultimately right and true in God's eyes (R. Niebuhr 1943, 45). The God of the Christian story makes a postulate of practical reason explicit. This God tells practical reason its rationally grounded hopes are well founded. Here the *telos* of practical reason and the promises of the Christian story unite and reinforce each other. This contribution of religion to practical reason detailed by Kant is just one of many that the Christian story makes to a fuller functioning of practical reason. Kant's insight is part of the story, but only a small part.

SENSE OF SECURITY AND FREEDOM

The doctrines of sin, grace, and forgiveness make it possible for practical-reason to become relatively free from the inordinate self-interest and self-justifying maneuvers that typically corrupt and distort practical reason. The very acknowledgment of the reality of sin gives practical reason a tool of self-criticism. It makes it suspicious of its own motives and its own claims to impartiality. But forgiveness and grace liberate the faithful in principle from the inordinate self-interest of sin. The person using practical reason does so out of a new sense of security and a deeper sense of justification before the final measure of all worth and dignity. Although the power of sin still lurks in the background for the Christian who has accepted the forgiveness and grace of God, it has been defeated in principle. The Christian should be both freer and more empowered to exercise undistorted practical reason and live the life of equal regard with family, friends, and the larger public.

ETHIC OF AGAPE

The Christian narrative of the cross adds an element of supererogation to the ethic of *agapē* as equal regard. The story of Jesus' life and ministry; his confrontation with the Pharisees, Sadducees, and Roman authorities; his trial and crucifixion; and the mingling of these historical events with the motifs of the Suffering Servant from Isaiah 53—all these add an element of self-sacrificial love to Christian love as mutuality and equal regard. Although, as I argued, Niebuhr's elevation of sacrificial love over mutuality should be reversed, the demands of the cross do still add a unique element to love as equal regard. Although Niebuhr was wrong to say that self-sacrificial love is the end and goal of the Christian life, he was right to find a definite role for it.

My argument has been that the Christian ethic is not the only ethic that guides practical reason with the principle of equal regard. But the Christian story brings a host of special values to this ethic that may be absent from other expressions of it. Besides the values listed above, this narrative commands the Christian to go the second mile, to make sacrifices to restore a situation of imbalance to equal regard. As Niebuhr and Ricoeur both emphasize, although in different ways, self-sacrifice empowered by grace renews mutuality and equal regard and keeps them from degenerating to simple reciprocity or, even lower, to the talon principle. This is doubtless the unique and definitive contribution of the Christian narrative to the working of the inner core of practical reason.

RELIGION AND DISCOURSE ETHICS

I have claimed that Niebuhr had an embryonic form of what we now call discourse ethics. I have said this for two reasons. First, Niebuhr's basic unit for ethical thinking was not the isolated individual but a community of discourse and mutual criticism. Second, although Niebuhr fully recognized the role that balance of power and compromise play in communal ethical conversations, he believed there was a role for rational moral discourse. The Christian faith supports, criticizes, relativizes, and renews this rational moral discourse. This suggests that Niebuhr would have been open to what Jürgen Habermas has called "the redemption of validity claims" advanced in communities of moral and political deliberation. In my reconstruction of Niebuhr's ethics and my attempt to chart the subrationalities implicit in the larger idea of practical reasoning, I want to make it clearer than he thought necessary how validity claims are redeemed within a Niebuhrian understanding of the Christian narrative. In what follows, I will show how Niebuhr's nascent discourse ethic can be strengthened in light of Habermas's program. In return, I will show how the theologies of Niebuhr and Helmut Peukert contribute to the completion of that program.

HABERMAS'S COMMUNICATIVE ACTION

Jürgen Habermas stands in the tradition of the Frankfurt school and its scholars, Max Horkheimer, Theodor Adorno, Herbert Marcuse, and Walter Benjamin. The Frankfurt school is known for its critiques of logical positivism, its exposure of the illusion of value-free social science, and its synthesis of Marxist theory with psychoanalysis. Horkheimer's and Adorno's critiques of logical positivism, however, did not develop an alternative rationality for social ethics and political science. They criticized brilliantly the dehumanizing narrowing of rationality in the scientific positivisms of the modern era, but they offered no alternative method to guide human moral discourse. Although Habermas builds on their critique of positivism, he offers an alternative rational method for social and moral discourse. Habermas feared that, without such a method, social disputes would be settled increasingly by violence, revolution, power struggles, and appeals to mystifications of various kinds.

Habermas, like the Frankfurt school in general, rejects the claims of logical positivism that the only meaningful statements are those confirmable by appeals to sense experience (Ayer 1946; Habermas 1971, 81–90, 291; White 1988, 25–28). He turned to the study of language in various disciplines to show that there was a much wider way of thinking about meaning. In particular, he turned to the linguistic-analytic philosophy of the later Wittgenstein and the speech-act theories of J. L. Austin. When one analyzes the fullness of immediate face-to-face communication, one realizes that meaningful language has the character of an action that is aimed at producing understanding between the speakers (Habermas 1979, 34–36). Creating such an understanding assumes, according to Habermas, that speakers have three sorts of competence—competencies that make it possible to meet expectations that the speaker can, if required, form sentences and give reasons that will substantiate three kinds of validity claims. (There are four validity claims, but for the sake of clarity I will omit from discussion, as Habermas sometimes does, the claim of comprehensibility.) The capacity to have these competencies and fulfill these validity claims is presupposed by the participants of the communicative act.

What are these three competencies and what are the validity claims that they equip communicators to address? They are to speak the truth, establish normative moral claims, and express oneself authentically (Habermas 1979, 58, 63–64). To speak the truth here means to make factual utterances about things in the world that can be tested by experience. Positivists thought this validity claim exhausted the entire sphere of meaningful statements. To make normative claims means to say things that will help regulate our interpersonal relations. And to express oneself authentically means demonstrating that one is communicating one's true intentions and is therefore trustworthy.

It may, at first glance, seem difficult to believe that all good communicative action assumes that the speakers are competent to say more, if pushed, on all three of these levels. Is this so for the uneducated or the primitive? Habermas believes so. He believes that, insofar as these competencies are lacking, communicative action breaks down. Further, Habermas claims that these competencies are internal obligations, that is, obligations presupposed by the very act of attempting to communicate. They are not imposed from the outside. To try to communicate and create understanding places upon one an obligation to meet these criteria. There is an ethic internal to the process of communication. Habermas calls it a "speech-act immanent *obligation*" (1979, 63–64). This brief statement of Habermas's position allows us to consider three points of possible interaction between his explicit and Niebuhr's implicit theory of discourse ethics.

First, Habermas can help extend Niebuhr's implicit discourse ethic. At first glance, Niebuhr might seem the quintessential antifoundationalist since reason, for him, is always historically situated and distorted by sin. And Habermas may appear as the quintessential foundationalist. But it is best to see Habermas's call for rationality in communication as a goal rather than a foundation for communication to stand on in the beginning. In both Niebuhr and Habermas, it is best to see rationality as extending a sphere of social objectivity or consensus rather than determining absolute objectivities of the kind foundationalists envision.

Second, Habermas himself can be extended by our reconstruction of Niebuhr in terms of the five dimensions of practical reason. It must first be noticed that Habermas does not really have a full theory of practical reasoning. His three validity claims and their related competencies may be assumed in all conversations. But they together do not constitute a theory of practical reasoning. The nearest that Habermas comes to such a theory is the peculiar way he develops his second validity claim—the one pertaining to normative claims that would regulate a community. Here, Habermas is something of a Kantian. He turns to Kant, and the neo-Kantian moral theories of John Rawls and structuralist moral theories of Jean Piaget and Lawrence Kohlberg, to understand what goes into morally competent speech acts. Turning to them does not mean that he accepts any of them without revision. Rather than affirming Kant's categorical imperative as such (or Rawls's theory of justice as fairness or Kohlberg's sixth stage of universalization), Habermas opts for a more procedural formal principle. In one of his more recent statements he says, "Only those norms may claim to be valid that could meet with the consent of all concerned, in their role as participants in a practical discourse" (Habermas 1991). The Kantian principle of generalizability has its meaning for Habermas within this formulation. The right is not just what is generalizable from the perspective of the solitary thinker. The right is what all can agree on who take part in the conversation. In shifting the criterion of generalizability away from Kant's more monological and individualistic formulation to what can receive generalized agreement in the context of free communication, Habermas feels he gives the Kantian formalist perspective a far more interactive meaning. It is a meaning more consistent with what modern social psychology (Mead) and sociology (Durkheim) tell us about the intersubjective character of human existence (White 1988, 83; Habermas 1979, 80–93).

Niebuhr could concur with Habermas in this more dialogical and social reformulation of the Kantian principle. Niebuhr's continued insistence that moral principles can never function abstractly or individualistically but instead emerge from concrete social interaction is certainly close to Habermas's point. This would be an appropriate extension of Niebuhr at my second level of practical moral discourse, an extension that I too feel is constructive.

The difference between Niebuhr and Habermas would be in their handling of basic human interests or what I have called the premoral good. Habermas, unlike Kant, lets human interests come into a discourse ethic. He has a teleological submoment in his discourse ethic, but human interests are tested only by their generalizability or, more specifically, by what the parties in moral dialogue agree can be generalized (Habermas 1979, 90; Habermas 1991). He believes that the parties can never use the subrationalities of practical reason (introspective induction, comparison, or objective empiricism) to discern the more basic and genuine human needs and tendencies beyond their individual self-assertion or communal consensus. Niebuhr admits a limited role for the *ius naturale* in this respect, and I have attempted to spell this out and push it further.

There is throughout Habermas a strange rejection of the idea that empirical reason (his first validity claim) can learn anything about human nature that would be relevant for a discourse ethic. In *The Politics of Social Theory* (1981) Russell Keat pointed out this deficiency in Habermas most tellingly. Habermas, Keat asserts, reduces humans to their linguisticality. In so doing, he divorces them from nature. The kind of study of the nature in human nature that we found in Mary Midgley, George Pugh, and others lacks a place in Habermas's discourse theory. When consensus about conflicting human interests cannot be achieved, there is no recourse to deeper insights concerning which inclinations and interests may be more central (Keat 1981, 84–91). There seems nothing that humans can learn, according to Habermas, about validity claims pertaining to human wants and needs (what Habermas calls validity claims pertaining to expressiveness) other than whether they are sincere, authentic, and reflect the real intentions of the speaker in the speech-act situation. This view deprives a discourse ethic of the possibility of relevant knowledge about human wants and needs. It also deprives it of any method for determining, once superficial agreements are exhausted, how human needs and associated interests relate to the selective power of social and ecological environments (dimension four).

In general, Habermas has not integrated the three validity claims into a workable theory of practical reason. One does not have to be a naive empiricist or realist to believe that relatively adequate descriptions of the regularities of human nature can be achieved and that these descriptions can help stabilize practical reason's efforts to clarify its teleological submoments. For instance, contemporary discussion about whether there is a biosocial substratum to parenting, as Alice Rossi and others have argued, is not meaningless scholarly debate (Rossi 1977, 1–32). One need not claim that such insights can be handled in a culturally neutral way to believe that things can be said for or against these arguments that can stabilize contemporary discussions over the ethics of the family and obligations of child care.

PEUKERT'S RELIGIOUS AMPLIFICATIONS

Helmut Peukert has pointed out that certain presuppositions entailed in Habermas's theory of the "ideal speech situation" require religious amplification. Both Peukert and Niebuhr can help with this amplification. Although the three validity claims are, according to Habermas, immanent obligations of all speech-act situations, he also believes that such situations imply additional assumptions if these three claims are to be satisfactorily redeemed. For people to have an open conversation in which validity claims are freely questioned and defended, what Habermas has called an "ideal speech situation," additional conditions must be met. Conversants must acknowledge that all relevant parties to the conversation have equal voices, must have a sense of solidarity with their conversation partners, and must renounce the use of force and deceit as tools for settling disputes. They must permit the persuasive power of reasons and defended validity claims to determine the consensus (McCarthy 1978, 306-10; Peukert 1984, 184-91). The ideal speech situation even has, as well, a certain attitude toward the future; it suggests that the conversation could in principle include all persons who might someday wish to enter it, make statements, and raise questions. In this it is like C. S. Peirce's "indefinite community of investigators" or Josiah Royce's "community of interpretation" (Peukert 1984, 194; Habermas 1971, 91-113).

Peukert has argued in *Science, Action, and Fundamental Theology* (1984) that these so-called immanent presuppositions and conditions about equality, solidarity, renunciation of force, and openness to the future actually entail transcendental assumptions of a theological kind. The weight of these ideals is simply too great to be carried by the speech situation itself. This is especially true of the ideal of solidarity. Habermas's idea of solidarity cannot, according to Peukert, include the great hordes of people who have unjustly suffered and died in the past. There is a fundamental contradiction, limit, or aporia in Habermas's theory of the ideal speech act: His concept of solidarity and equality excludes those lost to injustice in bygone eras. The entire history of Israel and the story of the early Christian community—especially the resurrection—are directed toward overcoming this limitation in the concept of an ideal speech community. These traditions, Peukert holds, tell of a God of both the living and the dead who, through the resurrection, will bring people of all ages into a community of genuinely free and equal communicative action (216-27).

This extension of solidarity and equality to include both the living and the dead may be seen as a radicalization of transcendental thinking like one finds in the Kantian practical postulate. Peukert, however, develops the idea more with the help of his former teachers Johann Baptist Metz and Karl Rahner. He argues that the Jewish and Christian story about God's universal redemptive activity clarifies and fills out what the immanent obligations of ideal speech logically require. Habermas's ideal speech situation runs into a limit—a limit that is a contradiction. It calls for the inclusion of everyone, but it cannot fulfill what it demands. Without the idea of a God who resurrects the dead, the immanent universalistic trends of the speech-act situation are aborted.

Peukert's point is arresting but overstated. The Judeo-Christian tradition and its narrative, as I have argued, contribute to a discourse ethic. But it goes too far to say that the dead must contribute to the discourse situation. The doctrine of the communion of the saints is important and must be retained, but its relevance for discourse ethics is primarily motivational, not substantive. The image of the unjustly dead motivates us in our discourse to avoid the tragedy of injustice; it gives us a promise and hope of a restored community beyond this life. But the dead themselves cannot figure in the discourse in this life. They cannot be part of the intersubjective principle of generalizability as Habermas describes it. There is no way to include their interests in any generalizable discourse, and there is no way to test the interests of the living in a generalizable situation that includes the dead.

Peukert was the first to state the relevance of the Christian narrative to a discourse ethic. The valid aspect of his argument overlaps with my earlier discussion on the contribution of the Christian narrative to practical reason. My leading point was that this narrative gives additional weight, as Basil Mitchell has insisted, to the more implicit claims of experience about the equality of humans and the need to take them all with equal seriousness. This general Kantian claim, of which Habermas's speech-act obligations are a variation, has a heavier weight when informed by the Christian doctrine of the *imago dei*. Also, our own experiential intuitions, according to Mitchell, cry out for this weightier religious understanding of the status of humans.

But then, as we saw above, there are at least five other ways in which Christian narrative and tradition can inform practical reason in regard to a discourse ethic. Everything I said about the relation of the Christian narrative to practical reason can apply to the intersubjective model of practical reason that Niebuhr hinted at but that Habermas demands. First, we saw how the Christian doctrine of the goodness of creation affirms all basic premoral goods and interests. This provides a meaning situation that permits, even encourages, all parties to bring their interests into the beginning of the conversation although not all will find an equal place at its end. Second, the idea of the creatureliness of humans and the finitude of the world provides a limit to all discourse ethics and all intersubjective generalizability. What can be agreed by all parties must also face the limits of the environment and the central tendencies of human nature. Third, as we saw, the idea of God the Governor reveals and reinforces the impartiality and generalizability of a discourse ethic. Not only are there speech-act immanent obligations in this direction, the nature of God both points to and reinforces them. Fourth, this same justice of God assures the eventual convergence of justice and happiness, if not in this world, then certainly in the next. Fifth, the doctrines of sin, forgiveness, and grace enable Christians to become aware of the distortions of sin, to be freed from these distortions through forgiveness, and to have the grace and power to be renewed in the capacity to pursue more nearly distortion-free communication.

Finally, the Christian narrative of the cross adds an obligation to go the second mile in the communicative situation. This is the point about the Christian narrative that Peukert most completely and sadly overlooks. This is the meaning of the demand for self-sacrificial living that is implicit in love as *agapē*. Although the genuine discourse situation is one of mutuality and equal regard, for moral discourse to be renewed when it breaks down, the symbol of the cross calls for self-sacrifice in order to endure and eventually, with the grace and power of God, restore genuine mutuality. This is what the Christian narrative contributes to a discourse ethic both within and outside the Christian community. This is what the Christian community has to contribute to the common discourse of the secular community. Christians should be freer than most to enter honestly into the statement and redemption of validity claims. They should be able to do this as undistorted communication requires. Neither Habermas nor Peukert supplies what is required to persist in the communicative act when distortion, resistance, frustration, and breakdown occur repeatedly. An account of the immanent obligations, as useful and suggestive as it is, is not sufficient to comprehend how discourse is renewed after turmoil and strife set in. Set within the context of discourse theory, the Christian narrative contributes to freer and less distorted communication as well as its revitalization and renewal.

One last comment about Habermas's inadequate theory of practical reason is in order. Although developing a dialogical and intersubjective theory of impartiality and generalizability is an important step, Habermas has not tied his validity claims into a full theory of practical reason. As we already have seen, Habermas believes claims about our needs cannot be tested by truth claims. In regard to claims about religion that might enter the discourse situation, Habermas says that, at most, they constitute aesthetic statements. He believes that metaphysical discourse is impossible. Consequently, religious and metaphysical claims cannot be tested rationally in the discourse situation (Tracy 1991). Habermas is left contending that claims about truth can apply only to empirical-analytic statements—the statements that so preoccupied logical positivism. They cannot apply to human nature, as we have seen. Nor do they apply to religious statements. Neither can the claims of religion be validated definitively; nor, according to Habermas, can reasons be given for their plausibility. In the end, Habermas severs his discourse theory from any rational discussion of either human nature or the ultimate context of experience. If I am right, practical reason needs concepts about both dimensions of human life—dimensions my theory discusses under the first and third levels of practical reasoning. The theory of the relation of practical reason to religion developed above provides, I contend, for fuller redemption of validity claims than Habermas's theory. And it does this in a manner relevant to the concrete functioning of practical reason.

PART FOUR

STRATEGIC PRACTICAL THEOLOGY

9

RELIGIOUS EDUCATION IN THE CHURCH OF THE COVENANT

T he central question facing the Church of the Covenant has already been stated: When Paul Williams asked the church to extend hospitality to a small group of Salvadoran refugees, he placed a major challenge on its doorstep. To offer this simple gesture of hospitality, the Church of the Covenant had to decide to break the law. It was not an abstract question. It was a question of what this conservative church with its traditional youth ministry would do with this challenge. It was a question about the relation of the requirements of citizenship to the demands of Christian discipleship. How do we reconcile the Christian demand that we offer hospitality to the homeless, the persecuted, and the refugees of this world, and the demand of citizenship to obey the law? More specifically, how do we reconcile discipleship with citizenship when this law has been established in a liberal democracy?

These questions became part of Christian education at the Church of the Covenant. They became part of a process of communal inquiry that involved most of the church. This inquiry was a practical reflective process designed to determine how the congregation should act on this issue. The revised correlational model of practical theology (with its critical hermeneutical underpinnings) can throw light on this educational process. Our research group was interdisciplinary, as was the group that studied the Wiltshire Church. We were convened to think about Christian education— indeed, challenged to think new and creative thoughts, if possible. To give our work concreteness, we decided to study an actual congregation undergoing an educational process. The record of this study can be found in two books, *Education for Citizenship and Discipleship* (Boys 1989b) and *Tensions between Citizenship and Discipleship* (Slater 1989).

The team studying the Church of the Covenant went further than the Wiltshire team in understanding its research as a hermeneutic dialogue. We had sessions where we shared with one another our personal histories and our social locations. We knew that these beginning points would affect what we saw at the Church of the Covenant. But only a few of us took this seriously in our final writings on this church. In the end, we still functioned like Olympian, objective, and basically detached scholars giving the Church of the Covenant little opportunity to confront and challenge our pre-understandings. We were academicians who blended liberal-to-left political philosophies with our various theological convictions. We almost all criticized the Church of the Covenant for not going far enough in dealing with the sanctuary issue. Yet very few of us belonged to sanctuary churches. I belonged to a sanctuary church; I think I was the only one. I left this experience suspecting that it is too easy and too uncostly for academics to hold their political views. They risked little. Some members of the Church of the Covenant risked a lot.

THE PLAY OF HERMENEUTICS

The revised correlational model of practical theology is not just a method imposed on the Christian message. Christianity itself demands it. The analogical correlation of the Christian message with personal and cultural experience is demanded by the interplay between the metaphors of God as Creator and God as Redeemer. The praxis-oriented correlation advocated in these pages is not just a dated vestige of the social gospel movement and liberal theology. We saw it in the neoorthodox theology of Reinhold Niebuhr, who appealed simultaneously to revelation and experience. Although I take the critical moment in theology further than Niebuhr, it was present in his thought. Also, he helps us see how far certain forms of narrative theology—for example, the thought of Stanley Hauerwas and William Willimon in their *Resident Aliens* (1989)—have gone in attempting to remove the Christian gospel from all appeals to experience and rationality and from any commonality with human culture.

The critical correlational model has profound implications for religious education. It is grounded, as we have seen, in a hermeneutical model of understanding that has built within it a strong critical moment. As a model of understanding, it has implications for all educational theory, secular or religious. Its implications for secular education have not been exploited fully. For instance, Gadamer's concept of effective history suggests ways in which all humanistic knowledge can be seen to have a religious dimension. The central monuments of our culture, both Hebrew-Christian and Greco-Roman, have religious dimensions, and their effective history still shapes the horizon of understanding and practice today, even of the secularized.

Furthermore, hermeneutic theory has implications for explicitly Christian education. Christian education too can be seen as a process of understanding. Because understanding, as Gadamer has taught us, is a practical process in which the concern with application is present from the beginning, it is possible to see all Christian education as exhibiting the structure of practical theological thinking. Or to say it more directly, all Christian education should be seen as education in fundamental practical theological reflection and action.

The structure of fundamental practical theology and the structure of Christian education are the same. Christian education, like fundamental practical theology, moves from descriptive theology backward to historical and systematic theology and forward to strategic practical theology. It does this in elementary ways for the young and immature in the faith; it does it in increasingly complex ways for the older and more mature in the faith.

All Christian education, like all practical theology, takes place in communities of faith, inquiry, and action. Like practical theology, Christian education should first describe the questions that emerge from the situated praxis of a Christian community and other communities with which it has dialogue. Christian education then takes these questions back to the classic sources of Christian ideals and norms. This sets up a *play* between question and text, a to-and-fro process of questioning the text, listening to the text, and being questioned by the text. As the practical educational process becomes more serious (more like work), it tries to gain a more systematic and critical grasp of both situated practice and text. Finally, the educational process returns to the concrete problems that stimulated the practical reflective process in the beginning. This last step is parallel to the moment I call strategic practical theology.

RELIGIOUS AND CHRISTIAN EDUCATION

Both the religious educator and the Christian educator are stimulators, guides, coaches, and to some extent umpires of this communal inquiry. The religious educator helps the civil community understand how the religious dimension of effective history has shaped its culture, institutions, and personal sensibilities. There is a great need for religious education in this sense. Public schools at all levels should employ experts in religious education. Their task should be to help craft a civil religion that will provide the larger framework of meanings required for democratic institutions. In addition, they should develop a critical understanding of the religious and philosophical sources of these institutions. What has been said about the relevance of hermeneutics to the humanities and social sciences suggests that religious education in this sense should be supported more vigorously than in the past. If Gadamer, Bellah, Hekman, and others are right that the modern academic disciplines have hermeneutical foundations, this has profound implications for the role of religious inquiry in all our academic inquiries and socializations. Since the model of hermeneutics I propose contains a strong critical moment, socialization into the civil religion of democratic institutions should be a critical socialization. The idea of a critical socialization is not an oxymoron. It simply entails an appreciative and critical inquiry into the values, meanings, and symbols in which we are already embedded.

In Western societies there must always be a vital link between religious education and Christian education. There must be a significant link between education for Christian *discipleship* and education for *citizenship* in democratic republics. The goal of Christian education is discipleship. The goal of religious education is citizenship. The task of religious education is not to produce Christians as such. It is not primarily a confessional and ecclesial task. The goal of religious education is to examine the resources of the classic religious and philosophical monuments for what they contribute to deepening skills in democratic citizenship. Indeed, religious education can examine the contributions to citizenship of other religious traditions as well.

Religious education in this sense is no substitute for confessionally oriented education and socialization. Religious education is no substitute for Christian education, or Jewish education, or Hindu education. Although religious education can take no responsibility for making us better Christians, Jews, or Hindus, Christian education does have the twofold task of making us both better disciples *and* better citizens. One great challenge of our time is to help Christians know how to be simultaneously Christian *disciples* and *citizens* in democratic liberal societies.

To know how to relate discipleship and citizenship, however, is also to distinguish them. Stanley Hauerwas, more than any other theologian of our time, has emphatically insisted that Christian discipleship and liberal democratic citizenship are not identical. Some liberal Christians find this increasingly difficult to understand (Hauerwas 1975b, 410–11; 1981, 11). The temptation to reduce

Christianity to the civil religion of democratic liberalism remains strong. In spite of this costly confusion, I claim Christian education has the task of educating for both discipleship and citizenship while helping people understand the distinction between the two. What I did in chapter 8 in relating Christian narrative to practical reason should help with this twofold task. It will help us relate yet distinguish discipleship and citizenship in Christian education.

MODELS OF CHRISTIAN EDUCATION

Critical hermeneutics is another term for the revised correlational method. Critical hermeneutics blends the practical philosophies of Gadamer and Habermas. It follows Gadamer in affirming the situated, historical, and dialogical nature of practical understanding. It follows Habermas in affirming that understanding requires a critical moment when people advance reasons in support of their validity claims. In their famous debate (McCarthy 1978, 187-93), Gadamer is convincing at the level of overall framework. Habermas, reworked by my five levels, provides a much needed critical moment. Understanding can develop both within specific traditions and between traditions because, as David Tracy has shown, people have the capacity for analogical imagination (Tracy 1981, 405-38). They can move toward understanding and consensus not because they start from agreement but because they see analogies between what they and others are saying. These analogies can constitute the grounds for arguments and reasons that people can understand across traditions. People especially can see analogies between the ways they observe the natural structures of the world—what I have called the naturalistic moment of ethical deliberation.

There are various contemporary approaches to Christian education. Christian education, as a subdiscipline of strategic practical theology, has a history. The cutting edge of my proposal will be advanced if I make a few broad comments about the history of religious education in the United States. Mary Boys has twice offered helpful sketches of the historical development of Christian education (Boys 1989a; 1989b, 98-129). In two books Jack Seymour and Donald Miller have developed topologies of contemporary options (Seymour and Miller 1982, 1990).

Boys believes Christian education in the United States has four classic expressions. Each has received older and more recent reformulations. The *evangelistic* approach emphasizes conversion and assumes a sharp distinction between the natural and the supernatural, the sacred and the secular. The critical hermeneutical model does not disvalue conversion and transformation. Learning

to confront the manifestations of truth in the classic witness should
lead to transformation. But transformation and conversion do not
necessarily have the emotional qualities associated with revivalism.
Transformation comes from the to-and-fro play between our questions thickly understood and the manifestation of truth contained
in the classic texts.

What Boys calls the *religious education* model emerged early in
this century and was influenced strongly by the progressive educational philosophies of John Dewey and George Albert Coe. This
view had a practice-theory-practice model of knowledge close to
what I advocate. Like my model, it assumed that religious education
should transform society. But it did not take the Christian classics
as seriously as the critical hermeneutical model. On the whole, it
reduced Christian discipleship to liberal democratic citizenship. It
was education for the civil religion of democratic liberalism. It was
close to what I earlier called religious education, but it differed.
The older religious education model tried to dominate the entire
field of Christian education; I, however, distinguish between religious and Christian education and place my emphasis in this book
on the latter.

Boys's third type, *Christian education*, takes the Christian classics more seriously than did the religious education model. Steeped
as it was in a watered-down neoorthodoxy, it failed, from my perspective, to take the moment of descriptive theology seriously. It
functioned out of a theory-to-practice model.

Finally, Boys describes the *Catholic catechetical* approach with
its strong emphasis on instruction in religious and moral beliefs.
Education in the religious and moral beliefs of the faith can definitely be a part of the critical hermeneutical approach to Christian
education. Such learnings would come as a smaller moment within
a larger practice-theory-practice circle. Along such a circle specific
Christian beliefs about faith and morals would be confronted within
a situated description of the ongoing practices to be reconstructed
and revitalized.

Seymour and Miller develop an alternative typology. Their interests are less historical. They deal more with present options in
the professional field of Christian education. Their categories and
those of Mary Boys overlap somewhat. For instance, they speak of
an *instructional* approach to Christian education, an approach that
has similarities with Boys's catechetical approach. Their other four
types are more distinguishable from Boys's. They speak of the *faith
community* approach, which emphasizes education as a process of
socialization within the life of the ongoing Christian community.
C. Ellis Nelson and John Westerhoff are the foremost representa-

tives of this view. More recently Robert Browning and Roy Reed have added a strong new voice on the role of liturgy in Christian education (Browning and Reed 1985). In this view, liturgy and the full experience of Christian living in the "intentional, covenantal, tradition-bearing faith community" become very important (Seymour and Miller 1982, 21). As we will see, the critical hermeneutical approach also has a strong place for socialization. It acknowledges that all education begins in particular communities. Both the community of faith approach and the critical hermeneutical approach are Aristotelian in this sense. But the community of faith approach seems not to envision either the need for or the possibility of developing a critical reflective praxis of the kind I am advocating.

Miller and Seymour speak of a *developmental* approach that relies heavily on the contributions of Piaget, Erikson, Kohlberg, Gilligan, and Fowler. This perspective also would be included within a revised correlational and critical hermeneutical model. This attempt to grasp the naturalistic timetables and structures of human development would have a status something analogous to the naturalistic moment in Christian ethical reflection. The developmental perspective can play a role in stabilizing our understanding of some regularities of human development, regularities that work themselves out uniquely in different communities and traditions. That perspective, however, can never stand alone but must be situated in traditions. The developmental perspective can never tell, all by itself, what it means to become a Christian disciple. Nor, for that matter, can it give a full account of citizenship. At best, the developmental perspective helps us understand the interrelations, tensions, and complementarities between our natural developmental structures and the historical transformative processes of becoming a Christian and becoming a citizen.

The last two perspectives discussed by Seymour and Miller are the *liberation* and *interpretation* approaches. They are very similar. The liberation approach builds on the theories of Paulo Freire (Freire 1970). Thomas Groome best exemplifies the interpretation approach. Both perspectives are very similar to the revised correlational or critical hermeneutical approach I propose. Both emphasize a practice-theory-practice model of reflection. Both make the practical life of the Christian the center of education, not doctrine or church teachings as such. Both relate tradition to a process of social transformation.

Groome's ground-breaking *Christian Religious Education* (1980) combines most of the features of both the liberation and interpretation perspectives. His book is one of the most important contributions to religious education in several decades. His position is close to mine, but differs in many ways. So his work is a fit subject for special review. A critique of this fine book and some of his subsequent writings will convey more fully what the critical hermeneutical approach offers to Christian education.

SHARED PRAXIS AND CRITICAL HERMENEUTICS

Groome's position is a practical theological approach to Christian religious education. This was implicit in his *Christian Religious Education*, but it has become explicit in his more recent writings. Increasingly his writings on Christian education have become a general critique of how theology is done and taught. Groome is critical of the theory-to-practice model in which theology and theological education seem trapped. He calls it a "trickle-down" process by which theologians at the top hope that their theological knowledge will "spill over on the baptized but non-theologically trained Christian below" (Groome 1987, 57). For Groome, as for me, the structure of theological reflection and the dynamics of Christian education should be the same. Doing theology and doing Christian education entail the same procedures. What students learn in theology courses and what they learn in religious education courses should have a striking continuity. Both should have continuity with what Christian educators do in churches and other contexts. Doing and teaching theology in all these settings should follow a practice-theory-practice model.

Groome joins a growing number of religious educators who place their theories of Christian education within a framework of practical theology (Fowler 1983; Miller 1987; Westerhoff 1983). But they often exhibit slightly different emphases in their understanding of practical theology. The tensions between the cultural-linguistic or narrative approach and the revised correlational approach to practical theology can be seen in the debates in Christian education. For instance, Westerhoff tends more toward the cultural-linguistic and Miller more toward the correlational approach. Fowler stands somewhere between. Even Miller does not go as far as he should, from my standpoint, in facing the need for a fully critical moment within the correlational approach. Nor does Groome. To economize space, I confine my remarks to Groome's complex and forcefully stated position.

Groome calls his educational methodology the "shared praxis" approach. In using the word *shared*, he puts himself in the company of Peirce, Royce, and Habermas in attempting to go beyond monological models of practical thinking. Christian education is education for the praxis of the Christian life and is education in a communal or shared context for life and reflection with other Christians. This shared praxis takes place in a situation of group dialogue. It is a matter of critical reflection on the shared Christian practices of that group. It is the critical reflection on present shared practices that makes this dialogue an intentional educational process (Groome 1980, 184).

Groome believes this critical reflection includes five movements. They closely parallel the four movements of fundamental practical theology that I introduced in chapter 2. In an essay Groome lists the five movements as: (1) expressing present praxis; (2) critical reflection on present praxis; (3) making accessible the Christian Story and Vision (Groome capitalizes *Story* and *Vision* in relation to Christianity to emphasize their normative claims and to distinguish them from the stories and visions implicit in our various communal practices); (4) a dialectical hermeneutic between present praxis and interpretations of the Christian Story and Vision; and (5) decision and response for renewed Christian praxis (Groome 1989, 89–90).

I can best show the meaning of these five movements by comparing them with the four movements of a fundamental practical theology that I claim are the key to both theology and Christian education. Groome's movements one and two are similar to what I have called descriptive theology. His movements three and four are analogous to what I have called respectively historical and systematic theology. His movement five is similar to what I have called strategic practical theology. The entire process is practical through and through. To recognize this, I call the entire range of movements a fundamental practical theology. Groome, in recent writings, now offers his model of Christian education as comprehending all theological reflection. My pilgrimage is just the reverse. Although I offered my four movements of a fundamental practical theology at the beginning of this book as a model for all theological reflection, it is now being offered as a model of religious and Christian education as well. Despite the different directions we are moving, we are on the same track.

Groome's model is similar in several ways to the one I propose. First, Groome's method is hermeneutical in the Gadamerian sense of that term. This is true though Groome has not to date discussed extensively either Gadamer or hermeneutics. He speaks of his fourth movement as a dialectical hermeneutic between descriptions of our present practices (and the stories and visions implicit in them) and the normative claims of the Christian Story and Vision.

Although Groome's perspective is implicitly hermeneutical, he does not use Gadamer's central point that *phronēsis* is a model for hermeneutics—a crucial point for my appropriation of Gadamer. Nor does he use Gadamer's concepts of effective history, dialogue as play, and meaning as fusion of horizons.

Second, Groome's view of education assumes a revised correlational model of theology. This is partially what is meant by his idea of a dialectical hermeneutic between present praxis and the Christian Story and Vision. Because of the strong emphasis on beginning and ending in praxis, it is really a praxis correlational model in the way Lamb, Chopp, and I have reworked Tracy. Groome in his 1980 book gave passing acknowledgment to the similarities of his position to Tracy's (232). In his 1987 article titled "Theology on Our Feet," he says this more directly: "While my own genesis in this approach was not initially influenced by Tracy's work . . . , I certainly found it affirming and clarifying when I encountered it" (78).

Besides being hermeneutical and correlational, Groome's approach also champions a critical moment in his educational theory. He emphasizes critical reflection throughout his writing. Groome affirms, yet goes beyond, a confessional stance in theology and a socialization stance in educational methodology. He is fully aware that faith first emerges out of the confessional stance of the worshiping, believing, and practicing religious community, as C. Ellis Nelson (1971, 1989), John Westerhoff (1983), and Craig Dykstra (1981) have insisted. But he also believes that Christian maturity within the conflicting perspectives of a pluralistic society requires submitting faith's confessional beginnings to critical reflection. Groome is not clear what he means by critical reflection but speaks of critiquing the Christian Story in light of our personal stories and critiquing our personal stories in light of the Christian Story (1980, 217).

This suggests a critical conversation, of the kind Tracy has in mind, between interpretations of our present practices and interpretations of the normative Christian Story. But Groome's view of critical reflection is more modest than Tracy's. It is both more cautious and less fully worked out than is needed for a revised correlational perspective. Groome spends little time developing a critical method that would guide this critical process responsibly. Groome's idea of critique seems to have several meanings. Sometimes it refers to how the gospel can critique our lives. Sometimes it refers to an ideology critique that would remove faulty and distorted interpretations of the gospel. Sometimes it is a limited critique of the Christian Story that would dispense with certain unessential practices and beliefs at the "lower echelon of the 'hierarchy of truths.'" But Groome cannot imagine an educational process where critical reflection might end in "total discontinuity with the previous tradition and with the primordial revelation on which Christianity rests" (1980, 199). Yet this is the risk that a fully critical educational process is willing to take. In a fully critical practical theology, the openness of the discussion must be established in principle.

Although few conversations push to the limit the validity claims that can be raised at any of the five levels of practical reason, the possibility of carrying the conversation that far must always be allowed. Communities of critical practical conversation (shared praxis groups), both in the church and outside the church, must be open to an indefinite process of critique. In spite of the situated and confessional nature of beginning points, progress can be made in bits and pieces as we struggle to give reasons for what first comes to us in faith. Groome does not carry the idea of critical reflection as far as I recommend.

Groome has not developed the critical element sufficiently because he has not, to date, considered adequately the theological ethical method that should guide reflection in a shared praxis situation. Although most Christian education will not discuss the two forms of theological ethics I have identified in these pages, these moments are present nonetheless in embryonic form. They must be brought out and made explicit when the complexity of the issue demands it. Groome is willing to face this and has some important things to say about it. But he does not go far enough.

At one point he gives us three principles to guide the ethical dimensions of a shared praxis dialogue—"consequences, continuity, and community/church" (1980, 198). What do these principles mean and how far do they carry us? By *consequences*, he means whether a particular praxis contributes to the coming of the kingdom. This, it must be admitted, would be difficult to determine unless one has a more precise definition of the love and justice of the kingdom than Groome advances. In saying this, I admit readily that Groome's *Christian Religious Education* contains splendid discussions of the meaning of the kingdom of God (1980, 35–51). But within these discussions, he does not set forth more refined accounts of the ethical meaning of the love and justice of the kingdom. It is not clear whether Groome's concept of justice moves toward teleological or more strictly deontological perspectives. Clearly the kingdom is seen as a realm for the fulfillment of all "authentic yearnings of the human heart and the needs of humankind" (1980, 37). But whether Groome interprets this as a situation ethic, a utilitarian ethic, or as some mixed deontological principle of the kind advanced by Frankena, Ricoeur, and my own reconstruction of Niebuhr is not clear. Without a clearer understanding of justice than Groome provides, his emphasis on consequences that promote the kingdom would leave, I fear, his shared praxis groups afloat.

By *continuity* Groome means that decisions "made by people in a shared praxis group must be in continuity with the Story of the Christian community before them" (1980, 198). Again, without more discussion of the central ethical meaning of the kingdom, one lacks the criteria to determine continuity. One would lack also a critical method for determining whether what was continuous with the central witness of the tradition is also humanly and ethically justifiable.

Finally, by *community/church* Groome means that decisions guided by the Holy Spirit will be sounder than those made without this communally shared guidance (1980, 198). How would Groome know that such decisions are wiser unless they are consistent with some understanding of the basic ethical principles implicit within the work of the Spirit? Although the meaning of any ethical principle varies depending on the questions brought to it, there is a moment within practical reflection when the reigning ethical principles must be, as Habermas would say, redeemed. This is true even if the principle is, like Habermas's principle of generalizability, basically the formal character of communicative action itself. The point is that these three criteria cannot themselves guide praxis; they assume criteria for the redemption of validity claims that Groome has not provided.

This is especially important for the transition from discipleship to citizenship. When Christians speak among themselves they often intuit the moral meanings of their narratives without making explicit their validity claims. But when Christians speak as citizens with the desire to inform citizenship with discipleship, they must become explicit about their Christian ethics in ways that Groome has not addressed fully. In his brief discussion of the famous debate between Gadamer and Habermas, Groome sides with Gadamer (Groome 1980, 174, 182, 203-4). I agree. The critical redemption of validity claims cannot proceed autonomously from tradition. The reverse is also true; the redemption of validity claims occurs within and helps extend our tradition-saturated and theory-laden practical reflection. But the five levels of practical reason are precisely an internal diagnostic of the claims that tradition-informed reason puts forward. These levels help detect these claims and offer modest ways for testing them. Groome can retain his preference for Gadamer and still take steps toward Habermas. Bernstein is right; the worlds of situated tradition and reasoned claims are not diametrically opposed. Our reasons always begin with tradition, and their claims beyond this beginning are humble and limited. Yet these reasons can make a difference in our conversations.

DESCRIPTIVE THEOLOGY

Descriptive theology begins with questions about present practices, the symbols and legitimations of these practices, and challenges to these practices. I will concentrate here primarily on educational practices. I will be concerned with the ecology of education that shaped the life of the Church of the Covenant. This concept, first put forth by Lawrence Cremin in his *Public Education* (1976), became very important for our research team. It is a broader concept than Groome's shared praxis. Groome's concept applies to a discernible and intentional group with specific boundaries—a group where the individuals are in dialogue with one another. I agree—this is the heart of Christian education. Such groups have analogies to Habermas's community of discourse in an ideal speech situation.

But the idea of an ecology of education is broader. It includes intentional and bounded groups, but it involves more. It includes the full range of influencing institutions and messages as they interact to shape the mind of a community and its individuals. In the case of the Church of the Covenant, the ecology of education includes the educational influences of the church, the news media, the public schools, the neighboring institutions of higher education, the family, and the various diffuse forms of public opinion. It entails all these as they interact over time. The task of shared praxis groups would be to interact with this ecology of education with as much critical intentionality as possible.

In the description that follows I will let the five dimensions loosely guide my description. Because in real life we do not have time to follow any grid in a lock-step fashion, I will try not to do it here. Paul Williams is described as a conservative Republican businessman. When he spoke at the congregational retreat, he was speaking to people like himself—they were conservative, largely Republican, midwestern, Presbyterian, and had considerable civic pride and interest. When he phoned the church asking that it provide hospitality to a group of touring Salvadoran refugees, the session of the church referred the touchy issue to the mission committee.

When the members of the committee began assessing the situation of the church in light of this challenge, they described some things explicitly and others were implied—the latter were known and felt but tucked away in the back of their minds. The two most prominent members of the committee were women—the chair, Nan Carr, and Hilda Mann. Nan was a somewhat new member of the congregation and a wife, mother, nurse, teacher of nurses, and graduate student. Hilda was a long-time, but somewhat lapsed, member who was also a wife, mother, professor at a nearby university, and graduate student concentrating on both Latin American and Reformation studies. She returned to the church primarily because Nan invited her to be a member of the mission committee. It was a way to give her academic studies some concrete focus.

Nan and Hilda were clearly the dominant actors on the sanctuary issue, but not without much existential search and agony between them. Nan and Hilda had long telephone conversations with one another. Both had politically conservative parents. They were aware that the Church of the Covenant was conservative and traditional. They knew that offering sanctuary to undocumented persons would be breaking the law. They wondered whether they were prepared to pay the price (Slater 1989, 6).

The conservatism of the church and their own histories were uppermost in their minds. When the Church of the Covenant, a few months later, did become a sanctuary church, an NBC national news team descended on Centerville to cover the story. John Hart on the evening news played the contrast between the church's image and its sanctuary action for all it was worth: "If there is a true-blue America, it is here on Federal Street in Centerville, population thirty-thousand, politics conservative, old houses, old values, safe for kids, a church town. If there is a mainline establishment church here in true-blue America, it is the Church of the Covenant, 133 years old" (Bass 1989, 27). The conservatism was mainline Presbyterian, not fundamentalist. The church was conservative in the sense of conserving tradition; it was not reactionary. In the early days, the church had formed an easy relation with the town government and the school system, providing many early leaders of both. Little effort was required to achieve congruence between the values of the church and the values of the wider civic life. This was especially true with regard to the education in the church and the education in the public schools. Dorothy Bass, who studied the community's history in some detail, reports that this ecology of mutually supporting and overlapping educational spheres endured well into this century. The tensions between citizenship and discipleship were minimal. To be a good Presbyterian was to be a good, loyal, law-abiding, and probably entrepreneurial citizen. The church and the town grew in size and prosperity together.

In the earlier days, Christian education was an important part of the church's life. But the educational programs deteriorated during the tenure of two social-activist ministers in the 1960s. One was forced to resign after participating in the March on Washington with Martin Luther King, Jr. The minister who followed resigned after a short time as well. The church's school programs and the youth programs became almost nonexistent during this period, or at least that is the way things are remembered. The present minister places great emphasis on a ministry to youth. Approximately 150 youth meet each Thursday for dinner and a program. But the adult education program is emphasized as well.

In many ways, the Wiltshire Methodist Church and the Presbyterian Church of the Covenant are embedded in the same convergence of liberal democracy and technical rationality. Wiltshire was at the top of this system socio-economically; the Church of the Covenant was plugged into the middle. Both groups of people struggled to hold the various components of their lives together—they especially struggled to bring together their private domestic lives and their jobs and vocations. Covenant was doing a better job than Wiltshire. Wiltshire people commuted to the high-tech, financial, and insurance industries of Springfield. Centerville, although less of a bedroom community, was beginning to feel the strains of an increasingly decentralized life. While Covenant debated the sanctuary issue, it also was making plans to leave its magisterial, grey-stone building in the center of the town and build a new church at its edge. Technical rationality was present in Centerville and fed by the middle-class drive toward an increasingly comfortable private life. Both Wiltshire and Covenant tried to hold together the lives of their people through programs for children and youth. A worthy cause, but is there more?

The practices that had been historically important at Covenant were not the only *practices* the mission committee needed to understand. Covenant's history of practices was more or less tacit. These practices were Covenant's ominous and assumed background that we onlookers needed to make explicit but that were implicit in the very bones of the congregation. The mission committee also was interested in the practices of the government of El Salvador, its armed forces, and the revolutionaries. It was also interested in the practices of the United States government, its Immigration and Naturalization Service, and its response to the sanctuary movement throughout the nation. In looking at this larger context of practices, in collecting information, reading, consulting, and conversing, the mission committee rather rapidly made a judgment about several aspects of these practices. It concluded that there were refugees who legitimately feared that if they were returned to El Salvador their lives would be endangered by death squads and irrational Central American governmental forces; that these refugees were appealing to become political refugees in the United States; and that the Immigration and Naturalization Service contradicted its own legal framework and certain established international traditions in refusing them this status. Also, the committee recognized that it must handle these issues within the conservative political traditions and practices of Centerville. Finally, it became painfully aware of the severe penalties, entailing imprisonment and fines, that the law had decreed should fall on those who house or transport illegal aliens.

All these realities need to be included in the description of practices impinging on the sanctuary issue at the Church of the Covenant. These realities created a situation in which addressing this issue entailed potential costs to the committee members—costs of being suspected of radical and traitorous acts and costs of possible imprisonment and humiliation. These consequences raised the question of the cost of discipleship and its relation to citizenship.

The committee members also analyzed the human *needs* at stake. This showed up in their first official report to the session of the church. The committee wrote, "We do believe that all people have the right to live without fear of torture, persecution, or murder. We recognize that there are people in Central America as well as other parts of the world who exist under the constant threat of torture, persecution, and murder" (Slater 1989, 6). The needs recognized in this paragraph are basic—to live, to avoid pain and torture. There may be a wide range of other primary and secondary needs that bear on decisions regarding various other associated problems. Some of these—such as food, clothing, shelter, and employment—were recognized and dealt with when the refugee group (Rosa, Oscar, and Juan) arrived at the church. The needs mentioned in this report are basic because all other human needs depend upon them. Something very fundamental is at stake for these refugees— life. The desire, need, and tendency to live are deemed so basic that they are almost universally acknowledged as a right, a right that can be given theological justification, although the committee did not attempt to provide it. Here, as always, the committee's descriptive theology anticipated normative ideas about both discipleship and citizenship. Description is never neutral.

Practices are always theory-laden. The description of practices is theory-laden as well. This raises questions about the *obligational* and *visional* levels behind the various practices. The Church of the Covenant, being Presbyterian, doubtless heard in its early days many sermons on the sovereignty of God and God's free election of those to be saved. Most doubtless interpreted membership in the Presbyterian church as a sign of their salvation. If Max Weber's analysis of the Reformed tradition is correct, they probably interpreted their success in the secular sphere as further evidence of election. At the unconscious semiotic level, for most Presbyterians in the nineteenth century, to be Presbyterian was to be elected for salvation in both the sacred and secular realms. Education was important in both realms; it equipped one to know the will of God in the sacred realm and to have the skills for financial success and effective citizenship in the secular realm. That was why there was such an intimate bond between citizenship and discipleship in Centerville. It was a bond made all the more easy by the manageable size of the town. It was precisely this bond that threatened to break apart in the sanctuary case. For the first time in the history of the church, discipleship could lead to what some might call bad citizenship, to being called a traitor, to imprisonment, to financial and social ruin. The Constantinian identity between discipleship and citizenship could collapse.

In contrast to the 1970s with its emphasis on social action, Hal Roberts's sermons had emphasized more classic Christian themes. In recent years, the dialectic of law and gospel had become central to his preaching. He seldom addressed concrete social issues; the obligations of social justice were not emphasized. He declined to preach on the sanctuary issue but allowed his associate, Carl Gordon, to carry that assignment. Roberts never took a public stand for or against Covenant becoming a sanctuary church. Perhaps he thought the new pluralism that marked both Centerville and Covenant required the minister to be the host and referee of an open conversation rather than its chief participant. Hal Roberts permitted, even encouraged, the hermeneutical conversation that emerged at Covenant. He only indirectly participated in it. His constant attention to the law-gospel dialectic served as a cushion to the tensions of the dialogue. His message implied that winners of debates are not justified before God by winning and losers do not lose their justification when defeated. We will soon see that Hal Roberts's sermons made a unique contribution to how Covenant saw the relation of the Christian narrative to practical reason. But they did not provide the entire model of how this narrative relates to *phronēsis*. Other parts of the congregation contributed as well. Roberts's law-gospel dialectic freed Nan and Hilda to ask good questions and recognize there was a problem to be faced. But this dialectic provided no immediate answers. Answers came from other parts of the Christian narrative and other parts of practical reason.

HISTORICAL AND SYSTEMATIC THEOLOGY

It may sound pretentious to refer to the historical and systematic theological moments of Christian education in a local church. But historical and systematic theologies are simple analogues to Groome's third and fourth movements. When we recall this, my claim sounds more reasonable. I propose that to describe present action in the thick way leads a community to ask not only, What are we doing? but also What should we do? and What are the ideals that should guide us? It says: "These *appear* to be the ideals that guide us, but what do we *really* believe and what *really* is the meaning of our beliefs?" When one asks these questions, the educational process truly begins.

In Christian education, such practical questions lead one to confront afresh the classic texts, events, and monuments of the faith, both Hebrew and Christian. These are the submoments of historical and systematic theology. Can we see something like this process happening at the Church of the Covenant? I think that we can. Although we can interpret any text in terms of all five levels of practical moral thinking, because our social and ecological contexts are so different from those of the classic texts, we primarily gain from these texts orientation at the visional and obligational levels. In the paragraphs that follow, I will confine my discussion to these two dimensions.

THE OBLIGATIONAL LEVEL

Our research team gave considerable attention to the textuality of the Covenant Church. Textuality refers to the Scriptures, books, works of art, and other resources chosen to show what the classic Vision and Story, as Groome says, really mean. Because application, as Gadamer claims, guides interpretation from the beginning, we can see immediately the practical nature of this historical and systematic task. The entire educational task is an act of *phronēsis*, an act of practical historical reconstruction.

Walter Brueggemann was a member of our team. In an essay titled "Textuality in the Church" (1989), he makes two important observations about Covenant's hermeneutical retrieval of its classic texts. First, he says only a few biblical selections were used in discussing sanctuary. Second, the textuality was two-tiered; the wider congregation used one group of texts and a vigorous lay leadership another.

The texts that stimulated the sanctuary discussion were popular and used widely throughout the congregation. They were texts pertaining to loving the neighbor as the self and the parable of the Good Samaritan. Paul Williams used them both at the church retreat. Slater writes about that retreat, "Williams shared his belief that the church that is not involved in loving its neighbor by reaching out to the world is not really the church" (Slater 1989, 3). He also told the story of the Good Samaritan as an example of neighbor love. A good neighbor and good Samaritan would offer sanctuary to homeless and fleeing Salvadoran refugees. A good neighbor would treat refugees as he or she would want to be treated. Brueggemann calls this level of textuality important but also *thin*. He feels it promotes neighborliness within the limits of conventionally defined law and good manners.

But there was a second level of textuality informing the Covenant discussions. It included the textuality used in Carl Gordon's sermon (the only sermon that ever addressed the sanctuary issue) on Matthew 2:12, a passage about the "civil disobedience of the wise men who went home another way and so protected the child, and about the sanctuary offered the holy family in Egypt" (Brueggemann 1989, 53). Beyond this, there was the textuality that informed Nan Carr and Hilda Mann, the real leaders of the moral conversation at Covenant. This included the enigmatic injunction to "give to the emperor the things that are the emperor's" (Mark 12:13-17), the difficult teaching of obedience to authority in Romans 13, and the call in the Sermon on the Mount to be willing to endure persecution for "righteousness' sake" (Matt. 5:10). Brueggemann believes "these texts invite a seriousness and dangerousness in faithful obedience that the first two texts popularly interpreted do not." Finally, Dietrich Bonhoeffer's *The Cost of Discipleship* deeply impressed the mission committee. This text gave Nan and Hilda a new understanding of the law-gospel tension. It led them to see law not just as God's ordained rules but as the conventional wisdom of governmental powers that kept suffering refugees from haven in our country. It led them to see some forms of law as the governmental policies that forced these refugees to flee their homeland. Bonhoeffer's book led them to understand discipleship as entailing the sacrifice of defying such laws and extending hospitality.

Brueggemann believes that this second level of textuality, used primarily by an inner group of leaders, extended and deepened the blander textuality that consisted of the neighbor love passages and the parable of the Good Samaritan. It provided the real motivating power that led the rest of the congregation to its final courageous vote on sanctuary. It was this second set of texts that opened the possibility of real sacrificial discipleship—a hospitality and neighbor love that are willing to pay a price.

Brueggemann's analysis is helpful. There were indeed levels of textuality at Covenant just as there were levels of leadership. These levels of textuality and leadership play out different parts of the fullness of *phronēsis*. At first, Nan and Hilda were as afraid to break the civil law in the name of discipleship as the rest of the congregation. In confronting the "*eyewitness accounts of human suf-*

fering" from Paul Williams and doing fresh hermeneutical work on the biblical tradition, a *theological conversion* was wrought in the lives of these two women (Brueggemann 1989, 62–63). The conversion came by bringing the questions emerging from unjust suffering to these different levels of textuality. It came from asking, What do these classic texts that were a part of our effective history *really* say when confronted as honestly as possible? That a conversion occurred when the truth of these texts was manifested can hardly be doubted. The meaning that emerged was a *fusion of horizons* between the practical questions of the committee and the witness of these texts. In its own way, the congregation was enacting the movements of historical and systematic theology within a wider practical theological task.

These moments of historical and systematic theology occurred in rapid succession yet were distinguishable. More careful work could have been done. Had the people of Covenant had the command of biblical textuality that we will find at the Apostolic Church of God, a more extensive confrontation with Scripture could have occurred. Even without this some features of systematic theology in the more formal sense were considered. Brueggemann points out that more could have been done with both the general and contextual aspects of the parable of the Good Samaritan. Although its concrete historical context is the conflict between Jews and Samaritans, it opens up the more general issue of the conflict between insiders and outsiders, the ritually acceptable and ritually impure. Systematic theology, in the formal sense of the term, deals with these general themes. Because the themes are general, a text that first deals with the tensions between Jews and Samaritans can be related to the sanctuary issue. Told by Jesus to show that the Samaritan was really the neighbor, it can be retold by Paul Williams to show that the neighbor is also anyone genuinely in need, including undocumented Salvadoran refugees.

All this occurred quickly in the course of pressured discussions, but it covered the rudiments of systematic theological reflection. Note that an applicational concern guided the historical task of interpreting Scriptures; it was hermeneutically conceived historical theology. The meaning of the text was not taken as a thing-in-itself isolated from the questions brought to it. Yet these texts have limits. When confronted honestly, playfully, and repeatedly in the to-and-fro process, they stretch and transform our questions. They confront us as something over against us. Their truth shines through and transformation can occur, as it did for Nan and Hilda and later in the wider congregation. Sometimes texts are misused and bent to the narrow interests of our situations and their questions. The major purpose of the distancing procedures of biblical criticism is to prevent this. Although all these features were not developed, we see in the educational and hermeneutical inquiries of Covenant the embryonic features of historical and systematic moments of a fundamental practical theology. The movements of Christian education and the movements of fundamental practical theology are the same.

In genuine practical theology, thought and action go hand in hand. At Covenant biblical texts were interpreted at committee meetings, meetings of the session, worship services, educational programs, congregational votes, and actual encounters with Paul Williams's Salvadoran refugees. The course of events went something like this: The mission committee began meeting in March and formed its first statements. In April, Hilda Mann, in spite of her energizing presence, resigned in reaction to being called a communist. Another member of the committee had previously resigned. In May, an initial plan of education was drawn up using materials from the Chicago Religious Task Force on Central America. The session approved the idea of an adult education program on sanctuary for the autumn. In June, partially under the influence of Paul Williams, the mission committee asked the session to adopt a statement informing the government of Covenant's support of those churches that already had become sanctuary churches. The session did this. Hilda Mann rejoined the mission committee then and served on a subcommittee to design the autumn course.

A ten-week course called "Latin America: Paradise Lost" was projected. Hal Roberts insisted that it be "balanced" but refused to preach any special sermons on the issue. Bonhoeffer's *The Cost of Discipleship* was chosen as the text for the course. In November, at the conclusion of the course, a special study group was appointed to draft a resolution on Covenant becoming a sanctuary church. Simultaneously, Paul Williams announced that three Salvadoran refugees had arrived in Centerville. Four members of Covenant, but not the church itself, provided temporary support. At a January annual meeting of the congregation, the proposal to become a sanctuary church was approved by a vote of 151 to 91. At a special service in February, the refugees were officially received into the church. This is the bare outline of events that made up the sanctuary action. But the events are not the full praxis. We see the full praxis only when we understand how thought and action relate.

Brueggemann's view of the two levels of textuality at Covenant is basically correct. Niebuhr, however, might see this somewhat differently. This is certainly true if we keep in mind my reconstruction of Niebuhr. From this perspective, Covenant is exercising a religiously inspired form of practical reason. This is one way to look at Paul Williams's appeal to the principle of neighbor love and the narrative of the Good Samaritan. To illustrate the meaning of neighbor love, Williams reversed the main point of the parable of the Good Samaritan. Jesus told the story to illustrate that the Samaritan, not the priest or the Levite, was the neighbor to the Jew from Jerusalem who fell among robbers and was left by the side of the road (Luke 10:25-37). As Williams said at the church retreat, to him the story meant that we should "see who is bleeding by the side of the road." To him, the neighbor was the person who was in need. For him, the principle of neighbor love meant that as each of us would want care if we were in need so too should we give care to others. Brueggemann was incorrect in concluding that Williams interpreted the love commandment as conventional neighborliness. It was far more boundary breaking than this. It went beyond the boundaries of the community of Centerville to include Rosa, Juan, and Oscar. It went against public opinion in Centerville and the initial sentiments of the people of the Church of the Covenant. It went beyond the limits of the federal law. It was not conventional, as Brueggemann suggests. It was boundary breaking and prophetic.

Although it shared the formal elements of generalizability and reversibility characteristic of Kant's categorical imperative and its restatements by Rawls, Kohlberg, and Habermas, it was different. Being distinctively Christian, Williams's formulation grounded respect for the other on the Christian concept of the *imago dei* in humans and not on appeals to rational agency. Williams was not just advocating bland respect for the other; he was promoting active care for the needy. He held an ethic of equal regard that also contained a strong teleological element. Although the equal regard of neighbor love was his dominant principle, he, like Janssens, Frankena, and Ricoeur, said it should also justly *promote benevolence* and the *welfare* of broken and suffering people. In adding this, he went beyond most Kantian formulations. He went even further beyond Kantian views when he exhorted us to be willing to sacrifice in living out neighbor love. As indeed it did for Jesus, neighbor love should extend to include all people. It is to include all even at the cost of suffering. This dramatic extension of the formal and rational reversibility of neighbor love was inspired by the way the Christian narrative informed neighbor love for Williams.

Moral philosophers have noticed the formal similarities between the reversibility of neighbor love and Kantian moral principles. Williams added something more—the symbol of the cross.

This extension of neighbor love captured the imagination of the mission committee, especially Nan and Hilda. From there it was taken to the congregation. My point is this: Christian neighbor love and Kantian or neo-Kantian moral principles are formally the same, but the symbol of the cross adds a dimension that the Kantian principle lacks.

This means that the principle of neighbor love has formal similarity to one powerful theory of democratic citizenship. Citizenship can sometimes be defined as a simple conventional matter of obeying the customs and laws of a society. This is citizenship at Kohlberg's second of three levels of moral development. It is his level of conventionality in contrast to preconventional egocentric stages of childhood or the two postconventional stages that people sometimes achieve in adulthood (Kohlberg 1981, 17–19).

Democratic citizenship also can be defined by either of these two postconventional stages, the utilitarian or the more universalistic. It can be, and often is, defined as the capacity to act as a utilitarian and promote the greatest good for the largest number of people (Hardin 1988). It can be defined in terms of the neo-Kantian theories of John Rawls. Here democratic citizenship is the capacity to think and act with fairness when fairness has the formal characteristics of reversibility.

There is an analogy (in the revised correlational sense of the word) between the principle of neighbor love and neo-Kantian principles of citizenship. In Tracy's terms, they are neither identical nor nonidentical. They are analogous. They are analogous and not identical because of the different ways in which the two perspectives ground their views of human dignity and respect. Although the Declaration of Independence indeed anchors respect for humans in the *image of God*, neo-Kantians would anchor it in human agency and rationality. Nonetheless, when the church educates for the discipleship of neighbor love, it is also educating for the highest level of citizenship. It is not the citizenship of uncritical conformity and unreflective conventionality; it is the citizenship of true democratic reversibility and equal regard. It is what Niebuhr called brotherhood and sisterhood. At this level, education for discipleship and education for citizenship are roughly the same.

This is why, as Glenn Tinder has argued, education for Christian discipleship can be, and often has been when rightly done, the very best education for citizenship (Tinder 1989a). At this level, education for discipleship and education for citizenship overlap; both can be explicit and self-conscious goals of the church, as they were implicitly at the Church of the Covenant. Both participate in the rational core of equal regard.

THE VISIONAL LEVEL

We have discovered the structure of practical reason functioning in the appeals of Paul Williams, the deliberations of Nan and Hilda, and the final decisions of the congregation. It was abstractly similar to some philosophical formulations of practical reason. And the adequacy of the church's practical wisdom could be tested, in part, by these contemporary philosophical discussions. Nonetheless, it was a practical reason functioning within a Christian narrative. This narrative fulfilled this practical reason in various ways.

In the preceding chapter, I listed seven ways in which the Christian narrative (at least Niebuhr's version) enlivens, activates, and fulfills the core of practical reason. Several of these are visible in the sanctuary discussions at Covenant Church. The first, and most obvious, is how the concept of the image of God in all humans served to expand and universalize Covenant's identification of the neighbor. Behind the idea that the neighbor was anyone in need was the idea that all humans (including persecuted refugees such as Rosa, Juan, and Oscar) are made in this image. For the believer, this gives weight to the concern for strangers that appeals to their status as rational agents could never give.

Second, perpetual preaching on grace and forgiveness doubtless contributed to the fulfillment of practical reason, as I have suggested already. Earlier I stated that the doctrines of sin, grace, and forgiveness make it possible for practical reason to be relatively free from inordinate self-interest and self-justifying maneuvers. There may have been wisdom in Hal Roberts's attempt to stay above the fray and continuously preach this truth. It may have helped people relax their self-justifying maneuvers and pursue more arduously the moral truth of this situation. But the gospel of grace and forgiveness contributes to practical reason at this level only if other aspects of the Christian narrative are functioning. Fortunately, other dimensions of the Christian narrative operated in these discussions, that is, Williams's appeal to neighbor love and the ethic of the cross from Bonhoeffer. Without other players besides the ministerial leadership of the church, the full orchestration of the core of practical reason with its narrative envelope would not have occurred as it did.

Third, there is the appeal of the cross. It is one thing to show equal regard and love of neighbor as self. It is another thing to do this against opposition and at risk to one's health, freedom, and safety. It is one thing to exercise practical reason; it is another to endure in its exercise when it hurts. Nan Carr and Hilda Mann were inspired to endure the costs of discipleship by reading Bonhoeffer.

Hilda used his book to lead the concluding session of the ten educational programs. Reinhold Niebuhr's view of the cross could have added further theological backing. In my reconstructed view of Niebuhr, mutuality and equal regard become the norm of the Christian life. This is how Christians are to live even amid the world of sin and brokenness. It also, as I argued above, constitutes a viable ethic for life in democratic societies. In addition, Christians are called to the sacrifice of the cross. It is a sacrifice designed to balance mutuality and help it to endure when it has fallen into disarray. Sacrifice is not an end in itself. The theology of the cross contributed to practical reason. It helps it endure when it is under threat.

There are other aspects of the relation of Christian narrativity to the inner core of practical reason that, although not very evident at the Church of the Covenant, are either implicit or could easily come into play. Implicit in the practical acts of provision for Rosa, Juan, and Oscar is an affirmation of the goodness of their basic human needs. The metaphor of God creating a good creation is behind this positive response to their fundamental needs. In addition, had persecution of Nan, Hilda, and the mission committee actually developed, some understanding of how virtue and happiness finally meet might have been extremely important to support their ministry to the refugees. Which parts of Christian narrativity will be called upon to support practical reason will change from situation to situation, problem to problem. But the resources of this narrative for *phronēsis* are rich and incalculable. This is why the Christian narrative inspires both discipleship and citizenship.

STRATEGIC PRACTICAL THEOLOGY

The rhythms of Christian education follow the movements of practical theology. This is even more true if Christian education is seen as a process of practical communal inquiry. I have affirmed Groome's shared praxis approach but suggested that the inquiry sometimes takes a complex communal form. It also takes the form of a critical dialogue between a believing community and the various communities around it. Christian education in pluralistic modern societies draws on an ecology of interacting resources located both within and outside the church.

The Christian education at the Church of the Covenant was not confined to the ten-week course that preceded the final sanctuary vote. We should see the entire process that began with Williams's challenge and that climaxed, although it did not end, with the reception of the refugees into sanctuary as Christian education. It began, like all good education, with a practical question. This question stimulated the descriptive and normative inquiry that made up the educational process. The total ecology of education contained many elements: Paul Williams's question and his own preliminary answers, the theological education of Hilda Mann at a secular university, the theological leadership and sermons of Hal Roberts and Carl Gordon, the biblical tradition, the publications of the Chicago Religious Task Force on Central America, the thought and leadership of Nan and Hilda, the self-interpretations of the Immigration and Naturalization Service, and finally a dialogue with the larger community of Centerville. From my perspective, there was a grand revised correlational dialogue at Covenant between these various groups. It was a critical hermeneutical conversation between a variety of parties with special attention given to the biblical tradition. This was the heart of the educational process at Covenant.

The wider community of Centerville was very much a part of the conversation. Newspaper columnists commented on Covenant's work and deeds on the sanctuary issue. Nonmembers of Covenant attended the ten-week course and entered the dialogue. Some were secular and unchurched. Some were from other churches. They did not share the religious narratives of the people of Covenant. Yet their convictions had sufficient *analogies* with those of the members of Covenant to make discourse possible. The conversation did not exhibit all the features of a critical dialogue as I have presented this concept. But it contained many of these features.

Although representatives of the Immigration and Naturalization Service (INS) were invited to make presentations during the ten-week course, they refused. If they had accepted, there would have been discussions about the meaning of citizenship. Generally speaking, the image of citizenship that the INS projected during this period was one that Kohlberg would call conventional. It entailed conformity to the laws of the state whether or not they could be defended morally. Had there been such a critical dialogue between the INS and Covenant, the question of validity claims would have come to the fore. All three of Habermas's validity claims would have come into play. Eventually, all five of mine could have been invoked. A variety of validity claims were at stake in this discussion, some of which the Church of the Covenant itself had to face.

I can illustrate only some of them. Covenant would have needed to answer truth claims (Habermas's term) about the factual reality of the Salvadoran refugees. Were they really persecuted? Were they political refugees or were they, as the government claimed, really economic refugees? The government would need to satisfy its truth claims as well. There would have been moral validity claims advanced—assertions that Habermas calls claims about the "right" or what I call claims about obligation. The government might, as it often did during this period, base its claims on models of obedience to the civil law—an argument based on conventionality. Had there been a confrontation between Covenant and the INS, there would have been a redemption of validity claims about different moralities of citizenship. Even at the level of citizenship, is simple conventionality morally adequate? Can it solve more human conflicts and meet more human needs than the equal regard morality of citizenship that developed at Covenant?

Posing this big question serves my main point. It illustrates the kind of critical conversation that the educational program at Covenant might eventually have to face and to some extent did face. Much of what the congregation did was intended to anticipate just such an encounter with the government. In educating themselves for the sanctuary vote, they were not just talking to themselves; they were implicitly talking to the wider community and even to the government. They were, in reality, functioning within a critical correlational dialogue, imagining and anticipating the responses of the other.

THE DEBATE ABOUT TRANSFORMATION

In presenting the five dimensions of practical reason I have made no firm distinction between what moral philosophers call deontic and aretaic judgments. Deontic judgments pertain to the actions and principles we call moral. Aretaic judgments refer to the kind of character or virtue, in contrast to explicit actions, that we consider morally good (Frankena 1973, 9). I have not invoked this traditional distinction because I simply have assumed that, although useful in some respects, on the whole it is artificial. Our images of good action and our images of good character are dialectical and imply each other. Talk about one soon implies talk about the other.

The five dimensions can be looked at from the perspective of aretaic judgments—judgments about character and virtue. Those dimensions have implications not only for the principles we should follow; they also have implications for the kinds of character and virtue that constitute readiness for moral action. This is enormously important for Christian education for discipleship and religious education for citizenship. To educate is to form the *character* and *virtue* of persons so that they *act* in certain ways. If the characterological implications of the five dimensions of practical reason can be stated, their relevance for Christian education becomes even clearer.

There is a vigorous debate in both secular and religious education about how humans are formed. The major parties in the debate are the narrativists, the deontologists, and the teleologists. These three parties parallel the first three levels of my model of practical reason—the visional, the obligational, and the tendency-need. I have chosen with purpose the terms narrativist, deontologist, and teleologist from moral philosophy to illuminate a discussion in education and developmental psychology. This dramatizes the parallels between the two fields of inquiry. The narrativists believe that humans are formed by participation in communities of memory that have powerful stories to tell about their origins and destinies. The foremost narrativist in religious education is Craig Dykstra, who has himself been strongly influenced by Stanley Hauerwas (Dykstra 1981). Those emphasizing how faith communities socialize persons, such as Nelson, Westerhoff, and Miller, also have affinities with the narrativists. This perspective even influences Groome's shared praxis approach with its emphasis on the correlation of classic Stories and Visions with our individual stories and visions.

Deontologists, in contrast, are the structuralists of Christian education. They are the educators who have been influenced by Piaget and Kohlberg and who hold that our intellectual operations mature through specific phases and structural transformations. Socialization is not as important as the continuous process of differentiation and integration of our mental and emotional patterns under the impact of diverse experiences—experiences that stimulate humans to increasingly more comprehensive cognitive structures. This complexification of cognitive structures helps us mature in our emotional responses and in our broader faith attitudes toward life. James Fowler (1981) and Mary Wilcox (1979) are leading representatives of this approach though Fowler at times counts himself as a narrativist as well.

Finally, there is the teleological approach. Don Miller calls it the "emotive" approach (Miller 1987, 185). These two terms— *teleological approach* and *emotive approach*—refer to that strand of developmental thinking that emphasizes the importance of affections and emotions. By using the word *teleological*, I am simply observing that our affections pursue experiences of the satisfying, the actualizing, or the loving—various ways psychologists talk about the *good*. Teleological theories of development and transformation are associated with psychoanalysis, notably with Freud, Erikson, and others of this tradition.

It is often thought that these three models of learning and development are in tension with one another, possibly in total contradiction. There is tension between them, yes, but not contradiction. One does not have to choose between them. If we examine the educational process at the Church of the Covenant, we see all three models functioning. We see their counterparts in moral theory as well.

From the hermeneutical perspective developed in this book, we should see most strikingly the importance of narratives in the sanctuary debate at Covenant. And it is true—narratives and stories abound. Paul Williams got the attention of Covenant by telling stories about his visits to refugee camps. He told the story of his own conversion to a deeper Christianity the day he concluded "that Christ might be who he said he was" (Slater 1989, 3). Then there were the stories of the refugees themselves—Rosa, Juan, and Oscar. There was the politically and culturally conservative story of the Church of the Covenant. There was the master story of the life, death, and resurrection of Jesus and its meaning for both love as equal regard and love as sacrificial giving that renews equal regard. But the predominance of narrativity in the educational situation of Covenant does not mean that deontological and teleological elements are totally absent. They are simply encased by narrativity just as I have argued that historical location and tradition encase our moral reasoning and our emotional needs. This does not mean that our moral thinking and affections have no possibility of independence from narrativity. By using the word *encase*, I mean to suggest something more like a permeable envelope than a firmly bounded container. In education, just as in moral theology and philosophy, an interactional model will serve us better. Hence there are times when our feelings and cognitive moral patterns break out of the confines of our narrative envelops. But on the whole, these cognitive moral operations and emotional patterns are shaped significantly, as the narrativists have argued, by our inherited stories.

To say, however, that there are no ways of feeling and knowing characteristic of the human species (no species-characteristic instincts, emotions, or modes of thought) and that our narrative contexts determine our feelings and cognitions *in all respects*—such claims fly in the face of general experience. The young man who has always heard that the United States was on the right side of God in all affairs but who receives unjust and murderous orders from his company commander in Vietnam may have experiences that force him to revise his narrative.

There were conflicting narratives at Covenant. There was Covenant's own history—a narrative about a white, middle-class people firmly anchored at the center of established power in Centerville. It was a story of conventional and established respectability. This was the semiotic story at Covenant analogous to the myth of Zeus at the Wiltshire Church. This is the story Hopewell would have discovered. He doubtless would have found an appropriate Greek myth to capture its symbolic form. The Bonhoefferian view of the Christian story finally transformed, at least for a time, this latent story at Covenant.

That is true, and the narrativist vision of Christian education appears right. But if carried too far, it denies the role that experience, reason, and emotion play as well. It overlooks Paul Williams's appeals to the reversibility of the principle of neighbor love. True, the principle has a narrative context as he uses it, but it also appeals to our own moral rationality. As we would want to be helped if we were abandoned by the side of the road, so too would others. As we would want hospitality were we fleeing from the terrors of persecution, so too did Rosa, Juan, and Oscar. Paul Williams simply asked us to recognize the humanity of Rosa, Juan, and Oscar. He was functioning little differently from Kant, Kohlberg, Rawls, Donagan, or any other neo-Kantian who anchors reversibility and generalizability on a simple recognition of the status of the other as a thinking, feeling, rational agent like ourselves. Because this level of appeal was present at Covenant, it attracted sympathetic citizens from the community who had little interest in the specifically religious premises of Covenant's action but who were attracted to the possibility of extending sanctuary to the refugees on other grounds. That, finally, the larger Christian story shone through and most of the congregation saw the refugees as children of God and not only as human rational agents—this means only that the Christian story *adds to* but does not necessarily oppose our natural practical reason.

This may have functioned all the more strikingly when Rosa, Juan, and Oscar arrived in the community. This event must be seen as part of the educational process. Their arrival, with Paul Williams's appeal on their behalf, constituted a claim that had to be dealt with. I can't help thinking that there were experiential dimensions to that claim that stimulated, as some structuralists and deontologists believe, the moral cognitive reflectiveness of some people of Covenant. These refugees who stood before them were human beings with feelings, thoughts, and rational capacities similar to their own. I believe such concrete experience stimulates our reversible thinking. It leads us to ask: Since they are like us, how would we want to be treated were we in their shoes? I also think that the Christian story deepens, intensifies, and makes more explicit our human moral intuitions and thought. The refugees' physical presence before the congregation influenced its moral thinking and was itself an educational experience.

We need not make a mutually exclusive choice between deontologists such as Kohlberg and Rawls and narrativists such as Hauerwas, Metz, and Dykstra. Narrativists sometimes write as though this choice is necessary, but it is not. Our Christian stories add to, deepen, and reinforce certain fundamental human tendencies toward reversible moral thinking. We need both to tell our stories (as the narrativists would have us do) and to expose ourselves to increasingly diverse and complex claims from others (as the structuralists and deontologists would have us do) in order to educate Christians for both the cost of discipleship and the justice of citizenship.

Nor do we need to make a choice between the narrativist approach and what I have called the teleological or emotive approach to learning. The teleological approach emphasizes the importance of emotional attachments in the development of our moral lives. Freud set the stage for this view. He believed that our consciences are formed when as children we seek to retain the love and approval of those who raise us. For fear of losing the love of the parental figures in their lives, children internalize the prohibitions and ideals of these figures (Freud [1933] 1964, 66–67). Freud did not speak of these prohibitions and ideals in terms of narratives, but he clearly was aware that they reflect the traditions within which parents stand. The psychoanalytic emphasis on the tradition-laden character of the superego can accommodate easily to the narrativist perspective. One might argue that prohibitions and ideals always are carried in narrative and tradition-based forms. If this is true, psychoanalysis adds an insight that the narrativists sometimes miss. We take over the narratives of the people we love because we have an affectional dependence on them and are afraid of losing them. It is not just the narratives that we are told that shape our lives; it is the narratives we are told by people we love. Or, to say it more in the parlance of contemporary object-relations theory, we take on the narratives of those we have internalized deeply into our inner psychological worlds. We adopt the narratives of those who fulfill our emotional needs. Seen from a psychoanalytic perspective, narrative theory has a teleological substratum.

Both teleological or emotive theories and narrative theories give conservative accounts of the transformative process. Both help us understand how we are socialized into inherited traditions. Our affection for authoritative figures leads us to make their stories our own. Certainly these two closely associated perspectives help account for some of the education on sanctuary that occurred at Covenant. But they account primarily for the more conservative and tradition-preserving features. They help us see how difficult it was for the mission committee to go against the tradition of Presbyterianism that had made being a good Christian and a law-abiding citizen almost identical. They do not go far in accounting for the transformation—the shift of the church from conservatism and caution to venture and risk.

To comprehend this, we must invoke the hermeneutical dialogue between the old story of Covenant and the new story that emerged from a *deeper* play with the classic Christian texts. The emotive point of view helps us, to a degree, to understand this as well. The affections motivating socialization at Covenant led people—the Nans, Hildas, and others—to take the Christian story *seriously.* If the latent story of Covenant proved inadequate before the cognitive and moral disequilibria created by the sanctuary issue, these people at least took their faith seriously enough to look deeper and have a more thorough hermeneutical confrontation with the tradition. The affections that led them to reexamine the Christian narratives were first conveyed to them by loved ones. Our affections motivate the hermeneutical process in ways that narrativists, including Gadamer himself, often overlook.

The tensions between the narrativists, deontologists, and teleologists are creative yet superficial. These diverse positions are only misleading when any one is used to exclude the others. The narrativist perspective is the most inclusive. But there are species-characteristic cognitive and emotional capacities that sometimes break through our narratives and restructure our inherited traditions. Both at the level of critical normative thought and at the level of learning, our principles of obligation and our affections are situated within our narrative traditions. But in both learning and moral thinking, our moral rationality and affections occasionally are small but effective voices exerting transformative pressure on these narratives.

I have tried to show in this chapter that Christian education can be seen as a critical hermeneutical and revised correlational process. So can pastoral or congregational care. It is to this subject that I now turn.

10

CONGREGATIONAL CARE
IN A BLACK PENTECOSTAL CHURCH

From one perspective, the Apostolic Church of God appears
to strain to the breaking point the hermeneutical model of
practical theology. This especially seems true if we try to
apply the model to the pastoral and congregational care of this
church. The powerful preaching and the firm biblical and moral
stance with which Arthur Brazier supports the Apostolic Church's
congregational care may seem to make the church far more authoritarian than a hermeneutic and correlational model would allow.
But I am convinced that a vigorous hermeneutical conversation is
present in that church. The authoritative voice of the Scriptures is
at the heart of this conversation. The Scriptures are the clear and
unambiguous classics of this church. The minister and the congregation are in a playful yet serious dialogue with them. It affects
all aspects of the church, including pastoral and congregational
care.

HERMENEUTICS AND PLAY

Gadamer often speaks of the hermeneutical process as having
the give-and-take—that is, responsive—quality of play. In earlier
chapters I have called the cultural reconstructive task of practical
theology a process of play. Although practical theology is conversation, it is playful conversation where the imagination—its questions,
inquiries, and syntheses—is given free reign. Such a conversation,
both grandly playful and gravely serious, permeates the worship
at the Apostolic Church of God and radiates to all aspects of its
life.

The entire worship service is a playful dialogue between choir
and congregation, soloists and congregation, and minister and congregation. Much has been written about the antiphonal, call, and
response character of the spirituals in black or African American

churches (Lovell 1972, 42–43). I was surprised to notice there were no hymnals at the Apostolic Church. The members of the congregation did not so much sing with the choir as respond physically and emotionally to what the choir and soloists were doing. The congregational responses came as shouts of joy or applause or by extending a hand toward choir and minister as if to receive and send communications directly by touch.

Not only music but also preaching and prayer took the form of dialogue. They had the form of playful dialogues that encouraged the use of imaginative rhetoric by the minister and active responses, amens, and applause from the congregation. At the center of the dialogue was a scriptural text. In Brazier's preaching, this text was given the respect of an authoritative classic but often was accurately contextualized as well. The sermon was a complex dialogue between Brazier and the text, the questions of the congregation and the text, and Brazier's interpretation of the text and the congregation's questions. Pastoral prayers had much the same character; the needs, concerns, and questions of the congregation were brought to prayer without being edited. God both encourages and permits this. Pastoral and congregational care at the Apostolic Church proceeded in this context of dialogical worship, preaching, and prayer.

In what follows I will have a hermeneutical dialogue with the Apostolic Church of God. Although a hermeneutical stance guided my reports on Wiltshire Methodist Church and the Church of the Covenant, my hermeneutical dialogue with the Apostolic Church was more immediate, direct, and intimate. I personally did the research at the Apostolic Church. The research at Wiltshire and Covenant was done by intermediaries who pursued the questions that came from our teams. As I have shown, there was a hermeneutical dimension in this research as in all social science research. But it was not self-conscious and acknowledged. In my work with the Apostolic Church, it was direct and obvious. It was all the more obvious in view of the proximity of the Apostolic Church to my home and work. Within a few blocks, vastly different ways of life unfold. To describe the Apostolic Church is to have a critical conversation between the world of that church, the world I inhabit in the university, the university's immediate neighborhood, and the surrounding churches. The conversation must, in the end, be mutually critical. The Apostolic Church affirmed and judged my world in a variety of ways. In turn, my world both affirmed and judged the Apostolic Church. This was true at several points; it was acutely true at the level of congregational care.

CONGREGATIONAL CARE OF FAMILIES

I went to the Apostolic Church of God to study how an African American congregation deep in the poorer sections of the inner city handles its care of families and their children. I had an interest in both care and discipline. I imagined that under the pressures of inner-city life, discipline was as important as care. I wanted to understand just how this discipline takes place.

I was interested in congregational care, not just the care delivered by the pastor. A new interest in congregational care had emerged in the professional literature of Protestant pastoral care and theology. For decades, under the growing influence of the modern psychotherapies, there was in this literature a preoccupation with the counseling done by the individual minister. Recently, under the impact of the congregational studies movement, an attempt has arisen to go beyond the clerical paradigm of pastoral counseling and look at what congregations as a whole do in their care (Browning 1988). This includes how the pastor guides the congregation, but it concentrates on the caring ministries of the entire congregation.

My interest in the Apostolic Church was not just idle curiosity. I wanted to know what a pressured, inner-city church did for its families because of my fear that mainline, white congregations were losing their capacity to cope with the growing pressures on their families.

THE RECENT HISTORY OF PROTESTANT CARE

The literature of Protestant pastoral care has gone through a variety of turns in recent decades. With the rise in the 1930s of clinical pastoral education, the psychotherapeutic psychologies have had increasing influence on both Protestant and Catholic care and counseling. Brooks Holifield in the final chapters of *A History of Pastoral Care in America* (1983) and Allison Stokes in *Ministry after Freud* (1985) have told this story well. These historical works, with the writings of Rieff (1966), Bellah et al. (1985), and Lasch (1978), show how the modern psychotherapies have helped make the church's care increasingly more individualistic, subjectivistic, and normless. Holifield, Gerkin (1984), and I (Browning 1976, 1983b) have pointed to the growing dominance of the goal of self-realization in Protestant care and counseling. Gone are the older motifs of self-denial, self-control, and self-mastery once prominent in pastoral care in the United States (Holifield 1983, 12). Long gone are the courts of conscience, the Celtic penitentials, the practices of penance, and the moral and legal structures of Catholic canon law that once dominated pastoral care before the Protestant Reformation (McNeill 1951; Brundage 1987). The moral context of care has become increasingly relativistic and individualistic, even in the church.

Since the early 1950s, mainline Protestant pastoral care theory has gone through three stages. Outside this stream, the Apostolic Church of God has been influenced by elements of this history but has gone in a different direction. The first stage ran from the end of World War II to the mid-1960s. During this phase there was emphasis on a one-to-one, psychologically oriented counseling model. Although Freudian psychoanalytic psychology provided the general framework, the client-centered counseling theories of Carl Rogers (1957) were the main resource. Seward Hiltner (1949), Carol Wise (1951), and Wayne Oates (1962), with different emphases, were the key mediators of this view. The emphasis was placed on educing moral and psychological resources from within the troubled person. It was a method supremely attuned to the growing pluralism of North American life and the weakening moral authority of the Protestant churches.

The second phase began with the early writings in the commanding career of Howard Clinebell (1966). He advocated a more complex model of counseling that entailed both uncovering the hidden resources of the troubled person and helping the person consolidate new habits and ego strengths. His work had a slightly more directive tone. It is widely believed, however, that Clinebell has only recently begun to develop the ethical and theological foundations for this suggestive model (Clinebell 1984; Gerkin 1984, 16).

The third phase is composed of several trends. They hold the common goal of recovering the theological, ethical, and ecclesial foundations of Christian care. These movements want to retain the contributions of the modern psychologies without losing the essential Christian contexts of care. This phase includes Thomas Oden's plea to return to the classic sources of Christian care and counsel in Scripture, the church fathers, Luther, Calvin, and Wesley (Oden 1980). It includes my attempts to reject the alleged *value-neutrality* of the modern psychotherapies and their uncritical acceptance in pastoral care, and my attempt to develop a theological ethics to inform the moral context of care (Browning 1976, 1983b, 1987). It includes the turn toward a hermeneutical model of pastoral counseling that is explicit in the writings of Charles Gerkin and Archie Smith (Gerkin 1984, 1986; Smith 1982). Finally, it includes the trend to go beyond the clerical paradigm of the ordained minister's care and examine the care of the congregation (Browning 1988; Fowler 1987).

HERMENEUTICAL APPROACHES TO CARE

A word is in order about the recent turn to hermeneutical models of care and counseling. What does this entail and how might it help us understand the congregational care of the Apostolic Church of God? Can the critical and correlational hermeneutical model for practical theology I have been developing clarify congregational care in general and the specific care of the Apostolic Church?

In answering these questions, I do not start from scratch. In the 1980s, two writers made significant contributions to a hermeneutical approach to Christian care. One is Archie Smith in *The Relational Self: Ethics and Therapy from a Black Church Perspective* (1982). The other is Charles Gerkin in *The Living Human Document: Revisioning Pastoral Counseling in a Hermeneutical Mode* (1984) and *Widening the Horizons: Pastoral Responses to a Fragmented Society* (1986). Smith's approach is implicitly hermeneutical. In his 1982 book he does not refer to Gadamer or formal hermeneutical theory. Yet many hermeneutical concepts are there implicitly. Gerkin's two books are built explicitly on Gadamerian theory and constitute a complex and sophisticated model of a practical theology of care.

Smith develops a hermeneutical view by emphasizing the importance of dialogue in both pastoral counseling and social transformation. He specifically addresses the African American community and church and their oppression by the racism and domination of the white community. Although he addresses the black church, he believes his view is relevant to the whole church. He uses the concept of ministry as dialogue to synthesize both individual and social transformation in one model. Changing the individual and changing society are not opposed to one another; they are related dialectically. For individuals to be free to change social structures that oppress them, they must be liberated from their psychologically internalized structures of oppression. Hence, therapy with individuals and prophetic ministries of social change should go hand in hand in the black church (27).

Although he never mentions Gadamer or the hermeneutic tradition, Smith gets many of the same values from his use of H. Richard Niebuhr (Smith 1982, 79–96). All individuals are historically situated, tradition-formed, value-rich social selves. All social interaction, even that between therapists and clients, takes the shape of historically situated dialogue. This is why ministers and Christian counselors have the right to bring their religious commitments into their helping dialogues with others. In truth, there is no way to escape it.

Gerkin's position explicitly draws on Gadamer's hermeneutic theory. In *The Living Human Document*, Gerkin addresses the situation of pastoral counseling both in the congregational and specialized settings. Gerkin's position is strikingly similar to Groome's in Christian education. Pastoral counseling is for Gerkin a dialogue or correlation between the life story of the troubled person and the grand themes of the Christian story. The difference between education and counseling is, I think, found in two things. One is the detailed care with which the counselor tries to understand the storied-self of the troubled person. The other is the quality of interaction between care giver and receiver. Counseling attempts to get to know the storied-self of the troubled person in a deeper way than occurs in education. Furthermore, counseling permits a longer and deeper relation between counselor and client than most educational settings. Transference issues are more likely to emerge in counseling. But these distinctions are not categorical. They are matters of degree. In counseling and care, according to Gerkin, there is a dialogue between counselor and client. It is an extended, playful dialogue in which the counselor creates what Gerkin, following Winnicott, calls a "transitional space" (Gerkin 1984, 137, 153–54). By transitional space, Gerkin means a nonthreatening relation of warmth and acceptance with the counselor that permits a growing interaction or play. This play is between the story of the troubled person, the Christian story, and the direct workings of the Holy Spirit.

Gerkin uses the modern psychologies, especially psychoanalytic object-relations theory, in an important but subordinate way. The object-relations theory is primarily a tool for uncovering the depths of the personal story of the receiver of care and counseling. It also helps uncover the storied-self of the counselor (1984, 143–60). The counselor creates change by becoming simultaneously a metaphor both for past figures in the person's life and for the Spirit of God and Christ (174–75). The troubled person *plays out* attitudes and expectations created by failed relations with mother, father, sibling, or spouse and projects them on the Christian counselor. The counselor responds by becoming a metaphor or parable of a more redemptive relation with a morally just, forgiving, and loving God. Where other relations were flawed, the counselor witnesses to a relation with a God who is just, loving, and transformative. But this occurs only when the new relation is tested repeatedly by the play and projection of old expectations.

In his later *Widening the Horizons*, Gerkin develops this view into an explicit "narrative hermeneutic practical theology of care" (1986, 22, 50). He extends his model beyond one-to-one counseling to include a wider care for individuals in their total social-systemic contexts. He takes a giant step toward Smith in seeing a dialectical relation between individual transformation and social transformation. The care and counseling of the church should take responsibility for both, understand their intimate relation, and see each as requiring the other.

Gerkin's narrative hermeneutic practical theology of care obviously is very close to the approach I propose. Although Smith never uses the phrase, it is close to his dialogical approach. But Gerkin and Smith are more consistently confessional than I. I agree that the confessional moment is the center of fundamental practical theology. Faith precedes critical reflection. The narrative of faith precedes our critical reflection upon it. My approach, however, is a critical correlational or critical hermeneutic method. It is not just a narrative or hermeneutical practical theology. It is a critical hermeneutical practical theology; it not only confesses its narrative beginning point; it also accepts responsibility for advancing reasons for its plausibility. Both Gerkin and Smith call for critical reflection on the praxis of the faith. They call for a moment of ideology critique within the practical theological task (Smith 1982, 156–86; Gerkin 1986, 64, 141). But neither develops anything approaching methods for redeeming validity claims in the way Habermas does or the way I attempted in chapters 7 and 8.

Although practical theological reflection can go a long way in the confessional mode, in our pluralistic and conflicted society, if the church is to have sustained impact on the public world, it must take a more genuinely critical step. We will see this in the Apostolic Church of God. It has developed a practical theology of families that may have some validity outside that church. But it can never communicate what it has to offer to the secular world on strictly confessional grounds. In fact, the Apostolic Church understands clearly the difference between the ethic it can demand for itself and the ethic it can expect from society beyond its membership. Brazier's approach to public life is neither sectarian nor Constantinian. He does not lead the church to retreat from public life. Nor does he use the power of his pulpit and the strength of his congregation to dominate public affairs. He occupies an unclear middle ground that must be located intuitively. The more general validity of his view of the family cannot be argued before the public on strictly confessional grounds. Yet clearly he and his congregation would like to see contemporary society follow the lead of the Apostolic Church in its views on the family, male-female relationships, and the method and standards for raising the young. A *critical* hermeneutical practical theology is needed to take that next step.

DESCRIPTIVE THEOLOGY

Practical theology always reflects the angle of vision from which it is done. In the paragraphs to follow, I will first look at the practical theology of the Apostolic Church of God. Gradually my voice will enter. This voice will be my practical reflections on what I find in that church. In this, my identity as a white, male, liberal theologian connected with an establishment university will become all too evident. We will witness a hermeneutical dialogue between the Apostolic Church and me. It surprised me that there were wider areas of agreement between us than I would have guessed before the dialogue began.

What is the descriptive theology of the Apostolic Church? How does it describe its context and practices? What is the theory behind its descriptions? The five dimensions will be used as guides again, but as unobtrusively as possible.

PRACTICES AND CONTEXTS

The main interpretive perspective at the Apostolic Church of God comes from the sermons, speeches, and writings of Arthur Brazier. Yet it is an interpretation that the congregation ratifies continuously. It has emerged out of decades of dialogue, shared experience, and shared praxis. Brazier and his congregation are fully aware of what has happened to the Woodlawn community. There is little tendency to repeat obsessively the statistics documenting the community's demise. They only have to look around them to realize that more than a fourth of the people have left the community since the early 1950s. To drive into the community is to observe directly the vacant lots, the abandoned buildings, and the boarded-up store fronts along the once bustling and affluent Sixty-third Street. The Apostolic Church is the only healthy establishment on the east end of Sixty-third. By the time these pages are read, its present large building and sanctuary will be joined by a second huge sanctuary seating over two thousand people. Brazier sometimes refers to the Apostolic Church as the "miracle of Sixty-third Street."

The people of the church are well aware of the history of gang warfare that has afflicted Woodlawn. In the 1960s and 1970s the Blackstone Rangers and the Disciples recruited hundreds of boys and young men into their ranks. Jeff Fort, the leader of the Rangers who later became the kingpin of an extensive drug operation, has been in jail for years. But he is still remembered. The people of the church know how many of their neighbors populate the prisons of Illinois or receive monthly checks from Aid to Dependent Children. They are aware that nearly 60 percent of the births in the black community are out-of-wedlock (Popenoe 1989). They know about the new crack houses in the run-down homes and apartments of the area. They know of the large number of unemployed men who roam the bars and back alleys of their neighborhood. They know that a fourth of black men between the ages of twenty and twenty-nine are in prison or on parole (Wilkerman 1990).

It is interesting to see how they interpret the cause of this. Brazier is fully aware of racism. In his 1969 book titled *Black Self-determination*, he applies this concept without hesitation to the white power structure of Chicago (Brazier 1969, 134). But he did not use the word once in the ten months that I attended the Apostolic Church. Racism was assumed, but it was not a preoccupation. He does not believe that racism is now systematic in U.S. society. "White Americans," he once said in an interview, "are not like the South Africans. Martin Luther King knew that, underneath it all, most white Americans do have the right values. These values can be appealed to. It is not clear that they exist in South Africa at all." Although Brazier, in The Woodlawn Organization (TWO) and in his church, has empowered blacks to fight racism, it has not been the center of his ministry. The center has been a spiritual empowerment that he claims is deeper than political empowerment. Spiritual empowerment makes political empowerment possible.

In his early writings and recent sermons, Brazier demonstrates awareness of the dynamics of technical or purposive rationality. He generally just calls it *technology*. He rails against it bitterly, not unlike the liberal ministers in the churches around the University of Chicago. He and his church members seem aware of the collusion between purposive rationality and racism that devastates inner-city black neighborhoods. When in the early 1960s the University of Chicago wanted to expand into the northern edge of Woodlawn and displace its poor black residents, this was interpreted as a compounding of racism and purposive rationality. The university wanted to expand its research (purposive rationality) and was willing to do it at the expense of the black community (racism). This was coupled, as Julius Wilson has shown, with the retreat of industry and jobs from the inner city (William Wilson 1987). Purposive rationality, in its capitalist forms, aims only to improve efficiency and profits. If this requires abandoning the inner-city work force, it generally is done. This abandonment might come all the more easily if the work force is African American.

It might be argued that the devastation of Woodlawn was the reverse side of the problems of the Wiltshire community and the Wiltshire Methodist Church. Purposive rationality there, largely controlled by white people, produced the affluence, the waste, the consumption, and the split between public and private worlds that had such dire consequences for the Wiltshire families. The purposive rationality that strains Wiltshire works to devastate Woodlawn. The purposive rationality that makes Wiltshire rich displaces people in Woodlawn or takes industry to the suburbs. Both churches live in a world of technical rationality. But they live at opposite ends of the continuum of strains and dislocations caused by the rationalizing process.

Neither the Wiltshire Methodist Church nor the Apostolic Church of God rejects purposive rationality. Not Wiltshire, because the people there are aware of its goods and are largely unconscious of its evils. Not the Apostolic Church, because the people there want to participate in its goods and are optimistic that they can control its evils. Brazier is not afraid of power and believes political power can be used for the good (Brazier 1969, 128–33). But more fundamental than political power and liberation is redemption or salvation. This is what he preaches. It is what his congregation talks about. In one sermon he said, "I have been tempted by politics. Many people have wanted me to enter politics. Many have wanted us to have a political ministry in this church. But I have tried over the years to keep my mind primarily on one thing—the salvation of souls in the name of Jesus Christ."

In spite of this denial, the Apostolic Church does have a political ministry. It gives handsomely to Operation Push. Although Brazier is no longer president of TWO, the church still works with this and other organizations to bring in low- and middle-income housing, improve schools, fight drugs, and bring business and banking institutions back into the community. But these activities never gain the central spotlight at Sunday morning worship or Wednesday evening Bible study. There is a theology of liberation preached at the Apostolic Church, but it is subservient to a theology of salvation and redemption. Some Latin American liberation theologians say oppression is the central problem of the human condition, but Brazier would say that the central problem is sin. Brazier would agree with Schubert Ogden that, although Christianity is interested in political liberation, it is more interested in liberation from the bondage of idolatry, sin, and death (Ogden 1979, 36–37). The issue of salvation is central to the worship life of the Apostolic Church. At every turn, the Apostolic Church resists considering itself a victim.

CONGREGATIONAL CARE AND DISCIPLINE

The Apostolic Church of God is very thoroughly organized. Every new member (and it takes in between fifty and seventy a month) is soon challenged to develop a ministry. Many departments and groups of the church are concerned with congregational care. I will concentrate primarily on them. Brazier, I was told, is unusual among the ministers of the Pentecostal Assemblies of the World in his willingness to delegate pastoral care responsibilities. Yet clearly he supervises all care activities energetically. More specifically, he works to create a shared theology and ethics of that care. As Helen Barnes said, "Many important religious beliefs and values are communicated by the way we care for one another." Brazier is open to new proposals about care. Church members come to him constantly with new ideas for ministries of care. Many of these he supports; some he does not. Some are institutionalized and become permanent parts of the congregation's ministry of care.

This is what happened when Helen Barnes recommended the creation of CALM (Christian Action Lay Ministry program). It is one of several programs aimed at meeting the care needs of the Apostolic Church and its neighborhood. Older and more established care programs include the Ministerial Alliance, the Men's Ministry, and the Visitation and Medical group of the Women's Fellowship. The Ministerial Alliance is made up of about forty lay ministers of the church. They are mostly men. Besides generally assisting Brazier, they visit the sick in hospitals and the elderly in nursing homes, take communion to shut-ins, and run a "prayer line." The Men's Ministry runs an outreach ministry to prisons and to poor families in selected Chicago housing projects. In addition, it is constantly sponsoring programs, services, dinners, and retreats that investigate the topic of what it means to be a "responsible man" and a Christian in the black community. The Women's Fellowship, among other programs, has a remarkable team of nurses and health care professionals who visit the people of the Apostolic Church who become ill and have difficulty caring for themselves.

CALM was the newest and most daring ministry of care. Helen Barnes, who sold the idea to Brazier, holds a Ph.D. in psychology and is a full-time child abuse counselor at a South Side community mental health center. The idea came to her while she was driving her automobile. She considers it an inspiration from God. She spoke to Brazier, who was himself looking for a social service program, and he liked her proposal. She puts in from eight to ten volunteer hours each week running CALM. Brazier can call any time while she is at her regular job. There is clearly, in her mind, only a very thin line that separates her ministry at the church and her profession at the community mental health center.

CALM has a professional-looking brochure that describes its ministries. It has fifteen specialized ministries. It has a legal advocacy program, a health ministry, a child welfare program, a counseling ministry (which works with families, couples, and singles), and an education and college planning program. It offers financial counseling, job counseling, drug and alcohol counseling, general legal services counseling, and helps with housing problems. It addresses juvenile delinquency, the needs of the elderly, teenage pregnancy, veteran services, and general issues in public aid. There are directors or chairs of each of these services. Most of them are professionals, generally well established in the Chicago mental health, educational, and social service network. Much of CALM's work is referrals—helping people learn where to go and how to handle the system. Much of its ministry is direct-service counseling and assistance.

As a professor who had written rather widely in pastoral care for over two decades, I was astounded by the range and depth of CALM and by the philosophy behind it. I had not expected to find anything like it when I started my research at the Apostolic Church. In the middle-class, white churches that I knew, there was little concern with concrete issues of welfare, housing, employment, and financial counseling. I wondered if these churches might broaden their membership were they to address these concerns. Also, I wondered whether white churches have problems in these areas that they overlook in the name of respecting the privacy of their members.

The crystal-clear value framework that surrounded the CALM ministries impressed me. It was far different from the value assumptions behind much of mainline Protestant care and counseling where the values of the troubled persons and the autonomy of their decision making are the basic moral framework. The moral context of care at the Apostolic Church was different from that in the middle-class, white churches I know.

The entire concept of CALM strains some theological stances of the Pentecostal tradition. Members of a Pentecostal church are supposed to be saints. They are supposed to be sanctified. This means, as Brazier constantly explained, "set aside" and "different from the standards of the world." Some authoritative interpretations say that sanctified people should not have certain kinds of problems such as alcoholism, drug addiction, divorce, teenage pregnancy, and so forth. To some extent, this is the position of the Apostolic Church. Helen Barnes said that most of these problems were with new members who had been converted but had not yet received the gift of the Holy Spirit. Or they were individuals who had received the Spirit and who had turned around but who were still growing. Also, as Helen Barnes insisted, many services of CALM were for the extended family and friends of members, not necessarily for the members themselves. However it is justified, the very existence of CALM suggested that a note of realism had crept into the Apostolic Church. The saints may be saved, but they also may have their problems.

Yet it was the universal testimony of the members of the Apostolic Church that there was far less alcoholism, drug addiction, teenage pregnancy, divorce, and juvenile delinquency among its members than in comparable groups in the black, inner-city community outside its boundaries. My experience in that church confirms that judgment. Saints in the Pentecostal tradition cannot drink alcohol, smoke, have premarital sex, use drugs, or commit adultery. In short, they follow the conventional moral codes, which they feel are biblical, which were once more firmly implanted in the mainline Protestant churches, but which have been in increasing decline in recent years. It seems these codes are adhered to widely at the Apostolic Church, even among the middle- and upper-middle-class educated and professional people of the church.

Brazier, however, was one of the first ministers in the tradition to alter the dress codes for women. Women can now wear cosmetics and jewelry. In fact, both men and women at the Apostolic Church were among the best-dressed people I have been around for years. In contrast to the churches near the university, where it has been fashionable for people to wear more casual clothes to Sunday worship than they do for their jobs, the people at the Apostolic Church put on their very best—that was very good indeed. Well-off or not, people at the Apostolic Church were well dressed.

In my interviews with Helen Barnes, I began to see the importance of the modern psychologies for the counseling ministries of the Apostolic Church. I had for years written about the widespread impact of the modern psychotherapeutic psychologies in modern societies. I had joined Rieff, Lasch, Bellah, and others concerned about the pervasive therapeutic ethic in our society. By a therapeutic ethic, we all seemed to mean an overgeneralization of the client-oriented, supportive, expressive, and self-actualizing atmosphere that most therapists offer their clients. Although none of these writers wanted to get rid of the psychotherapies, they all felt that an overgeneralization of the therapeutic ethic was pulling our society toward a philosophy of ethical egoism and individualism and a preoccupation with the self. All of them sounded cries of alarm, or at least of warning, asking the culture to pull back in the name of the common good.

In *The Moral Context of Pastoral Care* (1976), I had argued that this individualistic ethic of the therapies was pervading the churches, partially because of the wide use of the modern psychotherapies by ministers and pastoral counselors. Soon Charles

Gerkin, Thomas Oden, and others joined in this critique. They called for a recovery of the theological and ethical foundations of Christian care and counseling. Given this part of my background, it surprised me to see the extent of psychological language, insights, and attitudes in this African American Pentecostal church. The number of mental health professionals, school counselors, social workers, and teachers trained in psychology far exceeded my expectations. But the moral and theological framework that guided the use of these psychologies was not the framework of most mainline Protestant churches. There was no "triumph of the therapeutic," to use Rieff's felicitous phrase, at the Apostolic Church.

In his preaching, teaching, and example Brazier set the theological and ethical framework for using the modern psychologies. Yet it grew out of the similarities between his experience and the experiences of his people in the inner city and in their confrontation with Scripture. It was an ethic that pertained primarily to married couples, families, and the task of raising children. The importance of the black family and its reconstruction was a theme in almost every sermon and speech I heard. I hasten to add, however, that the family was *not* the most important value at the Apostolic Church. The most important thing was getting saved and receiving the gift of the Holy Spirit. After this, it simply was assumed that most people would want to be married and raise a family. It also was assumed that every member of the congregation, single or married, was interested in creating strong and healthy black families.

Because salvation rather than marriage was the major value, there was also a strong ministry to singles. Many young people (the congregation was mainly under fifty years of age) came to the church, in part, to find spouses or get help with marriage. But the message to singles also was strong. As Margo Bauer, the volunteer head of the singles ministry, said, "Christianity does not say that one must be married. A person need not be married to be whole. If a person has a relation with Jesus, that person always has a companion and never is really alone." Nonetheless, preparing people for marriage and helping them maintain their commitment were central objectives of both Brazier's preaching and the ministry of CALM. Heterosexual covenanted marriage and the capacity for a life of marital faithfulness were seen as clear signs and fruits of having the Holy Spirit.

The moral rules of the Apostolic Church—especially those concerning sexuality, marriage, and the family—were backed up with sanctions. They were administered by Brazier. Although there appeared to be very few teenage pregnancies, there were some. During an earlier period, Brazier would christen the babies of unwed mothers at Sunday morning worship. Gradually, however, "he began holding these christening services in his office. This was his way of being human yet setting some limits." Infidelity and lack of cooperation in attempting to save one's marriage also can receive sanctions. Brazier said, "The sanctions come primarily in the form of silencing. I may very discreetly withdraw the privilege to be a member of the choir or sit on a certain committee. I will inform a few of the lay leaders of the congregation. After a few months if there is genuine repentance and a change of behavior, I will restore full standing in the congregation." Sanctions apply to other areas of behavior beside marital and family issues. Law-breaking, alcoholism, overt greed, and other such actions also can bring these sanctions.

Pastor Brazier took the initiative in matters of discipline. All the members I interviewed thoroughly supported the process. More than that, they had a detailed grasp of the biblical sources supporting the church's care and discipline. The degree of biblical literacy was astoundingly high in comparison to what I observe in the mainline churches. Members' Bibles were underlined in various colors. Lay leaders I interviewed could quote passages readily that undergirded their ministries. Most could advance nuanced interpretations of these passages.

Although these standards and punishments were in place, the atmosphere of the church was extremely positive. The preaching, the music, the upbeat greetings of "praise the Lord" whenever members met, the general optimism and sense of mutual support, indeed, the overtly sensual atmosphere of hundreds of happily married couples who seemed delighted to have found each other and to be learning to live together—all this gave the church a decidedly unrepressed and unoppressed atmosphere. In some ways, the entire church was a school on making marriage and raising children work under the pressures of inner-city life. The church was almost completely devoid of the cynicism, confusion, and depression that sometimes appear to characterize relations among young men and women in the community around the University of Chicago, both in and out of the churches. For example, a young woman who is a graduate student at the university recently told me, "I know of no one my age who is happy with his or her relationship." Based on my experience, this is an overstatement. But it is a generalization clearly headed in the right direction.

The young couples at the Apostolic Church did not make such statements. They admitted that male-female relationships require hard work, but they were optimistic. Sustaining, enriching, and deepening these relationships are the objects of much work at that church. Besides the marriage counseling of CALM, there are other

resources. Ivory Smith heads the Youth Department. In connection
with her long-term work with the youth of the church, she and Gwen
Martin have for years headed a marriage support group for young
couples. Although she too has a professional mental health background, Ivory says the group primarily shares experiences, helps
one another, challenges one another to be loyal, and interprets a
scriptural understanding of male-female relationships.

PERCEIVED NEEDS

The Apostolic Church of God assumes that all humans have a full
range of creaturely needs for food, clothing, warmth, family relations, sex, friendship, and the development of their God-given talents (what psychologists would call the need for self-actualization).
Many ministries of CALM, the Women's and Men's Fellowship, and
the Ministerial Alliance are intended to meet some of these basic
needs of life. The contrast with the Wiltshire Methodist Church is
striking. People went to Wiltshire largely to find fellowship, address
their existential anxieties, confirm and maintain their upper-middle-
class values, and socialize their children into these same values.
The Apostolic Church was far more mobilized to help people with
subsistence needs in the area of jobs, housing, finances, and both
physical and mental health. It provided fellowship, but it was an empowering rather than a maintaining fellowship. There was clearly a
striving for middle-class values at the Apostolic Church. But a firm
distinction was made between them and the realities of salvation
and redemption. Although children were educated and the family supported, as at Wiltshire, the needs behind these values were
taken both more and less seriously at the Apostolic Church. From
one perspective, the family and children were everything at the
Apostolic Church; from another, they were subordinate to salvation
and the gift of the Holy Spirit. At Wiltshire Methodist, the distinction between salvation and upper-middle-class values was difficult
to discern. God's love at Wiltshire supported people in their struggle to maintain the social status they had achieved. At the Apostolic
Church, the gift of the Holy Spirit empowered the saints to aspire
for a higher socio-economic class, but becoming a member of that
class was not equated with salvation.

In Niebuhr's and Janssens's terms, creaturely needs (the *ordo
bonorum*) were simultaneously more freely expressed and more
severely limited at the Apostolic Church of God than at either Wiltshire Methodist Church or the Church of the Covenant. For instance,
it is permissible to enjoy wealth at the Apostolic Church as long as
one does it in principled ways, does not let it measure one's life,

and gives a tithe to the church. Sexuality is good, sensual pleasure is good, food is good, recreation and rest are good—all these things are good as long as they are ordered properly before God. Nor is the church prudish. Helen Barnes once said, "Nothing can defile the marital bed," hinting that the married couples of the Apostolic Church were experimenting with sexual techniques far beyond the traditional missionary position. All this seemed to have Brazier's approval.

The handling of human needs was seen most strikingly in the church's philosophy of prayer. In one of his sermons, Brazier said that Christians should feel free to bring all their wants and wishes to God in prayer. Christians should not edit their needs before God. They should not hide their frailties, their hopes, their goals, and their wishes. They should bring their full humanness to God in prayer. "But," Brazier continued, "this does not mean that God in his sovereignty will grant us everything we want. God in his wisdom knows what is good for us; some prayers will be answered and others will not." Nonetheless, the saints are encouraged to bring everything to God. Brazier explicitly contrasted this view with the philosophy of prayer put forth by the evangelists Jim Bakker and Jimmy Swaggart. They lead people to believe that if they ask with sufficient faith, God will grant all their petitions. This was not the position of the Apostolic Church.

In the end, the Apostolic Church has a less abstemious and ascetic life style than one might first think. Members are permitted to ask God for things that people in the liberal churches around the university would think inappropriate. The people of the Apostolic Church are more willing to let their human and childish needs show.

The pattern for expressing human needs at the Apostolic Church is different, for example, from Wiltshire Methodist. Evans and Reed's psychological analysis and Hopewell's semiotic analysis both showed Wiltshire in the waning days of a period of expectancy. For a decade the future had been bright, human needs found fulfillment, aging and death were defeated, dependencies of the past were overcome, and joviality reigned. Now this was coming to an end. Sid Carlson like Zeus was becoming old and saturnine. The congregation was calling for something more solid, more spiritual—something that transcended the limitless increase of finite life.

The Apostolic Church too is in an emotional attitude of expectancy. Human needs are fulfilled. The oppressed are freed and become successful. But the Apostolic Church distinguishes salvation and finite human fulfillment more clearly. The expectancy at the Apostolic Church is more about spiritual fulfillment and less

about economic and class fulfillment. Although Brazier is a powerful leader, the congregation may be less dependent on him than
Wiltshire Methodist was on Sid Carlson. Carlson was fifty years old
when he and his church met their crises. When I did my research,
Brazier was sixty-nine and no crisis was in sight. Brazier worked
harder than Carlson to make himself a metaphor of a force beyond
himself that was the real source of empowerment for the Apostolic
Church.

A semiotic analysis of the three churches' codes and signs
shows that membership in them signaled one's social and cultural
success. At Wiltshire Methodist people who had slain old and use-
less giants were supported in their efforts to *hold on* to their success.
At Covenant, good and responsible citizens were helped to *maintain*
their establishment credentials. At the Apostolic Church people recently on the margins were empowered to *go up* the socio-economic
ladder. It would be interesting to have Hopewell do his magic on
Covenant and the Apostolic Church and discover the deep myths
that animate their unconscious aspirations. In each church, the latent myth was in tension with its interpretation of the Christian
story. But to varying degrees, the latent stories were transformed by
versions of the Christian story. Possibly that tension and transformation were least dramatic at the Wiltshire Methodist Church. Even
there, as Joseph Hough perceptively observed, transformation was
occurring. The tension and transformation were most dramatic at
Covenant where an establishment Presbyterian church risked itself
through an act of civil disobedience. The tension and transformation are quite evident at the Apostolic Church where the upward
mobility of an African American congregation is simultaneously
affirmed, critiqued, and transformed.

In all three cases the natural *telos* of human eros expressed itself through latent myths and unconscious stories. The Jewish and
Christian doctrines of creation affirm the eros behind these myths.
These strivings and myths are not in themselves sinful. They express the natural needs and tendencies that make up our humanity
and creatureliness. What is sinful is their rigid, anxious, and inordinate overextension and resistance to transformation. All these
congregations are, to varying degrees, genuinely the church. Evidence of transformation is visible in each. The full semiotic analysis
of these churches—of their interacting systems of signs—should
not be identified solely with their latent myths, as Hopewell and
others have tended to do. Ricoeur is more correct in seeing the
full semiotic system as the tension and transformative dynamics
between the latent myth and the more explicit confessions of the
gospel story.

VISION AND OBLIGATION

The descriptive theology I recounted, with its interweaving of social observation and theological interpretation, helps us understand how the Apostolic Church of God asks its theological questions. Once we start with its descriptive theology, we see how the theological reflection of the Apostolic Church is practical through and through. The theological ideas of the Apostolic Church *accomplish work* and *get something done.* They gather the experience of the congregation, interpret that experience, and then search the tradition hermeneutically to establish a new horizon of meaning.

The Christian narrative at the Apostolic Church and its pattern of ethical obligations are closely intertwined. They also are distinguishable. We already have discovered, in our analysis of its practices, much about the ethics of the Apostolic Church, especially in marriage and family matters. Brazier and his congregation believe they anchor this ethic in Scripture, particularly Ephesians 5 and the Pastoral Letters. They often speak of the biblical model of the family. It seems to them visible, comprehensible, and applicable to their situation. Ethics, for most of the congregation, is made up of explicit rules that are quite clear and known by all. More liberal churches may harbor considerable ambiguity about such rules, particularly as applied to personal life, but there is little such ambiguity at the Apostolic Church. At first glance, there appears to be no general principle that controls these concrete rules. In one sermon, Brazier explicitly denounced the "liberal tendency to derive the entirety of the Christian ethic from the principle of neighbor love." He and his congregation saw Scriptures as providing concrete moral models and rules that are binding on Christians. The Christian is not saved by these rules. The Christian is saved by faith and the gift of the Holy Spirit. Nonetheless, the saved person will follow these rules joyfully and, indeed, be empowered by the Holy Spirit to do so. Yet there are ways in which Brazier, in spite of what he says, does use general principles such as neighbor love. We will discover ways in which the principle of neighbor love mediates between Brazier's theological vision and his understanding of human needs to create his ethic governing the life of families.

The church's ethic of the family is situated within a theology that combines Calvinist understandings of God's sovereignty with a Wesleyan theology of sanctification. God is the initiator of salvation. God is the ground of creation, the source of its goodness, the provider of the moral laws that fulfill creation, and the author of the love that pursues us when we fall. Although Brazier does not systematically use the metaphors of God the Creator, Governor, and

Redeemer, as the Niebuhr brothers did, the metaphors are present in his theology.

I referred in chapter 1 to the paradigmatic sermon that summarized what I heard time and again. It dealt with 2 Corinthians 8:9, "For you know the generous act of our Lord Jesus Christ, that though he was rich, yet for your sakes he became poor, so that by his poverty you might become rich." Brazier began, as he did so often, with a moving description of the richness of God. It was a description of the superabundance of God's being. God in heaven is rich. With God there is beauty, peace, joy, the singing of angels, light, health, wholeness, fellowship, love—many qualities that medieval scholars described under the aseity of God. Brazier in his description of God's fullness did not, like the Scholastics, speak of God's immovability and unneediness. God is rich, but not so rich as to be uninterested in restoring relationship with God's fallen creation. So God who was rich became human and poor so that we could once again become rich.

What kind of richness was Brazier describing? It was a richness of selfhood that comes to those with faith. It was not a material richness. It was not money, clothes, houses, or high-salaried jobs. It is, as Brazier said, "a richness at the core of your selfhood." Because the rich God became human in the form of Jesus, those who accept Jesus and the Holy Spirit become rich in their selfhood. This is the meaning of sanctification. This is the meaning of becoming a Christian. One receives the Spirit of God (the Holy Spirit), is freed of past sins, and finds a new richness of selfhood. As one recent convert said, "My mind cleared, I felt at ease, I had new energy, I felt refreshed and clean, I had a new sense of power." This corresponded with accounts I heard Brazier give from the pulpit. He would add, "To be sanctified—to have the Holy Spirit—does not necessarily mean that you will not sin, but it means that sin is no longer normal." On another occasion he said, "It means that you now have the power to *grow*, fight sin, and move toward a higher maturity." This new richness of the self is *power*. Even more, this richness and power give the self transcendence over former dependencies, co-dependencies, idolatries, and bondages.

This power of the self gives one the freedom to pursue the relative goods of life without making them idolatries. Here the affirmative, inner-worldly character of the Apostolic Church's theology emerges with full force. In this sermon, Brazier said it was permissible for a Christian to pursue wealth. In fact, the person with the gift of the Holy Spirit will have a richer and more powerful self to do that very thing. The Christian with the Spirit will have the strength to pursue a good job, education, and decent salary. The "Christian can do this *freely* precisely because salvation does not depend on material riches." Whether one succeeds in worldly things or fails makes no difference to one's ultimate standing before God. Even if a person fails, with the Holy Spirit that person will "have the power to try again." If one succeeds, "the Christian knows it adds nothing to one's salvation before God." But if the successful person does not share his or her wealth, if "you do not tithe and use your wealth responsibly for the good of others, you are not living the Christian life."

The same is true with personal relations. The person with a rich self that comes from the Spirit has the power to have better relations with loved ones. Clearly loved ones include girlfriend, boyfriend, fiancé(e), husband, or wife. One can pursue these relations precisely because one's salvation does not depend upon them. Whether "you win or lose" you are still in Christ. In fact, if you lose, "you will have the power to try again, either with the person you have loved or someone new." Then Brazier, who in developing these thoughts had been striding widely from one side of the chancel to the other, concluded his crescendo with a final point: "When Christians have a rich self that comes from the Holy Spirit, they will have the power to acknowledge failed relationships. They will have the strength to face this, disconnect themselves from the relationship, and start again. For after all, *they're not the only tin can in the alley. They're not the only pebble on the beach.*" At this moment, three-quarters of the twelve hundred people in the congregation rose to their feet in wild applause. In this picturesque statement, Brazier had liberated his people to both love and face the realities of loss and grief.

The gift of the Spirit strengthens the self, gives it power, makes it less dependent on finite values, and renders it freer to be genuinely responsible. In one of his long Wednesday evening Bible studies, attended by a thousand people, Brazier argued that there is no fundamental conflict between the writings of Paul and the epistle of James. Paul's emphasis on salvation by grace and James's emphasis on works are, for Brazier, two sides of the same coin. The priority falls on justification by faith through grace, but good works necessarily flow from this. The freedom and power to enact good works are central marks of the gift of the Holy Spirit. And the good works of "being a good parent and creating a good marriage" are central. Brazier and the people from the Apostolic Church hold an unusual doctrine that I have never heard in a white, mainstream church. One lay woman stated it this way: "God created the institution of the family before he created the institution of the church. Being a good Christian means being a good family member first and a good church member second." But one is not saved by one's

family. This teaching simply identified the family as a central arena
for Christian vocation.

Because I have a background in psychology, I could not resist thinking about the psychological implications of the Apostolic
Church's theological vision. There is much talk of the richness of
God. There is also much talk about having a personal, direct, face-
to-face relation with Jesus. No one has seen the face of God, but
most everyone at this church, I'm convinced, had a powerful, deeply
internalized image of Jesus. Jesus, for most, symbolizes the richness
of God's being and the richness of God's regard for humans. One
senses this most directly in the music of the church. It is full of such
phrases as "meeting Jesus face to face," "the power of Jesus," the
"love of Jesus," "Jesus' help" in times of discouragement, Jesus as
"the center of my joy," and "the light of Jesus." When the soloists
and choir sang, members of the congregation would rise to their
feet, close their eyes, and hold out their hands. They seemed to be
conjuring in their mind an image of Jesus that became mixed with
the transporting cadences of the spirituals.

I concluded that these experiences were sources of self-
cohesion for members of the congregation. They were not unlike
the experiences of developing self-cohesion that therapists produce in their clients. The self-psychology of the late Heinz Kohut
is useful to understand this (Kohut 1971). The consistent regard of
the therapist provides people who have diffuse self-images an empathic relationship that helps them rebuild their selves around this
predictable and constant regard. In formal therapy, the counselor's
task is to help the client handle the therapist's inevitable failures of
empathy and still maintain a sense of self-cohesion. The Apostolic
Church claimed, however, that God in Jesus is precisely the one who
never fails in his empathy and regard. The image of Jesus depicted
by this music emphasizes a countenance full of empathy, positive
regard, and constancy. Because God never fails, the saints can better
handle all other fragile and contingent human relationships.

Although there are analogies between the religious experience
of the Apostolic Church and some psychotherapies' goals of building self-cohesion, there are clear differences. Not only does the face
of Jesus communicate affirmation; it communicates judgment and
the power of the Holy Spirit. The subtle way in which the religious
experience of the Apostolic Church combines these themes is more
complex than most therapeutic analogies suggest. A philosophical
point is also relevant. It is philosophically justifiable to speak of
the psychological *consequences* of the religious experience of the
Apostolic Church. But these consequences must be distinguished
from arguments about psychological *origins.* On these matters, I

recommend the position of William James. In a day when positivism and scientism are in decline, it is best simply to describe phenomenologically the thick dimensions of the religious experiences we study. In the end, the Apostolic Church's claims about the work of the Spirit may be on as firm ground as other more academically fashionable ways of talking about the ultimate context of experience. It is best to eschew all psychologies of the origins of religious experience and stay at the level of describing and assessing its consequences. Here I had to admit that the emphasis on the power of the Spirit and the affirming face of Jesus seemed to have genuine empowering, differentiating, and cohesion-building consequences for the selves of these people. These people were strengthened to handle both their intimate and occupational lives without basing their salvation on either.

This broader theological framework gave support to a more specific theology of marriage and family. The model for the sanctified family can be found in Ephesians 5:21—6:4. To understand the situation in the black community behind the interpretation of this text, we should remember the large number of absentee fathers, out-of-wedlock births (approximately 60 percent in 1985), and children under age eighteen who live in single-parent families (53 percent in 1986) (Popenoe 1989). We also should remember that black men are not present abundantly in most black churches. Therefore, it is indeed noteworthy that approximately 35 percent of the membership of the Apostolic Church is black males with about the same percentage participating in Sunday worship.

Against this background we can better understand the centrality of the text from Ephesians for the Apostolic Church of God. The congregation was aware that it begins with the instruction to husbands and wives, "Be subject to one another out of reverence for Christ" (5:21). Two lay women who are leaders in the church said that this "meant that husband and wife are to be in tune with one another." Husband and wife should be open, sensitive, listening, and empathic with each other. This was how these women interpreted the next verse, "Wives, be subject to your husbands as you are to the Lord" (5:22). They interpreted this to mean that they should be in tune with their husbands—responsive, trusting, and supportive. They fully accepted the words, "For the husband is the head of the wife just as Christ is the head of the church" (5:23). This meant to everyone I interviewed that the man was to be Christlike. The husband's spiritual and moral leadership of the family meant that he was to be the "chief servant." As Helen Barnes said, "The man is the leader because he is the sacrificial servant of the family; it is in this that his moral and spiritual authority rests."

This leadership does not entitle the husband and father to be a tyrant. In his servantlike spiritual leadership he must treat all members of the family with respect. He must consult his wife and always take her views into account. This exegesis of the passage amounted to a strong appeal to black men to be responsible husbands and fathers. In a context where centuries of discrimination and misguided social programs had more and more induced black men to neglect their families, the logic and rhetoric of these interpretations gave black men the leadership so that they also might exercise appropriate responsibility.

Brazier would say from the pulpit and in his other speeches, "Men must never mistreat their wives or children." If husbands and fathers used their authority to mistreat their families, the church instructed wives and children not to obey or submit. Wives were thought fully capable of knowing how a sanctified husband should act. If husbands did not act correctly, that was to be brought to the attention of the pastor.

Finally, Brazier would end his meditations on the family referring to Ephesians 5:28-31: "Husbands should love their wives as they do their own bodies. He who loves his wife loves himself. For no one ever hates his own body, but he nourishes and tenderly cares for it, just as Christ does for the church, because we are members of his body. 'For this reason a man will leave his father and mother and be joined to his wife, and the two will become one flesh.' " Here Brazier inserted an implicit ethic of equal regard, not unlike the position that results when Niebuhr is reconstructed with Janssens's theory of the *ordo caritatis*. As husbands would not mistreat their own bodies, so they should not mistreat their wives. Stated more positively, as husbands instinctively would cherish their own bodies, they should nourish and cherish their wives. What appeared at first glance to be a rhetoric and ethic of male authority worked out in the end to be an ethic of male responsibility guided by an ethic of equal regard. The husband was to treat wife and children as he would his own body.

Being a sanctified and set-aside saint, the husband will have the gift of the Holy Spirit. This should give him the power and moral strength to be the kind of husband that this ethic demands. It should give him the strength to endure, to try again, to accept transitory failures, and to go the second mile. Despite the rhetoric, genuine mutuality between husband and wife seemed the goal of this ethic. The Christlike servanthood and authority of the husband required from him the sacrificial qualities needed to restore mutuality where there had been momentary brokenness.

STRATEGIC PRACTICAL THEOLOGY

The rhetoric of this family ethic seems to contradict the liberal democratic theory of the family that dominates the intellectual and religious circles in the university neighborhood where I live. Although the rhetoric is different, the actual functioning of these theories may have similarities. In what follows, I will enter a critical conversation with Brazier and the members of the Apostolic Church of God. The situation I found myself in when studying this church illustrates the nature of both practical theology and a hermeneutic approach to the study of other people. Studying the Apostolic Church brought into vivid relief the horizon of my own practices, my own implicit liberal beliefs, and the theory-laden practices of the communities in which I dwell. There was no honest way to study this church without becoming more conscious of the pre-understandings I brought with me. What I saw had meaning to me in contrast to these understandings. The questions bringing me to the Apostolic Church had been practical from the beginning. I wanted to know how an embattled inner-city minority group, discriminated against by a dominant white community and racked by the "negative dialectics" (to use a phrase of the Frankfurt school) of technical rationality, expressed its congregational care—especially for families. I soon found myself in a complex hermeneutical conversation with that congregation. My pre-understandings encountered the pre-understandings of the people of that church.

This resulted in a friendly critical conversation with the church. Not only must there be a Gadamerian moment that creates a fusion of horizons between our respective situations and the classic texts, there must also be a Habermasian moment as well. I finally had to ask, What are the claims of these texts and are they true? I had to ask, Are the interpretations of the Apostolic Church correct or are the liberal interpretations of my community correct? I asked, Can these texts legitimately shape the views of marriage and the family that either community should hold?

LIBERAL VIEWS OF THE FAMILY

The liberal theory of the family uses Lockean and Kantian models of individual autonomy and universalizability to fashion its family ethic (Okin 1989, 110–33; Elshtain 1988, 80–95). In this view, the husband and the wife are seen as two autonomous individuals of equal worth and equal dignity. In their autonomy, they form a marital alliance. The emphasis on the autonomy of the individuals is the Lockean aspect of liberal marital theory. From this beginning in the autonomy of the two individuals, the theory may go in a variety of ways. Some view the marriage bond as a contract for the fulfillment of the two individuals. This is what Lawrence Houlgate calls the individualistic view of the marital relation (Houlgate 1988, 78). Other views can begin with the autonomy of each member and move to a far more rigorous ethics of duty. This is what Houlgate calls the organic model of the family (60–67). Here the good of individual members of the family must be sacrificed for the good of the whole family. There are ways to justify this view of the family on liberal Kantian grounds. Some interpreters of the Kantian perspective suggest that the parties in the marriage contract use their autonomy to submit themselves to an ethic of universalization that suppresses their own quests for individual fulfillment or satisfaction. Either view would have genuine difficulty with an ethic such as Brazier's that gives the man a special spiritual and moral authority in the marital relation. The liberal view, whether individualistic or organic, has not in recent years countenanced such male authority.

Enlightenment philosophical liberalism of Lockean or Kantian varieties has undergirded the dominant philosophy of women's liberation since the 1960s, at least in the United States. Such a view would have immense problems with granting men any ontologically grounded spiritual or moral authority no matter how beneficial the final consequences of this might appear to be. This view has permeated deeply the mainline white denominations, especially in liberal, university-related communities. I too had drunk deeply of those waters before coming to the Apostolic Church. They had fed the pre-understandings that I brought to my reading of Scripture and to my efforts to understand that church.

This liberal view of the family has many sources. Modern liberal feminism is both a product and further development of this view of the family. Although there are many forms of contemporary feminism (socialist, radical, psychoanalytic, and so forth), liberal feminism has had the most influence in the United States in recent decades (Koch 1989). It has made its deepest impact on women who live in urban areas of the United States and who are middle- and upper-middle-class, educated, and professional. In many ways, it was an attempt to purify the liberal vision of the family by eliminating the last vestiges of patriarchal authority left from medieval and early modern institutions (Okin 1989, 18–19). Some of this vision has affected modern feminist theological thought. On the whole, however, modern feminist theology has been somewhat more communal and less individualistic than the classic liberal view of women and the family (Ruether 1975, 181–83; McFague 1982, 1987). Nonetheless, in the context of the individualistic commitments of much of Western life, the communal dimension of theological feminism gets lost when it finally filters down to concrete practical living. In addition, its communal spirit is further blunted by its habit of addressing women without speaking of their relation to families. Without addressing feminist issues in relation to larger issues of marriage and the family, much of communally oriented theological feminism still has a liberal, individualistic tone.

FEMINIST VIEWS OF THE FAMILY

Communally oriented feminist perspectives on the New Testament are relevant to my hermeneutical dialogue with the Apostolic Church. They have helped form the thinking in seminaries and university-related divinity schools in liberal or mainline circles. The most powerful of these perspectives is found in Elisabeth Schüssler Fiorenza's *In Memory of Her* (1983). Schüssler Fiorenza's view of Ephesians 5:21-33 is in tension with the Apostolic Church's interpretation. But the tension is not as serious as one might first think. Also, if Schüssler Fiorenza applied her hermeneutical principles to an understanding of the Apostolic Church, she might have genuine sympathy for what is said there. For the situation of black men, women, and their families differs vastly from the situation of white, middle-class, professional women who argue their case with little reference to the situation of the modern family. If one keeps their respective hermeneutical beginning points in mind, the Apostolic Church looks less patriarchal than most liberals would think.

In her ground-breaking book, Elisabeth Schüssler Fiorenza argues that the Jesus movement was in tension with the patriarchal structures of both ancient Judaism and Hellenism. She admits that Jesus develops no frontal attack on these structures, but she argues that an indirect critique of them clearly is evident: "Jesus' proclamation does not address critically the structures of oppression. It implicitly subverts them by envisioning a different future and different human relationships on the grounds that all persons in Israel are created and elected by the gracious goodness of Jesus' Sophia-God" (142). Evidence of this subtle undermining of patriarchal institutions can be found in Q and other Christian sources that predate the Gospels—that is, in the earliest sources of the Christian movement. Later, in the formation of the Gospels' accounts of Jesus' ministry and in the institutionalization of the Christian church in the non-Pauline Letters, the emerging church gradually accommodated to the inherited patriarchal assumptions so prevalent in the ancient world.

To illustrate her argument, Schüssler Fiorenza discusses a variety of pre-Markan texts (texts found in Mark but which Mark incorporated from even earlier documents) that depict the Jesus movement as a discipleship of equals. Her views can best be illustrated by her comments on Mark 10:2-9. This Scripture deals with a question put by the Pharisees to Jesus, "Is it lawful for a man to divorce his wife?" Schüssler Fiorenza believes that Jesus' response was an indirect attack on patriarchy. We see this when Jesus says that the tradition of divorcing wives by granting them a certificate of divorce was permitted by Moses for "your hardness of heart" (Mark 10:5). From the beginning of creation, "God made them male and female" (Mark 10:6). Jesus continues, "For this reason a man shall leave his father and mother and be joined to his wife, and the two shall become one flesh (sarx)" (Mark 10:7). Schüssler Fiorenza believes this undercuts the tradition of patriarchy that had developed the arbitrary male prerogative of dispensing with wives simply by issuing them a certificate of divorce. She believes Jesus is basically saying, "God did not create or intend patriarchy but created persons as male and female human beings" (142). The woman in the beginning was not given into the hands of the man; both were to leave the patriarchal family and become one flesh (sarx). She concludes by saying this about the passage regarding the one flesh (sarx) of the man and woman:

> Therefore, the passage is best translated as "the two persons— man and woman—enter into a common human life and social relationship because they are created as equals." The text does not allude to the myth of an androgynous primal man but to the equal partnership of men and women in human marriage intended and made possible by the creator God. What, therefore, God has joined in equal partnership (yoked together; cf. the yoke of Sophia-Jesus as a symbol of discipleship), a human being should not separate (143).

Schüssler Fiorenza would say to the Apostolic Church that Ephesians cannot be handled on the same level as this earlier pre-Markan text. Ephesians reflects a later period in the Jesus movement when issues of institutional accommodation with existing patriarchal structures were re-entering the life of the church. Even here, when Ephesians 5:21-33 is placed in the context of the entire letter, the themes of equality of discipleship apply to all relations in the Christian community. All who have been baptized in the Lord—be they Gentile or Jew, slave or free, male or female—are equal in the Lord. But, as Schüssler Fiorenza points out, this equality is not realized for women and slaves until the eschatological consummation (268). Shadows of accommodation to the existing patriarchal structures can be discerned in the eschatological delay of the full realization of this equality.

There are ways, Schüssler Fiorenza admits, in which the equality of discipleship of the early Jesus movement lingers on and mitigates the returning patriarchy. This observation moves her closer to the position of the Apostolic Church. She points out that the ancient patriarchal societal code is modified significantly in Ephesians. She tells us that two things happen in this regard. First, "Jesus' commandment 'to love your neighbor as yourself'... is applied to the marriage relationship of the husband." Second, "Christ's self-giving love for the church is to be the model for the love relationship of the husband and his wife. Patriarchal domination thus is questioned radically with reference to the paradigmatic love relationship of Christ to the church" (269–70).

We saw both of those features at the Apostolic Church. First, the husband had the moral and spiritual authority, but it was the authority of servanthood not domination. Second, the love commandment was implicit in the assertion that the husband should treat his wife with the care and nurture he would lavish on his own body. Building its family ethic on Ephesians leaves the Apostolic Church at most with a chastened, tamed, and greatly modified patriarchalism—one perhaps that does not even justify the word *patriarchalism* to describe it. It also leaves the church with a family ethic that greatly increases male responsibility, male self-worth, and equal regard between husband and wife.

The hermeneutical situation governing my interaction with the Apostolic Church is this: Before I came to that church I identified more with the thought of an Elisabeth Schüssler Fiorenza than with that of the Apostolic Church. But I soon was impressed with how its family ethic—including its rhetoric—functioned to transform lives and families in that context. In spite of Brazier's disclaimers, I discerned an ethic of equal regard and mutuality of the kind that I developed with the help of Niebuhr and Janssens. His appeals to the image of servanthood functioned to energize and extend *agapē* as mutuality and equal regard. As one recently married young woman named Sandy said, "We are not supposed to just give 50 percent to each other. Husband and wife are supposed to each give 100 percent. Marriage is not 50-50; it's 100-100." In her colloquial but highly precise way, she stated well the essential ideas of Janssens's concept of equal regard. To show equal regard, one is to take the needs and interests of the other as seriously as one's own. In the marital relation, this formal principle applies to a wide range of premoral goods—such as affection, sexual relations, and security—that should not be a part of formal relations in the public world.

The difference between equal regard in the workplace (what Niebuhr called brotherhood and sisterhood) and equal regard in the marital relation is the range of premoral goods that equal regard organizes. The goods of the workplace and marriage overlap but differ in many ways. When sexual relations enter the workplace, the results are almost always problematic.

In this respect, the formal aspects of the Apostolic Church's ethic of the family pass some of the philosophical and theological tests that a critical practical theology must encounter. But the formal dimensions are encased in highly contextualized rhetoric that, at first glance, the spirit of feminism and most modern liberal culture finds alien. The recent black "womanist" perspectives on feminism associated with Jacquelyn Grant, Cheryl Sanders, and others have put this rhetoric in better perspective (Grant 1989; Sanders 1989). A new dialogue is now emerging between black feminists, Third World feminists, and white, middle-class feminists. That dialogue should increase the mainline, white religious understandings of the Apostolic Church's family ethic.

A CRITICAL DIALOGUE

The Apostolic Church of God's family ethic may be more than rhetoric. The language of male servanthood and responsibility may be more than a compensatory language designed to bolster the egos of oppressed African American men. The situation of the black male in Western society may be closer to the situation of all males in modern societies than we might first think. And the situation of the black family may be closer to the situation of all families in modern societies. Clearly, discrimination and racism have fallen on the black male and the black family with devastating effects. As Helen Barnes said, "We black women support our men; the traumas of racial discrimination fell more heavily on them than on us women." Yet racism is not the only force in modern societies racking the framework of families. New insights into the social dislocations of men of all races and walks of life are emerging (Ehrenreich 1983). Inner-city black families have fought both the oppression of racism and the dislocations of purposive rationality expressed in urbanism and modernity. Their strategies of response to these threats may give us insights into how to deal with the latter as it affects all families. Not all groups face racial discrimination, but increasingly all face the dislocations of purposive rationality expressed in urbanism and modernity.

To develop a deeper assessment of the Apostolic Church, I need to have a critical correlational dialogue between its family theology and some modern perspectives. Let it be clear: I need to do this for my theology. The Apostolic Church may not need this for its theology. Some of its women, many of whom are educated and exposed to liberal social philosophy, occasionally object to the rhetoric and substance of this family ethic, but the vast majority do not. They fully affirm it. Someday this may change. If it does, Brazier's practical theology of the family may need to develop a critical correlational perspective. I need to take that extra critical step now if I am to communicate a positive appreciation of the richness and particularity of the Apostolic Church's views to the diverse communities in which I stand. The scope of practical theology varies according to the communities in which it is done. In the pluralistic, liberal, skeptical communities where I live, a critical correlational second step must supplement the hermeneutical first step. The Gadamerian turn must include a Habermasian sub-moment. The fusion of horizons between situation and classic text must include heuristic reasons.

To further this, I turn to the creative work of the social psychologist David Gutman. Although Gutman works with the tools of comparative anthropology and evolutionary biology, he could understand, I believe, both the rhetoric and the ethic of the family theology of the Apostolic Church. In a series of articles (1968, 1969, 1974) and in his more recent *Reclaimed Powers: Toward a New Psychology of Men and Women in Later Life* (1987), Gutman has developed a novel theory of the human life cycle. It invites dialogue with, yet contrasts sharply with, positions such as the one found at the Apostolic Church. Instead of a Christian theological view, Gutman presents an evolutionary-adaptive point of view. He examines the family and male-female relations from the perspective of how they contribute to creative and life-sustaining responses to the selective powers of the environment. Gutman's overall goal is to throw light on the dynamics of aging for both males and females. In the process, he illumines general patterns of male-female relations as they have developed in a variety of cultures. Using categories I have discussed earlier, it can be said that Gutman illumines some of the premoral values that men and women bring to the principles of equal regard and mutuality. The liberal family project, of which liberal feminism is a part, has developed flat and unnuanced conceptions of equality. These ideas of equality sometimes have overlooked the truth that people have different needs and tendencies at different stages of life. This includes men, women, parents, and children. Clearly parents and their children have different and changing needs, needs significantly shaped by the biological time clocks of their respective life cycles. There are analogous emerging and waning needs in parents that sometimes synchronize with, but sometimes conflict with, the needs of their children.

I have argued throughout this book that basic needs and tendencies are the grounds of the premoral values relevant to the moral process. But they do not exhaust that which is moral. Basic needs constitute, as Mary Midgley has stated wisely, "central tendencies" that higher-order moral principles such as equal regard must stay within and further enhance. Gutman has provided an interpretive perspective on these fundamental male-female and parental tendencies. But they require further refinement by a higher-order moral principle that Gutman intuits but does not make explicit. Such a principle can be found in our reconstruction of Niebuhr in light of Janssens and Outka. But the principle of equal regard is abstract and formal. To become concrete, it requires something like Gutman's theory of the shifts in human needs through the human life cycle. Human beings need different things at different times in life, and our interpretation of equal regard must be nuanced enough to account for these shifting premoral values. Liberal family theory and liberal feminism often overlook this. The complicated and highly contextualized practical theology of the family at the Apostolic Church may understand it more profoundly.

For three decades Gutman has dedicated himself to the clinical and cross-cultural study of aging and the human life cycle. He has done extensive anthropological field studies of Mayan, Navajo, and Druze traditional societies. These studies have convinced Gutman that parenthood is the center of normative images of adulthood in most cultures. The goals of adulthood for the bulk of human history have been dominated by the evolutionary requirements of parenthood, that is, by what is required in different contexts to fulfill the "generative task" (to use a phrase of Erik Erikson's) of maintaining and revitalizing the human life cycle (Gutman 1987, 186–87; Erikson 1963, 131; Browning 1973). Evolutionary history has left men and women with different psychobiological tendencies for parenthood. In hunter-gatherer societies, men specialize in the perimeter tasks of hunting for food and defending women and children from animal and human predators. Women, who fashion "the baby in their own flesh," gravitate toward secure areas to supply the formative experiences that guarantee emotional security in children (Gutman 1987, 195–97). Together men and women meet the basic needs of the children for physical and emotional security.

The birth of a child creates what Gutman calls the "parental emergency" (195–99). The parental emergency mobilizes and transforms the narcissistic energies of both the man and woman toward the care of the highly dependent human infant. Rather than remaining on the periphery of society, the male now must focus his energies on the protection and security of the highly vulnerable female and infant. The birth of the child limits narcissistic investment in what Gutman calls the "omnipotentiality" of both the male and the female—but especially the male (194). Both the male and the female have a wide range of potentialities that must be sacrificed during the long period of infant and child dependency. These sacrifices are difficult for both. They are most difficult for the male. His potentialities are more centrifugal and more focused on the periphery of social life than the female's. The dedication by the male and female to the parental emergency is absolutely crucial for human survival and flourishing. It is the presupposition of the long period of learning that carries the human infant beyond the strict dictates of nature and into the realm of culture and freedom.

At first glance, Gutman's perspective, backed up strongly by anthropological research, appears antithetical to liberal family theory and liberal feminism. Some will see it as chauvinistic to the core. Used to gain insight into the Apostolic Church, some will expect it to bring out that church's worst features. But then Gutman does something surprising. He points out that the parental emergency is *transitional.* It does not consume the entire life cycle, even in more traditional societies. The initiative and protectiveness of the male are transitional. The centeredness and nurturance of the female are transitional. Both behaviors build on central tendencies in males and females but also limit the expression of other genuine potentialities. The parental emergency of both female and male occurs in response to the infant's need for physical and emotional security. As the transitional demands of the parental emergency subside, both men and women in cultures throughout the world reclaim dimensions of their personalities that of necessity had been de-emphasized to care for children.

During the parental emergency, couples throughout the world show "more sex-role stereotype" behavior (201). After the emergency, the female recaptures more of the aggressive, executive, and less nurturing aspects of her personality, and the male begins to express more of the nurturant, passive, and softer aspects of his personality. The sex-role stereotype, according to Gutman, is not a result of male chauvinism as such. It is a transitional product of the parental emergency that subsides, at least at the psychological level, as the couple moves to later stages of the life cycle.

In traditional societies, men often express the more passive and nurturant aspects of their personalities in religion, contemplation, or ritual. They lose the power of physical aggression but gain the power of being sacred and wise bearers of culture (220–26). The premium in modern societies on experimentation and change undercuts this culture-bearing role of the elderly. Advanced cultures dedicated to the innovations of purposive rationality undermine the cultural role of older men. The dynamics of purposive rationality stimulate a perpetual Oedipal crisis between younger and older men, rewarding innovation, experimentation, creativity, and omnipotentiality at the expense of wisdom and tradition. These dynamics limit the transmission of values needed to teach younger men to focus their aggression to meet the parental emergency. As older men become irrelevant, younger men become irresponsible.

Gutman's theories, and the extensive anthropological data they display, throw light on the human tendencies and needs being ordered at the Apostolic Church. It is too strong to say that Gutman gives Brazier definitive arguments to meet the validity claims that might be thrust upon Brazier in an open discourse situation. As long as Brazier is speaking to his own congregation, such analogies are not extensively used or needed. Yet they are used, as a matter of fact, both by Brazier and certain members of his congregation. As we have seen, some church leaders have extensive education in the social sciences and the mental health disciplines. Some leaders speak freely about basic human needs—what children, men, and women *really* need. The language of the social sciences comes into play. Insights such as Gutman's are brought into contact with the more biblically based family ethic of the Apostolic Church. When this happens, these social science insights function as "diagnostic indicators" (to use Ricoeur's phrase) of human potentials that the gospel ethic addresses and successfully patterns (Ricoeur 1966, 87–88, 221–22). "Men need to feel needed," one school counselor told me. "We take them off the streets and give them something important to do in the church. We make them somebody." In these informal sentences, this modern counselor/saint used the language of psychology (with its evolutionary-adaptive overtones) as a code or script to open a certain level of meaning in the more explicit family theology of the church. In doing this, she tried to support the validity claims implicit in her discourse.

She was speaking to me—an outsider. She was addressing the validity of her remarks at my level three of the five levels of practical moral thinking. She was saying that the active, periphery-searching initiatives of men need a settled focus. At the Apostolic Church they get focused into the parental emergency, and the parental emergency itself is given sacred meaning. It is difficult to say how far she could have gone in redeeming her validity claims. I do not say that she did the full task that Habermas envisions. I am saying that she used more than one language. She used, as Brazier sometimes does from the pulpit, various languages to provide an extended correlational reasonableness to what Brazier says.

The parental emergency is not the center of the theology of the Apostolic Church. Getting saved is at the center. But, as we have seen, salvation gives all who receive it the new strength of selfhood required to meet the parental emergency. The family ethic of the Apostolic Church has within it an ethic of mutuality and equal regard, buttressed by the servanthood and sacrificial authority of the male. Reading the New Testament under the growing influence of either a Gutman or liberal feminist theory may lead the Apostolic Church eventually to soften or at least nuance its rhetoric of male spiritual authority. It may lead the Apostolic Church to speak of that authority as more transitional, more shareable, and more specific to the pressures of the parental emergency.

Even during the parental emergency, that authority is not one of domination. It is an authority of servanthood and responsibility. If we consider Gutman's insights about the human tendencies and premoral values involved in the parental emergency, it seems an authority attuned to the requirements of parenting. The Apostolic Church may recognize these needs and premoral values better than the liberal theory of the family and feminist theory. In spite of its patriarchal surface language, the Apostolic Church's rhetoric and ethic may point to something the liberal community misses. The Apostolic Church recognizes that the ethic of mutuality means different things for men, women, and children at different moments in the life cycle. The ethic of mutuality and equal regard must guide the life cycle as a whole. It should not be used simplistically and mathematically to enforce momentary equalities that are mindless of fundamental human tendencies and their shifting places within the total human project.

11

TRANSFORMATION

T ransformation is extremely difficult to define. Some people equate it with change. But not all change is good. Nor, for that matter, is all transformation good. When practitioners saw the traditional disciplines of practical theology as applied specializations, they often limited their work to the dynamics of transformation. They assumed that systematic theology provided the norms of transformation and that practical theology investigated the means for effecting it.

THE NEED FOR A THEOLOGICAL BRIDGE

Frequently the bridge between the norms and the technical dynamics of transformation was not established. Transformation became transformation for the sake of transformation. Change became change for change's sake. Because these disciplines generally were allied closely with cognate secular disciplines, the norms of transformation were often borrowed from them. The most notorious example of this was in Christian education and pastoral care where models of adjustment, adaptation, self-actualization, or individuation (all concepts from the social sciences) began to dominate Christian concepts of human fulfillment.

RHETORIC, ETHICS, AND MANIPULATION

In ancient Greece, Aristotle in his *Rhetoric* accused the sophists of splitting ethical norms and rational argument from the techniques and dynamics of changing people's minds. When we attempt to change other people but can neither articulate nor justify the norms and reasons that guide the transformative process, we approach the cynicism of the sophists (Aristotle 1941b, bk. 1, ch. 1.1355b:17–20).

This book has attempted to join together the discussion of the norms of change and the discussion of the dynamics of change. This is the basic goal of a fundamental practical theology. The question of the dynamics and conditions of transformation is a topic of special interest to strategic practical theology. All the concerns of a fundamental practical theology culminate in fully or strategic practical theology and join with new attention to the conditions of transformation. Much that I have said already bears on the conditions of transformation. But I need to assemble the bits and pieces of this discussion.

CHURCH CONSULTANTS

In Dudley's book, professional church consultants wrote four chapters. These chapters give us excellent insights into the important new profession of church consultation. The chapters—all of which discuss the Wiltshire Church—also can give us insight into how church consultants might intervene in a situation like that at Wiltshire. These four chapters, however, show the difficulty that this profession has in determining its epistemological status. Only two of the authors—Lyle Schaller (1983, 160) and James Anderson (1983, 192)—seemed to clearly and joyously consider church development as a thoroughly practical enterprise functioning out of a practice-theory-practice model. Loren Mead (1983, 155) and Newton Malony (1983, 175) saw it as an "applied" field. They presented it as applying theory that was worked out in more foundational disciplines. They seemed to hold a theory-to-practice model. The comments of these four men, however, will be useful in developing a few propositions about the dynamics of transformation. The Wiltshire Church will help illustrate many of my points, but the Church of the Covenant and the Apostolic Church of God will prove helpful as well.

DIALOGICAL DYNAMICS OF TRANSFORMATION

In my view transformation follows the dynamics of dialogue in a practice-theory-practice rhythm. Because it is dialogical, the transformative process is mutual. From a Christian theological perspective, God is always finally the agent of transformation. All other agents of transformation—community, minister, lay leader—are metaphors of God's deeper transformative love. Their transformative work always has the form of a dialogue. Both the witnessing person and the person or community witnessed to are transformed in varying degrees in the dialogue.

There are important analogies between the transformative processes in individuals and in communities. And there are important differences. In the propositions that follow, I will try to point out both.

PROCESS FOLLOWS THE FIVE DIMENSIONS

Transformation is a multidimensional process following the five dimensions of practical reasoning. The transformative process is very complex and can be seen from several angles. The multidimensional nature of practical reasoning helps us see this.

Sometimes transformation is basically an alteration at the *visional* level. An old narrative of a person or community proves inadequate and a new or amended story is introduced and gradually replaces it. Sometimes this change of stories comes at the level of the latent or unconscious myth in the community. Sometimes the more conscious narrative is retold or reframed. Sometimes the transformation comes at the *obligational* level. A more adequate principle of obligation is introduced. Or a fresh and more deeply assimilated interpretation of an old principle of obligation is introduced. Sometimes transformation comes when fresh experiences challenge us to relate old principles of obligation to new situations, thereby learning more deeply what the principles truly mean. Sometimes transformation comes primarily at the *tendency-need* level. The narrative may stay largely intact. A person's or community's moral principles, conscience, or superego may stay much the same. But very slight changes may occur that permit persons or communities to deal with their needs and wants in a more conscious, less repressed, more direct, and more principled way. This is often what happens in psychotherapy with people whose personalities are basically intact. It probably accounts for certain types of transformation in groups and even churches. Then there may be transformations in assessments of a person's or group's *environmental-social* context. Aspects of the environment that were not known adequately are now understood and better assessed. A person's or group's narrative and ethics can now be used more effectively to address those aspects of their situation.

Transformation can come even at the level of *rules and roles.* In fact, transformation at any of the other levels always will have implications for these most concrete patterns of life organization. The reverse is also true. Change the rules and roles we enact, and this will eventually alter other dimensions of practical thinking. These wider connections are present from the beginning but sometimes are not clear and obvious. Our concrete practices are theory-laden; a change in these rules implies a change in our view of the fundamental structure of our narratives, deep metaphors, and world views. It may change the unconscious narratives as well. Forcing a change in rules can be coercive; it can place pressures on a person's or group's entire symbolic structure and cause changes that have not been consciously considered or chosen.

When a transformation is effected at the higher levels of practical thinking—the visional and obligational—and is both genuine and deep, we are likely to call this a *conversion*. We saw some elements of a conversion at the Church of the Covenant where the hermeneutical inquiry deepened the congregation's understanding of the cost of discipleship, its understanding of the meaning of the cross, and its understanding of how this should deepen and strengthen its ethic of equal regard with the Salvadoran refugees. We saw deep conversion in some lay leaders of the Covenant congregation and less deep yet meaningful conversion of many in the wider congregation. In the Apostolic Church of God, the pattern was different. I concluded my study there believing that when new members come into that church, most do receive a radically different self-understanding—a new narrative in which to reorganize their life histories. They have powerful emotional experiences and receive a well-formed ethic to support this new narrative. The process was more individualistic. It also may have addressed deeper aspects of the personality.

When the five dimensions of practical reason are filled in with content from the Christian narrative, they are a useful tool for diagnosis or assessment. Groups and individuals can be described in terms of where they are at the five levels. I did this in some detail for the Wiltshire Church. Each of the five levels can be looked at historically and developmentally in the life of an individual or group. I do this in some detail in chapter 8 of *Religious Ethics and Pastoral Care* (1983b). Although transformation can occur at any of the five levels, it is sometimes needed more at one level than another. Descriptive theology is implicitly a preliminary and tentative act of theological assessment.

CRISIS IS NEEDED

Crisis is a necessary but insufficient condition for transformation. Crisis destabilizes older, inadequate structures of practical reasoning exposing their inadequacies. Older organizations of practical reason may be inadequate for at least two reasons. They may be inadequate normatively: They may be theologically and philosophically skewed or deficient when tested against the classics of tradition and the demands of experience. They also may be inadequate in a second sense: The individuals or groups may not be deeply socialized into these structures. They may be held superficially.

Whatever the reason, when crisis comes, destabilization occurs. With destabilization comes a possibility for spiritual movement. This spiritual movement may come in the form of the breakup and reconstruction of the old structure of practical reason. Or it may come as a deepening and consolidation of the existing envelope and inner core of practical reason. At Wiltshire, the crisis of Sid Carlson's demands produced a breakup of the old structure, especially the narrative envelope of its practical reasoning. We saw only a desire and promise for reconstruction, but this may have been genuine and something tangible to build on. Joseph Hough thought there was evidence of grace and new hope. I tend to agree.

Crisis came to Covenant in the form of Paul Williams's challenge and the physical presence of the Salvadoran refugees. One might criticize Covenant for not following the dictates of religiously informed practical reason far enough to question basic policies of the United States. Such a criticism overlooks the great expansion of practical reason that occurred at Covenant. The people of Covenant capitalized on the destabilizing factors of their crisis and launched a reconstructive practical inquiry. Much the same thing happens at the Apostolic Church but in an ongoing fashion. African American communities experience themselves as perpetually in crisis. But no special crisis was central during my ten-month study.

WITNESS TO GOD EFFECTS AND SUPPORTS

Witnesses to the affirming, empowering, and consistent love of God both effect and support transformation. Nearly every word in this proposition has a special meaning. I will first comment on the words *effect* and *support*. Clearly love and positive regard are central to genuine transformation. But we often make too much of love, whether it be the love of a parent, the love and positive regard of a therapist, or the love and gracious countenance of God. Love and affirming regard transform in a context of other factors. These other factors are important. I already have mentioned one of these factors—crisis. From a psychoanalytic perspective, under every crisis is the deeper threat of separation from meaningful and life-sustaining relationships.

Hence, love transforms in dialectical relation to crisis and separation. Remove, downplay, repress, or attempt to avoid crisis and separation, and love may not work its transforming miracles. If the crises at any one of these three churches had been denied, witnessing to the transcendent love of God by minister or congregation would not have had its deepest effects. In fact, appeals to a sentimental view of love that denies crises and possible separation can confirm people in their various idolatries, sins, or pathologies.

I have used the word *effect* to suggest that love is a positive force. I have used the word *support* to say that love undergirds the selves of the faithful, provides a ground of trust, and bestows a sense of self-cohesion and power that holds people together while other factors in the total gestalt of transformation have time to do their work. Here the psychotherapeutic theories of Carl Rogers (Rogers 1957) and Heinz Kohut (Kohut 1971, 1978, 1984) are helpful; more helpful are the perennial testimonies of Jewish and Christian theology. The love of a minister or church leader witnesses to (is a metaphor of) the deeper love of God. Some have argued that this is also true for the love or positive regard of the therapist in secular situations. Even here, the positive regard of the therapist is a metaphor of a deeper set of unarticulated assumptions that point to the love of God for the client (Oden 1966, 1967; Browning 1966). Love transforms partially because it relaxes our defensive and self-justifying maneuvers designed to defend ourselves from anxiety. The warmth, positive regard, and constancy of attention of a therapist can do this for a client. The love and constancy of God can do the same for a religious community. Love overcomes sin because it lowers anxiety and the need to hold on desperately to our self-justifying maneuvers.

This was the wisdom in Hal Roberts's continued concentration on the law-gospel dialectic during the difficult times of the sanctuary discussion at Covenant. Roberts created what Donald Winnicott called a "holding environment" (Winnicott 1965). In this holding environment inquiry could take place into what practical reason and the justice of God required. Roberts's theology provided a support and holding environment for Nan and Hilda to energize a tension-producing education program that organized a congregation-wide practical conversation. Brazier's appeals to the love and empowerment of the Holy Spirit did something similar at the Apostolic Church. Those appeals bestowed on individuals a new sense of self (new self-cohesion) that made it possible for them to take new initiatives and think more freely about their vocations and interpersonal relationships. Instead of encouraging a cult of irrationalism, Brazier's presentation of the gospel produced a holding environment for individuals to exercise a higher degree of practical rationality.

DESCRIPTIVE THEOLOGY HELPS RESTORATION

Doing descriptive theology helps implement love and positive regard. The very act of doing descriptive theology is restorative. Individuals and groups like to be understood. If we have learned anything from the confluence of hermeneutic theory and psychotherapy, we have learned that being understood is a deep hunger of the human spirit. It gets to the heart of the universal human tendency to maintain a workable sense of self-esteem and self-cohesion. It is difficult to maintain either an individual or group identity if people feel deeply misunderstood. Nor is it possible to change people or groups (except through coercion or conditioning) if they feel deeply misunderstood. Our sense of self or identity (the two are closely related) depends heavily on the attitudes of others toward us. North American social psychology, North American pragmatism, the philosophy of Hegel, and the concept of intersubjectivity in existentialism and Habermasian critical theory all testify that individual and group identities are social phenomena. Identity is an internalization of familial, interpersonal, and socio-cultural others. Although particularly reflective individuals and groups transcend—to a degree—their social identities, this partial transcendence is precisely over socially constructed identities. This is why being understood by others, especially those others who offer transformation, is so important.

Descriptive theology attempts this deep understanding of others, their situations, and their identities. Descriptive theology is an act of empathy expressed within the limits of a historically situated dialogue. This very act communicates affirmation. It also helps discern the points of continuity between the witnessing initiators of transformation and the persons or groups addressed. This is an old rhetorical device, but a good one. Find common ground. Or, in terms of the revised correlational method, find the analogies and the identities. In fact, the nonidentities must not be ignored if mutual change is to take place. But the nonidentities should not be allowed to blot out analogies and continuities that can be named, affirmed, and built on for the future.

Descriptive theology, in attempting to understand people and groups in their concrete situations, communicates affirmation, preserves the cohesion of selves and identities, and builds on strengths. Seasoned church consultant Lyle Schaller, without the benefit of the concept of descriptive theology, recognizes the value of building on a congregation's strengths (Schaller 1983, 171). Howard Clinebell's revised model of pastoral counseling builds on the strengths of the troubled person (Clinebell 1984). Although

Schaller works with groups and Clinebell primarily with individuals, there is an analogy between their philosophies of transformation. But before one can build on strengths, some description must be done and some assessment made. The approaches to transformation of these two leaders require the movements of descriptive theology to describe, assess, and identify the strengths. But descriptive theology does more than build on strengths; it affirms and builds cohesion. The main task of descriptive theology, however, is to form questions that are brought back to the classics for the creation of new horizons of meaning. These horizons of meaning are the most basic, most threatening, and finally most truly powerful sources of transformation. These new horizons transform our fundamental visions and narratives that provide the envelope for practical reason.

Much that church development consultants do can be comprehended under the rubric of descriptive theology. They use various instruments and procedures to describe a congregation. James Anderson describes a church in terms of its identity, structure, leadership, and surrounding community (Anderson 1983, 193). This is roughly analogous to my five levels. Identity corresponds to vision and obligation. Structure and leadership are useful differentiations of the rule-role level. The community surrounding the church corresponds to my social-systemic and environmental-social levels. I mention these correspondences in order to emphasize my point that church consultants use some descriptive or diagnostic framework to gain a picture of the church. They then place this description before the congregation so that it can make freer and more informed decisions. Some church consultants see this descriptive task as primarily a social science task. Some see it as an objective and value-neutral task. Insofar as they have this self-image, they completely miss the significance of what they are doing and what they have to offer. The descriptive task of church consultants is neither strictly social scientific nor value-neutral. Rather the description emerges out of a historically located dialogue between the consultant and the congregation. Tools that are used—questionnaires, surveys, demographic information, interviews—provide slightly distanciating moments in this dialogue. The feedback to the congregation by the value-laden otherness of a seasoned and widely experienced consultant is part of what is valuable. Most church development consultants do not go far in helping the congregation move through the next three movements of fundamental practical theology—the movements of historical, systematic, and strategic practical theology. Congregations are generally expected to use their own leadership and resources to do that.

This may be the right way to proceed. But the church consultant might be useful in helping congregations comprehend the later stages of the practical theological task. In its concentration on the stage of descriptive theology (or in its too quick move from descriptive to strategic practical theology), church development is like clinical pastoral education. Although extremely helpful for stimulating the early stages of self-reflection and self-description in individuals and groups, neither is strong in carrying through the last three stages of practical theological reflection. Who does have the skills to facilitate and lead this process? To educate such persons is the central purpose of theological education.

The listening and empathy so fundamental to pastoral counseling also should be understood under the rubric of descriptive theology. When we listen, we do not simply receive information passively. We listen in order to describe, and the description comes from a particular perspective. We hear, listen, and empathize out of a particular social and historical dialogue. Listening is the first part of conversation and dialogue. Listening is never perfectly neutral, objective, or internal to what the other person or group is saying. The listener's attempt to get deeply into the internal frame of reference of the other is transitional and partial. We understand the other largely in analogy to our own experiences, although even here, as in all experience, new elements from the other's experience occasionally break through our fore-concepts. Part of the usefulness of listening in counseling (and in all human relations) is that what we gain from it can be used when it comes to communicating our understanding to the people or groups we are helping. The communication of understanding, as I said earlier, affirms, increases self-cohesion, and helps build on strengths. Pastoral counselors in communicating understanding should really see themselves as communicating their descriptive theological understanding to the troubled person. This may be done lightly, artfully, and without a heavy hand, but that is really what is being done. If pastoral counselors (and possibly all counselors who stand in the effective history of Western societies) were to bring a hermeneutical understanding to the epistemology of their work, they would see listening as a moment within the larger structure of dialogue. They also would see listening as an act of descriptive theology—an act that in itself witnesses to God's grace in creation and redemption.

Just as descriptive theology can integrate the other human sciences (psychology, sociology, anthropology, and so on) as submoments, so it can integrate the moments of listening and description characteristic of all the practical ministerial arts—counseling, education, preaching, worship, church development, social ministries

of various kinds, and so on. We can listen, at times, with a psychological, sociological, or anthropological ear, but that act is really
secondary or tertiary to listening to the fullness of the situated
dialogue.

DEMANDS OF POSITIVE IDEALS NEEDED

In order for love to be fully transformative, it must be experienced
in tension with the demands of positive ideals. Love and positive
regard that are not experienced in association with positive ideals
for responsible living do not fully stimulate the reconstructive process. For example, the moral demands at the Wiltshire Church were
minimal. They primarily pertained to individuals' capacity to persist
in the struggle to actualize themselves professionally. In contrast,
moral demands, especially concerning personal ethics, were very
high at the Apostolic Church of God. The love of God and the gift
of the Holy Spirit were available to all people, regardless of their
morality, but God's love, witnessed to by the love of the minister and church leaders, liberated and empowered the repentant to
fulfill these moral demands. One cannot understand the transformation at the Apostolic Church, or the lack of it at Wiltshire, without
attending to the differing roles of moral expectations in the two
communities.

The Church of the Covenant stands in the middle. The consistent dialectic between law and gospel that was preached there
framed a role for moral expectations although they were not the
grounds for salvation. Nor were moral expectations, we should be
reminded, the grounds for salvation at the Apostolic Church. One
difference between the churches was that moral expectations at
Covenant were stated more generally and abstractly. The law and
justice were talked about in the sermons, but their specific content
was seldom defined. At the Apostolic Church, the law and moral
expectations were crystal-clear, and Brazier was their authoritative
interpreter.

The general and abstract manner in which moral expectations
were stated at Covenant Church had its usefulness. It made it possible for the church community to participate in an active process of
moral inquiry to fill in the concrete content. I am sure some moral
questions were clear even at Covenant Church. I am sure that Hal
Roberts as the minister would not have hesitated to take a position
on many issues. On some matters, he saw his task as stimulating
inquiry. I would call this inquiry a revised correlational practical dialogue about the church's responsibility to the Salvadoran refugees.
Since the content of the law was stated vaguely, abstractly, and gen-

erally, it was possible to take this moral issue as a matter of inquiry. The minister did not have a clear answer; he knew only that there was a moral obligation to discern an answer. This made it possible for the church to move into an ambiguous new area where the answer was not entirely clear. Hal Roberts's preaching had established fully that moral demands must be taken seriously in the Christian life. He had also established that not all claims to law (not all moral demands) are on the same level. This made it possible for the congregation to take a reflective and critical attitude about which laws should be taken as appropriate guides in particular situations. Inherited or conventional law was taken seriously, but it was also taken critically. Or at least that was the case in the matter of the Salvadoran refugees.

Transformation will be either incomplete or nonexistent if the tension between moral ideals and love is not present. Agents of transformation must be able either to articulate these moral expectations or lead a community into a critical hermeneutical dialogue that aims to construct or reconstruct ideals that the community and its individuals can own. Increasingly, in this pluralistic and rapidly changing society where new moral challenges are constantly emerging, the establishment and maintenance of moral ideals will occur through critical hermeneutical dialogue of the kind I have been describing.

The deliberation at the Church of the Covenant best demonstrates how this can occur. Our research committee may have missed the point in criticizing Hal Roberts for not taking a clear stand on the sanctuary issue. He clearly took a strong moral stand on the importance of a fair and balanced moral inquiry into the matter. His leadership may have more to tell us than our team first comprehended. This leads us to the next proposition.

LEADERSHIP GUIDES THE PROCESS

Leadership is a matter of energizing, contributing to, and orchestrating the various levels of practical reasoning that function in a group. Religious groups are not always in the full heat of the reconstruction of their experience. They are not always exercising and testing the envelope and inner core of their practical reasoning. Most of the time they are functioning out of their achieved consolidations and helping their members internalize and deepen the group's settled tradition and culture.

This is good. If churches and religious groups cannot develop wisdom to pass on to their members in more or less uncomplicated processes of socialization, the gravitation and centeredness of religious institutions and the church will collapse. Nothing that I have said about the reconstruction of experience is intended to disparage settled tradition.

We must learn more about how religious groups reconstruct experience not because settled tradition is unimportant but because it is insufficient. Brazier had achieved a remarkably cohesive tradition at the Apostolic Church. Although he took the initiative in creating this tradition, there was evidence he did this over the last thirty years in dialogue with his congregation. Furthermore, changes had occurred even at the Apostolic Church. Women once could not wear cosmetics; now they can. Out-of-wedlock babies were once christened before the entire congregation; now this is done in the privacy of the pastor's study before a few family members. But I never observed or heard about a major congregation-wide process of moral inquiry at the Apostolic Church of the kind that occurred at Covenant Church. The more or less settled and piece-by-piece reconstruction at the Apostolic Church has its place, but increasingly churches will face challenges from new issues that require Covenant's type of response. Those who lead the kind of transformation that occurred at Covenant will be stronger if they envision themselves as stimulating, blessing, contributing to, and orchestrating the various dimensions of practical reasoning that play themselves out in the group. In chapter 9 we saw how the various dimensions came together at Covenant. These dimensions of practical reasoning also functioned at the Apostolic Church, but differently. We saw their presence in Brazier's complicated theory of the family and male-female relationships. In spite of that church's rhetoric of male spiritual and moral authority, we saw both an inner core of practical reason (the logic of equal regard organizing certain premoral goods) and a narrative envelope that infused this core with energy and a call to self-sacrifice. It is true, the chief agent and center of practical moral thinking at the Apostolic Church was Brazier himself. He initiated the thinking that others modeled, extended, and communicated.

The exercise of practical reasoning was more of a total group process at Covenant. Contributions to the different levels came from different sources. Clearly Hal Roberts contributed to the first two levels—the visional and obligational. He contributed a narrative about God's redeeming love, grace, and forgiveness. In his preaching on the law-gospel dialectic, he stated abstractly the importance of moral norms although he warned that they were not the grounds of salvation. Other parts of the narrative envelope came from other sources. The importance of sacrifice and the willingness to bear the cost of discipleship are parts of the emerging narrative at Covenant that came mainly from Nan and Hilda and their use of Bonhoeffer. Paul Williams himself stimulated the inner core of practical reasoning around his use of neighbor love and equal regard. He further extended this by confronting Covenant with the actual physical presence of the Salvadoran refugees. Nan Carr's mission committee determined some of the premoral goods—life, food, health, self-respect—that were at stake. Large portions of the church were involved in this practical thinking. The leadership stimulated and orchestrated this process. The structure of practical reasoning was distributed among the church's various committees and leadership groups. No single person was doing the practical reasoning for the group as a whole.

Recognizing the strengths of the process of group practical reasoning at Covenant does not invalidate the leadership-centered reasoning at the Apostolic Church. A leader often makes the chief contribution. Such leadership can be either growth-producing or infantalizing depending on how deeply the followers are permitted to process, review, and test the leader's practical moral initiatives. The quality of the leadership also depends on how thoroughly the leader shares his or her thinking and reasons with the religious group. The playful, to-and-fro character of the dialogical process at the Apostolic Church permitted much of this kind of review and testing. Also, Brazier was extremely careful to provide detailed exegetical and logical accounts of his thinking. The people trusted his practical wisdom partially because they understood it and partially because they had witnessed and tested his practical moral leadership over many years. In the total economy of religious communities in North American life, there is a place for Brazier's style.

Increasingly, however, the broad-based moral inquiry of the kind we saw at Covenant Church will be the style. This is the style that "the prophetic" will take in modern societies both in and outside religious communities. Such inquiry requires a discourse ethic of the kind I described in chapter 8. It requires a critical hermeneutical process and procedures for the redemption of validity claims. This is all the more important if the discourse of the religious community addresses secular groups in the surrounding society. In these cases, leaders will not enact the entire process of practical reasoning for the rest of the religious community to model. Some issues are so novel, so complex, and so delicate that we cannot expect any leader or group of leaders to master all the exegetical, factual, and logical demands. While leaders will contribute to practical reflection, they also must establish the conditions upon which the church or religious group can shape practical reasoning through its own study and deliberations. More and more, the concrete ideals that must be kept in tension with love will be established through critical dialogue and communicative action.

It may seem unheroic to associate the prophetic with the processes of communicative action and the ethics of discourse. But there is something positive to be said about this idea. Since the victories of the civil rights movement in the United States, many people have thought that social change must always take the form of confrontation, demonstration, and prophetic pronouncement. Although there is doubtless a time for this, the development of high levels of religio-ethical culture in our religious denominations, churches, and other religious groups is more important. The prophetic in the more dramatic sense of the word cannot function well unless it works in close conjunction with high levels of ongoing moral and religious sensibility in our religious communities. Hence the task of an ethics of discourse that guides moral inquiry is to help establish this ongoing level of religio-moral sensibility and culture. Crises can be handled better if we bring a rich and tested culture to them. The primary task of a religiously informed practical reason is to establish and maintain this religio-moral culture.

COMMUNICATIVE ACTION IS CRUCIAL

Skills in communicative action are crucial for the development of a rich and life-enhancing religio-ethical culture for churches and religious communities. A revised correlational approach to strategic practical theology is basically an approach to communication. It assumes that communication and understanding are aspects of dialogue. Dialogue between people who hold similar assumptions is challenging. It is even more challenging between those whose basic assumptions differ. A revised correlational approach to strategic practical theology can foster dialogue even when basic assumptions either are not shared or are unclear. The revised correlational approach is an apologetic approach to practical theology that enhances the noncoercive communication of the Christian faith. It should help communicate the Christian faith to the wider world. It should help communicate its wisdom as a crucial element in the reconstruction of the wider civil order. It should help guide the communication process in the churches' work of education and care both within their institutional boundaries and beyond.

As a communication process, the revised correlational approach looks for identities, nonidentities, and analogies between the Christian message and the cultures and practices of the people it addresses. It does this for the communication within the churches. It does it for the communication between the churches and the world. It sees communication as rich and multidimensional. All communication contains the dimensions of practical reason that I have discussed in this book. Surface communications have depth. The surface rules and roles of all communications are thick and theory-laden. Specific communicative messages come out of particular narrative traditions. Understanding these communications is a mutually transformative dialogue. It is a dialogue with many levels of meaning that are tested by several different kinds of rationality.

COMMUNICATIVE ACTION AND DIALOGUE

Communication is important in all of strategic practical theology's disciplines—care, education, worship, preaching, and social service. We should add church development to that list. This may be the newest and in some ways the most important of the practical theological disciplines. Almost all church consultants understand their work as contributing to the improvement of communication in the churches or religious groups they help. Newton Malony says this well in his chapter on the Wiltshire Church. Malony gave Sid Carlson and members of his official board questionnaires for rating what skills they valued in a minister. As we might expect, what Sid valued about his leadership and what the board valued were beginning to diverge significantly.

After discussing these findings, Malony says something very important: "The dialogue that is prompted by the administration of such instruments is far more important than the measures themselves" (Malony 1983, 188). Then Malony advances an intersubjective theory of truth that even Habermas might bless. He writes that most church development consultants agree that "truth exists in the interaction *between* persons rather than inside them." Truth is discovered "in the dialogue persons have with one another and...change comes through group action rather than individual insight" (189). These words say more than Malony may realize. Nearly all the theoretical discussions in the present book could be used to amplify the possible meaning of Malony's statements. It is also possible to give these sentences a trite and subjectivistic meaning that would de-emphasize the complexities of both the hermeneutical process and the five dimensions of practical reasoning.

If dialogue has the full meaning laid out in Gadamer's theory of hermeneutics and if communication entails the redemption of validity claims as outlined by Habermas, then the concerns with communication and dialogue found among educators, counselors, organization consultants, and many others are profound. They can point to a new understanding of theology of the kind attempted in this book. They can point to the need for a fundamental practical theology with the movements of descriptive, historical, systematic, and fully practical theology.

BIBLIOGRAPHY

Allen, Charles
  1989   "The Primacy of *Phronēsis.*" *The Journal of Religion* 69, no. 3:359–74.

Ames, Edward S.
  1929   *Religion.* New York: Henry Holt and Co.

Anderson, James
  1983   "Crisis, Communication and Courage." In *Building Effective Ministry*, edited by Carl Dudley, 192–210. San Francisco: Harper and Row.

Andolsen, Barbara
  1981   "Agape in Feminist Ethics." *The Journal of Religion* 9:69–83

Aristotle
  1941a   *Nichomachean Ethics.* In *The Basic Works of Aristotle*, edited by Richard McKeon, 332–581. New York: Random House.

  1941b   *Rhetoric.* In *The Basic Works of Aristotle*, edited by Richard McKeon, 716–59. New York: Random House.

Ayer, A. J.
  1946   *Language, Truth, and Logic.* New York: Dover.

Bakan, David
  1958   *Sigmund Freud and the Jewish Mystical Tradition.* Princeton, N.J.: D. van Nostrand.

Ballard, Paul, ed.
  1986   *Foundations of Pastoral Studies and Practical Theology.* Cardiff:
          Faculty of Theology.

Barth, Karl
  1936   *Church Dogmatics,* I/1. Edinburgh: T. and T. Clark.

Bass, Dorothy
  1989   "A Church Town: A History of Presbyterians and Education in
          Centerville." In *Tensions between Citizenship and Discipleship: A
          Case Study,* edited by Nelle Slater, 27–40. New York: Pilgrim Press.

Bellah, Robert
  1983a   "The Ethical Aims of Social Inquiry." In *Social Sciences as Moral
          Inquiry,* edited by Norma Haan et al., 360–82. New York: Columbia
          University Press.

  1983b   "Social Science as Practical Reason." In *Ethics, Social Sciences,
          and Policy Analysis,* edited by Daniel Callahan and Bruce Jen-
          nings, 37–64. New York: Plenum Press.

Bellah, Robert, et al.
  1985   *Habits of the Heart.* Berkeley: University of California Press.

Bernstein, Richard
  1983   *Beyond Objectivism and Relativism.* Philadelphia: University of
          Pennsylvania Press.

Betz, Hans Dieter
  1979   *Galatians.* Philadelphia: Fortress Press.

Bion, W. R.
  1961   *Experiences in Groups.* New York: Basic Books.

Bonhoeffer, Dietrich
  1949   *The Cost of Discipleship.* New York: Macmillan.

Bowlby, John
  1969   *Attachment and Loss.* New York: Basic Books.

  1973   *Separation.* New York: Basic Books.

Boys, Mary
  1989a   *Education in Faith: Maps and Visions.* San Francisco: Harper and
          Row.

1989b "Religious Education: A Map of the Field." In *Education for Citizenship and Discipleship*, edited by Mary Boys, 98–129. New York: Pilgrim Press.

Brandt, Lewis
1982   *Psychologist Caught.* Toronto: University of Toronto Press.

Brandt, R. B.
1959   *Ethical Theory.* Englewood Cliffs, N.J.: Prentice Hall.

Brazier, Arthur
1969   *Black Self-determination.* Grand Rapids, Mich.: William B. Eerdmans.

Browning, Don
1966   *Atonement and Psychotherapy.* Philadelphia: Westminster Press.

1973   *Generative Man.* Philadelphia: Westminster Press.

1976   *The Moral Context of Pastoral Care.* Philadelphia: Westminster Press.

1980   *Pluralism and Personality.* Lewisburg, Pa.: Bucknell University Press.

1983a Ed. *Practical Theology.* San Francisco: Harper and Row.

1983b *Religious Ethics and Pastoral Care.* Philadelphia: Fortress Press.

1986   "Globalization and the Task of Theological Education." *Theological Education* 33:43–59.

1987   *Religious Thought and the Modern Psychologies.* Philadelphia: Fortress Press.

1988   "Congregational Care in an Activist Church." In *Beyond Clericalism*, edited by Barbara Wheeler and Joseph Hough, 103–18. Atlanta: Scholars Press.

Browning, Don, David Polk, and Ian Evison, eds.
1989   *The Education of the Practical Theologian: Responses to Joseph Hough and John Cobb's "Christian Identity and Theological Education."* Atlanta: Scholars Press.

Browning, Robert, and Roy Reed
1985   *The Sacraments in Religious Education.* Birmingham, Ala.: Religious Education Press.

Brueggemann, Walter
  1989   "Textuality in the Church." In *Tensions between Citizenship and Discipleship: A Case Study*, edited by Nelle Slater, 48–69. New York: Pilgrim Press.

Brundage, James
  1987   *Law and Sex in Christian Society in Medieval Europe.* Chicago: University of Chicago Press.

Burkhart, John E.
  1983   "Schleiermacher's Vision for Theology." In *Practical Theology*, edited by Don Browning, 42–57. San Francisco: Harper and Row.

Campbell, Alistair
  1972   "Is Practical Theology Possible?" *Scottish Journal of Theology* 25:217–27.

Carroll, Jackson, William McKinney, and Wade Clark Roof
  1983   "From the Outside In and the Inside Out." In *Building Effective Ministry*, edited by Carl Dudley, 84–111. San Francisco: Harper and Row.

Chopp, Rebecca
  1987   "Practical Theology and Liberation." In *Formation and Reflection*, edited by Lewis Mudge and James Poling, 120–38. Philadelphia: Fortress Press.

Clinebell, Howard
  1966   *Basic Types of Pastoral Counseling.* Nashville: Abingdon Press. Revised edition 1984.

Corrington, Robert
  1987   *The Community of Interpreters: On the Hermeneutics of Nature and the Bible in the American Philosophical Tradition.* Macon, Ga.: Mercer University Press.

Cremin, Lawrence
  1976   *Public Education.* New York: Basic Books.

Dahl, Norman
  1984   *Practical Reason, Aristotle, and Weakness of the Will.* Minneapolis: University of Minnesota Press.

D'Arcy, Martin
1959 *The Mind and Heart of Love.* New York: Meridian Books.

Dean, William
1986 *American Religious Empiricism.* Albany: State University of New York Press.

Dewey, John
1934 *A Common Faith.* New Haven: Yale University Press.

Dilthey, Wilhelm
1972 "The Rise of Hermeneutics." *New Literary History* 3 (Winter): 229–44. Originally published 1900.

Donagan, Alan
1977 *The Theory of Morality.* Chicago: University of Chicago Press.

Dudley, Carl, ed.
1983 *Building Effective Ministry.* San Francisco: Harper and Row.

Dykstra, Craig
1981 *Vision and Character.* New York: Paulist Press.

Ehrenreich, Barbara
1983 *The Hearts of Men.* Garden City, N.Y.: Anchor Press/Doubleday.

Elshtain, Jean Bethke
1988 *The Family in Political Theory.* Grand Rapids, Mich.: William B. Eerdmans.

Erikson, Erik
1963 *Childhood and Society.* New York: W. W. Norton.

Evans, Barry, and Bruce Reed
1983 "The Success and Failure of a Religious Club." In *Building Effective Ministry,* edited by Carl Dudley, 33–54. San Francisco: Harper and Row.

Ewing, J. W.
1965 *Ethics.* New York: The Free Press.

Farley, Edward
1983a *Theologia.* Philadelphia: Fortress Press.

1983b   "Theology and Practice Outside the Clerical Paradigm." In *Practical Theology*, edited by Don Browning, 21–41. San Francisco: Harper and Row.

1987   "Interpreting Situations: An Inquiry into the Nature of Practical Theology." In *Formation and Reflection*, edited by Lewis Mudge and James Poling, 1–26. Philadelphia: Fortress Press.

1988   *The Fragility of Knowledge.* Philadelphia: Fortress Press.

Fiorenza, Elisabeth Schüssler
1983   *In Memory of Her.* New York: Crossroad.

Firet, J.
1987   *Dynamics in Pastoring.* Grand Rapids, Mich.: William B. Eerdmans.

Fish, John
1973   *Black Power/White Control.* Princeton, N.J.: Princeton University Press.

Fletcher, Joseph
1966   *Situation Ethics.* San Francisco: Harper and Row.

Fowler, James
1981   *The Stages of Faith.* San Francisco: Harper and Row.

1983   "Practical Theology and the Shaping of Christian Lives." In *Practical Theology*, edited by Don Browning, 148–66. San Francisco: Harper and Row.

1987   *Faith, Development, and Pastoral Care.* Philadelphia: Fortress Press.

Frankena, William
1973   *Ethics.* Englewood Cliffs, N.J.: Prentice Hall.

Frankenberry, Nancy
1987   *Religion and Radical Empiricism.* Albany: State University of New York Press.

Frei, Hans
1974   *The Eclipse of Biblical Narrative.* New Haven: Yale University Press.

Freire, Paulo
1970   *The Pedagogy of the Oppressed.* New York: Seabury Press.

Freud, Sigmund
1964   *New Introductory Lectures on Psycho-Analysis.* In vol. 22 of *The Standard Edition of the Complete Psychological Works of Sigmund Freud,* 3–182. London: Hogarth Press. Originally published 1933.

Frye, Northrop
1957   *Anatomy of Criticism.* Princeton, N.J.: Princeton University Press.

Fuller, Robert
1986   *Americans and the Unconscious.* New York: Oxford University Press.

Gadamer, Hans-Georg
1982   *Truth and Method.* New York: Crossroad.

Gager, John
1975   *Kingdom and Community.* Englewood Cliffs, N.J.: Prentice Hall.

Geertz, Clifford
1973   *The Interpretation of Culture.* New York: Basic Books.

Gendlin, Eugene
1962   *Experiencing and the Creation of Meaning.* New York: Free Press of Glencoe.

Gergen, Kenneth
1973   "Social Psychology as History." *Journal of Personality and Social Psychology* 26:309–20.

1982   *Toward Transformation of Social Knowledge.* New York: Springer-Verlag.

Gerkin, Charles
1984   *The Living Human Document: Revisioning Pastoral Counseling in a Hermeneutical Mode.* Nashville: Abingdon Press.

1986   *Widening the Horizons: Pastoral Responses to a Fragmented Society.* Philadelphia: Westminster Press.

Gewirth, Alan
1978   *Reason and Morality.* Chicago: University of Chicago Press.

Gilligan, Carol
 1982   *In a Different Voice.* Cambridge: Harvard University Press.

Goldberg, Michael
 1982   *Theology and Narrative.* Nashville: Abingdon Press.

Goldstein, Valerie
 1960   "The Human Situation: A Feminine View." *The Journal of Religion*
         40, no. 2 (April): 100–112.

Grant, Jacquelyn
 1989   *White Woman's Christ and Black Woman's Jesus.* Atlanta: Scholars
         Press.

Green, Ronald
 1978   *Religious Reason.* New York: Oxford University Press.

Gresser, Moshe
 1989   "Sigmund Freud's Jewish Identity: A Study of His Correspon-
         dence." Ph.D. diss., University of Chicago.

Groome, Thomas
 1980   *Christian Religious Education.* New York: Harper and Row.

 1987   "Theology on Our Feet: A Revisionist Pedagogy for Healing
         the Gap between Academia and Ecclesia." In *Formation and
         Reflection,* edited by Lewis Mudge and James Poling, 55–78.
         Philadelphia: Fortress Press.

 1989   "A Religious Educator's Response." In *The Education of the Prac-
         tical Theologian,* edited by Don Browning, David Polk, and Ian
         Evison, 77–91. Atlanta: Scholars Press.

Gudorf, Christine
 1985   "Parenting, Mutual Love, and Sacrifice." In *Women's Conscious-
         ness, Women's Conscience,* edited by Barbara Andolsen et al.,
         175–91. New York: Seabury Press.

Gustafson, James
 1970   *The Church as Moral Decision Maker.* New York: Pilgrim Press.

Gutman, David
 1968   "Aging among the Highland Maya." *Journal of Personality and
         Social Psychology* 7:28–35.

1969   *The Country of Old Men.* Occasional Papers in Gerontology, no. 5. Ann Arbor: University of Michigan Press.

1974   "Alternatives to Disengagement: The Old Men of the Highland Druze." In *Culture and Personality,* edited by Robert A. LeVine, 232–45. Chicago: Aldine.

1987   *Reclaimed Powers: Toward a New Psychology of Men and Women in Later Life.* New York: Basic Books.

Habermas, Jürgen
1971   *Knowledge and Human Interests.* Boston: Beacon Press.

1973   *Theory and Practice.* Boston: Beacon Press.

1979   *Communication and the Evolution of Society.* Boston: Beacon Press.

1984   *Theory of Communicative Action.* Vol. 1, *Reason and the Rationalization of Society.* Boston: Beacon Press.

1987   *Theory of Communicative Action.* Vol. 2, *Lifeworld and System: A Critique of Functionalist Reason.* Boston: Beacon Press.

1990   *Moral Consciousness and Communicative Action.* Cambridge: MIT Press.

1991   "Response." In *Habermas, Modernity, and Public Theology,* edited by Don S. Browning and Francis Schüssler Fiorenza. New York: Crossroad.

Hadden, Jeffrey
1969   *The Gathering Storm in the Churches.* Garden City, N.J.: Doubleday.

Hardin, Russell
1988   *Morality within the Limits of Reason.* Chicago: University of Chicago Press.

Hare, R. M.
1952   *The Language of Morals.* Oxford: Clarendon Press.

Harlow, Harry F., and Margaret K. Harlow
1965   "The Affectional Systems." In *Behavior of Nonhuman Primates: Modern Research Trends,* edited by A. M. Schrier et al., 287–334. London and New York: Academic Press.

Hartshorne, Charles

    1953   *Reality as Social Process.* Boston: Beacon Press.

Hauerwas, Stanley

    1974   *Vision and Virtue.* Notre Dame, Ind.: Fides Publishers.

    1975a *Character and the Christian Life.* San Antonio: Trinity University Press.

    1975b "The Ethicist as Theologian." *Christian Century* 92, no. 15 (April): 408–12.

    1977   *Truthfulness and Tragedy.* Notre Dame, Ind.: University of Notre Dame Press.

    1982   *A Community of Character.* Notre Dame, Ind.: University of Notre Dame Press.

Hauerwas, Stanley, and William Willimon

    1989   *Resident Aliens: Life in the Christian Colony.* Nashville: Abingdon Press.

Hekman, Susan

    1986   *Hermeneutics and the Sociology of Knowledge.* Notre Dame, Ind.: University of Notre Dame Press.

Hiltner, Seward

    1949   *Pastoral Counseling.* Nashville: Abingdon Press.

Holifield, Brooks

    1983   *A History of Pastoral Care in America.* Nashville: Abingdon Press.

Hopewell, James

    1983   "The Jovial Church: Narrative in Local Church Life." In *Building Effective Ministry,* edited by Carl Dudley, 68–83. San Francisco: Harper and Row.

    1987   *Congregation: Stories and Structures.* Philadelphia: Fortress Press.

Hough, Joseph

    1983   "Theologian at Work: Theological Ethics." In *Building Effective Ministry,* edited by Carl Dudley, 112–32. San Francisco: Harper and Row.

Hough, Joseph, and John Cobb
  1985   *Christian Identity and Theological Education.* Atlanta: Scholars
          Press.

Houlgate, Lawrence
  1988   *Family and State.* Totowa, N.J.: Rowman and Littlefield.

Hume, David
  1957   *An Inquiry concerning the Principles of Morals.* Indianapolis:
          Bobbs-Merrill. Originally published 1751.

Husserl, Edmund
  1970   *The Crisis of European Science and Transcendental Phenomenol-
          ogy.* Evanston, Ill.: Northwestern University Press. Originally
          published 1936.

James, William
  1955   *Pragmatism.* New York: Meridian Books. Originally published
          1907.

  1956   *The Will to Believe.* New York: Dover Publications. Originally
          published 1897.

  1970   *The Meaning of Truth.* Ann Arbor: University of Michigan Press.
          Originally published 1909.

  1971   *Essays in Radical Empiricism and a Pluralistic Universe.* New York:
          E. P. Dutton. Originally published 1912 and 1908, respectively.

Janssens, Louis
  1977   "Norms and Priorities in a Love Ethics." *Louvain Studies* 6:207–38.

Johann, Robert
  1955   *The Meaning of Love.* Westminster, Md.: Newman Press.

Johnson, Benton
  1982   "Taking Stock: Reflections on the End of Another Era." *Journal
          for the Scientific Study of Religion* 21:189–200.

Kant, Immanuel
  1956   *Critique of Practical Reason.* Indianapolis: Bobbs-Merrill. Origi-
          nally published 1788.

  1959   *Foundations of the Metaphysics of Morals.* Indianapolis: Bobbs-
          Merrill. Originally published 1785.

Karier, Clarence
   1986   *Scientists of the Mind.* Urbana: University of Illinois Press.

Keat, Russell
   1981   *The Politics of Social Theory.* Chicago: University of Chicago Press.

Klein, Dennis B.
   1985   *Jewish Origins of the Psychoanalytic Movement.* Chicago: University of Chicago Press.

Klostermann, Ferdinand, and Rolf Zerfass
   1974   *Praktische Theologie heute.* München-Mainz: Kaiser.

Koch, Margaret
   1989   "Feminism through the Lens of History." Paper presented at the Calvin Center for Christian Scholarship, Calvin College, Grand Rapids, Mich.

Kohlberg, Lawrence
   1981   *The Philosophy of Moral Development: Moral Stages and the Idea of Justice.* San Francisco: Harper and Row.

Kohut, Heinz
   1971   *The Analysis of the Self.* New York: International Universities Press.

   1978   *The Restoration of the Self.* New York: International Universities Press.

   1984   *How Does Analysis Cure?* Chicago: University of Chicago Press.

Kuhn, Thomas
   1970   *The Structure of Scientific Revolutions.* 2d, enl. ed. Chicago: University of Chicago Press.

Lamb, Matthew
   1976   "The Theory-Praxis Relationship in Contemporary Christian Theologies." *Catholic Theological Society Proceedings* 31:149–78.

   1982   *Solidarity with Victims.* New York: Crossroad.

Lasch, Christopher
   1978   *The Culture of Narcissism.* New York: W. W. Norton.

Lewin, Kurt

   1951   *Field in Social Science*. New York: Harper.

Lindbeck, George

   1984   *The Nature of Doctrine*. Philadelphia: Westminster Press.

Lovell, John

   1972   *Black Song: The Forge and the Flame; the Story of How the Afro-American Spiritual Was Hammered Out*. New York: Macmillan.

McCann, Dennis, and C. Strain

   1985   *Polity and Praxis*. New York: Winston Press.

McCarthy, Thomas

   1978   *The Critical Theory of Jürgen Habermas*. Cambridge: MIT Press.

McClendon, William

   1974   *Biography as Theology*. Nashville: Abingdon Press.

McCormick, Richard

   1984   *Health and Medicine in the Catholic Tradition*. New York: Crossroad.

McFague, Sallie

   1982   *Metaphorical Theology*. Philadelphia: Fortress Press.

   1987   *Models of God: Theology for an Ecological Nuclear Age*. Philadelphia: Fortress Press.

MacIntyre, Alasdair

   1981   *After Virtue*. Notre Dame, Ind.: University of Notre Dame Press.

   1988   *Whose Justice? Which Rationality?* Notre Dame, Ind.: University of Notre Dame Press.

McNeill, John T.

   1951   *A History of the Cure of Souls*. New York: Harper and Brothers.

Malherbe, Abraham J.

   1987   *Paul and Thessalonians: The Philosophical Tradition of Pastoral Care*. Philadelphia: Fortress Press.

Malony, Newton
>   1983   "A Framework for Understanding and Helping the Church." In
>   *Building Effective Ministry*, edited by Carl Dudley, 175–91. San
>   Francisco: Harper and Row.

Maslow, Abraham
>   1954   *Motivation and Personality*. New York: Harper and Brothers.

Mead, Loren
>   1983   "Seeking Significant Intervention." In *Building Effective Ministry*,
>   edited by Carl Dudley, 155–59. San Francisco: Harper and Row.

Meeks, Wayne
>   1986   *The Moral World of the First Christians*. Philadelphia: Westminster
>   Press.

Mette, Norbert
>   1980   *Theorie der Praxis*. Düsseldorf: Patmos Verlag.

Metz, Johann Baptist
>   1980   *Faith in History and Society*. New York: Crossroad.

Midgley, Mary
>   1978   *Beast and Man: The Roots of Human Nature*. Ithaca, N.Y.: Cornell
>   University Press.

Miller, Donald
>   1987   *Story and Context*. Nashville: Abingdon Press.

Miller, Donald, and James Poling
>   1985   *Foundations for a Practical Theology of Ministry*. Nashville: Abing-
>   don Press.

Mitchell, Basil
>   1980   *Morality: Religious and Secular*. Oxford: Clarendon Press.

Moore, G. E.
>   1965   *Ethics*. New York: Oxford University Press.

Mudge, Lewis, and James Poling
>   1987   *Formation and Reflection*. Philadelphia: Fortress Press.

Murdoch, Iris
   1970   *The Sovereignty of Good.* New York: Schocken Books.

Nelson, C. Ellis
   1971   *Where Faith Begins.* Atlanta: John Knox Press.

   1989   *How Faith Matures.* Louisville: Westminster/John Knox Press.

Nelson, James
   1979   *Embodiment: An Approach to Sexuality and Christian Theology.* Minneapolis: Augsburg.

Nelson, Paul
   1987   *Narrative and Morality.* University Park: Pennsylvania State University Press.

Niebuhr, H. Richard
   1963   *The Responsible Self.* New York: Harper and Brothers.

Niebuhr, Reinhold R.
   1941   *The Nature and Destiny of Man.* Vol. 1, *Nature.* New York: Charles Scribner's Sons.

   1943   *The Nature and Destiny of Man.* Vol. 2, *Destiny.* New York: Charles Scribner's Sons.

   1955   *The Self and the Dramas of History.* New York: Charles Scribner's Sons.

Nygren, Anders
   1953   *Agape and Eros.* Philadelphia: Westminster Press.

Oates, Wayne
   1962   *Protestant Pastoral Counseling.* Philadelphia: Westminster Press.

Oden, Thomas
   1966   *Kerygma and Counseling.* Philadelphia: Westminster Press.

   1967   *Contemporary Theology and Psychotherapy.* Philadelphia: Westminster Press.

   1980   "Recovering Lost Identity." *Journal of Pastoral Care* 34, no. 1 (March): 4-19.

Ogden, Schubert

   1979   *Faith and Freedom.* Nashville: Abingdon Press.

   1986   *On Theology.* San Francisco: Harper and Row.

Okin, Susan Moller

   1989   *Justice, Gender and the Family.* New York: Basic Books.

Outka, Gene

   1972   *Agape: An Ethical Analysis.* New Haven: Yale University Press.

Pacini, David

   1983   "Professionalism, Breakdown, and Revelation: Philosophical Theology." In *Building Effective Ministry*, edited by Carl Dudley, 133–52. San Francisco: Harper and Row.

Pannenberg, Wolfhart

   1976   *Theology and the Philosophy of Science.* Philadelphia: Westminster Press.

Parsons, Talcott

   1960   *Structure and Process in Modern Societies.* New York: The Free Press.

   1964   *Social Structure and Personality.* New York: The Free Press.

Parsons, Talcott, and R. Bales

   1955   *Family Socialization and Interaction Process.* New York: The Free Press of Glencoe.

Peukert, Helmut

   1984   *Science, Action, and Fundamental Theology.* Cambridge: MIT Press.

Popenoe, David

   1988   *Disturbing the Nest: Family Change and Decline in Modern Societies.* New York: Aldine-DeGruyter.

   1989   "The Family Transformed." *Family Affairs* 2:1–5.

Pugh, George

   1977   *The Biological Origin of Human Values.* New York: Basic Books.

Rawls, John
  1971   *A Theory of Justice.* Cambridge: Harvard University Press.

Ricoeur, Paul
  1966   *Freedom and Nature.* Evanston, Ill.: Northwestern University Press.

  1970   *Freud and Philosophy.* New Haven: Yale University Press.

  1974   *The Conflict of Interpretations.* Evanston, Ill.: Northwestern University Press.

  1981   *Hermeneutics and the Human Sciences.* Cambridge: Cambridge University Press.

  1989   "Entre philosophie et theologie: La regle d'or en question." *Revue d'historie et de philosophie religieuses* 69:3-9.

Rieff, Philip
  1959   *Freud: The Mind of a Moralist.* New York: Harper and Row.

  1966   *Triumph of the Therapeutic.* New York: Harper and Row.

Rogers, Carl
  1957   *Client-centered Therapy.* Boston: Houghton Mifflin.

Roof, W. C., and W. McKinney
  1987   *American Mainline Religion.* New Brunswick, N.J.: Rutgers University Press.

Rorty, Richard
  1979   *Philosophy and the Mirror of Nature.* Princeton, N.J.: Princeton University Press.

  1982   *Consequences of Pragmatism (Essays: 1972-1980).* Minneapolis: University of Minnesota Press.

Rossi, Alice
  1977   "A Biosocial Perspective on Parenting." *Daedalus* 106:1-32.

Rössler, Dietrich
  1986   *Grundriss der praktischen Theologie.* Berlin: Walter de Gruyter.

Ruether, Rosemary
  1975   *New Woman, New Earth.* New York: Seabury Press.

1983   *Sexism and God-talk.* Boston: Beacon Press.

Ruse, Michael
1985   "The Morality of the Gene." *The Monist* 67 (April): 167–99.

Sanders, Cheryl
1989   "Christian Ethics and Theology in Womanist Perspective." *Journal of Feminist Studies in Religion* 5 (Fall): 83–91.

Schafer, Roy
1980   "Narration in the Psychoanalytic Dialogue." *Critical Inquiry* 7, no. 1 (Fall): 29–53.

Schaller, Lyle
1983   "A Practitioner's Perspective: Policy Planning." In *Building Effective Ministry,* edited by Carl Dudley, 160–79. San Francisco: Harper and Row.

Schleiermacher, Friedrich
1966   *Brief Outline on the Study of Theology.* Richmond, Va.: John Knox Press. Originally published 1830.

Schön, Donald
1983   *The Reflective Practitioner: How Professionals Think in Action.* New York: Basic Books.

Schreiter, Robert
1985   *Constructing Local Theologies.* Maryknoll, N.Y.: Orbis Books.

Segundo, Juan
1976   *Liberation of Theology.* Maryknoll, N.Y.: Orbis Books.

Seymour, Jack, and Donald Miller
1982   *Contemporary Approaches to Christian Education.* Nashville: Abingdon Press.

1990   *Theological Perspectives in Christian Education.* Nashville: Abingdon Press.

Shea, Daniel
1974   "B. F. Skinner: The Puritan Within." *The Virginia Quarterly Review* 1 (Summer): 416–37.

Sidgwick, Henry
    1962   *The Methods of Ethics.* Chicago: University of Chicago Press.

Silberman, Charles
    1964   *Crisis in Black and White.* New York: Random House.

Singer, Peter
    1981   *The Expanding Circle: Ethics and Sociobiology.* New York: Farrar, Straus, and Giroux.

Slater, Nelle, ed.
    1989   *Tensions between Citizenship and Discipleship: A Case Study.* New York: Pilgrim Press.

Smith, Archie
    1982   *The Relational Self: Ethics and Therapy from a Black Church Perspective.* Nashville: Abingdon Press.

Spence, Donald
    1982   *Narrative Truth and Historical Truth.* New York: W. W. Norton and Co.

Stokes, Allison
    1985   *Ministry after Freud.* New York: Pilgrim Press.

Stout, Jeffrey
    1981   *The Flight from Authority.* Notre Dame, Ind.: University of Notre Dame Press.

    1988   *Ethics after Babel.* Boston: Beacon Press.

Strawson, Peter F.
    1966   "Social Morality and Individual Ideals." In *Christian Ethics and Contemporary Philosophy*, edited by Ian T. Ramsey, 280–98. New York: Macmillan.

Theissen, Gerd
    1978   *Sociology of Early Palestinian Christianity.* Philadelphia: Fortress Press.

Thielicke, Helmut
    1964   *The Ethics of Sex.* New York: Harper and Row.

Tillich, Paul

    1951   *Systematic Theology.* Vol. 1. Chicago: University of Chicago Press.

    1952   *The Courage to Be.* New Haven: Yale University Press.

    1963   *Systematic Theology.* Vol. 3. Chicago: University of Chicago Press.

    1966   *On the Boundary.* New York: Charles Scribner's Sons.

Tinder, Glenn

    1989a   "Can We Be Good without God?" *The Atlantic Monthly* 264 (December): 69–85.

    1989b   *The Political Meaning of Christianity.* Baton Rouge: Louisiana State University Press.

Tipton, Steven

    1982   *Getting Saved from the Sixties.* Berkeley: University of California Press.

Tracy, David

    1975   *Blessed Rage for Order.* Minneapolis: Seabury Press.

    1981   *The Analogical Imagination.* New York: Crossroad.

    1983   "Foundations of Practical Theology." In *Practical Theology*, edited by Don Browning, 61–82. San Francisco: Harper and Row.

    1991   "Theology, Critical Social Theory, and the Public Realm." In *Habermas, Modernity, and Public Theology*, edited by Don S. Browning and Francis Schüssler Fiorenza. New York: Crossroad.

Turner, Victor

    1969   *The Ritual Process.* Chicago: Aldine.

van der Ven, Johannes

    1988   "Practical Theology: From Applied to Empirical Theology." *Journal of Empirical Theology* 1:7–28.

Viau, Marcel

    1987   *Introduction aux études pastorales.* Montreal: Paulines.

Vitz, Paul

    1988   *Sigmund Freud's Christian Unconscious.* New York: Guilford Press.

    1990   "The Use of Stories in Moral Development." *American Psychologist* 45:706–20.

Walzer, Michael
1983 *Spheres of Justice.* New York: Basic Books.

Warner, Stephen
1988 *New Wine in Old Wineskins: Evangelicals and Liberals in a Small-town Church.* Berkeley: University of California Press.

Weber, Max
1958 *The Protestant Ethic and the Spirit of Capitalism.* New York: Charles Scribner's Sons. Originally published 1904–5.

Weinreb, Lloyd
1987 *Natural Law and Justice.* Cambridge: Harvard University Press.

Westerhoff, John
1983 *Building God's People.* New York: Seabury Press.

Wheeler, Barbara, and Joseph Hough
1988 *Beyond Clericalism: The Congregation as a Focus for Theological Education.* Atlanta: Scholars Press.

White, Stephen
1988 *The Recent Work of Jürgen Habermas.* Cambridge: Cambridge University Press.

Whitehead, Alfred N.
1960 *Process and Reality.* New York: Harper Brothers. Originally published 1929.

Whitehead, James, and Evelyn Whitehead
1980 *Method in Ministry.* New York: Seabury Press.

Wilcox, Mary
1979 *Developmental Journey.* Nashville: Abingdon Press.

Wilkerman, Isabel
1990 "Facing Grim Data on Young Males." *New York Times,* July 17, sec. A, p. 14.

Williams, Daniel Day
1968 *The Spirit and the Forms of Love.* New York: Harper and Row.

Williams, Melvin
    1974   *Community in a Black Pentecostal Church: An Anthropological Study.* Pittsburgh: University of Pittsburgh Press.

    1983   "The Conflict of Corporate Church and Spiritual Church." In *Building Effective Ministry,* edited by Carl Dudley, 55–67. San Francisco: Harper and Row.

Wilson, E. O.
    1975   *Sociobiology.* Cambridge: Harvard University Press.

    1978   *On Human Nature.* Cambridge: Harvard University Press.

Wilson, William J.
    1987   *The Truly Disadvantaged.* Chicago: University of Chicago Press.

Winnicott, Donald
    1965   *The Maturational Process and the Facilitating Environment.* London: Hogarth Press.

Winquist, Charles
    1981   *Practical Hermeneutics.* Chico, Calif.: Scholars Press.

Winter, Gibson
    1962   *The Suburban Captivity of the Churches.* New York: Macmillan.

Wise, Carol
    1951   *Pastoral Counseling.* New York: Harper and Brothers.

Wood, Charles
    1985   *Vision and Discernment.* Atlanta: Scholars Press.

INDEX OF NAMES

INDEX OF SUBJECTS

practical reason (cont.)
    rule-role dimensions of practical
    reason, and *phronēsis*
    dimensions of, x, 2, 16, 17, 26, 56,
    66, 71, 84, 93, 94, 97, 104–13, 116,
    120–22, 127, 130, 135, 139–42, 146,
    149–51, 156, 158, 164, 165, 170, 173,
    183, 184, 191, 194, 196, 197, 201–3,
    207, 215, 221–23, 228, 234, 237, 250,
    276, 280, 281, 285, 288, 289, 292
    inner core, 10–12, 26, 40, 93, 104, 107,
    150, 151, 158–60, 162, 170, 173, 194,
    196, 197, 234, 235, 282, 288–90
    levels of. *See* practical reason,
    dimensions of
    outer envelope of, 10–12, 26, 40, 93,
    106, 107, 150, 194, 234, 239, 282,
    285, 288, 289
practical theology, ix, xi, xii, 3–5, 7–9, 12,
    15, 16, 33, 34, 35–38, 42–44, 46–49,
    51, 52, 54–62, 64–72, 74, 81, 82,
    92–94, 96–98, 102, 122, 132, 134,
    135, 139, 140–42, 148–51, 154, 155,
    158, 166, 170, 179, 211–13, 215, 218,
    219, 221, 231, 235, 243, 247, 248–50,
    267, 272–74, 278, 279, 285, 286, 291,
    292, 293
    practice-theory-practice model, 9, 39,
    97, 123, 132, 213, 216–18, 228, 230,
    279
    theory-to-practice or applicational
    model, 5, 7, 39, 41, 43, 51, 56, 57,
    60, 66, 67, 78–80
pragmatism, 2, 8, 15, 40, 50–52, 63, 69,
    70, 91, 174, 175, 179–81, 284
praxis, 3, 4, 17, 38, 47, 49, 51, 54–57,
    59–62, 66–68, 71, 84, 94, 96, 107,
    139, 212, 213, 217–23, 231, 235, 238,
    249, 250
prayer, 32, 244, 253, 259
preaching, ix, 8, 9, 20, 25, 27, 29, 31, 57,
    58, 97, 129, 132, 172, 227, 234, 243,
    244, 256, 257, 286, 288, 289, 292
premoral good, x, 71, 100, 102–4, 107,
    161–64, 166–69, 183, 187, 189,
    193–95, 202, 205, 271–74, 277, 289,
    290
pre-understanding, x, xi, 17, 38, 41, 48,
    74, 82, 83, 89, 128
privatism, 67, 117–20, 122, 133, 134, 149,
    168, 170, 252
process philosophy, 63, 91, 191
psychiatry, 31, 72, 80, 98
psychoanalysis, 61, 65, 83–85, 200, 238,
    241, 246, 248, 268, 282
psychobiology, 103, 106, 111, 114, 167–69,
    181, 274
psychology, x, 31, 37, 48, 60, 61, 65,
    77–83, 85, 89–92, 98, 99, 101, 110,
    111, 113–16, 121, 122, 126, 127, 130,
    131, 142, 149, 162, 169, 190, 202,

    238, 241, 245, 246, 255, 256, 258,
    264, 265, 273, 276, 284, 286, 287
psychotherapy, 31, 84, 85, 89, 90, 98, 99,
    126, 142, 184, 185, 245–47, 255, 256,
    264, 280, 282–84
public ministry, 8, 21, 23, 31, 35, 57, 58,
    68, 72, 114, 227, 252, 286
purposive rationality. *See* technical
    reason

racism, 31, 247, 251, 272
radical empiricism, 149, 179–82, 188, 195,
    196
reason, 1, 10, 18, 38, 43, 45, 102–5, 116,
    144, 145, 153, 154, 165, 168, 173,
    176, 179, 182, 188–90, 201, 202, 222,
    240. *See also phronēsis,* practical
    reason, technical reason, and
    theoretical reason
relativism, 69, 168, 173, 183
religious education, ix, 8, 9, 12, 22, 23, 51,
    56, 57, 81, 95–97, 132, 211, 212–22,
    223, 224, 227, 228, 231, 235, 237,
    238, 240, 242, 248, 278
religious experience, 17, 31, 32, 45, 53,
    54, 61, 65, 143, 264, 265
resurrection, 68, 148, 204, 239
revelation, 5, 10, 54, 188, 197, 212, 220
    general, 143, 144, 180, 181
    special, 146, 147, 180, 181
revised correlational method, 33, 5ꞁ, 60,
    61, 63, 68–71, 97, 98, 102, 179, 181,
    211, 212, 215, 217, 218, 220, 233,
    236, 242, 284, 287, 291
rhetoric, 56, 57, 244, 266, 267, 271–73,
    277, 278, 289
rule-role dimension of practical reason,
    x, 71, 104–7, 111, 112, 142, 153, 154,
    184, 192, 229, 256, 261, 280, 281,
    285, 292

sacrifice. *See* self-sacrifice
sanctuary of undocumented persons,
    23–25, 35, 49, 57, 64, 212, 224–31,
    234–37, 239–42, 283, 288
scriptures, 5, 7, 8, 35, 36, 39, 60, 66, 143,
    146, 196, 228, 230, 243, 246, 252,
    256, 261, 263, 268, 270
self, 29, 152, 154, 158, 228, 234, 255,
    262–64, 283, 284
self-actualization, 117, 119, 129, 143, 150,
    155, 163, 166, 169, 245, 255, 258,
    271, 278
self-cohesion, 106, 155, 165, 264, 283, 286
self-regard, 106, 159, 166, 169, 194, 284,
    290
self-sacrifice, 26, 140, 143, 147, 148,
    150–54, 158, 160, 163, 170–72, 199,
    206, 229, 232, 235, 239, 265, 266,
    268, 271, 275, 277, 289